Social Studies for the Preschool/Primary Child

NINTH EDITION

Carol Seefeldt
PROFESSOR EMERITUS, LATE OF THE INSTITUTE FOR CHILD STUDY
UNIVERSITY OF MARYLAND, COLLEGE PARK

Sharon Castle
GEORGE MASON UNIVERSITY

Renee C. Falconer
GEORGE MASON UNIVERSITY

PEARSON

Boston   Columbus   Indianapolis   New York   San Francisco   Upper Saddle River
Amsterdam   Cape Town   Dubai   London   Madrid   Milan   Munich   Paris   Montreal   Toronto
Delhi   Mexico City   São Paulo   Sydney   Hong Kong   Seoul   Singapore   Taipei   Tokyo

Vice President and Editorial Director: Jeffery W. Johnston
Senior Acquisitions Editor: Julie Peters
Editorial Assistant: Andrea Hall
Vice President and Director of Marketing: Margaret Waples
Senior Marketing Manager: Christopher Barry
Senior Managing Editor: Pamela D. Bennett
Production Editor: Carrie Mollette
Production Project Manager: Liz Napolitano
Manager, Central Design: Jayne Conte
Cover Designer: Suzanne Duda
Cover Art: ©Don Smith/Alamy
Full-Service Project Management:
  Munesh Kumar/Aptara®, Inc.
Composition: Aptara®, Inc.
Printer/Binder/Cover Printer: Courier Westford
Text Font: 10/12 Berling LT Std

Credits and acknowledgments for material borrowed from other sources and reproduced, with permission, in this textbook appear on the appropriate page within the text.

Photo Credits: Laura DeSantis/Artville, Inc., pp. iv, 1, 26, 68, 111, 139, 176, 204, 238, 276, 300, 321; Laima Druskis/PH College, p. 3; Anne Vega/Merrill, pp. 4, 40, 86, 132, 165, 185, 288, 291; © Monkey Business/Fotolia, pp. 7, 261; Todd Yarrington/Merrill, p. 10; Pearson Learning Photo Studio, p. 29; PH College, p. 31; Kenneth P. Davis/PH College, p. 36; Barbara Schwartz/Merrill, pp. 61, 121, 173, 302; Anthony Magnacca/Merrill, pp. 72, 75, 97, 105, 240, 287, 314, 332; Shirley Zeiberg/PH College, p. 80; © Anatoliy Samara/Fotolia, p. 92; Ken Karp/PH College, p. 112; Jo Hall/Merrill, p. 115; © Michael Newman/PhotoEdit, p. 124; Karen Mancinelli/Pearson Learning Photo Studio, p. 144; Scott Cunningham/Merrill, pp. 146, 157, 181, 188; © Stanislav Komogorov/Fotolia, p. 194; Silver Burdett Ginn, pp. 168, 211, 326; © photos1st/Fotolia, p. 208; © Bill Aron/PhotoEdit, p. 218; © Andres Rodriguez/Fotolia, p. 222; © Hemeroskopion/Fotolia, p. 228; Carol Seedfeldt, p. 230; Eugene Gordon/PH College, p. 246; Morgan Lane Photography/Shutterstock.com, p. 251; John Paul Endress/Silver Burdett Ginn, p. 255; © Iuliia Metkalova/Fotolia, p. 266; KS Studios/Merrill, p. 272; L. Morris Nantz/PH College, p. 279; © studio beam/Alamy, p. 309; Dan Floss/Merrill, p. 324.

Every effort has been made to provide accurate and current Internet information in this book. However, the Internet and information posted on it are constantly changing, so it is inevitable that some of the Internet addresses listed in this textbook will change.

Copyright © 2014, 2010, 2005 by Pearson Education, Inc. All rights reserved. Manufactured in the United States of America. This publication is protected by Copyright, and permission should be obtained from the publisher prior to any prohibited reproduction, storage in a retrieval system, or transmission in any form or by any means, electronic, mechanical, photocopying, recording, or likewise. To obtain permission(s) to use material from this work, please submit a written request to Pearson Education, Inc., Permissions Department, One Lake Street, Upper Saddle River, New Jersey 07458, or you may fax your request to 201-236-3290.

Library of Congress Cataloging-in-Publication Data

Seefeldt, Carol.
  Social studies for the preschool/primary child / Carol Seefeldt, professor emeritus, late of the Institute for Child Study, University of Maryland, College Park, Sharon Castle, George Mason University, Renee C. Falconer, George Mason University.—Ninth edition.
      pages cm
  ISBN-13: 978-0-13-286798-6
  ISBN-10: 0-13-286798-2
  1. Social sciences—Study and teaching (Primary)—United States. 2. Social sciences—Study and teaching (Preschool)—United States. I. Title.
  LB1530.S37 2014
  372.83—dc23
                                                                         2012043921

10 9 8 7 6 5 4 3 2 1

PEARSON

ISBN 10:   0-13-286798-2
ISBN 13: 978-0-13-286798-6

Dedication

In memory of Carol Seefeldt

Dedicated to Iola Powell Cadwallader, my first early childhood mentor; she taught me the wonder of children's development and creativity. —S. C.

Also to Mrs. Goodfellow, my kindergarten teacher many, many years ago in 1949 at Kowloon Junior School in Hong Kong; she taught me that school could be an adventure. —R. C. F.

About the Authors

At her death in 2005, **Carol Seefeldt, Ph.D.,** was Professor Emeritus of human development at the Institute for Child Study, University of Maryland, College Park. She received the Distinguished Scholar-Researcher award from the university and published 25 books and over 100 scholarly and research articles for teachers and parents. Her books include *Social Studies for the Preschool/Primary Child*, *Active Experiences for Active Children* (Science, Social Studies, and Mathematics), and *Current Issues in Early Childhood Education* (all with Alice Galper). She also wrote *Playing to Learn* and *Creating Rooms of Wonder*. She coauthored *Early Childhood: Where Learning Begins-Geography* for the U.S. Department of Education.

During her 40 years in the field, Dr. Seefeldt taught at every level from nursery school for 2-year-olds through third grade. She frequently conducted teacher-training programs in the United States, Japan, and Ukraine. Carol's research revolved around program development and evaluation. Her contributions to the field were extraordinary and her influence carries on.

Sharon Castle is a retired associate professor of education at George Mason University. She taught early childhood and elementary social studies, fine arts, creativity and play, and research courses. Her most recent area of research was professional development schools, and her most recent publication was "The Impact of Professional Development School Preparation on Teacher Candidates" in the 110th NSSE Yearbook, *Taking Stock of Professional Development Schools*. She also studied children's creative and artistic development and school change. She received her master's in child development from Iowa State University and her Ph.D. in curriculum and instruction from the University of Maryland, College Park.

Renee C. Falconer is a semi-retired associate professor of education at George Mason University. She still teaches child development and curriculum courses and works with a professional development school. She taught children in countries all over the world (including the United Kingdom, Canada, Australia, Kenya, and the United States) for 20 years and has taught teachers in the eastern, western, and southern United States. She received her master's in early childhood education (ages 3–8) from the University of South Carolina and her Ph.D. in curriculum and instruction/early childhood and multicultural education from Utah State University.

Preface

Social Studies for the Preschool/Primary Child was designed as a text for early childhood pre-service teachers and a resource for in-service teachers, and it has been a standard text in the field through many editions. We are pleased to continue the authorship of the text with the ninth edition and continue to make Carol Seefeldt's fine work available and up-to-date. This edition retains the continuity while addressing contemporary changes in early childhood education and the social studies.

CHILD GROWTH, DEVELOPMENT, AND LEARNING

The ninth edition continues to be based on knowledge of children. Although the world has changed, children have not. Today's children grow, develop, and learn in much the same ways as they always have. This edition of *Social Studies for the Preschool/Primary Child* is based on a solid theoretical and research foundation of child growth, development, and learning. Each chapter incorporates current research and theory on child growth, development, and learning into all areas of the social studies.

NEW TO THIS EDITION

- Newly revised National Council for Social Studies (2010) themes
- New Focus Questions at the beginning of each chapter

- New Children's Literature Boxes, many of which list NCSS Notable Books
- New ideas for using current technologies in today's classrooms, including examples from real classrooms
- New questions for group discussion (online or in person) at the end of each chapter
- Additional developmental theories that explain how children are socialized
- Updated research and references
- Expanded planning and assessment chapter with rubrics and other examples
- More suggestions for expanding and extending teacher candidate knowledge, skills, and attitudes

LEARNING THROUGH ACTIVITY

Play is children's work. This text assumes that all young children will be educated in enriching, stimulating educational environments that foster and promote play as well as mental, physical, and social activities that are known to lead to learning. Research clearly documents that humans learn best when they are active—when they can play with things, objects, others, and ideas. Because play is so critical to learning, it serves as the integrator of the social studies curriculum and is viewed as the basic mode for children's learning. Play and activity are featured in each chapter; however, a separate chapter on resources for children's learning gives teachers ideas for arranging the environment to enable children to learn through their activities.

AN INTEGRATED APPROACH

The wholeness of the child is honored in this text through the advocacy of an integrated social studies curriculum. The wholeness of learning—the intimate relationship between children's cognitive growth and their social, physical, and emotional growth—is recognized and respected.

Social studies are approached as an integrated experience, one that involves the school, parents, and community. The social studies are also presented as a continual experience, one that builds as children move from a child-care setting or a preschool to kindergarten and the primary grades.

Even though the text presents separate chapters for teaching social studies content, it is based on the theory that learning is a continuous, integrated activity. Thus, teaching social studies involves all curriculum content areas. Integrated throughout this edition of *Social Studies for the Preschool/Primary Child* are suggestions for incorporating content and activities from the visual arts, music, movement, science, health, mathematics, and language arts.

CULTURE, DIVERSITY, AND INCLUSION

This edition features culture, diversity, and inclusion. A separate chapter on culture and diversity offers pre-service and in-service teachers a solid foundation of curriculum methods and practices based on the latest theory on and research into teaching young children to value themselves, each other, and the world we share. The chapters also include ideas and practices designed to celebrate culture and diversity and provide full inclusion into the social studies curriculum for all children, regardless of special needs or individual differences.

CHANGES IN THE FIELD

While children and children's development have not changed since the first edition of *Social Studies for the Preschool/Primary Child* in 1977, the world has changed—dramatically so. The world has become smaller and our communities more diverse. The world sometimes feels less safe and the economy less secure. The expansion of technology has affected worldwide changes.

Technology brings us closer to information and knowledge as well as each other. Children today have more knowledge of and experience with technology than ever before and at younger ages. Thus, this edition offers teachers ideas for using current technologies in today's classrooms, from using digital cameras to obtaining resources from the Internet.

Changes in the field of early childhood education itself form another underpinning for this text. As the field of early childhood education enters the future, it does so with a sense of professionalism and established standards. The National Association for the Education of Young Children has set standards for quality in programs serving children from birth through age 8, standards for appropriate curricula, and standards for the professional preparation of early childhood teachers. The assumption that all children will be taught by professional, highly intelligent, and qualified early childhood teachers continues in this edition. Teachers are needed who take their cues from children, who understand children and their development, and who know how to follow their lead. This text offers a multitude of practical ideas, suggestions, and guides for teaching social studies; but the most important component of any social studies program is a reflective, thoughtful, highly educated teacher who will plan, implement, and assess the social studies concepts, skills, attitudes, and learning experiences found herein.

STANDARDS

Recognizing the need to prepare children to become effective, fully functioning citizens in a rapidly changing world, authorities have called for reforms in social studies education. National standards and position papers in history, geography, economics, and civics education suggest the directions for the social studies curriculum. This ninth edition addresses all 10 of the newly revised National Council for Social Studies (2010) themes.

These standards lead to the conclusion that social studies has been a long-neglected topic in schools for young children. *Social Studies for the Preschool/Primary Child* can remedy this neglect. Structured around the concepts considered key to the social science disciplines—the knowledge, skills, attitudes, and values believed essential for citizens of a democratic society—this text presents a multitude of ideas for introducing children to social studies content and experiences. These suggestions will give young children an opportunity to build a foundation of knowledge in history, geography, economics, civics, and other social science disciplines as well as skills and attitudes that will enable them to become fully functioning members of a democratic society in the future.

SPECIAL FEATURES

In this teacher-friendly and student-friendly text, each chapter does the following:

- Begins with focus questions that serve as advanced organizers and objectives
- Concludes with a summary that organizes the information presented
- Includes questions for group discussion at the end of each chapter
- Offers suggestions for expanding and extending teacher candidate knowledge, skills, and attitudes
- Provides resources for teachers
- Integrates children's literature into each chapter; some chapters include a Children's Literature Box as well
- Provides examples and ideas for inclusion and valuing culture and diversity
- Is replete with examples and ideas of how to translate social studies theory and research into practice
- Integrates ideas for using technology

STRUCTURE OF THE NINTH EDITION

Social Studies for the Preschool/Primary Child is organized into three parts. The first part introduces the social studies with chapters on defining the social studies, planning and assessment, and resources for learning (Chapters 1 through 3).

The second part focuses on child development by providing information about thinking and concept formation; social skills; and culture, diversity, and values. Chapters 4 through 6 discuss development of these processes and how teachers foster them through experiences with the social studies.

The third part is devoted to content from the social studies disciplines of history, geography, economics, and civics (Chapters 7 through 10), plus a chapter on global connections (Chapter 11). Current standards and position papers from these fields are reflected throughout these chapters.

INSTRUCTOR'S RESOURCES

The following online supplements are available to instructors and can be downloaded at www.pearsonhighered.com:

- Online Instructor's Manual. This manual provides a variety of resources that support the text.
- Online Test Bank. The Test Bank features evaluation items, such as multiple choice, true–false, and short answer questions.
- Online PowerPoint® Slides. PowerPoint® presentations accompany each chapter of the text. These slides can be customized by adding comments.

ACKNOWLEDGMENTS

We are deeply grateful to the late Carol Seefeldt for this text and for her work on behalf of children and their teachers. She continues to be our standard-bearer and our inspiration.

We thank Joan Isenberg, who encouraged us to take on this task. We appreciate her faith in us.

We give enormous gratitude to Julie Peters, our editor, for her invaluable support and patience. Our sincere thanks for the assistance of Kathleen Reilly and Andrea Hall. Our sincere thanks as well to Carrie Mollette and everyone who worked on the production process.

We also wish to express our appreciation for those individuals who reviewed the manuscript throughout its development: Ruth Kennedy, Bloomsburg University; Leslie A. Sevey, Rhode Island College; Latisha Shipley, Northwestern Oklahoma State University; and Josephine Wilson, Bowie State University.

Last but not least, we are grateful to our husbands, Dana Pless and Allan Falconer, for the many large and small ways in which they love and support us.

Brief Contents

Chapter 1 / These Are the Social Studies — 1

Chapter 2 / Planning and Assessment — 26

Chapter 3 / Resources for Learning: School, Family, Community — 68

Chapter 4 / Thinking and Concept Formation — 111

Chapter 5 / Self, Others, and the Community: Social Skills — 139

Chapter 6 / Culture, Diversity, and Values — 176

Chapter 7 / Children's Study of Time, Continuity, and Change: History — 204

Chapter 8 / People, Places, and Environments: Geography — 238

Chapter 9 / Production, Consumption, and Decision Making: Economics — 276

Chapter 10 / Developing Citizenship: Civics and Government — 300

Chapter 11 / Global Connections — 321

Contents

Chapter 1 / These Are the Social Studies   1
    THE PURPOSE OF SOCIAL STUDIES   1
    PAST APPROACHES TO THE SOCIAL STUDIES   3
        Progressive Education and the Here-and-Now Curriculum   3
        Social-Living Curriculum   5
        Holiday Curriculum   7
        Social Forces and Theories Affecting the Curriculum   8
    SOCIAL STUDIES TODAY   12
        Active Learning   13
        Integrated   14
        Meaningful   15
        Of High Interest   15
        Standards for Knowledge, Skills, and Attitudes   16
        Scope and Sequence   19
        Curriculum Models for Early Childhood Education   20
    SUMMARY   23
    DISCUSSION QUESTIONS   23

EXTEND YOUR KNOWLEDGE   24
RESOURCES   24

Chapter 2 / Planning and Assessment   26

KNOWLEDGE OF CHILDREN   27
    Children Are Alike   28
    So Alike, So Different   29
    Special Needs   30
KNOWLEDGE OF THE COMMUNITY   35
    The Child's Physical World   35
    Cultural Knowledge and Values   36
KNOWLEDGE OF THE SOCIAL STUDIES   37
SHORT- AND LONG-TERM PLANNING   38
    Involving the Children   38
    Planning for the Spontaneous   40
    Lesson Plans   41
    Units, Projects, and Thematic Learning   46
ASSESSMENT OF THE SOCIAL STUDIES CURRICULUM   57
    Observation   59
    Checklists   60
    Informal Interviews   60
    Performance Tasks   61
    Products   62
    Portfolios   64
    Standardized Tests   64
SUMMARY   65
DISCUSSION QUESTIONS   65
EXTEND YOUR KNOWLEDGE   66
RESOURCES   66

Chapter 3 / Resources for Learning: School, Family, Community   68

THE CHILDREN   69
THE FAMILY   69
    Informal Involvement   70
    Formal Involvement   71

THE SCHOOL 73
COMMUNITY 73
    Fieldwork 74
    Planning Fieldwork 76
    Guest Speakers 79
    Community Service 79
THE CLASSROOM 79
    Deciding on Learning Centers 81
    Introducing Centers 81
    Types of Centers 83
    Vicarious Materials in the Classroom 95
TECHNOLOGY RESOURCES 104
SUMMARY 108
DISCUSSION QUESTIONS 109
EXTEND YOUR KNOWLEDGE 109
RESOURCES 110

Chapter 4 / Thinking and Concept Formation — 111

PLANNING THINKING EXPERIENCES 114
    Firsthand Experiences 114
    Experiences Involving Others 114
    Experiences Requiring Language 115
FOSTERING THINKING PROCESSES 117
    Questioning and Sensing Problems 117
    Locating Information: Field Trips 118
    Organizing and Interpreting Information 121
    Seeing Relationships and Beginning to Generalize 125
    Interpreting, Reflecting, and Reaching Conclusions 127
    Jokes and Riddles 129
CONCEPT FORMATION 130
    Key Concepts 131
    Concept Development 132
NURTURING CONCEPT FORMATION 133
    The Problem of the Match 133

Guidelines for Concept Formation   135
Helping All Children Form Concepts   137
SUMMARY   137
DISCUSSION QUESTIONS   138
EXTEND YOUR KNOWLEDGE   138
RESOURCES   138

Chapter 5 / Self, Others, and the Community: Social Skills   139

INDIVIDUAL DEVELOPMENT AND IDENTITY AND INDIVIDUALS, GROUPS, AND INSTITUTIONS   140
SOCIAL SKILLS DEVELOP   140
THEORIES OF SOCIALIZATION   143
Behavioral Theories   143
Erickson's Theory of Psychosocial Development   144
Social–Cognitive Theories   146
Cognitive–Developmental Theories   147
Vygotsky's Sociocultural Theory.   148
Developmental Systems Theories   149
FACTORS AFFECTING SOCIAL DEVELOPMENT   149
The Family   149
Role of Community   150
Role of the School   152
SELF-CONCEPT   153
General Identity: Names   154
The Physical Self   155
Self-Efficacy/Self-Worth   157
Assessing Self-Concept, Self-Esteem, and Self-Efficacy   158
RELATING TO OTHERS   158
Communicating   159
Sharing   164
Cooperating   168
Making and Having Friends   169
Conflict Resolution   172
SUMMARY   174

DISCUSSION QUESTIONS   174
EXTEND YOUR KNOWLEDGE   175
RESOURCES   175

Chapter 6 / Culture, Diversity, and Values   176

CULTURE   177
   What Is "Culture"?   177
   Communities   179
   Friendship   179
DIVERSITY   179
WHAT ARE YOUR ATTITUDES?   180
HOW CHILDREN LEARN ABOUT OTHERS   184
KEY CONCEPTS   186
ATTITUDES AND VALUES   186
HOW CHILDREN LEARN VALUES   188
   Modeling   188
   Reinforcement   190
   Learning   190
WHICH THEORY?   192
   Indoctrination   192
   Value Clarification Theory   193
   Value Analysis Theory   193
WHICH VALUES SHOULD BE TAUGHT?   195
   Encouraging Anti-Bias Values in the Classroom   197
   Teaching Peace, Understanding War   199
SUMMARY   201
DISCUSSION QUESTIONS   202
EXTEND YOUR KNOWLEDGE   202
RESOURCES   203

Chapter 7 / Children's Study of Time, Continuity, and Change: History   204

SCIENCE, TECHNOLOGY, AND SOCIETY   205
HISTORY   207
KEY CONCEPTS   207

TIME   209
- Development of Time Concepts   209
- Routines that Teach Time   211
- Measuring Time   212
- The Passage of Time   213

CHANGE   214
- In School   214
- In the Neighborhood or Community   215
- In Nature   216
- In Children   216

THE CONTINUITY OF HUMAN LIFE   219
- The Family   219
- Intergenerational Contacts   221
- Holiday Celebrations and Traditions   223
- Cultural Universals   227

THE PAST   228
- People   229
- Primary Sources   229
- Narratives and the Arts   232

METHODS OF THE HISTORIAN   233
SUMMARY   236
DISCUSSION QUESTIONS   236
EXTEND YOUR KNOWLEDGE   236
RESOURCES   237

Chapter 8 / People, Places, and Environments: Geography   238

GEOGRAPHY SKILLS FOR YOUNG CHILDREN   239
KEY CONCEPTS   240
THE EARTH IS THE PLACE WHERE WE LIVE   241
- Our Environment   242
- Land and Water   243
- Caring for Our Earth   246
- A Nearly Round Sphere in a Solar System   252

DIRECTION AND LOCATION 254
    Movement Exploration 256
    Directional Terms 257
    Distance and Measurement 259
    Maps and Globes 260
RELATIONSHIPS WITHIN PLACES 269
SPATIAL INTERACTIONS 270
REGIONS 271
    Physical Regions 271
    Cultural Regions 272
SUMMARY 273
DISCUSSION QUESTIONS 273
EXTEND YOUR KNOWLEDGE 274
RESOURCES 274

Chapter 9 / Production, Consumption, and Decision Making: Economics 276

ECONOMIC LITERACY 277
DEVELOPMENT OF ECONOMIC CONCEPTS 278
KEY CONCEPTS 282
SCARCITY AND DECISION MAKING 282
    Wants and Needs 282
    Decision Making 285
PRODUCTION AND CONSUMPTION 287
    Consumers 287
    Consuming Services 290
    Production and Distribution of Goods and Provision of Services 291
JOBS AND CAREERS 293
    Jobs 293
    Attitudes and Values 294
    Essential Skills 296
SUMMARY 296
DISCUSSION QUESTIONS 297
EXTEND YOUR KNOWLEDGE 298
RESOURCES 298

Chapter 10 / Developing Citizenship: Civics and Government — 300

    KEY CONCEPTS   301
    DEMOCRATIC VALUES   302
        Civic Participation   306
    POLITICAL CONCEPTS   311
        Research   312
        Voting   313
        Symbols of Democratic Government   315
    OWNERSHIP AND PRIDE   318
        School and Community   318
        Nation   318
    SUMMARY   318
    DISCUSSION QUESTIONS   319
    EXTEND YOUR KNOWLEDGE   319
    RESOURCES   320

Chapter 11 / Global Connections — 321

    KEY CONCEPTS   323
    INTERCONNECTEDNESS AND INTERDEPENDENCY   323
        Similarities   325
        Trade   331
        Technology   331
    RESOURCES FOR LEARNING ABOUT OTHERS   331
    GLOBAL EDUCATION   333
    SUMMARY   334
    DISCUSSION QUESTIONS   335
    EXTEND YOUR KNOWLEDGE   335
    RESOURCES   335

References   336

Index   355

CHAPTER 1

These Are the Social Studies

> **Focus Questions**
>
> After you read this chapter, you should be prepared to respond to the following questions:
>
> - What is the definition of the social studies? Why is it important to teach social studies?
> - How were the social studies taught in the past?
> - What theories and models have most influenced social studies today?
> - What characterizes social studies today?

THE PURPOSE OF SOCIAL STUDIES

After the Fourth of July fireworks and parades, Carol Seefeldt's grandfather would take a key from his pocket and open a metal box containing his important papers. From the box he would take a small package wrapped in a soft chamois cloth. Carefully he would unwrap the package. They knew what was inside—a small leather folder holding his citizenship paper. Opening the folder, he would unfold the paper declaring him a citizen of the United States. Then he would tell the story of how he came to America, his trip across the ocean, and the sorrow he experienced when he said goodbye to parents, brother, and sisters, knowing he would never see them again. He would finish the story by saying, "You do not have to leave your home to be a citizen of the United States. All you need to do is go to school, and there you will learn how to be a citizen of this wonderful country."

Her grandfather was right. By participating in the small democracies of their classrooms, young children gain the knowledge, skills, and attitudes required to become good citizens. Although all of children's early educational experiences are designed to prepare children for the role of citizen in a democratic society, the integrated study of the social sciences—the social studies—is uniquely suited to do so. Through the social studies, children have the opportunity to learn that they are deeply respected as individuals and at the same time learn to give up some of their individuality for the good of the group.

As defined by the National Council for the Social Studies (NCSS), social studies are

> the integrated study of the social sciences and humanities to promote civic competence. . . . social studies provides coordinated, systematic study drawing upon such disciplines as anthropology, archaeology, economics, geography, law, history, philosophy, political science, psychology, religion and sociology, as well as appropriate content from the humanities, mathematics and natural sciences. (NCSS, 2010, p. 3)

The two main purposes of the social studies—to prepare children to assume "the office of citizen" and to integrate knowledge, skills, and attitudes within and across disciplines—distinguish the social studies from other subjects.

It seems overwhelming. The field of social studies is enormous, and children are so young. Preschool and primary children are too new to this earth to be expected to learn all about economics, history, and geography, much less the attitudes and skills necessary to participate in a democratic society. Yet it is because children are so young that the subject of social studies is critical during early childhood. In these early years, the foundation for later and increasingly mature understanding is constructed (National Research Council [NRC], 2000, 2001).

Realizing that children have a long time in which to grow and learn makes teaching social studies in the preschool–primary classroom less overwhelming. During their early years, children need to develop anticipatory, intuitive ideas and interests and gain basic knowledge that will serve as a foundation for the elaboration of more complex understandings, attitudes, and skills (NCSS, 1994; NRC, 2001).

Then, too, social studies learning takes place naturally as children participate in preschool or primary classrooms, which are themselves small democratic societies. Within these classrooms, the rights of the individual are constantly balanced with those of the group; children naturally learn and use the knowledge, skills, processes, dispositions, and attitudes that will serve as a foundation for later social studies learning (Mitchell, 2000; Pohan, 2003).

Looking to the past helps today's educators understand how social studies and young children can be brought together in meaningful, appropriate ways. Over the years, many approaches to social studies education for young children have been developed and implemented and have brought us to where we are today.

Social studies takes place naturally in good schools for young children.

As you read about historic approaches to the social studies curriculum, think about how each of these approaches continues to influence today's social studies. You might recall your own experiences with social studies education or observe how social studies is being taught in today's schools.

PAST APPROACHES TO THE SOCIAL STUDIES

Progressive Education and the Here-and-Now Curriculum

Before the 1930s, the social studies were concerned with an unchanging body of facts—facts to be memorized. Appalled by this dry memorization of things children knew nothing about and had no experience with, Lucy Sprague Mitchell (1934) developed a practical and detailed account of the ways in which teachers could enlarge and enrich children's understanding of the world around them and their place in it. Mitchell was encouraged and influenced by the child development theory and progressive education movement of John Dewey (1900a, 1902, 1944), who described the importance of an education that is child centered, active and hands-on, choice based, resource rich, and directed toward "doing" social studies rather than memorizing social studies facts. Based on Dewey's philosophy, Mitchell created a curriculum that was a direct attack on the elementary school's concentration on facts totally unrelated to children's lives.

Mitchell's basic educational concept was that children need to experience things for themselves. She believed that the social studies curriculum should be based on children's experiences and their discovery of the things and culture of the world around them—on the "here and now."

Mitchell believed it was dangerous to teach anything to children before they had an opportunity to experience it. The teacher should not pour in information

Children's world expands to the study of the community.

but should provide experiences that would enable the child to absorb information through firsthand manipulation and encounter.

In some ways, the dominant organizational pattern for sequencing social studies topics has been based on Mitchell's work (Wade, 2003). For example, the typical social studies curriculum began with the child in the neighborhood and then expanded as the child was introduced to societies farther away in time and space. This is known as the spiral curriculum or the expanding horizons/expanding communities curriculum.

Grade	Emphasis
K	Home and neighborhood
1	Community and community helpers
2	United States
3	People in other lands

Unfortunately, many misinterpreted Mitchell's theories and ideas. Although convinced that social studies for young children should be solidly based on the here and now of children's lives, teachers ignored the complexities of children's here-and-now world. Instead of focusing on the relationships of things in the environment or the web of interdependency within it, social studies instruction revolved around the trite. Kindergarten children learned that they live in a family, first-graders that firefighters help them, and third-graders that they live in a neighborhood. In the end, Mitchell's strong concern for relationship thinking and intellectual development was ignored (Wade, 2003).

Mitchell (1934), however, saw the children's world—"whatever and where ever it may be"—as complex and full of opportunities to enhance their knowledge and foster thinking (p. 16). At first glance, her suggestion that geography learning begins with children's explorations of their immediate environment seems preposterous because the environment is too complex. "Modern children are born into an appallingly complicated world. The complications of their surrounding culture, however, instead of making this attack impossible, make it imperative" (p. 8). By enlarging and enriching children's understanding of their immediate environment, their world, and their place in it, Mitchell aimed to develop children's intellectual capabilities in terms of "relationship thinking, generalization from experience and the re-creation of concrete experience through symbolic, dramatic play" (p. 11).

Mitchell's insights into the intellectual processes of young children—in terms of relationship thinking, generalizing from experience, and re-creating concrete experience through symbolic or dramatic play—are consistent with the theories of Piaget (Piaget & Inhelder, 1969) and Vygotsky (1986). Further, the philosophy articulated in *Developmentally Appropriate Practice* (Bredekamp & Copple, 1997) is congruent with Mitchell's ideas. Subsequent research and theory (NRC, 2000, 2001; Piaget & Inhelder, 1969; Vygotsky, 1986) support the principles she first advocated:

- The younger the child, the greater the need for firsthand sensory experiences.
- One experience, fact, or idea needs to be connected in some way to another; two facts and a relation joining them are and should be an invitation to generalize, extrapolate, and make a tentative intuitive leap—even to build a theory.
- What children learn must be useful to them in some way and related to daily life.
- Play and active learning are necessary.

Certainly, nothing can be more potent for fostering intellectual development than real experiences, and the here and now of children's lives can provide a foundation for social studies experiences—that is, if the total of children's here-and-now lives is considered.

Today, children's here-and-now world has expanded; it is increasingly diverse, multicultural and global. "Will my school get bombed?" asked 5-year-old Kala after the bombing of Baghdad. This does not mean that 5-year-olds should study maps to locate Iraq, but it does mean that the spiral/expanding horizons curriculum may be overly simplistic in our global, technological society. Today's teachers should recognize the complexities and totality of children's here-and-now environment. Building on children's interests and fostering their understandings of both their immediate world and what is far away in space and time are part of teaching social studies to young children.

Social-Living Curriculum

As Mitchell (1934) was formulating her theories, Patty Smith Hill (1923), in an attempt to apply the principles of democracy to school organization, initiated a curriculum with the goal of habit and social skill development: Training children in the skills and habits necessary to function in a democratic society would prepare them to participate in a democracy. Her book, *A Conduct Curriculum for the Kindergarten and First Grade*, specified all the social skills and habits that children should learn, stated in measurable form. It focused primarily on the realm of moral and social conduct.

Hill's social-living curriculum grew from child development and psychoanalytic theories coupled with the growing concern in the 1930s about education for citizenship. The social-living approach maintained that young children are developmentally ready to learn skills required for them to live with a group. Having learned in infancy and early childhood who they are and how they fit into their family unit, children were then ready to develop the social skills necessary for nursery school and kindergarten.

Psychoanalytic theory, with its strong emphasis on the psychosocial segment of life, lent support to the social-living curriculum. The concepts that children should learn to express feelings and to find emotional and social support in the school situation were readily translated into the social-living curriculum.

Curricula in many nursery schools established in the 1930s and 1940s were based on the social-living curriculum. Some of these schools were established by faculty wives at universities to provide socializing experiences for their young children; others were established for children of immigrants or poverty-stricken families. They shared the goal of supporting and fostering the social and emotional growth of young children by leading children to do the following:

- Learn to share materials and ideas
- Develop healthy relationships with others
- Become self-reliant
- Feel responsibility for their own behavior
- Develop interest and attention span
- Cooperate with others in a friendly, willing spirit
- Appreciate the worth and contribution of others
- Develop self-concept and self-respect

Implementation of these goals led to social studies programs that included large blocks of time for free play, interaction with others, discussions of feelings, emphasis on sharing, and cooperating behaviors and rule learning. Rather than becoming a strong, interdisciplinary, interrelated curriculum based on an individual's relationship with others and the environment or focusing on complex social studies concepts such as interaction, cooperation, and interdependency, the social studies curriculum called social living became a curriculum of benign neglect. Children were given a rich environment of toys and materials and left alone to learn to live with themselves and others. Even worse, in some programs elaborate plans and procedures were developed and implemented to teach children how to share, hang up their coats, take care of materials, blow their noses, tie shoes, and cooperate, with little concern for their intellectual development.

Through the 1930s, the social studies curriculum continued to revolve around the promotion of social skills (Freeman & Hatch, 1989). Only recently has the social skills curriculum been pushed to the background. With the passage of the No Child Left Behind Act in 2001 and increasing pressure for academic accountability, the social-living approach to the curriculum has all but disappeared. Increasingly, the focus is on literacy and mathematics skills to the exclusion of social skills.

Perhaps the real failure of the social-living approach in social studies was proponents' inability to view the child holistically. Many teachers failed to understand that learning to relate to others, see another's point of view, and understand the complex social rule system are cognitive as well as social tasks. Relating to others requires communication—a facility with language. The abilities to express ideas, share thoughts with others, listen, and speak are cognitive skills. Nevertheless, fostering children's

To express ideas and to work with others are both social and cognitive skills.

language development, enhancing their cognitive growth, and even developing concepts of rules, moral values, and understandings—which should have been an integral part of the curriculum designed to foster social living—were neglected or ignored.

Holiday Curriculum

Another common approach to social studies in early childhood education—a total embarrassment to those teachers who guide children through valuable learning episodes—is the holiday curriculum. Celebrating holidays is an enjoyable diversion from the regular school routine. Unfortunately, in too many cases these celebrations have become the basis for teaching social studies. Year after year, the same celebrations are repeated without much concern for the knowledge, skills, attitudes, or values gained from them (Myers & Myers, 2002).

Commercial companies have fostered the holiday approach with unit plans, posters, and entire curriculum packages, all centering on the celebration of holidays. Children follow a pattern to make Pilgrim hats, cut out a pumpkin at Halloween, sing songs, and listen to contrived stories that are more myth and legend than fact. Given this curriculum, children's social studies learning is superficial—an unrealistic perpetuation of myths that are untrue at best, and stereotyping groups of people at its worst.

This does not mean, however, that there is no place for the recognition of holidays in the social studies curriculum. Celebration of holidays can promote identification with family, community, and nation (Vygotsky, 1986). Further, acquaintance with the holiday customs of many lands, when appropriately introduced, fosters an appreciation of other cultures and global connections. The use of stories, videos, role-playing, music, bulletin boards, and discussions to clarify the meaning of virtues such as honesty, bravery, and kindness can help children develop historical understandings (National Center for History in the Schools, 1994; NCSS, 1998).

Figure 1.1 summarizes the strengths and weaknesses of historical approaches to the social studies.

Date	Approach	Concept	Weakness	Strength
1920s–1930s	Social skills	Social skills are necessary for living in a democracy.	Translated into habit training and formation. Ignored the complexities of social learning.	Social skills are required to function in a democracy. The ability to cooperate, share, negotiate, and give up some of oneself to consider the rights of others is necessary.
1934	Here-and-now	Children's learning is firsthand, based on experiences in their immediate environment.	Misunderstood and translated into meaningless simplistic units of "my family," "community helpers," etc.	When complexities of the immediate here-and-now world are considered and used to support thinking, this approach is current and supported by both theory and research.
1930s+	Holiday curriculum	None	Stereotypic and sterile in content, ideas; limits thinking, problem solving.	None

Figure 1.1 Historical foundations of social studies in early childhood education.

Social Forces and Theories Affecting the Curriculum

In the middle of the twentieth century, two major social forces influenced the social studies curriculum: the Soviet Union's launching of *Sputnik* and the civil rights movement of the 1960s. Theories, especially those of Piaget (Piaget & Inhelder, 1969) and Vygotsky (1978), also influenced the curriculum.

Sputnik's Challenge

After the launch of *Sputnik*, the first satellite to circle the earth, educators in the United States began reevaluating their theories and practices. In 1959, the famous Woods Hole Conference was held, where scientists and educators met to determine the content of various disciplines and how to present that content to children. After this conference Jerome Bruner (1960) stated that the "curriculum of a subject should be determined by the most fundamental understanding that can be achieved of the underlying principles that give structure to that subject" (p. 31).

This idea—that curriculum content should emphasize the structure of a discipline—caught the imagination of curriculum planners and educators and has guided curriculum development since that time. Concepts and theories key to a discipline became the core of the curriculum, and inductive thinking became the method of teaching. Many mathematics, science, and social studies curricula were developed based on this notion.

In 1965, Robison and Spodek published *New Directions in the Kindergarten*, a description of a program for 5-year-old kindergarten children that focused on the structure of subject matter and included curriculum content from science, mathematics, language, and social studies. Robison and Spodek concluded that young children could successfully learn concepts that once were believed to be beyond their grasp.

The ideas of the past are reinforced with current knowledge of how children learn (NRC, 2001):

- Children develop ideas and concepts about their world when they are very young.
- The embryonic concepts or pre-concepts children bring to school are the foundation for new and more conventional knowledge of their social world.
- Children's learning is continual. They deal with ideas over long periods of time.
- Children think. They pose questions and gather information in many ways.
- Children use the tools of the social scientist.
- Children transfer their understandings when approaching new situations.

Civil Rights

As this reexamination of curriculum and educational practices was taking place, Americans were becoming aware of the inequality of opportunities for many people in our society. The recognition that large groups of people had been systematically discriminated against for many years led to organized efforts to gain full civil rights and educational opportunity for all citizens, regardless of ethnic background or race. This drive for civil rights was manifest in the Johnson administration's War on Poverty.

The War on Poverty included the Elementary-Secondary Education Act of 1965 and the Head Start program. Using the theories of J. McVicker Hunt (1961) and Benjamin Bloom (1963), who believed that intelligence was malleable and could be influenced by early, enriching educational experiences, the government looked to early childhood education as a means of increasing children's intelligence and as an instrument to break the poverty cycle. Preschool programs that were enriching and stimulating and involved the child's total family were thought to increase young children's intelligence as well as change their attitudes and the attitudes of their families toward school. Thus, early childhood education was designed to increase children's motivation to learn and achieve while improving basic cognitive skills; all of this would, in turn, lead to success in later school experiences and in a chosen career.

Of all the programs within the War on Poverty, the Head Start program has had and continues to have the most influence. The program is not only popular with families, educators, and members of the community but has demonstrated long-lasting positive effects (NRC, 2001). Twenty years after participating in a model early-intervention program, children had repeated fewer grades, were less likely to be placed in special education programs or to be involved in delinquency, and had been more productive when compared with those of comparable backgrounds who had not participated in such a program (Washington & Bailey, 1995).

Because the social studies emphasize the development of self-concept, skills in relating with others, and multicultural understanding as well as knowledge, the discipline proved to be an excellent vehicle for fostering the goals of Head Start. Many social studies experiences—taking field trips, exploring the environment, observing adults at work, talking to classroom visitors—help Head Start children better understand themselves and their place in the world.

Piaget

Linked with renewed concern for providing equality of educational opportunity for all children was an emerging acceptance of the work of Jean Piaget (Piaget & Inhelder, 1969), a Swiss psychologist who had been exploring children's thought processes since the early 1900s. During the 1960s, his research and theories began receiving attention from psychologists and educators in the United States. Piaget's work may have become well known at this time because his writings were then being translated into English. On the other hand, the interest may have arisen because his theories offered psychologists a different way of looking at children's learning.

According to Piaget, children, like humans of any age, construct their own knowledge through maturation and interaction with the total environment. He

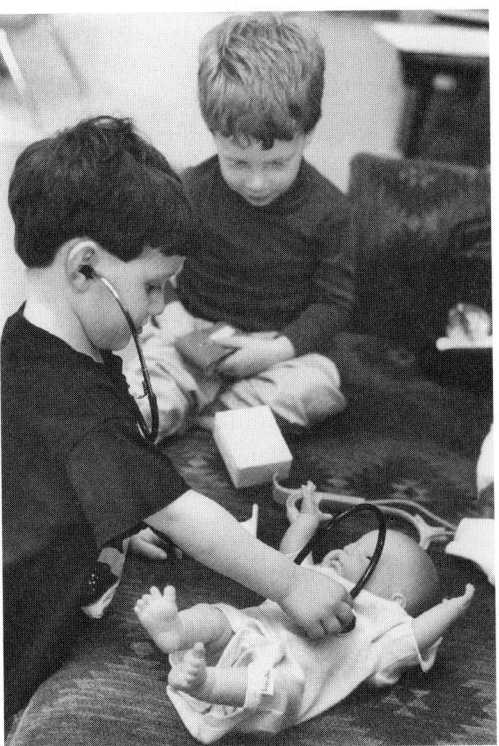

Piaget helped us realize that children construct knowledge through social, physical, and mental activity.

suggested that, as children mature, they pass through four stages of cognitive development: (1) the sensorimotor period, from birth through age 2; (2) the preoperational period, ages 2 through 7 or 8; (3) the concrete operational period, ages 8 to adolescence; and (4) formal thought, after adolescence. To progress through these stages requires mental activity and interaction with the physical environment.

The social studies curriculum was heavily influenced by knowledge of Piaget's stages of intellectual growth. His descriptions of young children's abilities and their conceptions of the world, time, and space offered insights for social studies curriculum planners and teachers. Further, the Piagetian interview—the probing technique used to uncover children's concepts—could be used as a model for evaluating the outcomes of lessons, units, and other teaching sequences.

Vygotsky

The current focus on the social and cultural influences of all aspects of children's development has promoted the ideas of another theorist, Lev Semenovich Vygotsky (Glassman, 2001). A student of literature, philosophy, and aesthetics, Vygotsky was born in the late 1800s into a middle-class Jewish family in Belorussia. He graduated from the University of Moscow in 1917 and entered the field of psychology in the 1920s. During the 1920s and 1930s, his written research was banned by the Soviet Union. Vygotsky died in 1934 before the ban was lifted. His works were translated into English in the 1960s and 1970s and gradually became popular. They are now used to support curriculum development (Glassman, 2001), especially social studies curricula and group work, particularly cooperative learning.

Vygotsky believed the following:

- A person's social and psychological worlds are connected.
- Child–adult interaction is important for cognitive development.
- The capacity to use language to regulate thought and action is distinctly human and the source of conscious mental life.
- Social experience is extremely important for cognitive growth.
- Education leads development.
- Teaching must be geared to the zone of proximal development; that is, it must match what is to be taught to what the child already knows and will be able to accomplish with adult help until it can be accomplished independently.

Vygotsky's ideas are similar in a number of ways to Piaget's: Both believed that learning is the result of firsthand experiences that stem from the child's environment; both regarded play and exploration as a major educative activity; and both believed that social interaction with others, whether peers or adults, is critical for learning to take place.

NCLB

The No Child Left Behind Act (NCLB) passed the U.S. Congress in 2001 in response to concerns over public education. NCLB instituted standards-based reform based on the premise that high standards and measurable goals would improve student outcomes. Among other provisions, it requires states to develop assessements and test students at specified grade levels. While this may sound logical on the surface, it has resulted in unintended consequences that do not fit the guildelines of developmentally appropriate practice, such as the following:

- Curriculum now centers more on test content and less on thinking (Anderson & Metzger, 2011; Boyle-Baise, Hsu, Johnson, Serriere, & Stewart, 2008).
- Teaching involves more "teaching to the test" than teaching to students' needs or the zone of proximal development.
- The arts and subjects not tested, including social studies in many states, have been marginalized.
- Standardized testing has grown as a method of evaluating not only students, but teachers and schools as well.

Although students do not take the state standardized tests until third grade, these impacts are felt in the primary grades and even, to some extent, in preschools. In this climate, it is up to teachers of young children to use developmentally appropriate practice guidelines to balance the following:

- Content knowledge with the thinking processes and attitudes necessary for civic participation (Boyle-Baise et al., 2008; Slekar, 2009)
- Covering required test material with student's background knowledge and zone of proximal development
- Reading and mathematics with social studies, science, and the arts through integration
- Standardized testing with authentic assessment that informs students, teachers, and parents about what students really know and understand

SOCIAL STUDIES TODAY

Today's social studies are based firmly on the past. The philosophy of John Dewey, the theories of both Piaget and Vygotsky, and the work of Mitchell continue to influence the field.

Social studies in today's schools, however, are based on more than just the past. Current learning theory and research as well as social and political forces such as NCLB are reflected in today's social studies curriculum. The implications of theory and research for teaching are many. The National Council for the Social Studies (2010) formulated a position statement that distills the theory and research into a vision for powerful social studies, which includes five principles. Social studies teaching and learning are powerful when they are:

- Active
- Meaningful
- Integrative
- Challenging
- Value-based

As the purpose of social studies states, learning for civic participation is of utmost importance. Plus, we are teaching and learning in a standards-based climate. Therefore, teaching socials studies to young children today needs to incorporate the following:

- Active learning
- Integrated subject areas
- Meaning and relevance
- High interest, engagement, and challenge
- Social and participatory skills
- Attitudes and values
- Standards for knowledge, skills, and attitudes

We will discuss these throughout the text.

Active Learning

"Active lessons require students to process and think about what they are learning (NCSS, 2010, p. 169). It is "hands-on" and "minds-on."

In order to learn, children from birth through the primary grades and even beyond must be physically, mentally, and socially active. Every type of play and active learning, whether alone or with others—sociodramatic play, play with materials, or physical play—provides children with physical, mental, and social opportunities to learn about themselves and their environment (Colker, 2002). Children learn by doing (see Figure 1.2).

The theories of both Vygotsky (1986) and Piaget and Inhelder (1969) support the premise that children's play and active learning with concrete objects and materials are necessary for concept formation. Play, according to the theorists, permits children to do the following:

- *Develop more hierarchical and long-term goals.* Play and active learning may be the first contexts in which children are able to delay gratification, to keep on working at something until they achieve their goal.

Today's social studies is integrated, meaningful, and of high interest. Whatever is introduced to children is

❏ *integrated* into and with children's cultural background, personal knowledge, family, and community and embedded into the total curriculum;

❏ filled with *meaning* because it is appropriate for their development, matching their cognitive, emotional, social, and physical maturity; and

❏ *of high interest* to children when based on their firsthand experiences, self-choice, and social interaction.

Figure 1.2 Social studies today.

- *Take the perspective of others, which is necessary to learning.* When children play and interact with others, they are forced to consider the ideas of others. If children did not consider each other's ideas, they could not play as if they were mothers, fathers, doctors, beauticians, and so on. This initial ability to coordinate, to think about multiple ideas, will develop into reflective thinking and metacognition (Bodrova & Leong, 2003).
- *Use mental representations.* Children often use objects as substitutions for other objects. For example, a child may use a block to represent scissors as he or she plays barbershop. To be able to use symbolic substitutes for real objects is essential to the development of language and abstract thought.

Because play and active learning are so critical to children's cognitive development, large blocks of time in child care, preschool, and kindergarten settings will be arranged for children's play. Throughout the primary grades, children need opportunities to continue to play with others, to explore and use materials in active ways, to process ideas in concrete, hands-on ways, and to play with board and other games to solidify their learning.

Slekar (2009) cautions that, although social studies should not be boring, it should be more than fun and stories. Well-planned, active social studies learning activities and experiences are most effective when rooted in meaningful content and the significance of ideas (such as democracy).

Integrated

Integrative social studies addresses "the totality of human experience over time and space, connecting with past, linked to the present, and looking ahead to the future (NCSS, 2010, p. 170).

Social studies are not isolated bits of information or knowledge that children memorize but, as Vygotsky (1986) indicated, are deeply rooted in children's cultural background and personal experience. The more situated in context and the more rooted in cultural background and personal knowledge an event is, the more readily it is understood, learned, and remembered (Popkewitz, 1999). Thus, today's social studies are embedded within the context of children's families, schools, neighborhoods, and world (Garcia, 2003).

No one social science discipline can be separated or segregated from another or from the development of skills, attitudes, and values. Just as the social studies are integrated, so is the entire early childhood curriculum. The social studies cannot be separated from any other subject matter of the school. Try to find a key concept or a suggested activity in any of the chapters of this text that does not involve children when they are studying other subjects in school. Most social studies concepts and activities involve children in using language through listening, speaking, reading, or writing; in applying mathematics or science concepts; or in expressing their ideas through art, music, or movement. Many social science concepts overlap those of science and mathematics (Jantz & Seefeldt, 1999a). Helping children to see these connections is an important aspect of social studies teaching.

Meaningful

Meaningful social studies builds networks of "knowledge, skills, beliefs, and attitudes that are structured around enduring understandings, essential questions, important ideas, and goals (NCSS, 2010, p. 170)

To be meaningful, social studies content must match children's intellectual growth, be connected to their experience, and help them to make sense of their world. Meaningful teaching requires matching the richness of the learning environment to the intellectual growth of the child. The richness of an environment for intellectual growth is a function of the appropriateness of this match between inner organizations (prior knowledge and experience) and external circumstances in a child's succession of encounters with his or her environment. Developmentally appropriate social studies is meaningful because children can connect it to their knowledge and experience and process it in order to make sense of it. Vygotsky (1978) explained the importance of matching what is to be learned with the nature of children's cognitive maturity: "It is a well known and empirically established fact that learning should be matched in some manner with the child's developmental level" (p. 85). Sue Bredekamp (1998) calls matching what one wants to teach children to their existing knowledge "teaching on the edge of children's knowledge."

Today, early childhood educators have increased their understanding of the problem of this match. The National Association for the Education of Young Children has published *Developmentally Appropriate Practice in Early Childhood Programs Serving Children from Birth Through Age 8* (Bredekamp & Copple, 1997) as well as *Reaching Potentials* in two volumes: *Appropriate Curriculum and Assessment for Young Children* (Bredekamp & Rosegrant, 1992) and *Transforming Early Childhood and Assessment* (Bredekamp & Rosegrant, 1995). These are important guides for teachers.

Recognizing that curriculum must match children's maturation as well as the context in which they live, the National Council for the Social Studies (2010) specifies ten general themes and includes purposes, questions for exploration, knowledge, processes, and products for each theme. It does specify content, scope, or sequence in its standards. These decisions, the council believes, are in the hands of those who teach social studies, the people who know the children, state standards, and the world in which they live.

The search for matching content to a child's intellectual development continues. By organizing the social science disciplines—knowledge, skills, and attitudes—around key concepts or principles and then describing what we do know about how children grow in understanding these principles, teachers have an opportunity to plan ways of presenting social studies material and content that will have meaning because it will match children's developmental levels, connect to their experiences, and enable them to make sense of new information.

Of High Interest

Social studies should reflect a "balance between retrieval and recitation of content and a thoughtful examination of concepts in order to provide intellectual challenges" (NCSS, 2010, p. 171).

Children learn when they are interested. Interest leads to "meaningful learning, promotes long-term storage of knowledge and provides motivation for further learning" (Hidi, 1990, p. 549). Whether studying history, geography, economics, civics, current events, or cultures, children must find the material of high interest. It is their interest that motivates them to satisfy their curiosity about themselves and the world in which they live, promoting a sense of competence (Wigfield, 2002). At least four factors stimulate children's interest in social studies: firsthand learning and connection to experience, choice, social interaction, and appropriate challenge (not too easy or too hard). All social studies teaching is grounded in children's firsthand experiences, play, and activity. Choice is encouraged. Children can select their own learning experiences, activities, topics, and materials. Children who are given choices are more likely to succeed because the problem of match and challenge is at least partially solved (Seefeldt & Galper, 2000). Learning centers are one way to provide choice since children can initiate their own learning experiences and activities, choose the centers in which they will work, and make choices within the centers.

As social beings, children want to be with others and learn to relate ever more effectively with them. Relating with others, children are exposed to different ways of thinking, knowing, and valuing—all of which lead to expanding cognitive powers (Pattnaik, 2003). Feeling competent socially and cognitively, children are fully motivated to continue to learn more about themselves, others, and the world in which they live (Stone, 2003).

Standards for Knowledge, Skills, and Attitudes

Today, standards guide the knowledge, skills, and attitudes that children must acquire. Using the recommendations of the NCSS (2010) and national history, geography, economics, and civics standards, today's social studies revolves around introducing children to the knowledge, skills, and attitudes required of citizens of a democracy in an interdependent world. Some states have developed their own social studies standards (social studies is not identified as a required subject by NCLB) that fit within the general themes, but focus on more specific content.

Focus on Standards and Knowledge

More than ever, children need knowledge and a basic understanding of the world in which they live. Without knowledge of history, geography, economics, current events, and global interrelationships, children will be ill prepared to assume responsible citizenship.

In the past, much of social studies content was limited in scope, trivial, and lacking in connection to major social education goals (Brophy & Alleman, 2002; 2006). Today, however, there is an awareness of the richness of concepts key to the social studies and how these concepts can be meaningfully introduced to very young children (Levstik, 2002).

National associations and state curriculum committees have identified social studies content that children are to learn during the primary grades. Geographers, historians, economists, civic educators, and social studies authorities have all identified what children should know and be able to do beginning in kindergarten. Prekindergarten standards developed by CTB/McGraw-Hill (2002) and reviewed by the Carnegie Corporation of New York articulate what children 3 to 5 years of age should know and be able to do in the field of the social studies. Additionally, NCSS (2010) identifies ten themes around which social studies teaching can be organized. All ten of those themes are reflected throughout this text.

- *Culture.* The study of culture—the art, language, history, and geography of different cultures—takes place across the total curriculum. To become a global citizen, children must recognize the universals of human cultures everywhere. Chapter 6, "Culture, Diversity, and Values," guides teachers on ways to develop children's ideas about the things that unite all humans everywhere, including themselves.
- *Time, continuity, and change.* In the context of their lives, children come to understand themselves in terms of the passage of time and develop the skills of the historian. This theme is reflected in Chapter 7, "Children's Study of Time, Continuity, and Change: History."
- *People, places, and environments.* Children learn to locate themselves in space, become familiar with landforms in their environment, and develop beginning understanding of the human–environment interaction. Chapter 8, "People, Places, and Environments: Geography," presents these themes.
- *Individual development and identity.* Personal identity is shaped by one's culture, by groups, and by institutional influences. How people learn, what they believe, and how people meet their basic needs in the context of culture are themes within this topic. Chapter 5, "Self, Others, and the Community: Social Skills," begins with a focus on developing children's sense of self.
- *Individuals, groups, and institutions.* Institutions such as schools, families, government agencies, and the courts play a role in people's lives. Children can develop beginning concepts of the role of institutions in their lives. Chapter 5, "Self, Others, and the Community: Social Skills," introduces children to the fact that within a democracy, individual rights are balanced with those of the group.
- *Power, authority, and governance.* Understanding how individual rights can be protected within the context of majority rule can be introduced to young children in the context of their classroom. The idea of power and rights is developed in Chapter 10, " Developing Citizenship: Civics and Government."
- *Production, distribution, and consumption.* Because people have wants and needs that often exceed the resources available to them, a variety of ways have evolved to answer questions such as "What is to be produced?" and "How is production to be organized?" Chapter 9, "Production, Consumption, and Decision Making: Economics," is designed to enable young children to develop beginning ideas of these concepts.
- *Science, technology, and society.* This theme deals with questions such as "How can we cope with change?" and "How can we manage technology so that all benefit from it?" The theme draws on the natural and physical sciences, social sciences, and the humanities. It is introduced in Chapter 7 and has implications

for chapters 7 through 11. Technological resources for the classroom are discussed in Chapter 3.
- *Global connections.* Global interdependence requires understanding and responsive action. Young children explore basic global connections issues and suggest or implement caring actions as described in Chapter 11, "Global Connections."
- *Civic ideals and practices.* This theme deals with what it means to be a citizen. Chapter 10, "Developing Citizenship: Civics and Government," deals with rights and responsibilities within a group.

Focus on Skills

Within the small democracy of the preschool or primary classroom, children begin to develop the social and participatory skills required of citizens in a democracy. They will gain the skills necessary to cooperate and share and begin to assume responsibility for themselves as part of the total group. The NCSS (2010) standards outline essential social studies skills for personal and collaborative interactions and civic engagement (see page 141). The *National Standards for Civics and Government* (Center for Civic Education, 1994) state that students in school should learn to do the following:

- Respect the rights of others
- Respect the privacy of others
- Promote the common good, clean up the environment, and care for the school
- Participate in voting and in developing class rules and constitutions

Civics and government standards suggest that these skills are best developed by "providing students [with] opportunities to practice these skills and to observe and interact with those in their community who are adept in exercising them" (Center for Civic Education, 1994, p. xiii). Good citizenship is not just a matter of the observance of outward forms but also a matter of reasoned conviction, the end result of people's thinking for themselves (Center for Civic Education, 1994).

Citizens of a democracy need to have the skills of thinking and inquiry. Those skills are promoted throughout the social studies curriculum. "Intellectual skills and civics are inseparable" (Center for Civic Education, 1994, p. xii), and being a citizen of a democracy means being "able to think critically" (p. xii). Wade (2003) suggested a civics curriculum focused on civic projects and aimed at developing concepts of a common good. In this way, young children are most likely to develop the concepts key to citizenship in a democracy.

Social studies involves learning many other skills in addition to social skills. Involving children in study of their world, whether the focus be history, economics, geography, or civics, gives them the platform for posing questions and finding answers. As children study their world, they collect data, observe, survey, weigh, measure, map, compare, and contrast things in their here-and-now world. After considering the information collected, children reach conclusions. Through inquiry, they use an array of tools appropriate for study of their world. Through historical inquiry, they study the past. Children learn the skill of map reading in geography, and counting money in economics.

Teachers scaffold children's use of tools and provide time and opportunity for children to practice new skills and reflect on the results of their activity. Only as children make sense of their own world, whatever or wherever that world is, will they develop the thinking skills and knowledge of content necessary for productive citizenship.

Focus on Attitudes and Values

"The values embodied in our democratic form of government with its commitment to justice, quality, and freedom of thought and speech, are reflected in social studies classroom practice" (NCSS, 2010, p. 170).

Children need to develop attitudes and values congruent with the democratic way of life if democracy is to continue, and congruent with the global village if the planet is to survive. The attitudes and values of respect for each individual—freedom of speech, setting and following rules, learning to make choices, participating in the democracy of the classroom, and caring for people and the planet—are fostered through the social studies.

The NCSS (2010) maintains that the focus of education is on how values are formed and how they influence human behavior rather than on building commitment to specific values. They outline basic individual rights, individual freedoms, individual responsibilities, and beliefs concerning social conditions and governmental responsibilities (see page 167). The values and attitudes of the fundamental rights to life, liberty, dignity, equality, and speech are first taught by helping students to weigh priorities in situations in which conflicts arise before more formal study of these concepts begins. Attitudes regarding the importance of participation in and responsibility to the group are taught first within the classroom, the school, and the community.

Misco and Shiveley (2010) propose a taxonomy of dispositions (attitudes and values) for social studies centered around the themes of open-mindedness, whole-mindedness, and responsibility. They suggest that these dispositions can be taught in developmentally appropriate ways through strategies such as community-based problem-solving, service learning, issues-centered curriculum, questioning and investigations, cooperative learning, and global education with accompanying projects. The projects can be assessed for knowledge, skills, and dispositions.

Scope and Sequence

Scope refers to what and how much will be taught, and sequence refers to the order in which it will be taught. While Mitchell's expanding horizons curriculum has been the dominant organizer for social studies scope and sequence in some ways, it has come under discussion for two reasons (Wade, 2003). First, research has shown that preschool and primary children are more adept at applying their here-and-now knowledge to other times and places than previously thought (Brophy & Alleman, 2006). Second, our global, media-based society exposes children to places beyond their local community earlier in their lives. The global village has become a greater part of children's here-and-now experience, at least virtually, through technology and the media. Many states have revised their social studies curriculum away from the spiral/expanding horizons framework in order to expose children to other times, places, and cultures earlier. For example, in highly diverse communities, it is not unusual to see a world map in a kindergarten classroom with stickpins indicating each child's home country; children are gaining firsthand experience of people from other countries at an early age.

Brophy and Alleman (2002, 2005a, 2006, 2007) have proposed an alternative framework called *cultural universals*. They define cultural universals as the human needs and experiences that are basic elements of all cultures, past and present. The universals include food, clothing, shelter, transportation, families, work, communication, government, and recreation. These are a part of students' everyday lives. Children have considerable prior knowledge and experience of these cultural universals in their here-and-now world. Such topics are, therefore, interesting and meaningful. They are also integrated in that each cultural universal has historical, economic, civic, geographic, multicultural, and global connections as well as science and mathematics connections.

Alleman and Brophy (2001, 2002, 2003) have developed instructional units on many of the cultural universals for K–3. Each focuses on major understandings with embedded content, skills, and attitudes. For example, one major understanding from the food unit is that food functions the same across time and cultures, but people eat different things or eat the same things differently. Food groups, nutrition, farming and plant growth, geographical influences, historical changes, production and distribution (Brophy, Alleman, & O'Mahony, 2003), needs and wants, choices, and holidays can all be integrated into a cultural universals framework.

Curriculum Models for Early Childhood Education

Three of the curriculum models currently in use in early childhood education provide the "what" and "how" for social studies (see Figure 1.3). "What" includes the knowledge put forward in the NCSS standards. The "how" addresses the way in which the learning environment is structured and focuses on the desired skills, attitudes, and values developed in the model. Each of the three curriculum models described is based on constructivist theories of active learning, integrated content, and meaningful experiences that are of high interest to children.

Reggio Emilia

The prevalent philosophy of the Reggio Emilia curriculum model is constructivist, and the "how" and "what" of that curriculum reflect the theories of Piaget, Vygotsky, and Dewey (Gandini, 1997). It is based on the premises that social interaction promotes learning and that children learn best through experiences on which they build to create new learning. The characteristics of Reggio Emilia schools are as follows (Hendrick, 2004):

- The emergent curriculum predominates.
- The children's ideas and feelings are encouraged and promoted.
- Inquiry projects are the framework for the curriculum, and the children and teachers actively collaborate to develop these.
- Creativity, expressed particularly through art, is predominant.

Curriculum Model	Connections with the Social Studies		
	Skills	Attitudes and Values	Standards and Knowledge
Reggio Emilia	Focus on collaboration promotes ability to share ideas, problem solve, explore.	Collaboration between all parties develops responsibility, autonomy, and respect.	Curriculum content is emergent; meaningful activity directed by teachers and based on children's interests.
High/Scope	Plan-do-review process promotes inquiry, problem solving, and reaching conclusions.	Plan-do-review process develops responsibility, autonomy, and respect for others. Six steps to conflict resolution taught and practiced.	Curriculum content is emergent; involves meaningful activity directed by teachers and children and is based on children's interests.
Montessori	Materials and activities help them learn to care for themselves and the environment.	Materials and activities encourage responsibility, autonomy, and sense of self.	History and geography: Preschoolers work with appropriately designed maps; learn names of countries and continents. Elementary age explore cultures: their own and those of others.

Figure 1.3   Curriculum models and the social studies.

- Parents are encouraged to participate in their child's learning.
- The classroom includes the whole community.
- Teachers stay with one group of children for 3 years.
- The teachers co-teach in all aspects of the learning environment.

Implications for the Social Studies.   Collaboration between children, teachers, and families is a key feature of this curriculum, reflecting the NCSS goals of promoting democracy, respect for every individual, and problem/conflict solving.

High/Scope

In response to the War on Poverty, David Weikart developed the High/Scope approach to early childhood education in 1970 (Weikart, 1998). It was based on the constructivist philosophy of Piaget. The central beliefs of the approach are as follows:

- Children are active learners.
- At the core of the curriculum are the children's interests.
- Teachers provide hands-on experiences and promote investigation and problem solving through open-ended questioning in their role as facilitators of learning.

The High/Scope program has curricula that extend through elementary school. At the elementary level more emphasis is placed on cooperative projects that develop social skills. Throughout the program, there are both child-directed and teacher-directed activities. During the child-directed activities, a process called "plan-do-review" is used. During planning time, the children decide what they will do and share their ideas with the teacher, who assists the children in getting started. The teachers move among the children as they "do" their work. During review time, the children meet in small groups with a teacher to discuss what they did.

High/Scope preschool programs place a special emphasis on five major social learning areas:

- Taking care of one's own needs
- Expressing feelings in words
- Building relationships with children and adults
- Creating and experiencing collaborative play
- Dealing with social conflict.

The High/Scope curriculum stipulates a six-step conflict-resolution process as a group of teaching strategies that teachers find especially useful in helping children settle conflicts and disagreements. By the end of the program, the children are usually able to use these on their own. These steps can be found on the Web at *www.highscope.org* (accessed August 2008).

The High/Scope program's effectiveness has been highly researched, with program completers being investigated until they reached the age of 40 (Schweinhart et al., 2005). The study inquires into the lives of 123 African Americans born into poverty who had been considered high-risk students. At age 40, those who had received a high-quality preschool experience based on the High/Scope philosophy and curriculum in comparison to the group who had received no preschool:

- Had higher earnings
- Were more likely to hold a job
- Had committed fewer crimes
- Were more likely to have graduated from high school.

Implications for the Social Studies. Through High/Scope, children are supported in developing independence along with collaboration and responsibility. The NCSS goals focusing on skills, attitudes, and values are promoted through the learning environment.

Montessori

The theory and beliefs of Maria Montessori are the foundation for contemporary American Montessori schools, some of which span the ages of 3 through 12. Montessori believed that children universally have four characteristics: the ability to concentrate, an interest and pleasure in meaningful work, self-discipline, and the desire to be a contributing member of a community (Montessori, 1949/1995). These beliefs lead to the following key educational theories:

- Active engagement in natural/spontaneous activity is essential for children.
- Mental stimulation and engagement through the senses promotes intellectual development.
- Learning experiences must be based on the child's needs.

The role of the educator in a Montessori school is to observe children carefully and establish what the children need to optimize academic and social development. Then the educator prepares a learning environment designed to capture the children's interests, stimulate their senses, and engage them in meaningful and active experiences through specially designed materials. The children progress through the graduated activities independently and at their own pace. While the children work, the teachers observe their progress and then prepare for the next set of needs.

Implications for the Social Studies. Children are encouraged to care for the learning environment, and cleaning and tidying up are an essential part of the school day. They work independently and are discouraged from interfering with the other children's work, although cooperation is encouraged. The materials are designed to promote problem solving and inquiry. Respect for others and their surroundings is promoted, as are autonomy and responsibility.

Geography and history are essential parts of the Montessori curriculum from the age of 3. Children play with specially designed maps, learning the names of countries and continents. At the elementary level, children study various aspects of their own culture and those of their peers in depth.

SUMMARY

Knowledge of the content, skills, and attitudes that make up the social studies is necessary if children are to be prepared to take their place as fully productive members of a democratic society. Only when social studies are active, integrated, meaningful, and of interest to children, however, will the discipline fulfill its purpose.

Today's social studies are also grounded in current thinking about social studies education. Using current theories of learning; developmentally appropriate practices; NCSS, discipline, and state standards; and current curriculum models, teachers have a basis for fulfilling the primary goals of the social studies: to prepare children to fulfill their role as citizens of a global world, and to integrate the total curriculum.

Discussion Questions

1. Think back to your early memories of social studies. What was your first experience with the subject? What were your positive experiences? What were your

negative experiences? Which memories are based on your feelings, which on knowledge? What are the implications for powerful social studies teaching?
2. Mitchell discussed the importance of "real-world experiences." Generate ideas of real-world experiences for children and discuss what and how they might learn from them.
3. What common themes do you see across the various theories and curriculum models? How do these align with developmentally appropriate practice? With the principles of powerful social studies teaching?
4. What do you see as the strengths and weaknesses of the standards-based reform movement? What are some ways that you as a teacher can balance the sometimes competing priorities of developmentally appropriate practice and a standards-based environment?
5. When young children are asked questions about what they learned in socials studies, they do not understand the term "social studies." Why do you think this might be the case?

Extend Your Knowledge

1. Observe a group of young children at play. As you observe, make a list of all the topics the children mention or discuss. Then write a description of the nature of the child's here-and-now world. What were the most frequently mentioned topics? Where did children become acquainted with these topics? Which topics have an element of social studies?
2. View online or obtain copies of social studies standards such as *National Curriculum Standards for Social Studies: A Framework for Teaching, Learning, and Assessment* (NCSS); *National Standards for Civics and Government* (Center for Civic Education); *National Standards for United States History: Exploring the American Experience, K–4* (National Center for History in the Schools); or *Geography for Life: National Geography Standards* (National Geographic Society). Read and discuss them with other students. How will your ideas about the standards affect how you teach social studies to young children?
3. Interview a teacher of young children. Ask him or her to define the social studies. What is included in this definition? How does the teacher decide what to include in the social studies curriculum? You may be able to interview a number of teachers, asking the same or similar questions. The goal is to determine how teachers define the social studies and make decisions about what to teach.

Resources

Successful teachers identify and use available resources. Your local school system, state department of education, and local affiliates of national associations have excellent resources to use in teaching social studies. Other organizations are also concerned with social studies education and the education of young children. These associations offer publications, educational materials, services, and other resources for teachers. Check out their websites:

Association for Childhood Education International
www.acei.org

U.S. Government Printing Office
www.gpo.gov

National Association for the Education of Young Children
www.naeyc.org

National Council for the Social Studies
www.ncss.org

Center for Civic Education
www.civiced.org

National Center for History in Schools
www.nchs.ucla.edu

National Geographic Society
www.nationalgeographic.com

Council for Economic Education
www.councilforeconed.org

CHAPTER 2

Planning and Assessment

> **Focus Questions**
>
> After you read this chapter, you should be prepared to respond to the following questions:
>
> - Why is knowledge of children's growth, development, and learning necessary for planning social studies?
> - How does the nature of the community in which children live affect planning?
> - How does social studies content affect planning?
> - What is the nature and purpose of long-term planning? Of short-term planning? What are the benefits of teaching through themes, units, and projects?
> - How will you know if children have learned what you planned to teach them?

"But what do I teach?" asked one teacher candidate after a discussion of the scope of the social studies. "I know social studies is a large, complex field, and I've read some of the standards, but isn't there a workbook or something we can use that tells what to teach?"

If social studies is to be meaningful and totally integrated into children's culture, background of experiences, and social interactions, the teacher must, based on his or her knowledge of the children, knowledge of the community in which they live, and knowledge of the social studies, "make [his/her] own curriculum for small children" (Mitchell, 1934, p. 12).

Throughout the years, reflective teachers have understood this need. They understand that, to bring children and the social studies together, curriculum must hold meaning and interest for each child and be based on children's firsthand interactions with their immediate environment.

Today, as in the past, the teacher is the decision maker. The decisions that teachers will make include the following:

- What short- and long-term goals and objectives will guide the curriculum?
- How will these goals and objectives be achieved?
- How can children's interactions with their environment and community be used to achieve these goals?
- What place will standards of learning and mandated curriculum plans hold in the curriculum? How can the goals and objectives of mandated curriculum be achieved in meaningful ways?
- How will the curriculum be assessed?

As in the past, these decisions cannot be made without (a) knowledge of children, (b) knowledge of the community in which the children live, and (c) knowledge of social studies content.

KNOWLEDGE OF CHILDREN

"I am advising you to retain Judy in kindergarten for another year," the teacher said to 6-year-old Judy's parents. "She doesn't know which day comes before or after another, nor can she tell you the name of the month or the months that came before or after. She just won't make it in first grade until she can do so."

This is the problem of the match that Vygotsky (1986) discussed and Bredekamp and Copple described in *Developmentally Appropriate Practice in Early Childhood Programs* (2009). If Judy's teacher had based her social studies instruction on knowledge of child growth and development, she would have known that isolated facts, such as the names of the days of the week or the months, have little meaning to children. Further, she would have known that children will learn these names automatically as they progress through the primary grades.

Without knowledge of children, teachers are unable to match the curriculum or its goals and expectations for children's learning to the developmental capabilities of children. Without this match, social studies is meaningless and uninteresting to children. As a result, children will dislike social studies. Once they have developed a negative attitude toward social studies, it is very difficult to overcome it.

Basing curriculum on the universal characteristics of children (i.e., those characteristics that make all children alike) and on the unique characteristics of each child (i.e., those things that make each an individual) is one way to ensure that children will live fully each day and be prepared to take their places in a democratic society.

Children Are Alike

Regardless of where children live, their ethnic background, or the structure of their family, they all have the same needs and share similar characteristics.

Children Have Similar Needs

Young children share certain characteristics. For instance, all young children need the following:

- Love, security, and the attention of a friendly, interested, sympathetic adult they can trust (NRC, 2001)
- Shelter, food, warmth, and clothing
- To feel good about themselves and learn to relate to others, make friends, and be a friend

Children Are Active Learners

If children's basic needs for security and love have been met, they are curious, interested in their environment, and filled with the desire to learn more about themselves and their world. Their active minds and bodies demand that they move about physically and interact with one another. Children need to talk, question, and take things apart in their attempts to find out about and make sense of their world (Bredekamp & Copple, 1997; Piaget & Inhelder, 1969).

Children Pass Through the Same Stages of Thought

Between the ages of 2 and 7 or 8, children's thinking is preoperational. They are beginning to think abstractly and use symbols, to represent their actions mentally, to anticipate consequences before an action actually occurs, and to develop some idea of causes; but they still need concrete referents to understand abstract ideas, and they need concrete referents to perform operations on abstract ideas.

For example, a child in the stage of preoperational thought relies heavily on the way things look. Perception dominates thought; the way things look is the way they are. Thus, a child under age 7 or 8 says there is more juice in a tall, skinny glass than in a short, squat one or that there are more candies in a long, spread-out row than there are in a bunched group.

At around age 7 or 8, children's thinking changes; they begin to think operationally. They can tell you that the amount of juice poured into two containers of different shapes stays the same because no juice has been added or taken away; they can perform the mental operation of translating the amount of juice between the two containers when they see it. But even though children after age 7 or 8 can reason this way, their thinking is still tied to the concrete. They do not think about the hypothetical or possible easily or naturally. Their thought is bound to the real, concrete world—hence the term *concrete operations*. Not until age 11 or 12 do children enter the last stage of thought, in which they can think formally about abstractions and have the ability to manipulate abstract ideas without concrete referents.

Because children cannot think in truly abstract ways until nearly age 11 or 12, most of the goals and objectives planned for early social studies learning are based on the concrete, hands-on experience. For example, when asked about the abstract concept of democracy, elementary-age children might be able to say that in a democracy people vote (a concrete act that they may have witnessed or heard about during an election), but they are not yet able to give a definition of democracy as a political structure. During the preschool and primary grades, children need to develop an interest in learning, a base of firsthand experiences, and basic content knowledge on which to build later, more abstract concepts and understandings.

So Alike, So Different

As individuals, however, young children are very different. Each child is unique. Understanding the general characteristics of all children, teachers recognize that each one brings to school a different background of experiences, interests, and motivations. Successful social studies are based on teachers' understanding of the experiences children have had before coming to school, the interests of each child, individual abilities, special needs, and the culture in which children live (Derman-Sparks, 2003; McCormick, Wong, & Yogi, 2003).

Experiences

For the most part, children entering school have a full, rich background of experience. Many have had opportunities to explore their immediate neighborhoods, become familiar with traffic systems and community helpers, discuss their experiences with adults, and recognize the relationships among their experiences. Teachers can determine children's background of experience in the following ways:

- Visiting their homes and talking with their parents about the things the children have done
- Walking around the children's neighborhoods to see what the community offers experientially

Children—so alike, yet so different.

- Interviewing the children, asking them to tell about the things they do, places they have been, and things they would like to do
- Studying the home countries or cultures of new or recent immigrant families

Whatever the children's backgrounds, they are important indicators of objectives and goals for the social studies program. Teachers plan curriculum to support past experiences of children, introduce new experiences that can be incorporated into the children's previous experiences, and extend, clarify, and expand all experiences.

Interests

As anyone who has contact with young children knows, they are interested in learning about everything. They enter preschool interested in learning about ants, worms, cars, boats, water, air, space, foreign countries, letters, machines, trees, colors, families, seeds, rocks, love, hate, birth, death, friendship, war, peace, cosmic forces, good, and evil. To plan a social studies curriculum, some understanding of what the group and each individual child within the group is interested in will be necessary. To begin, you could do these things:

- Talk with children informally; ask them what they would like to know more about, what they would like to do, or what they know a lot about.
- Observe children at play; note the things they play with, how they use materials, what they play, what they talk about, and which books they select.
- Discuss children's interests with their parents, and ask what the children like to do at home.

Abilities

Children not only bring a wide range of experiences and interests to the classroom, but they also bring great differences in social, emotional, physical, and intellectual developmental levels and abilities. These differences also help form the basis of goals and objectives of social studies for the group and for individual children.

To determine the developmental levels and abilities of children, you might take these steps:

- Review past records
- Observe children at play
- Structure tasks for children to complete
- Conduct a simple developmental assessment
- Review results of standardized measures

Special Needs

All children are special, and each has individual needs, strengths, and weaknesses. Some, however, have needs and characteristics that require special planning and care. Public laws have been passed to ensure that the special needs of these children

Teachers find ways to include all children.

will be met. P.L. 94-142, the Education of All Handicapped Children Act of 1975, protects children with special needs by requiring that every child, regardless of the handicapping condition, have access to free and appropriate educational experiences in the least restrictive environment.

P.L. 99-457, the Federal Preschool Program and Early Intervention Program Act of 1986, extends rights and services to handicapped infants, toddlers, and preschoolers. Until 1986, children between ages 3 and 5 received services only at each state's discretion. P.L. 99-457 requires appropriate public education for those children. From birth through age 2, the law requires that services be available for children who show signs of developmental delay, have identifiable physical or mental conditions, or are at risk because of medical or environmental problems (Diamond & Stacey, 2003).

Even without laws, teachers wishing to foster the principles of democracy in their classrooms would find ways to include all children and their families (see Figure 2.1).

When talking with families of children with special needs, try to do the following:

- *Reduce education or professional terms.* Instead of talking about methodologies or strategies, say, "This is what we will do," and "Here is how we will do it."
- *Use words instead of initials.* Rather than saying, "P.L. 94-142," say, "the law providing for equality of educational opportunity." Say, "individual education plan" instead of "IEP."
- *Accept parents' feelings.* Say, "Understandably, you are very worried," to parents who are expressing anxiety about their child. To angry parents, say, "Understandably, you are angry."
- *Use active listening.* To clarify what parents have said, you might say, "I heard you say. . . . Did I understand you correctly?"

Figure 2.1 Talking with families.

Democracy reflects the belief that young children, whatever their abilities or disabilities, can grow in self-confidence and increase their skills and abilities to interact socially with others when included in programs. As Diamond and Stacey (2003) asserted, all children have the right to a life that is as normal as possible.

Teaching children with special needs is not a new aspect of early childhood education. The needs of exceptional children in the regular preschool or primary classroom have been recognized for decades, long before implementation of these laws. So what was new about P.L. 94-142 and P.L. 99-457? They protect children with special needs by requiring educational experiences in the *least restrictive environment*. The preschool or primary classroom is often determined to be the least restrictive environment, for it gives children with special needs the opportunity to enter the mainstream of living and learning with other children their age (McDermott, 2003).

As a teacher of special children you need to (a) familiarize yourself with the complete text of P.L. 94-142; (b) ask your director, principal, or supervisor for your child-care center's or school system's guidelines for implementation of the law; (c) obtain resources and special assistance when mainstreaming children with special needs; and (d) perhaps request a classroom aide—a teacher of a specific skill, such as sign language—for assistance in acquiring specialized skills.

Children with special needs who benefit from being in the mainstream preschool or primary classroom are those who have visual or hearing impairments, physical disabilities, mental retardation, emotional problems, or speech or language impairments, as well as those who are not proficient in English and those who are gifted. While labeling of individual children is discouraged, it does help to know something about the specific conditions children bring to the classroom.

Visual Impairments

Children with visual impairments frequently can work and learn effectively in the regular classroom, and they can participate in many activities without special assistance. Teachers working with children who have visual impairments just have to remember the obvious: These children cannot see well, if at all. This means remembering that children with visual impairments do not learn by looking or by imitating others. They will need systematic and deliberate introduction to the physical environment of the room, school, and playground as well as the activities of the school. You will need to maintain consistency in the physical environment, provide tactile guides in the room, and communicate by touching as well as speaking. You will need to ensure that the child is comfortable, asking questions when he or she does not understand or needs assistance.

Hearing Impairments

Children with hearing impairments also find the mainstream preschool and primary classroom suited to their needs. You will want to learn how to communicate with the child who has a hearing impairment using the method the child uses and learn the care of hearing aids and how to assist the child with the aid.

Children with hearing impairments can participate in nearly all school activities. You need to communicate with these children in special ways. They learn by seeing, and they respond to touch. Marschark, Lang, and Albertin (2001) describe how a child with a hearing impairment was successfully included in a first-grade classroom through collaboration with children, the family, and others in the school.

One teacher and his student agreed on a sign—placing her finger beside her nose—to indicate to the teacher that she did not understand. This sign enabled the teacher to be helpful without disrupting the entire class.

Physical Disabilities

You may need to adapt the physical environment for children with physical disabilities and for those who use orthopedic aids. Ask specialists for assistance in adapting the physical plant to the needs of the child, both indoors and outdoors. Special chairs, tables, and play equipment can be purchased or made for children with physical disabilities, enabling them to participate in school activities.

You will want to learn all you can about the condition of a child with physical disabilities. You will need to know the child's limitations and potentials as well as how to care for orthopedic equipment and assist the child with the equipment.

Mental Disabilities

Children who differ from average or normal intelligence or who have learning disabilities are also frequently mainstreamed in the preschool and primary classroom. The open schedule, free activity times, and emphasis on concrete learning as well as social, emotional, and language development are well suited for children who have mental impairments (Molenarr-Klumper, 2002).

You will need to analyze each task so that you can present it to the child in small steps. Specific experiences and instruction in listening and speaking, social skills, and self-help skills will enable children who have mental impairments to be more successful.

Emotional Problems

Nearly everyone has lost control, felt afraid, or had difficulty interacting with others. At one time or another, all children experience difficulty handling strong emotions. Children who have more difficulty than most in handling their emotions find a preschool experience very beneficial. Here they can learn techniques for channeling emotions appropriately and strengthening their ability to control behavior.

Probably all preschool activities will benefit children who need to learn to handle emotions, and the primary classroom environment can be modified to permit more activities designed for this purpose. It will be important to have an agreed-upon behavior plan and a plan for how to handle a child who is totally out of control—hitting, kicking, hurting self and others—such as a timeout place or an aide or a volunteer to stay with the child for a while, offering the child support and guidance in learning to gain control over strong emotions (Greene, 2001.)

Speech and Language Impairments

For children who have language impairments, you can arrange assessment for specific diagnoses and plan appropriate activities in listening and speaking. Speech and hearing specialists can assist you as you plan for these children, and volunteers or aides may help you implement specific lessons.

Remember that all of the language activities of the preschool–primary classroom will benefit children with speech and language impairments. The stories, poems, creative dramatics, and dramatic play will be of great benefit.

Limited English Proficiency

Children whose first language is one other than English can benefit greatly from a classroom rich in language and multisensory experiences. Using simple sentence structures and known vocabulary; using pictures, songs, gestures, and kinesthetic experiences; and providing opportunities for play and social interaction will enable English language development.

Gifted Children

Children who demonstrate intelligence higher than the norm or who have specific gifts and talents deserve to have their special needs met (Walker, Hafenstein, & Crow-Enslow, 1999). Typically, the needs of children who are gifted have been met by acceleration, enrichment, placement in special schools, or advancement to a higher grade. The social studies offer these children many opportunities to explore interests, solve problems, and develop talents.

A Program of Inclusion

While public laws protect all children's rights to appropriate education, teaching children who have special needs requires much more than just being together in a classroom. Children with special needs require acceptance for who they are and an environment that fosters their autonomy and the development of alternative modes of interaction with the world (Diamond & Stacey, 2003).

Research suggests that early childhood programs should strive for the following goals:

- Develop an inclusive educational environment in which all children can succeed
- Enable children with disabilities to develop autonomy, independence, competency, confidence, and pride
- Provide all children with accurate, developmentally appropriate information about their own and others' disabilities, and foster understanding that a person with a disability differs from others in one respect but is similar in many others
- Enable all children to develop the ability to interact knowledgeably, comfortably, and fairly with people who have various disabilities
- Teach children with disabilities how to handle and challenge name calling, stereotypic attitudes, and physical barriers

- Teach nondisabled children how to resist and challenge stereotyping, name calling, and physical barriers directed against people with disabilities
- Encourage children to ask about their own and others' physical characteristics
- Enable children to feel pride, but not superiority, about their racial identity
- Enable children to develop ease with and respect for physical differences
- Help children become aware of our shared physical characteristics—what makes us all human beings

Regardless of the disability, these children will require some modifications or accommodations in order to be successful. Modifications can be made to content, learning activities, assessments, and/or the environment according to each child's needs. Children with an official special education designation will have an IEP (Individualized Education Plan) that helps guide the teacher's planning.

KNOWLEDGE OF THE COMMUNITY

"I found four signs with words and seven without," exclaimed an excited first-grader returning from a walk around the block.

As Mitchell (2000) suggested, teachers must become aware of the nature of the here-and-now world in which children live. Then they must develop knowledge of the culture and values of the community. Just as teachers cannot plan a social studies curriculum without knowledge of child growth and development, they cannot successfully implement it without knowledge of the community.

The Child's Physical World

"The practical tasks for each school are to study the relations in the environment into which their children are born and to watch the children's behavior in their environment, to note when they first discover relations and what they are" (Mitchell, 1934, p. 12). To do this, you might drive or walk through children's neighborhoods. You can encourage children to notice particular things as they walk or ride to school. One teacher asked a parent to guide her through the school's neighborhood. As they walked and talked together, they noted the following:

- The physical nature of the area
- Places children enjoyed going
- The history of the neighborhood
- Neighbors who had special skills or resources
- Places of business
- Other resources for learning

Another day the teacher walked through the neighborhood again. This time she noted where children played, the pathways they took on their way home from school, and the way they interacted with peers, adults, and their parents. She also noted how people functioned in the neighborhood. In communities that are spread

Teachers locate community resources for children's learning.

out and in which children ride the bus, teachers can follow bus routes to determine what children see as they ride to school. Insights into the children's community and here-and-now world can influence the teacher's decisions about the overall goals and objectives for the social studies curriculum.

Cultural Knowledge and Values

Less concrete than knowledge of the physical environment, but perhaps even more important, is knowledge of the culture and values of the community. Early in the school year, teachers try to become acquainted with each child's ethnic and subcultural backgrounds as well as the culture and values of the community as a whole (Garcia, 2003). This can be done in various ways:

- *Informal conversations.* Early in the school year, teachers can talk informally with parents and children. Teachers can ask them what the family does on weekends, in the evenings, before school starts, or on vacations. Teachers can note the traditions, customs, language, special foods, items of dress, and types of celebrations mentioned by the children or their parents during these conversations.
- *Talks with or visits from resource persons.* A resource person is someone with particular knowledge to share. The resource person might be within the school or from the community. Resource persons might be able to inform teachers about the traditions, history, and meaning of a group's practices.
- *Formal inservice activities.* Teachers and administrators can initiate a variety of activities and programs designed to acquaint them with different cultures and values. One school enrolled a large number of children from Cambodia. A resource person knowledgeable about Cambodian culture and its demands on children and their families was invited to talk with the teachers. In a short period of time, she was able to help the teachers build a base of knowledge useful for understanding and teaching these children (Newman, 1995).

Other meetings might be sponsored by community organizations or local businesses and involve parents and other community residents. Slides, videos, and photographs of the community are helpful in illustrating the culture of a community.

KNOWLEDGE OF THE SOCIAL STUDIES

"I have to take two more courses from the social sciences if I want to teach young children. What in the world does my taking geography, history, and economics have to do with young children?" complained an undergraduate student to her advisor. Well, just about everything. Without complete, in-depth knowledge of the social sciences and the skills and values considered to be a part of social studies, teachers cannot be effective.

To make this vast, even overwhelming, amount of information accessible to children, teachers must have a basic grasp of the key concepts in each social science discipline. Selected concepts must be complete and accurate as well as match what children already know and are capable of understanding (Brophy & Alleman, 2002, 2003, 2005b). Thus, knowledge of both child development and content is required. If a concept key in politics is setting and keeping rules, then 4-year-olds might decide on rules for using the woodworking bench, 5-year-olds could dictate a list of rules they will follow in their group for the coming year, and 6- and 7-year-olds might draw up rules for their class. Children in middle school/junior high school and high school could study the lawmaking bodies of the community, state, and nation.

Standards of developmentally appropriate practice as well as content-oriented national and state standards also guide teachers in planning and selecting social studies content. National professional organizations in the fields that form the social studies have identified key concepts in history, geography, economics, civic education, and other fields. These standards typically begin with kindergarten and may be grouped for kindergarten through Grade 3 or 4. In addition, most states have content standards organized by grade level. States and/or school districts often have curriculum frameworks, which serve as guides for scope and sequence. The standards, therefore, are a useful framework to guide teachers' planning. But teachers will still need to adjust the standards to accomplish the following:

- Provide for the needs of individual children and the unique group of children with whom they are working
- Match the standards with the resources in the community so children can learn from their here-and-now world
- Offer developmentally appropriate learning experiences

Teachers also need to be knowledgeable about social studies skills, attitudes, and values. Some of these are outlined in national and state standards. Teaching skills is part of both social studies and other areas of the curriculum. Some skills, however, are best fostered within the context of social studies, such as map reading. Other skills, such as thinking, finding and using information, and social skills, are present in social studies but are developed throughout the curriculum. Skill development begins at birth and continues throughout life. In gaining proficiency, children will have the opportunity to practice thinking and social skills throughout their preschool and primary experiences.

Attitudes and values constitute the third major area of social studies. Those included in social studies are necessary for the perpetuation and continuation of our society. Teachers select goals and objectives for children's learning of content and skills congruent with the values of a democracy and an interdependent world. The entire early childhood program is arranged around goals and objectives that will foster the following:

- Each child's own worth and dignity
- Respect for self and others
- Participation in and responsibility for the group
- The disposition of learning to learn

SHORT- AND LONG-TERM PLANNING

With an understanding of the children, their culture, and the social studies, you have a base from which to answer this question: "What am I trying to help the children learn, understand, and experience?" Before you begin to answer the question, consider some other factors:

- How can I involve the children in planning?
- How can I plan for spontaneous learning?
- How can I plan short-term lessons?
- How can I plan units, projects, and thematic learning?

Involving the Children

Everyone benefits when children and teachers plan together. Teachers benefit because children who have been involved in planning their own learning are more highly motivated to learn and less likely to disrupt the group. Children benefit because they know they belong. They feel in control.

Teacher–child planning implies cooperation between teacher and child. It does not mean that children take over. Young children would feel insecure if that were the case; they want and need an adult to make decisions and to protect and guide them. On the other hand, teacher–child planning does not mean that a teacher decides ahead of time and then fishes for answers until the children give the responses she had in mind. Here's an example of such fishing:

> "What should we make today?" asked a teacher.
> "I'm going to build a garage," answered one child and another said, "I'll make a painting." The teacher continued questioning until a child asked, "Are we going to make valentines?"
> "Yes, that's it. Today we're making valentines," said the teacher. Later, when asked why she proceeded this way, the teacher explained, "It's very important to involve the children in making plans."

Much teacher–child planning is informal and takes place when 3- and 4-year-olds are asked to plan what they will do next or during the morning. Five-year-olds may be able to make plans for a party next week or at the end of the month, and primary-age children can develop even more extended plans.

All children should be asked to take part in making plans. Those who may be too shy to speak in front of a group or are not quick enough to take their turn may need other opportunities besides group discussions to contribute their ideas. Some planning can be done by talking with individuals or small groups of children as they play and work.

Children can plan many things:

- What they will work and play with
- With whom they will work and play
- The materials they need to complete a project
- What things they would like to learn more about
- How they will celebrate a birthday or holiday
- Places they would like to visit to learn more about a specific topic

More formal ways of planning with children have been developed. Many teachers ask children to tell them what they *know* about a specific topic, what they *want* to learn, and (after the lesson) what they have *learned* (K-W-L) (Ogle, 1986) as a means of involving children in planning (see Figure 2.2).

K	*What do we Know about fire fighters?* They put out fires. Only men can be fire fighters, girls can't. Firemen are big.
W	*What do we Want to learn about fire fighters?* Where do they sleep? How do they slide down the pole? What do they eat? Do they like to ride on the truck?
L	*What have we Learned about fire fighters?* Men and women can be fire fighters. They sleep and eat at the fire station, but they have a home too. A computer tells them where there is a fire. Fire fighters put on boots, fireproof clothing, and helmets. They carry air with them. The truck has another computer, hoses, and equipment. Fire fighters go to school and learn everything. They know how to stop, drop, and roll. Fire fighters are daddies and mommies too. They have children. Fire fighter Bob's little boy is named Daniel, and his girl is Catlain. They're nice.

Figure 2.2   A K-W-L chart.

A teacher from the University of Maryland's Center for Young Children sent a letter to each kindergarten child before school started. She asked each to return the enclosed self-addressed postcard to her, listing the things the child wanted to learn in the coming year.

After the children had settled into the kindergarten routine, the teacher organized their postcards into a graph. The children discussed the graph, counting the cards in a given area. Most of the children responded that they wanted to learn to read and do math, but they also included many other topics that the teacher incorporated into her plans.

Planning for the Spontaneous

Teaching young children is never predictable. Their curiosity, interests, and creativity can jump from one exciting event to an equally thrilling moment, none of which may have been planned by a teacher or a curriculum guide. Being able to respond to children's spontaneous interests and to incidental events—whether it be a bird that flies against the window, a dead fish in the aquarium, snow, or the need for a repair person—is part of being an effective teacher. When teachers ignore the changing interests, immediate needs, or incidental experiences of children, they miss too many opportunities for teaching; and children miss opportunities to follow their curiosity and have their needs for knowledge met.

Although you cannot ignore the opportunities for social studies teaching and learning that arise spontaneously, planning is still critical. You can keep in mind the broad goals and objectives of social studies, the locally required standards (if any), as well as specific objectives for individual children and then use the spontaneous and incidental as a means of fostering the achievement of these objectives. With goals in mind, any number of spontaneous happenings becomes a lesson. For example, a visit from the school janitor to fix a leaky faucet might led to a unit on school helpers and then perhaps community helpers; or a lesson on toys might lead to a study of kites from children's home countries (DeGaetano, Williams, & Volk 1998).

Being able to respond spontaneously to incidental events is part of the planning process.

You can also keep complete lesson plans or even unit plans handy. A lot of things seem to happen spontaneously or incidentally, yet they are really very predictable. For instance, the apple tree outside the window will bloom one day, it will rain or be windy on another day, and children will fight and argue over a toy on another day. Aware of the many things that happen throughout the year, some teachers keep concept boxes on hand. These boxes contain props and equipment—perhaps a complete lesson plan with poems and books—on a variety of topics. They may focus on the weather, seasons, historical figures related to holidays (e.g., George Washington and President's Day), interpersonal disputes, recognition and safe release of feelings, the functions of school personnel, or mainstreaming children with special needs.

One day when an unpredicted wind came up, a teacher went to the storeroom and picked out a box labeled "wind." Using the small parachutes, kites, scarves, and poems about wind in the box, she led the children through a series of lessons that, although they seemed spontaneous, were in reality very carefully and thoughtfully planned to meet children's interests as well as specific goals and objectives of the curriculum.

Lesson Plans

Teachers make plans for day-to-day experiences and activities as well as long-range plans. *Lesson plans* are created for short-term, day-to-day learning experiences, while *units* or *projects* are planned for learning experiences that extend over time.

Daily lesson plans are one useful tool for short-term planning. They enable a teacher to plan meaningful activities for the present—for today, tomorrow, or next week. Once you get into the habit of making lesson plans, planning becomes second nature, like driving a car does. Once teachers internalize the process of planning lessons, they can focus on the broader aspects of teaching, meet individual differences, and take advantage of the spontaneous.

Lesson plans can revolve around an individual child, a small group, or the total group. They include elements such as the following:

- Arranging the room to provide different opportunities for children's play
- Presenting new materials or demonstrating possibilities with materials familiar to the children
- Providing opportunities for open-ended outcomes and creativity
- Giving teacher guidance in the form of feedback, listening to children, talking with them, and asking questions
- Planning for inclusion of children with special needs

Teachers use many types of lesson plans and formats. Regardless of the format, every lesson plan includes the following:

- Preparation
- A statement of goals and objectives
- Procedures to obtain the stated goals and objectives
- Ways to assess the stated goals and objectives

Preparation

"Is Jefferson City north or south of where we live?" a teacher asked a group of 6-year-olds. When no one answered, the teacher said, "I told you yesterday. Now listen: Jefferson City is north of us; north is always up," pointing to a globe she was holding.

If this teacher had been prepared, she would have known that the concepts of north and south are meaningless to young children. She also would not have given children inaccurate information—that north is always up.

Before planning, you must be fully certain that you understand the concept, attitude, or skill you want to present. You can obtain references from the library or Internet or discuss the topic with an authority on the subject. If you are planning experiences in geography, you might attend a lecture at the local library, community center, or university. Teachers need to understand content for two important reasons: (1) translating subject matter into experiences for children demands knowledge of the scope and structure of the discipline; and (2) facts (e.g., the names of countries or the number of chemical elements) change so rapidly in today's world that continually updating knowledge is required to ensure accuracy.

It is also important to assess children's prior knowledge so you can use it as a foundation on which to build and make connections. It can be useful to observe children as they work and play and to interview them to find out what they already know and would like to know about a topic. Some teachers simply ask children to "tell me everything you know about _____." The answers to this type of question provide valuable insights into children's ideas on any given topic. K-W-L charts are also useful. Other teachers ask children to make books about a topic. For example, they may have children make a booklet about dogs to discover their level of knowledge about the subject (Bredekamp & Rosegrant, 1995).

Your final preparation for planning involves locating resources for children's use, obtaining materials, arranging the room, or contacting experts who might visit the class. Outstanding resources in the community may lead you to select a goal you had not thought about; limited resources may cause you to eliminate an experience you were considering.

Objectives

The song "Happy Talk" from the musical *South Pacific* expresses the idea that you must first have a dream before you can make it come true. This same idea can be applied to teaching. How do you know when you have achieved your goals if you have never established any? Thus, the first and perhaps the most essential part of planning is determining your objectives.

State the lesson's major purpose. One or two carefully thought-out objectives stated in specific behavioral terms are more effective and realistic for a lesson plan than less specific goals are. Teachers decide on objectives based on goals/standards, knowledge of the children, the content of social studies, and knowledge of the environment.

Today, nearly every educator is familiar with behavioral objectives. Although writing objectives behaviorally may seem somewhat tedious, stating them behaviorally is not at all mysterious or difficult. A behavioral objective, unlike the more general objective just mentioned, is a precise statement of behavior that will be accepted as evidence of the child's having achieved what was set out to be accomplished. A behavioral objective answers the following questions:

1. What will we teach?
2. How will we know when we've taught it?
3. What materials and procedures will work best to teach what we wish to teach?

In writing behavioral objectives, you will want to pay particular attention to your use of language. Since behavioral objectives are specific, your language must also be specific, using verbs that are observable and measureable. Verbs must be observable or measureable in order for them to be assessed. Look at the following words and decide just how well each one communicates what will be taught and learned:

Too General	Measurable
Know	Name
Understand	Identify
Appreciate	Construct
Enjoy	Compare
Believe	Solve

For example, an objective that states, "The student will know about money" does not have a measurable component and it does not help you in planning what to do on a given day. An objective such as, "The student will be able to name 3 coins" is measurable and tells you something specific about what to teach and how you will know what the student learns about money. You might write objectives in one of the following ways:

1. Identify the terminal behavior you desire by name. ("Name four ways to travel on land.")
2. Try to define the desired behavior further by describing the conditions under which you expect the behavior to occur. ("When given a set of pictures of vehicles, the child will be able to identify and name those that travel on land.")
3. Specify the criteria of acceptable performance by describing how well the learner must perform. ("The child will select three of the five vehicles that travel on land.") (Figure 2.3)

Goals stated in these terms—specific student behaviors related to lesson content—facilitate the teaching–learning process as well as its assessment. Once you determine the lesson's behavioral objectives, you need only to teach those behaviors identified in the objective and, after the teaching, assess each child's performance in regard to the specified behavior.

Behavioral objectives have been in use for a number of years. But while they enable teachers to plan more precisely, they are not without problems. Because they always specify the outcome, they can limit children's learning by leading teachers to ignore children's behaviors or outcomes not prespecified by an objective. Assuming only one correct response may leave little room for divergent thinking, choice, or selection of materials. In addition, behavioral objectives are very specific,

Guide to Writing Objectives

Students will be able to MEASURABLE VERB + CONTENT NOUN + (optional) ACTIVITY

Each objective requires a verb and a noun. The verb describes the cognitive process or performance that is measurable and/or observable, and the noun describes the content/skill to be learned. The noun is the content/skill to be assessed; the verb is the process by which the content/skill is assessed. Note that the activity is optional, but helpful. The activity can usually be used as the assessment.

For example:

Students will be able to define (VERB) economic terms (CONTENT NOUN).

Students will be able to represent (VERB) economic terms (CONTENT NOUN) by drawing (ACTIVITY).

Students will be able to demonstrate knowledge of economic terms by answering Jeopardy questions.

Students will be able to classify living and nonliving things by sorting pictures.

Students will be able to diagram the water cycle by drawing.

Students will be able to identify three coins by pointing and naming.

Students will be able to recall George Washington as the first President of the United States by drawing, writing, or answering when questioned.

Students will be able to construct a simple map of the classroom with at least three details.

Students will be able to demonstrate the ability to use latitude and longitude by using coordinates to locate cities on a map.

Students will be able to distinguish between 3 kinds of Native American shelters by labeling.

Students will be able to explain how geography impacted 3 kinds of Native American shelters by drawing and/or writing.

Measurable Verbs for Learning Objectives
organized by Bloom's Taxonomy of Cognitive Processes (Arends, 2012)
(Use only the bulleted verbs.)

1. **Remember**
   - Retrieve
   - Recognize
   - Recall
   - Identify
   - List

2. **Understand**
   - Interpret
   - Give examples of
   - Classify
   - Summarize
   - Infer
   - Compare
   - Explain
   - Restate
   - Paraphrase
   - Define
   - Contrast
   - Describe
   - Illustrate
   - Represent (e.g., numbers, symbols)

Figure 2.3 Guide to writing objectives.

Source: Based on S. Castle and R. Falconer (2006/11), *Guide to Instructional Objectives*, Elementary Education Program, George Mason University.

3. **Apply**
   - Execute
   - Demonstrate
   - Implement
   - Determine
   - Locate
   - Match
   - Sequence
   - Show how to
   - Document (e.g., observations)

4. **Analyze**
   - Differentiate
   - Distinguish
   - Organize
   - Attribute
   - Diagram

5. **Evaluate**
   - Check
   - Critique
   - Verify
   - Judge
   - Prioritize
   - Justify
   - Rate

6. **Create**
   - Generate
   - Plan
   - Hypothesize
   - Speculate
   - Produce
   - Build
   - Design
   - Dramatize
   - Compose
   - Construct
   - Invent

Figure 2.3 (*Continued*)

breaking learning into isolated steps without considering the entire experience. A child can learn the 22 steps in shoe tying, yet never be able to put them together to actually tie a shoelace. It is up to the teacher to decide which learning experiences require behavioral objectives and corresponding assessments and which do not. For example, free play in the grocery store center is primarily experiential and may not require a behavioral objective. If play in the grocery store center is focused on counting money, a behavioral objective that states, "The student will be able to count money correctly," may be appropriate. This objective can then be assessed through observation and a checklist of who counts correctly and who does not.

Procedures

It is not necessary to excite or stimulate young children; however, every lesson begins with an introduction to involve children and hook their interest. An interesting picture, a photograph, a book, an object, a big question, or a finger play can engage children's interest and prepare them for the lesson.

Learning activities are then specified. The learning activities describe what the teacher and children will do to achieve the stated goals and objectives. There may be one or several learning activities. Some lesson plans will indicate the teaching strategy being used such as learning centers, cooperative learning, concept attainment, discussion, or problem-based learning. The activity that serves as the assessment is included.

Each lesson ends with a summary or closure in which the teacher or the students briefly review what they have learned in the lesson. It can be as simple as repeating the objective ("Today we learned to identify quarters") or asking the children what they learned ("What did we learn today?"); or it can be a little more complex, such as completing the L portion of a K-W-L chart. This helps to solidify the new knowledge in the children's minds (Arends, 2012).

Assessment

The beauty of stating objectives behaviorally is that, once stated, assessment is nearly complete. The teacher has only to check the children's work or behavior against the statement, and the lesson is assessed.

Most teachers now use authentic forms of assessment. Teachers familiar with authentic assessment techniques know how to evaluate the success of a lesson by (a) observing the children's behavior, (b) interviewing children informally to see if misconceptions have been corrected and concepts gained, and (c) structuring tasks for children to complete—for example, asking each child to follow a map of the room to find a hidden treasure, to describe the things happening in a picture, to tell the story of something, to draw and/or write about the objective, or to select the pictures showing what the objective taught.

Units, Projects, and Thematic Learning

Units, projects, and thematic learning share a number of similarities. Each is grounded solidly on theories of constructionism. In the mid-1900s, Dewey's (1944) assertion that meaningful curriculum is not just the memorization of isolated facts but a unified whole led to the development of unit planning. Over the years, Piagetian and Vygotskian ideas of children's construction of knowledge through social, physical, and mental activity supported project and thematic learning (Piaget & Inhelder, 1969; Vygotsky, 1986).

All three approaches revolve around a theme that unites activities and learning into a congruent, consistent whole. The learning experiences in a unit of study allow children the opportunity to learn concepts as parts of an integrated whole rather than isolated bits and pieces of information under a particular content area (see Figure 2.4).

Units are organized around a social studies or integrated theme and may include project work. They differ subtly from project and thematic learning in that they are more teacher directed. A unit is developed and planned in advance by the teacher to last for a specific amount of time—perhaps several days, a week, or even a month (Helm & Katz, 2001a). Although a unit plan allows room for children to initiate and teachers follow children's interests and cues as the unit is implemented, the teacher is the primary initiator. The integrated units on food, clothing, shelter, and transportation designed by Alleman and Brophy (2001, 2002, 2003; Brophy & Alleman, 2005b; Brophy, Alleman, & O'Mahony, 2003) are examples of such units.

As opposed to a preplanned unit, project work stems from children's interests and follows children's questions and needs. Children actively investigate, bring in

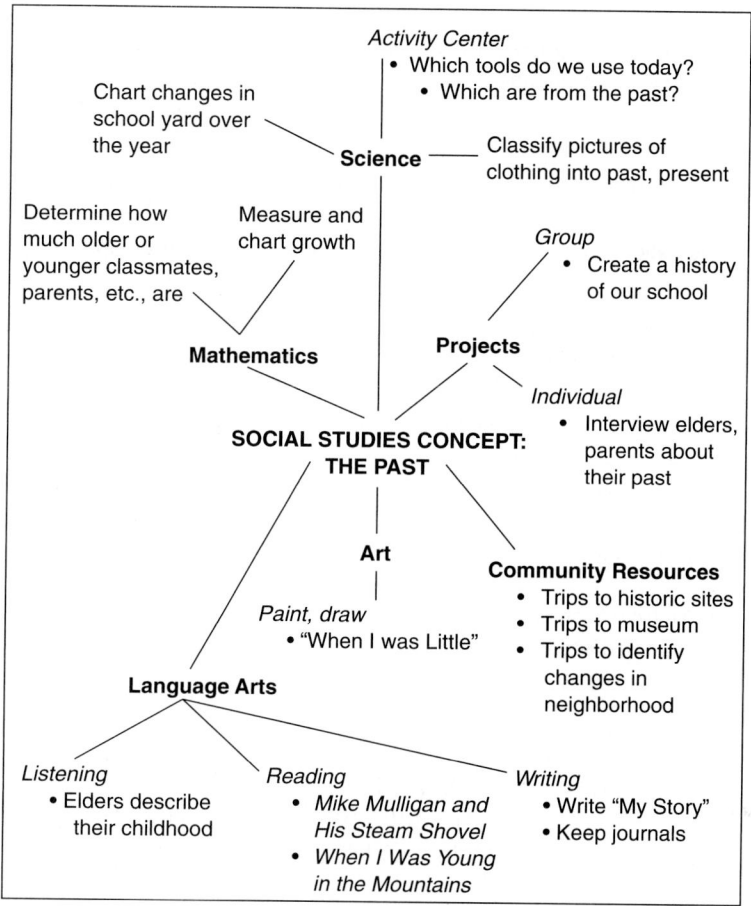

Figure 2.4 Social studies: An integrated web.

resources, and represent their ideas. Projects may last for several days, weeks, months, or even the entire year. An example of a year-long project is the Web-based learning site Journey North (*www.journeynorth.org*). Journey North is a free online educational service supported by Annenberg/CPB. The project uses media and communications to improve math, science, and social studies education for the nation's school children. Journey North tracks migratory species each spring. Children share their own field observations with classrooms across the hemisphere. In addition, students are linked with scientists who provide expertise directly to the classroom. You can choose the species you want to follow, and migration is tracked by satellite telemetry, providing live coverage of individual animals as they migrate. As spring sweeps across the hemisphere, students note changes in daylight, temperatures, and all living things as the food chain comes back to life.

Thematic learning is somewhere between units and projects. Thematic learning usually is more teacher directed than project learning is, but the word *theme* implies

> - They equip students with knowledge, skills, and attitudes they will find useful both in and outside of school.
> - They are based on goals selected to develop students' expertise, conceptual knowledge, and self-regulated application of skills.
> - They balance breadth with depth by addressing limited content but develop this content sufficiently to foster conceptual understanding.
> - They allow children to actively make sense and construct meaning.
> - They build on children's prior knowledge.
> - They foster children's higher-order thinking skills by relating what they are learning to their lives outside of school, thinking critically and creatively about it, or using it to solve problems and make decisions.
> - They take place within a classroom designed as a learning community.

Figure 2.5 Why we use projects, units, or themes.
Source: Based on J. Brophy and J. Alleman (2002), *Learning and Teaching About Cultural Universals in Primary Grade Social Studies*.

a more planned or crafted progression than the word *project* does. Thematic units are often interdisciplinary.

Units, projects, and thematic learning accomplish a number of goals (see Figure 2.5):

1. They offer opportunities for a group of children to *build a sense of community* by working together around a common interest, theme, or project. Working together on a project facilitates fruitful conflicts and investigations, permitting children to clarify and rethink their initial ideas (Helm & Beneke, 2003; New, 1999a, 1999b).
2. When children work together on a common theme or project, they have the chance to relate to one another. They check one another, spontaneously offering criticism and information as they exchange ideas and prior knowledge in a cooperative effort. Vygotsky (1986) saw this type of *social activity as the generator of thought*. He believed that individual consciousness is built from outside through relations with others.
3. They *give relevance to the curriculum*. When content is a part of an organized whole, children see it as useful and relevant to their daily lives. Conceptual organizers such as themes, units, and projects give children something meaningful and substantive on which to engage their minds. They foster memory, understanding, and real-world connections. It is difficult for children to make sense of or remember abstract concepts such as colors, mathematical symbols, letter sounds, or the importance of facts—such as George Washington was the first president—when they are presented at random or devoid of any meaningful context.
4. They *provide flexibility* for teaching and learning, following children's interests and building on their experiences. Because units, projects, and thematic learning are flexible, they are planned for varying lengths of time. Some seem to end as quickly as they begin if children satisfy their interests immediately. Others

extend for several weeks or even a semester as children expand their interests and seek other information (Bredekamp & Copple, 1997).
5. Units, projects, and thematic learning can *meet individual children's needs* through the variety of learning experiences and opportunities offered over time. They provide ample time to engage all of the multiple intelligences. Children can pace themselves, staying with a specific activity for a long period of time to satisfy their interests or needs or selecting tasks that permit them to practice skills or gain mastery over new skills.
6. Units, projects, and themes *provide opportunities for integration* and cross-disciplinary connections. One of the hallmarks of social studies is its connections to other subject areas: science, math, literature, and the arts. Therefore, social studies units, projects, and themes lend themselves easily to integration across social studies disciplines and the other content disciplines. Integration across subject areas helps children relate to their world, which is not divided into subjects. It also helps children see connections. In addition, with increasingly limited time in the school day for social studies, integration of social studies with science, math, literature, and the arts helps ensure that social studies is covered in the curriculum.

Planning Units, Projects, or Thematic Learning

Planning involves selecting a topic, specifying goals/standards and objectives, and identifying content for the entire group (see Figure 2.6). The plans also include specific ideas and experiences for individual children (Helm & Beneke, 2003).

Teachers need to make additional plans for children with disabilities so they can participate freely and fully. For example, a teacher who wanted his class to experience a field trip to a fast-food restaurant made special arrangements so that a child in a wheelchair could take part.

Plans are also made for children who are uninterested in the topic. In one second-grade class, a unit on fruits and where they come from bored two of the children. Observing them, the teacher noted their curiosity about an apple that was beginning to rot. She directed their attention to the molds growing on the apple. The two children completed an entire unit on that subject, concluding by presenting their findings to the class, while the others studied fruit.

Selecting Themes or Topics. The theme for a unit, project, or thematic learning can stem from a number of sources. Some themes or topics grow out of the children's interests or the immediate environment. The school system, state department of education, or local, state, or national standards may suggest other topics.

In the child-care programs in Reggio Emilia, the selection of a project topic is a complicated, child-centered process. The genesis may take a number of forms:

1. The teacher may observe something of interest and importance to the children and introduce it as a topic or theme.
2. A topic may stem from the teacher's interest or professional curiosity.
3. The topic or theme might stem from some serendipity that redirects the attention of the children and teacher to another focus. The topic may be concrete or

Geography standards

Children will understand the world in spatial terms.

Children will understand the characteristics and uses of maps, globes, and other geographic tools.

Goal

Children will create maps and use them to locate places.

Key Concepts

Maps represent places.

Maps help us locate places.

Objectives

Children will be able to:
- Name pieces of play equipment and their uses
- Locate play spaces and equipment when asked to do so
- Construct a map of their playground
- Locate a hidden object by following a map

Introduction
- Before they go out to play, ask children to sing: "What will we do when we all go out, all go out, all go out. What will we do when we all go out, we all go out to play." List responses on a chart.
- As children play, take candid photos of them in different areas using different equipment. Make sure each child is included in a photo, and you have a photo of each area of the playground and piece of equipment.

Continuing

Activity 1: After you print the photos, place them on a table for children to look at and discuss. Ask them to find the following:
- Themselves at play
- Their favorite piece of equipment
- Their favorite spot on the playground

Then ask children to group the pictures by their function, grouping equipment in terms of climbing, sand play, riding, swinging, and so on.

Assessment: Checklist and note taking on naming and functions.

Sing "What DID we do on the playground." List children's responses and compare them to the first list of what they thought they would do.

Activity 2: Provide each child with a large piece of paper on which you have drawn an outline of the playground. Project this outline on an overhead or computer screen and draw one landmark on the paper, perhaps the building with the entrance to the playground. Have children draw the same landmark in the same place (check to be sure each has it correctly placed). Have children draw the playground equipment or build it with unit cubes, then draw it. They can use the photos as guides. (An alternative is to have the class make one mural-sized map together on a large sheet of brown paper.)

Figure 2.6 Unit plan: Mapping the playground.

Assessment: Checklist and note taking on naming, locating, and creating a map.

Activity 3: Take the maps outside and ask children to check them for accuracy. Are there any changes they need to make? If so, make them. Collect the maps.

Assessment: Checklist and note taking to assess maps on locating, constructing a map, and key concepts.

Culminating Activity and Assessment

Draw an accurate map and duplicate one for each group of three. Hide objects on the playground, one for each group. Mark one object with an X on each map. Organize the children into groups of three and give each group a map. They are to use the map to find the object that is marked with an X on their map. Directions are to find the hidden object. Back in the classroom, discuss using maps to find their objects.

Assessment: Checklist and note-taking on locating and key concepts.

Summary/Conclusion:

Discussion: What did you like about our mapping the playground unit? What did we learn about maps this week? What are maps? Why do we use maps? How can they help us? Repeat the key concepts.

Assessment: Note-taking on understandings and misconceptions.

Mapping Unit Assessment Checklist

	Names equipment	Names function of equipment	Locates spaces and equipment	Constructs a map	Uses map to locate object	Shows understanding of key concepts	Notes
Child A							
Child B							
Child C							

Figure 2.6 (*Continued*)

abstract in nature, local or distant, present-day or historical, small or large scale; but whatever the topic, it should allow children to draw on their own prior understandings and should involve them in firsthand, relevant, and interactive experiences (Helm & Beneke, 2003).

Here is an example of how one unit, based on children's interests, progressed. In a kindergarten, a visiting police officer permitted children to sit in a police car. Following the visit, the children began building a police car in the classroom out of large blocks. A posted sign let others know what the block structure represented and that it was not to be disturbed. The teacher added a steering wheel, a piece that looked like an instrument panel, and some boards. The block structure expanded and became a more permanent car with seats, a dashboard, a horn, and a gearshift. The children did research as they strove to make the car more and more realistic.

NCSS (2010) Standard II: Time, Continuity, and Change

The learners will understand key people, events, and places associated with the history of the community, nation, and world.

Virginia Standards of Learning (2012): History

K.1 The student will recognize that history describes events and people of other times and places by
   a) identifying examples of past events in legends, stories, and historical accounts of Powhatan, Pocahontas, George Washington, Betsy Ross, and Abraham Lincoln;
   b) identifying the people and events honored by the holidays of Thanksgiving Day; Martin Luther King, Jr., Day; Presidents' Day; and Independence Day (Fourth of July).

Theme, topic, or unit focus: George Washington

Possible Objectives: Students will be able to identify George Washington as the first President of the United States. Students will be able to describe the jobs of George Washington as farmer, leader of soldiers, and President of the United States. Students will be able to demonstrate George Washington's modes of transportation (horse, boat) and compare them to transportation today. Students will be able to identify George Washington as one of the Presidents honored on President's Day. Students will be able to dramatize facts about George Washington's life. Students will be able to distinguish between George Washington as a past president and the current president.

Figure 2.7   Standards and objectives.

Finally, the teacher added wires, bulbs, and batteries. With the help of a volunteer who guided and directed them in their discovery, the children made the right connections and were able to turn the lights in their car on and off. They consulted books, compared different types of cars and trucks, and held discussions. Videos of police cars in action were shared when the police officer visited the class again. The entire unit lasted for more than 6 weeks.

Particularly in the primary grades, standards of learning are becoming increasingly important as frameworks for curriculum. They are useful guides when selecting topics or themes.

Standards tend to be broad and serve to focus the scope and sequence of learning. They are different from objectives, which are specific and serve to focus instruction and assessment in lesson and unit plans (see Figure 2.6). Standards must be broken down into smaller parts for daily learning, then tied back together for the big picture. Because objectives are small parts of a larger standard, many objectives may be required to "cover" one standard (Figure 2.7).

When using standards, a unit might focus on the following:

- One social studies standard such as history: Native Americans
- Two social standards from different disciplines such as history and geography: Native Americans and Where They Lived
- One or more social studies standards and one or more standards from other disciplines such as history, geography, and science: Native Americans and the Habitats in Which They Lived

- A transdisciplinary theme, which might include standards from all disciplines, such as Why People Live Where They Do or Harvest Festivals Around the World (including Thanksgiving), either of which would include history, economics, geography, science, math, and literature

It is the teacher's job to look across standards for connections and relationships that might help children better understand their world.

Each unit, project, or theme should have, in addition to goals and standards, one or more big ideas or essential understandings (see Figure 2.6). These are often found in the key concepts of the discipline (as described in the content chapters, Chapters 7–11) and in the disciplinary standards (NCSS for social studies as well as those for science, math, and literacy). Using these themes, key concepts for the unit might include the following:

- History is about people in the past.
- People in the past lived differently than we do now.
- Habitats are different and have different characteristics.
- Geography affects where and how people live.

Content. Once the theme, goals, standards, and key concepts have been identified, the content to be covered can be identified. The content lists the major points to be included. Again, local, state, or national standards or descriptions of developmentally appropriate practice provide a guide. You will want to organize and specify the facts, concepts, skills, and attitudes that will be included. You should also include a list of available materials, resources, people, and field trips. Flexibility is the key. Guided by the overall goals and objectives of the program, teachers select content that meets children's developmental and learning needs.

Objectives. Objectives derive from the overall goals or standards of the unit, project, or theme. They direct the teaching and learning. They tell what the unit, project, or thematic learning is to accomplish; describe how the children will change following the experience; and lead to appropriate assessments. Here again, your careful selection of a few well-thought-out measurable objectives related to the content and key concepts will be more effective than listing numerous general objectives. Focusing objectives on each area of the social studies—knowledge, skills, attitudes, and values—helps balance children's learning experiences (see Figure 2.6).

But objectives can be flexible as long as they address the relevant standards. At all times, teachers remain alert to children's progress and interests, continually looking for ways to extend rather than dampen children's learning and enthusiasm for the theme or topic.

Procedures. The procedures section includes three parts: the introduction, the learning experiences, and a culminating activity.

Introduction. Almost anything that motivates and stimulates the children's interest can be used to introduce a unit, project, or theme. The purpose of the introduction is to arouse children's curiosity, to get them "hooked," by stimulating their interest and prior knowledge on the topic. This could be done in any of the following ways:

- *A teacher-initiated question.* You might ask the children some questions to stimulate their thinking, such as, "I wonder where firefighters live." Or you could say directly, "We all have to ride the school bus, so what do we know about the safety rules for riding the bus?" Their answers could be listed on a K-W-L chart. Either of these questions could begin a unit on safety.
- *An incidental experience.* Sometimes a unit arises from an unplanned experience. A child's illness in school could begin a unit on health. Some event in the local community—fire prevention week, elections, construction—might initiate a unit. The discovery of a bird's nest could stimulate interest in a unit on birds.
- *A book.* Children love stories. A story, poem, or picture book stimulates interest in the topic. The story of Johnny Appleseed might serve to introduce a unit on plants and how they grow.
- *Enactments.* A play, reader's theater, or historical reenactment can create interest and motivation to learn more. You might ask children, "What do you think it would be like to sail on a ship to a new country?"
- *An audiovisual resource.* A television show, a song, a video, or a website could stimulate interest. You can make use of other media as well, such as newspapers or magazines.
- *Ongoing activities.* Units, projects, and themes can lead to other units and projects. The study of the grocery store might lead to the study of food, purchasers, consumers, or transportation. A unit or project on seashells can lead directly to a study of life in the sea and then to life on land.
- *An arranged environment.* You might display objects from some other country, place, or time; exhibit a poster or an open book; or prepare a bulletin board. Any of these steps would call children's attention to a topic and stimulate questions and interest. One teacher from a western state left a branding iron on the library table with a few books opened to pictures of cowhands at branding time. In this way he introduced a theme built around the history of the region.

Learning Experiences. Learning experiences are the heart of the unit or project. These experiences are not isolated activities but are planned to foster the goals and objectives of the unit.

Since the purpose is to build a strong relationship between learning experiences and content, you will want to design the learning experiences to work together as a whole. You can plan a sequential presentation of learning experiences around the objectives of the unit. Analysis of each objective will suggest activities that will foster children's attainment of the objective. You might ask yourself, "What experience will foster this goal?" "Which experiences should come first and provide a basis for further experiences?" "What will extend and clarify children's understanding?" (See Figures 2.4 and 2.6.)

You can plan some activities for individual children, others for small groups, and still others for the total group.

Creating learning centers is an ideal way to provide various experiences while giving children choices about their learning. Teachers make several decisions when planning learning centers (Castle, 2002 in Arends, 2012):

- Organization: by topic (such as fall); by content areas (such as math, science, language arts, fine arts); around a story (such as Johnny Appleseed); by multiple intelligences (visual-spatial, logical mathematical, interpersonal, musical, bodily-kinesthetic)
- Amount of student choice: free choice; choices within guidelines and conditions (such as finish 4 out of 5 centers this week); limited choice (small groups work together and choose together)
- Documentation: student work completed at centers; student checklist of centers completed; student folder of work; student portfolio of work plus reflections

Learning experiences may come from any of the following:

- *Language experiences.* Oral discussion, listening to records, recording ideas in writing, dictating to a teacher or a tape recorder, reporting to a group, and dictating or writing letters, booklets, or stories are all examples of language experiences you could plan to foster children's attainment of unit goals.
- *Community resources.* Field trips in the school neighborhood or the community can be part of any unit or project plan. You could ask individuals from the community to visit and share information with the class.
- *Audiovisual and technology-based experiences.* Videos, pictures, CDs, models, graphs, murals, websites, virtual field trips, simulations, and digital photos integrate seeing and hearing for engaging learning. Children could make their own graphs or murals or illustrate a topic by taking their own photographs.
- *Arts and crafts.* Painting, constructing, drawing, modeling with clay, paper weaving, and many other art activities can be coordinated with other learning experiences.
- *Music, drama, and physical activities.* Songs, games, plays, puppet shows, making and playing musical instruments, creative rhythms, and dance foster children's active involvement with the stated objectives.
- *Mathematics and science activities.* Opportunities to use mathematics include counting, ordering, and sorting; classifying; adding and subtracting; graphing; and judging groups of more or fewer objects. For science, one class, stimulated by the discovery of parsley caterpillars in their garden, recorded how many days the caterpillars spent eating, the caterpillars' length, how many days it took for each chrysalis to form, and the number of days it took for the butterflies to emerge. Because they were engaged in meaningful activities, the children gained not only counting, calendar, and information-gathering skills, but science knowledge as well.
- *Social skills.* Social skills are an integral part of the unit as children participate together in planning or work together on activities. Children's interests might dictate that they work together to investigate some subtopic; later, they could report to the group. Young children can also improve their social skills by working together on a mural, a painting, a skit, a scrapbook, or a construction project (Figure 2.8).

> **Theme: Harvest Festivals Around the World (including Thanksgiving in the United States)**
>
> **Field Trip** (real or virtual): Garden, farm or orchard.
>
> **History Center**: Draw farming then and now (horses and tractors); or draw Thanksgiving then and now
>
> **Geography Center**: Draw a picture that shows what living things need to grow; or locate the harvest festival countries on the globe; or use premade climate cards to find the climate of each harvest festival country and tell how each climate will or will not help things grow.
>
> **Civics Center**: List (drawing or writing) "Things I Am Thankful For."
>
> **Economics Center**: Where do foods come from? Match pictures of foods to their source.
>
> **Culture Center**: Photos from 3 harvest festivals. Find similarities and differences.
>
> **Math Center**: Sort and count beans, seeds, and Indian corn kernels; graph number of each.
>
> **Science Center:** Draw life cycle of a plant (including harvesting); match stages to seasons
>
> **Language Arts Center**: Look at/read picture books of harvest festivals; draw/write a story about a harvest festival; or sequence pictures for a harvest story (planting, growing, harvesting, celebrating) and tell the story.
>
> **Music/Dance Center**: Make/play instruments or dance to recorded music from harvest festival countries.
>
> **Dramatic Play Center**: Farmers (artifacts for planting, growing, harvesting)
>
> **Art Center:** What did they eat? On a paper plate, using beans, cotton, construction paper, etc., create a dinner from the first Thanksgiving; What do we eat? Create what your family eats on Thanksgiving.
>
> **Technology Center**: Do a Webquest on harvest festivals.

Figure 2.8   Examples of learning center activities.

Regardless of the number and type of learning experiences selected, continuity between experiences is planned. One experience builds on another. A thread of meaning runs through several experiences. Experiences and activities are juxtaposed to enable children to see the connections between past and present, among and between people, and between objects in their world.

Culminating Activity.   The culminating activity is time spent for reviewing, summing up, and assessing the unit; it provides closure for teacher and children. A concluding activity gives the teacher a chance to observe the children and assess what concepts they have formed about the topic or theme. It gives the children an opportunity to tie the pieces together. It also gives the teacher a chance to assess learning on the overall unit. Culminating activities may be short and simple or more complex. Units and projects could end simply with the children acting out stories or poems they have created or presenting their projects. Dictating experience charts or thank-you letters, compiling a booklet, or sharing experiences are other summary activities. Activities such as creating murals or designing brochures enable children to show what they have learned about the topic (see Figure 2.6).

Anne Daniels, a teacher of 5-year-olds at the Center for Young Children at the University of Maryland, concluded a unit on Winnie the Pooh with a trip to the university apiary to collect honey for a snack. This activity, in turn, led to a new theme—studying and identifying different types of insects, where and how they live, and what they contribute to our lives.

Assessing Units, Projects, or Thematic Learning

You will want to be able to describe what children have learned and the skills and attitudes they have gained. The behavioral objectives and culminating activity offer built-in assessment. In addition, it might be useful to ask the children to assess the unit themselves: "What did you learn? What did you like best? What can you do now that you could not do before? What would you like to do again? What could you do differently next time?" Children could dictate or write booklets reporting the "Things I've Learned." You can assess the success of the unit informally as you observe children and take notes on their play or work. Or you can structure the assessments by asking each child to tell about a topic, demonstrate a task, or respond to some questions (see Figure 2.4). Checklists, rubrics, or portfolios developed around the goals of the unit and the specified content and skills might be used.

In addition to assessing the children, teachers will want to evaluate their planning and teaching. A well-planned project or unit should include the following:

- Clear, realistic, obtainable goals and objectives
- Material of high interest to the children
- Activities that take into consideration children's different abilities, interests, and backgrounds
- Involvement of the children in planning the goals and activities of the unit
- Active experiences that fully involve the children
- Opportunities for children to work and play together
- Opportunities to assess children's learning

Following a unit, teachers should reflect on the unit and ask themselves the following:

- Whether it included all of the elements
- How it could be improved
- What parts were highly successful
- How could it be done differently next time

ASSESSMENT OF THE SOCIAL STUDIES CURRICULUM

Assessment is necessary and important. We all want and need good information about how and what children are learning. Teachers and parents want to know how their children are doing, school administrators want to know how effective their program is, and policy makers want to judge the worth of policies (National Education Goals Panel, 1998). When assessment is authentic, it benefits children, teachers, and parents. Authentic assessment takes place as a part of the curriculum.

The tasks used to assess children's learning in the social studies are real and they connect to children's daily experiences rather than detract from them (Helm & Beneke, 2003).

Authentic assessment can be used to do the following:

- *Assess developmental levels and/or prior knowledge*, enabling the teacher to plan goals and objectives that are appropriate to the children's learning, growth, and development
- *Give feedback to students*, enabling them to feel good about and become more involved in their own learning, and enabling the teacher to correct misconceptions
- *Assess attainment of learning objective(s)*, providing evidence for teachers of the extent to which children are attaining the desired goals and objectives
- *Guide instruction*, enabling teachers to adjust instruction based on children's learning
- *Improve instruction*, functioning as a quality-control system that permits teachers to determine which parts of the teaching–learning process have been effective and which have not and stimulate ideas for alternative procedures that may be more effective

A broad and complex process, assessment is not to be confused with evaluation or standardized testing. Authentic assessment is ongoing, comprehensive, and an integral part of classroom social studies instruction. Assessment procedures can focus on behavior (what they do), verbalizations (what they say), or products (what they make).

Creating assessments is not difficult when they are connected to learning goals and objectives; are based on children's behavior, verbalizations, or products; and follow principles of good assessments. Effective assessments:

- Are developmentally appropriate
- Match the goal or objective(s)
- Align with instructional strategy
- Are visibly documented
- Facilitate students showing what they know
- Are done often
- Use multiple measures
- Have clear scoring procedures, as appropriate
- Are made explicit to students
- Address all cognitive domains (knowledge, comprehension, application, analysis, synthesis)
- Access multiple intelligences
- Are motivating and interesting
- Can be accomplished with reasonable effort
- Are unbiased
- Drive subsequent instruction
- Are used to improve teaching and learning

There are many types of assessments, and you will want to choose ones that suit your children and your objective while keeping the principles of effective assessment in mind. Types of assessments include the following:

- Observation using anecdotal notes, checklists, rating scales
- Traditional (closed-ended):
  - Selected response (multiple choice, true/false, matching)
  - Constructed response (short answer, fill-in-the-blank, essay)
- Alternative (more open-ended) using rubrics, checklists, rating scales
  - Authentic (products, projects, problem-solving tasks)
  - Performance (demonstrations, performances, presentations)
- Portfolios (content, student choice and reflection, organization)

Observation

Children's learning can be observed in their behavior and talk and documented by observational notes. When they observe children's behavior systematically, teachers see indications of their achievement of social studies goals. Teachers look for and record behaviors that demonstrate children's skills, attitudes, values, or knowledge. Behavioral observation is a valid way to evaluate social studies goals relating to social skills, problem solving, decision making, and acceptance of the values of others.

Observing means noting only the behavior that is occurring without making inferences. Teachers can observe and record children's behavior at any time during the school day, including free play, center time, activity time, group time, on the playground, or during the routines of dressing, eating, cleaning up, and resting.

When you record repeated behaviors of children, you compile a record of their progress. You could structure your observations around the specific and general goals of the social studies program. You could observe and record children's behavior in applying knowledge, solving a problem, taking responsibility, or working with others; or you might structure your observations around more specific goals. Children's use of maps during block building and their drawing of maps for use with wheel toys give real indications of their mapping concepts. Shopping at the play store, children reveal economic concepts through their behavior. As children play, you might note when they (a) use new vocabulary correctly, (b) demonstrate their understanding of making change, purchasing, or producing, and (c) follow social rules and procedures.

Recording observations through anecdotal notes is essential in compiling a documented record. Each note should include the child's name and the date. These can then be ordered chronologically to see patterns and changes.

Digital and other photographs can help you observe and assess children's behaviors, knowledge, and progress. The photos let you reflect on what was happening and what children were doing when they were observed (Hoisington, 2002). The photos can also be e-mailed to families or included in a child's portfolio for parents to see. Discussing what the child in the photo was doing, why, and when can be a fruitful form of assessment. Videotapes can be useful in the same way.

Table 2.1 Example of a Social Skills Checklist

NAME:		DATE:	
Behavior	**Always**	**Sometimes**	**Never**
Completes a task Works with others Takes responsibility Cooperates in group work Listens to others			

Checklists

Some learning experiences and objectives lend themselves to checklists of behaviors or skills, and are a convenient way to document children's progress. You can construct a checklist for yourself designed around the specific concepts, goals, and objectives of the social studies unit or lesson plan. Other checklists are often provided by the school or by the county or state department of education and might be based on the general goals of social studies. Publishers of textbooks and instructional kits sometimes prepare checklists. Table 2.1 shows a checklist developed by a teacher to assess and document social skills with a group of 5-year-old children.

Rating scales are similar to checklists, except they enable the teacher to give a numeric score (Always = 2, Sometimes = 1, Never = 0), which may be helpful when letter grades need to be calculated.

Informal Interviews

Another, more specific form of assessment of children's progress in social studies is the informal interview method. You could conduct interviews during free play or anytime you and individual children are together. You should look for the following as you interview children:

1. *Consistency.* Does the child have a stable set of responses? Does the child reply in the same way to the same type of question?
2. *Accuracy.* Are the answers correct? The child may not include all of the possibilities, but is the response somewhat accurate?
3. *Clarity.* Is the response clear and acceptable?
4. *Fullness.* How complete was the response? How many aspects of the concept were covered by the response?
5. *Extensiveness.* How many illustrations of the concept were given?

As they conduct interviews to discover children's thinking about a social studies topic, teachers sometimes use pictures or objects for the children to manipulate in order to demonstrate or illustrate the concepts. Not all concepts can be expressed by children verbally; you could ask them to act out a concept, show it, draw all the

Planning and Assessment 61

Informal interviews with children yield information on children's thinking.

things they know about it, find an example of the concept in the pictures, or sort pictures into examples and nonexamples. In any case, the responses must be documented through teacher note-taking.

The work of Piaget (1969) provides other guidelines for interviewing young children. The questions Piaget asked and the way in which he built his questions on the child's responses to the first question exemplify the type of interview technique that reveals children's thinking. For example, one teacher wanted to find out what children knew about seeds and plants. He asked them to tell him what grows from a seed, where one looks for seeds, and how one gets seeds to grow.

In administering Piagetian interviews, you must establish an atmosphere of security and trust by communicating to the child that she is in a safe, nonthreatening position. When a child responds to your question, accept the answer without judgment. You might use a small tape recorder to record the answer or take notes. Children's responses are often short, so they are not difficult to record by hand.

When the child responds, continue questioning by asking for justification. Do not assume that if a child gives a correct answer, he has done the proper thinking. Several questions may be necessary to understand his perceptions and thinking processes. You might ask the child, "Could you show me?" "Would you tell me more?" or, "What if . . .?" You could ask the child to act out the answer, or you could challenge his answer by saying, "Well, another person said . . ." In this way, you will be able to uncover more of the child's thinking and ideas.

You will need to give the child plenty of time to answer. In many testing situations, time is limited. When conducting an individual interview, you will want to allow the child all the time necessary to think and answer.

Performance Tasks

Structuring tasks for children to do something that demonstrates skills or concepts is another kind of assessment. You might ask children to draw a map of the room, show on a graph which bus has the most riders, complete a puzzle, use latitude and longitude coordinates to find a location, or sort pictures into categories (e.g., needs and wants; past and present). One teacher used a set of pictures to assess children's awareness of selected concepts in physical geography by asking them to select the four pictures that represented the concept and the four that did not. Performances might also include plays, movement or dancing, signing, demonstrations, or presentations of the results of a problem-solving task. Performance tasks must be documented through note taking, checklists, rating scales, or rubrics.

Products

Structuring tasks for children to make something that demonstrates concepts or skills is another kind of assessment. Many lessons ask children to make something related to the objective: a drawing or diagram, a drawing with a written sentence, written work, a glued picture sort, a map, a poster, a brochure, and so on. In the geography sort example given earlier, the teacher could watch the children and note the number of correct pictures; or the teacher could ask the children to sort and glue the pictures into two labeled columns, creating a product for the teacher to assess after school. Units, projects, and thematic units often conclude with a complex product, such as a mural, newspaper, travel brochure, or some other product that ties the unit together and demonstrates the children's learning. These products might be assessed by a checklist or rating scale, but their complexity may require a more complex assessment tool such as a scoring rubric.

Rubrics enable the teacher to rate a child's work on multiple elements and the quality or level of each. A holistic rubric includes descriptions of expected performance that are numbered. For example the product or performance:

3 = Demonstrates complete understanding
2 = Demonstrates partial understanding
1 = Demonstrates little or no understanding
0 = No attempt was made.

An analytic rubric has concepts, skills, attitudes, or other criteria on one axis, scores or levels of performance on the other axis, and descriptions of performance in each cell. For example, teacher candidates in George Mason University's Elementary Education Program were required, as part of their social studies and fine arts course, to visit a historical museum and write a persuasive argument to their principal for why they should take their students there. They had to include the work the children would do and how it would be assessed as well as integrate fine arts. Figure 2.9 shows the rubric for this assignment.

Rubrics may take some time to create and refine, particularly revising the wording of the performances so they are clear to the children. Rubrics can also be made with Smiley, Neutral, and Frowny faces for nonreaders. Rubrics are now easy to find on the Internet, but not all of them are well done, and you will have to adapt them to your children and curriculum. When creating, using, or adapting rubrics, be sure that the criteria match your learning objectives, the content and skills children are expected to demonstrate. They should not focus on criteria that are not in the objectives such as neatness.

Rubric for Museum and the Arts Persuasive Argument

Criteria	Clear and Consistent Evidence; Meets All Requirements 3 points	Some Evidence; Meets Partial Requirements 2 points	Limited Evidence; Needs Improvement 1 point	No Evidence 0 points
Correct, complete information Is the required information present?	Includes the name of the site, type of site, link to objectives, types of programs provided (including websites), contact information	One or two of the required items are missing.	Three or four of the required items are missing.	Required items not included.
Persuasive argument based on social studies knowledge Does the presentation make a case for a social studies field trip? Does it reflect knowledge gained from texts and class discussions?	The presentation is well-written, clear, and complete so the intended target audience (principal or team) can understand the reasoning. References to texts and class discussions are well documented.	The presentation is well written, but some information is not clear or complete, so the intended audience may or may not understand the reasoning. References to text and class discussions are limited.	Presentation is not well written. Information is unclear and/or incomplete so the intended audience cannot understand the reasoning. There are few references to texts and class discussions.	Presentation is not a persuasive argument. No reasoning is included. No references to text or class discussion.
Integration of social studies and the arts Does it include examples of student work or project that integrates social studies and the arts?	Student work sample would allow creativity and integrate at least two of the fine arts.	Student work sample is somewhat creative and integrates one of the fine arts.	Student work sample is not creative and does not integrate the fine arts.	Student work not included.
Assessment Is an assessment included?	An appropriate assessment task and scoring tool/rubric are included.	An appropriate assessment task or scoring tool/rubric is included.	An assessment task is included but it is not appropriate.	Assessment not included.

Attach an "artifact" from the site = **3 points**

Total points _____ /15

Figure 2.9 Example of an analytic rubric in teacher education

Source: Adapted with permission from S. Castle and S. Shoob (2009), George Mason University Elementary Education Program.

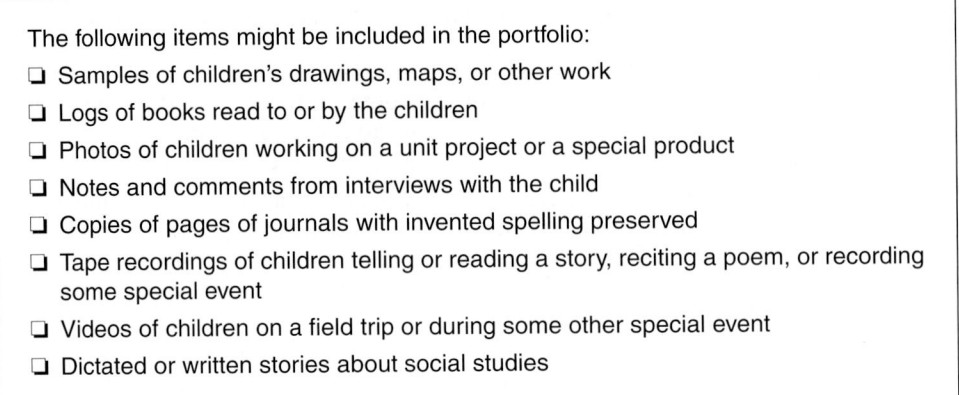

Figure 2.10   The portfolio.

Portfolios

Collecting samples of children's work in portfolios illustrates children's progress over time. Each child has an individual portfolio; whatever work or records are placed in the portfolio are dated, and often something about when, how, and under what conditions the work was completed is included. Growth charts, photos of children completing skills, and recordings of their speech can also be collected (see Figure 2.10).

Several times a year, teachers go over the portfolios and note the changing form of children's concepts, new vocabulary, expansion of ideas, and children's increasing ability to express their ideas. This analysis offers a base on which to assess both children's learning in the social studies as well as your teaching.

The child, as well as teachers and parents, should have the opportunity to select work samples to place in the portfolio. Teachers can guide children when asking them to contribute work samples. Teachers might ask children to select something that was difficult to do, that illustrates a special accomplishment, or that has special meaning and merit (Gronlund, 1998). Children may write or dictate reflections on their included work.

When the work in the portfolio is an accurate representation of a child's growth and achievement, teachers can use it to assess progress. The work can be analyzed and assessed for progress toward a standard of performance consistent with the individual child's growth and development; or the work can be assessed using a scoring rubric common across the classroom. Presenting the portfolio to the teacher and even to the parents helps children to become self-directed learners and to feel good about their accomplishments.

Standardized Tests

Standardized tests are based on goals and objectives decided by someone other than the classroom teacher and are intended to serve as large-scale evaluations. They may appear to have little to do with what goes on in preschool and primary classrooms. Although they may guide the scope of the curriculum, preschool and primary classrooms prepare children well beyond the scope of the tests (social skills, for example). Standardized tests are based primarily on verbal or mathematical intelligence and do not reflect the multiple forms of intelligence (Anderson, 1998; Seefeldt, 1998), so they do not access the strengths of all children. However, if you are responsible for teaching standards-based content on which your students will be tested, you will need to be sure that the content is embedded and assessed within your lessons, units, themes, and projects.

Recognizing that all children are special and unique, most early childhood teachers want to consider a combination of assessment techniques. In this way, they are better able to pinpoint children's strengths and needs. Using a variety of assessment techniques is useful for other reasons. Keeping records of the children's work, systematically observing their behavior, or using informal interviews might be helpful in reporting progress to parents, in giving insights on how to improve your teaching methods, or in indicating which experiences, activities, goals, and objectives are appropriate to introduce at a given time. This type of assessment, conducted by teachers for the purpose of assessing the teaching and the attainment of specific goals, is often called *formative*. It is the type of assessment that enables you to formulate your program, set goals, and know when the goals have been reached, what new goals should be set, and what goal modifications should be made (Shepard, Kagan, & Wurtz, 1998).

SUMMARY

Planning is essential for successful teaching and learning. Having a clear idea of what children are like, the goals of society and education, and content knowledge of the social studies, you are prepared to plan. In planning, you must consider the reality of your situation, provide balance throughout the program, involve the children, and allow for spontaneity.

Long-term planning of social studies units and short-term planning of the daily lessons involves designing appropriate learning objectives. In setting specific goals for your teaching and children's learning, assessment follows naturally as you assess the degree to which the goals have been reached.

Discussion Questions

1. Describe the difference between preoperational and concrete operational thinking. What are the implications for teaching?
2. What does the term "least restrictive environment" mean? Give examples. Discuss the implications.
3. What are some possible modifications or accommodations that teachers might make for children in each of the special needs groups?

4. Why is social studies content knowledge essential for teachers of young children?
5. Discuss the similarities and differences between units, projects, and themes. What would be important considerations when deciding which to use? Is it possible to combine them or not? If so, how?
6. What is the relationship between standards, objectives, and key concepts?
7. What is integration? Why is it important? Generate some themes that integrate social studies with other disciplines.
8. Discuss the principles of effective assessment. Why is each important? What are the implications for making assessment decisions? What are the variety of ways you might assess a kindergarten standard such as "The student will describe everyday life in the present and in the past and begin to recognize that things change over time" (Virginia Standards of Learning, 2012).

Extend Your Knowledge

1. When you are shopping, walking in a park, or attending a community gathering, observe children under the age of 8. List the ways in which these children are alike, regardless of their age and individual characteristics. Then observe again and make another list of the ways in which the children differ from one another as individuals.
2. Take a fresh look at the community your school is part of. What physical properties do you note that affect children's learning? For example, what kinds of stores are present? Are there gardens? Talk with some of the community members. Ask what they expect children to learn in school, how they think children should be taught, and what they would do to change education. From these responses, can you determine some of the cultural values of the community? List these values and compare and discuss them in class.
3. Curriculum libraries at colleges, universities, or school systems contain guides from school systems throughout your state and nation. Most states have their standards of learning and curriculum frameworks online. With a partner or in a small group, compare the goals and objectives of unit and project plans suggested in two or more of these guides.
4. Design both a lesson and a unit, project, or thematic learning plan. When you have completed the plans, ask the class to critique them.

Resources

Often, curriculum guides (sometimes called curriculum frameworks) are developed by local school systems or state departments of education. Inquire in your school system or at the state department of education about curriculum guides or search for them online. The guides offer suggestions for objectives in many subject areas, including the social studies. They also contain abundant information and ideas for lesson planning and things to do with children.

Resource Books

Katz, L. G., & Chard, S. C. (2000). Engaging children's minds: The project approach (2nd ed.). Stamford, CT: Ablex Publishing.

Singleton, L. R. (1997). *C is for citizenship: Children's literature and civic understanding.* Boulder, CO: Social Science Education Consortium.

Chick, K. A. (2008). *Teaching women's history through literature: Standards-based lesson plans for grades K–12.* Silver Spring, MD: National Council for Social Studies.

Websites for Unit Plans, Lesson Plans, and Materials

Population Connection
www.populationconnection.org

National Council for the Social Studies
www.socialstudies.org

National Archives
www.archives.gov

National Gallery of Art's Education Page
www.nga.gov/education

National Association for the Education of Young Children
www.naeyc.org

PBS
www.pbs.org

Social Science Education Consortium
Search for "Social Science Education Consortium" to find their publications on various websites.

CHAPTER 3

Resources for Learning: School, Family, Community

> **Focus Questions**
>
> After you read this chapter, you should be prepared to respond to the following questions:
>
> - In what ways are the children themselves resources for social studies?
> - How can teachers use each child's family as a resource for teaching social studies?
> - What resources in and around the school are useful in fostering the goals of the social studies?
> - How do you plan a field trip to use the resources in the community fully?
> - How does the teacher plan for active engagement in meaningful learning in the classroom? What are centers of interest? What are the various activities and materials important to social studies? What is the role of the teacher?
> - What are appropriate uses of technology with young children? What are the cautions?

Suppose you wanted to learn how to swim. Would you read books about swimming and listen to people tell you how to swim, or would you jump into a pool and, with the guidance of an expert swimmer, learn by doing?

People have long known that humans, whether adults or children, learn best by doing. This is why the social studies curriculum demands that children be able to learn through firsthand experiences grounded in their here-and-now environment. But the here-and-now environment is more than physical. It includes interaction with others, both adults and children, as well as children's actions in the physical environments of the classroom and community.

THE CHILDREN

Children themselves are resources for social studies learning. Each child brings a unique set of experiences and skills to share with others. To enrich the social studies curriculum, children can become involved in many ways:

- Share their experiences by telling others about how they do things in their own homes.
- Bring in objects, photographs or digital photo albums, cultural foods, and stories to share with classmates.
- Demonstrate how to make a bridge of blocks, how to paint, or how to make a replica of an Indian pot.
- Teach one another how to complete a puzzle, read a map, or sing a song from their culture.

THE FAMILY

The family offers a world of resources for the social studies! Think about it: Probably all of the content, attitudes, values, and skills included in the social studies could be fostered through study of the family (Helm & Katz, 2001b; Seefeldt & Denton, 1997). Families are different in some ways and similar in some ways.

Families have a history. Where did each family come from? What stories do they tell about how they got here and where they first settled? Do children's parents tell their children about their own childhoods? What about family celebrations?

Geography is also part of families. Find out where each family came from and locate the country on a map or Google Earth. How did the family travel here? Families move, even within the same city. Make a map and locate where each family once lived. You can explore these locations online for basic geographic information, such as climate.

Where do family members live? Who lives in the current household? Where do grandparents live? How many children are in the family?

What jobs do parents hold? How are tasks divided within the family? Who handles the money? Children find economic concepts meaningful when they are related to their own experiences in the family unit.

Weaving parents into the fabric of early childhood programs is a primary goal of educators. Parental involvement is particularly helpful in social studies, because all types of involvement—informal and formal—bring parents, teachers, and children together, serve as resources for social studies learning and teaching, and connect social studies to the child's world.

Informal Involvement

Here are some simple things that you might do to involve parents in the social studies program:

- Let parents know they are welcome in the classroom. Encourage them to visit the classroom anytime they can. Invite parents to visit during American Education Week or on special days. Parents may find themselves with an afternoon off, an hour or two at lunch, or a few hours free during the morning when they would be able to visit the classroom. Arrange a space at the school where parents can meet to chat, relax, or work on a task. When talking with parents about informal visits, be sure to keep in mind any policies your school has regarding parent visits.
- Send home a questionnaire at the beginning of the year inviting parents to indicate the kinds of things they would like their children to learn in social studies. It might be a good idea to list several choices, asking the parents to check the ones they like as well as leaving space for their suggestions. Other questionnaires could request suggestions for field trips or visitors to the class. If some parents have limited English proficiency, use a translator, pictures, or other ways to communicate so these parents feel included and valued. If most parents have access to computers, you can send an online survey.
- Send home a brief outline of each unit or project plan. A page of simple statements tells parents something about their children's activities: "For the next few days, we will study the concept of production. We will visit a store and . . ."
- Children in the primary grades can write a class newsletter. In the letter, you can include plans for parties or field trips, reviews of movies or books the children have enjoyed, or the things they have learned.
- Forward a booklet of children's favorite poems and songs.
- Send home individual notes with children telling parents about their child's progress—a new skill learned or how the child used new knowledge to solve a problem. Single sentences on the back of a picture or attached to some of the child's work do much to inform parents about the progress their children are making and the things that happen during the school day: "Please notice how well Aletha completed this map. It's a drawing of our playground, and it's quite accurate." "This is the first time John included a base line in his painting; it means . . ." "Toni's story shows imagination and thought."
- After children were familiar with *Brown Bear, Brown Bear* (Martin, 1969a), one second-grade teacher put a stuffed brown bear in a backpack along with a journal. Each child took turns taking home the bear and the journal. They wrote in the journal about what Brown Bear did in their home. The children then read their journal notations to the class.

- M. S. Gorter-Reu and J. M. Anderson (1998) developed home kits, which include music tapes and idea cards for making simple toys and games at home. Kindergarten and first-grade teachers in Texas and New Mexico have used these kits. Other teachers send home backpacks containing thematically related books with suggestions for their use.
- Give parents your e-mail address so they can keep in touch with you and ask questions. This not only opens communication between parent and teacher but lets both exchange thoughts about children's progress.
- Teachers at the Center for Young Children at the University of Maryland laminate class books created by the children. Children take turns bringing home the books. A sheet in the back of the book is provided for parents to sign and comment on the children's work.

Involving parents in the school's program implies respect for each child and family. To communicate the school's respect, you can do the following:

- Involve parents in the teaching–learning process. Letters telling the parents about the concepts being taught and asking them to extend these concepts at home are useful: "We're learning about traffic safety. The next time you go for a drive, could you point out the traffic signs and explain their meanings to the children?" Parents can also take part in children's homework—not the dreary pencil-and-paper kind but the homework that involves looking for all the tools in the house, counting the number of jobs that family members have, drawing a map of the block the child lives on, or watching a certain television program together. Many preschool programs foster children's cognitive growth by involving parents as teachers of their own children. You could send ideas, toys, books, games, puzzles, and other equipment home with the children, permitting parents to take an active part in their child's education.
- Show respect for each child's family structure. Be aware that attitudes are communicated subtly through language use. The term *broken home* or the comment "he doesn't have a father" implies stereotypical attitudes. Families who have experienced divorce may be more whole after the divorce rather than broken by it; and children of divorce do in fact have a mother and a father, who do not currently live in the same house. It is important to talk about families in a realistic, nonstereotypic way rather than an idealistic, stereotypic way (Brophy & Alleman, 2005c).
- Structure school activities for the parent in general, not specifying the mother or father. This shows your respect for the family unit as it may exist in many children's homes.
- Offer real support in recognizing the time limitations of working parents, and schedule conferences when parents are able to attend.

Formal Involvement

Informal parent-involvement activities often lead to more structured involvement of parents in the social studies program. At first, parents and teachers are comfortable communicating at the day-by-day informal level. As trust develops, parents find they

Families are asked to make decisions about their children's learning.

are interested in more structured involvement. Attending group meetings, working with children, and making decisions about the social studies program then take place.

Group Meetings

Parents are interested in seeing photos and videos of their children at school, and these can serve as the focus of a group meeting. One teacher took many digital photos of children participating in social studies activities. At the end of the year, she held a parent meeting and showed photos taken at the beginning, middle, and end of the year that illustrated the children's growth in skills and their progression in caring, sharing, cooperative attitudes, and school knowledge.

One school system instituted Family Nights Out. The school provided dinner for families, children, teachers, and the principal. After dinner the children played together while the parents met with a family therapist who led group discussions. Both teachers and parents said they benefited because they got to know one another as equals (Seefeldt & Goldsmith, 1998). Another school with a large English as a second language population sponsored English classes for parents at the school.

Working with Children

Parents may be able to work with individual children or help groups carry out projects. Some parents may serve as resources when children study various topics, themes, or jobs. Parent volunteers are needed for field trips as well as on a daily basis.

Decision Making

When parents are involved, they should eventually make decisions about the social studies program. They may help set some of the goals and objectives of the program, decide on topics or themes, or help generate ideas for how to implement certain topics or themes.

The Transition Demonstration is a national program that follows Head Start children through the third grade with Head Start–like services. In a number of cases, it involves parents in writing an Individual Transition Plan with their children's current and future teachers. Together, teachers and parents share what they know about the child's strengths, interests, and learning style and make decisions about the goals they will set for the child for the coming year.

THE SCHOOL

If you want to be a teacher of young children, you must be able to look at the world through the eyes of a child. Take a walk inside the school and on the playground and consider what would interest a child who is 3, 5, or 8 years of age. Look at the playground and pretend you are that child filled with wonder and curiosity. What do you see?

Following the theories of Mitchell (1934), Piaget (Piaget & Inhelder, 1969), and Vygotsky (1986), you can ground a great deal of your social studies in the here-and-now world of the school, both inside and outdoors. To provide children with this type of experience, you can take a number of steps:

- Identify building materials, how they got to the building, and who used them.
- Study communication systems—mail, computers, fax machines, cell phones, and telephones.
- Care for the school grounds; plant a butterfly garden.
- Examine various delivery systems for food, materials, and supplies.

The people in the school also serve as resources for children's learning. Every member of the school staff has some special skill or background to share with the children. Just observing the staff at work—art, music, and physical education teachers; media specialists, lunchroom personnel, office workers, custodians—puts children in touch with real-world learning. Some staff members might demonstrate a specific skill used in their jobs, or they could invite small groups to observe them completing a specific task. Just as the parents do, the staff might share something from their backgrounds with the children—a song, a favorite food, a game, or a custom enjoyed by the person's family.

The teacher is a resource for social studies learning. Your experiences—the different places you have worked, the things you did in college, the places you have visited—all can be used to enrich children's learning by giving them vicarious experiences on which to build concepts. Then, too, the skills, knowledge, and information you bring to your job are potent factors for children's learning. Regardless of the extent of materials available, the teacher's creativity is the most important learning resource in the classroom.

COMMUNITY

In the lovely northern Italian city of Reggio Emilia, children in the city-run child-care centers leave their centers frequently, taking trips into their community. They run in the poppy fields, sit on the stone lions guarding a building in the town square, go to the supermarket, and walk in the rain. On these trips children observe and they work. They measure, feel, compare and contrast, and keep records. Like teachers in Reggio Emilia, teachers in the United States have always valued taking children on excursions into the community. Today more than ever children need physical activity, experiences outdoors, and experiences with nature. The community may offer many such opportunities.

Fieldwork

Fieldwork and social studies seem to go together. Fieldwork has many benefits:

- It extends children's knowledge of their environment, providing them with firsthand experiences that could not be implemented in a classroom.
- It acquaints the children with their immediate environment and orients them to it by developing concepts of direction, maps, and spaces.
- It provides contact with adult models in the social world, increasing children's knowledge of the world of work.
- It allows children to use scientific methods as they gather information, observe the environment, and draw conclusions.
- It unifies children, providing a common core of experience for them to play out, problem solve, share, and discuss.
- It promotes parent involvement by taking children to visit one another's homes or the places where their parents work or by going to the same places they go with their parents. A field trip also involves parents as participants.
- It stimulates new ideas and new learning by enlivening children's interests and posing new questions that demand answers.

Types of Fieldwork

It is up to the teacher to identify, locate, and evaluate the possibilities for fieldwork within a community and to decide what type of work is best suited for the children. According to Mitchell (1934), no list of field trips can be provided. Each school and classroom determines its own field trips that fit the children, the environment, and the curriculum.

Lucy Sprague Mitchell probably would have chosen walking trips through children's immediate school and neighborhood environments. Other types—split group, repeated, those for a specific purpose, and virtual trips—can be taken as well.

Walking Trips. Perhaps the most valuable trips are walking field trips that can be taken once or twice a week in the school building, the schoolyard, or the neighborhood. There is much to see and learn within walking distance, and walking provides physical activity. These trips can be planned ahead by you or the children or can arise spontaneously as the children's interests dictate.

Small-Group Trips. Some trips will involve the total class, with the entire group visiting the library, the firehouse, or the florist. Other trips might involve a committee

Repeated field trips help children assimilate knowledge.

or a small group of children who are vitally interested in some specific place. Once children become accustomed to waiting their turn to go on a trip and the trips are frequent, there is no difficulty in planning committee trips.

With a volunteer adult, a committee can be sent to purchase a goldfish for the class or a soup bone to make "stone soup." Or the three children interested in engines can be allowed to go to the corner garage to observe a mechanic at work. On some whole-group trips, the class can be divided into committees with each having a specific purpose or a goal to fulfill. One group might be asked to investigate where the firefighters sleep, another what they eat, and another the answer to a question about fighting fires. On purchasing trips, each group of children can purchase a separate item.

Repeated Fieldwork. Why not return to a place? Children can gain from visiting the same place again, learning something new from each trip. Young children, excited about being away from their familiar classroom, often do not see everything or focus on the specific idea or purpose of the trip. Returning to the same place gives children a sense of mastery; being familiar with the place, they feel secure, competent, and safe enough to risk new learning.

Specific-Purpose Field Trips. You can plan fieldwork to fulfill specific purposes. A trip can be taken to observe all of the round things inside and outside the classroom, to record the sound that feet make on different materials in the building, or to find out the name of the street on which the school is located. You can also plan field trips to places such as parks, monuments, community helper sites, or museums. You might even create a field trip to an "archeological dig" in the sandbox or schoolyard.

Virtual Field Trips. Places that are not close by can be visited through virtual field trips via the Internet. Colonial Williamsburg is such an example. Although these are vicarious experiences, they enable children to learn about places they would not be able to experience otherwise.

WOW Trips. Once or twice a year, perhaps as a culminating activity or a traditional school trip, you might plan a WOW experience, with many of the parents involved. Trips to the zoo or end-of-the-year picnics are WOW trips. These trips, while still related to particular topics or themes, involve parents and provide the excitement of doing something new and different at school.

Planning Fieldwork

The longest, perhaps most important, part of fieldwork includes the hours that the teacher and the children spend getting ready for it. Just the thought of dealing with a group of young children away from the confines of the classroom can terrify an inexperienced teacher; yet once the teacher knows the group, this problem seems minor compared to the difficulty of planning meaningful trips: those that provide a continuity of experiences and fieldwork for the children. In planning for valuable fieldwork, you must do the following:

1. Survey the community to learn what is available, where places of interest are, who to contact, and what places welcome children. One teacher discovered a broom factory, one of only a few still in existence in the country, just a block away from the school. Another teacher made a card file of places of interest in the community, recording the telephone number, contact person, safety factors, and special things of interest for children.
2. Have a clear idea of the purpose of each trip. Writing a list of objectives, tied to national and/or local social studies standards, helps you clarify the purpose and internalize your goals.
3. Attempt to provide continuity among and between trips. Education is a continuous experience, and field trips should ensure the continuity of that experience rather than interrupt it.
4. Think in terms of a simple field trip. The world is so confusing to the young child that a simple trip to help the children understand his or her world might be more valuable than a complicated one.
5. Use the children's play to direct your planning. Observing the children at play, you can note their interests as well as misconceptions that might be clarified with a trip. If children are interested in transportation, a trip to visit a gas station might be more appropriate than a trip to a zoo. A teacher can also observe what ideas need to be extended or enriched and can plan trips accordingly.
6. Make a survey of the children and their parents to find out places the children have already visited, things parents would like their children to see and do, or places the children would like to know more about.
7. Consider the time of day, week, and year. It is wise to take walking trips when the children are fresh—early in the day or after a nap. You can plan returns to coincide with snack time, lunchtime, or rest periods. The weather and seasonal conditions will also affect the type of trip planned.

Before Fieldwork. Establish the goals and objectives for a trip and fieldwork and assure yourself that the trip will provide the children with a continuity of experience that is built on their backgrounds of interest and experience. You then begin the actual planning for the trip:

1. Visit the place first, checking for safety hazards, noting special needs for clothing or supervision, checking bathroom facilities, and confirming arrangements with the contact person.
2. Notify the parents that their children are leaving the school building. A blanket statement, given at the beginning of the year in a handbook or at a parents' meeting, can inform parents that their children will be going on many walking trips. Notices can still be sent home informing parents about the exact nature of the trip; however, they need to know that some trips will be spontaneous—walking in the rain, finding ice puddles, or looking for the rainbow. For more involved trips, permission slips prepared according to the dictates of the school board will need to be sent home, signed, and returned.
3. Discuss the trip with the children. Ask children what they know about where they are going. Record their answers. Have children list things they want to learn while on the trip. Write their questions on chart paper. Later you can cut the questions into strips and give one to each child to ask while on the trip.
4. Provide the children with a background of experiences. Stories, props for play, video clips, or pictures give children a foundation on which to build their new experiences.
5. Review simple safety and behavioral rules with the children. Definite standards of behavior can be established for field trips. It is important to review these standards with the children as well as with the adults going on the trip. When adults and children are certain about what is expected of them, trips are safer. Some rules might be recorded on a chart.
6. The teacher will want to involve as many adults as necessary for a safe trip; plan for emergencies, and include supplies such as tissues, adhesive bandages, and drinkable water.

During Fieldwork. The teacher must provide skillful and tactful guidance during the trip. The interest of the group will be somewhat restricted by the trip's location and activities, yet you may still need to focus children's attention on the goals of the trip and the work they have to do as well as keep them together as a group.

During the trip, you can do the following:

1. Encourage singing of marching songs to keep children together.
2. Repeat some of the safety rules: "Remember to stop at the corner." "Always stay on the sidewalk."
3. Follow a map showing the children their present location, where they will turn, and how they will return to the school.
4. Tell the children again what they will see.
5. Let the children take their own time, observing things that are of interest to them, making discoveries, asking questions, and discussing the things they see.

6. Help the children to observe, identify, and recognize different things in the environment. Empty paper-towel or toilet-paper tubes were given to one group of children on a nature field trip to use as field glasses or telescopes, which helped them focus on specific things in the environment.
7. Give children assignments to complete on clipboards or notepads. For example, divide the paper on the clipboard into four sections: on a trip to a hardware store, the four spaces on the paper are labeled "Flowers," "Not Flowers," "Plant Food," and "Tool." Children write and draw a corresponding object.
8. Take the chart with the list of questions children decided to ask. Cut it up before the trip. On the trip, give a question to each child to ask. The child who asks the question records the response on a clipboard or notepad. Or have two children serve as recorders, writing the answer to the questions.
9. Take pictures of the children or make audio recordings to use in the classroom for recall and discussion.

After the Trip. For very young children, the time immediately following a trip will be for resting and refreshment or some other relaxing activity. Young children may not be immediately ready to recall their experiences and may be too fatigued to react. At some time soon after the field trip, you provide follow-up activities, which increase the value of a field trip. Through these activities, children can reconstruct their experiences, use their memory, relate events to ideas, use language and creative expression, and become involved in dramatic play with others.

Discussions. Some discussion of the trip and the work children did can take place. The children should have the opportunity to tell about their impressions of the trip and raise questions. They might dictate or write a thank-you letter or a story about the trip. You can use this time to help them clarify their ideas and concepts and recall their experience. "What do you think the scale was for?" "Why did the people wear uniforms?" "How many types of beans did we see?"

Play. After a trip, you will want to add props to the housekeeping or dramatic play corner that will help the children act out their experiences. Pieces of hose after a trip to the fire station, gardening tools and equipment after a trip to the florist, and various hats and uniforms all encourage children to replay the trip.

Additional Experiences. You can structure additional experiences or learning tasks to reinforce the goals and purposes of the trip. Often the trip is the stimulus for a unit or more complete study of a concept. Vicarious experiences such as reading stories, seeing movies, listening to a resource person, and looking at pictures have more meaning after a trip.

Creative Expression. You can provide opportunities for creative expression after a trip. Make blocks available for constructing, and give the children paints, clay, and other materials for creating. Make books of the things you saw on the trip. Music, dance, and dramatics are also encouraged.

Increasing Knowledge. Depending on the type of field trip taken and the goals of the trip, you can structure activities that will enable you to assess the effectiveness of the trip and to increase children's knowledge:

- A discussion of near and nearer, left and right, far and farthest will help children understand time–space relationships.
- You might construct bingo games using the words children have noted on the trip.
- You and the children can use riddles: "I'm thinking of something we saw on the trip. It was made of metal and was red and white."
- Play absurdity games: "I put my mail in the supermarket. What is wrong?"
- Follow the trip route on a map, using a toy car or model of a person.
- Give the children pictures of houses, stores, workers, or whatever they saw on the trip to play with and sort into categories.

Guest Speakers

Children enjoy and learn from people coming to the school to teach them. Community helpers are a good example. Firefighters and police officers are often willing to visit classrooms and teach children not only about their jobs but about safety as well. Parents, people who live in the community, and people who work in the community are resources. Perhaps the groundskeeper at the local park could come and talk about care of plants. Or perhaps a local baker could come and talk about measuring or where the ingredients in bread come from. As with field trips, it is important to plan carefully, prepare the children, and provide follow-up activities including thank-you notes.

Community Service

As with everything else, children learn civic responsibility by doing; they learn to contribute to their community by contributing. The importance of contributing will be most readily internalized if the ideas come from the children. Ideas for contributing may be generated after a walk, a field trip, or a guest speaker or as a result of studying a particular topic such as recycling. The teacher's role is to prompt the children to think—"Is there something we could do? Is there some way we could help?"—and then help the children decide what can be done realistically and help them carry it out. In one school, children decided to recycle their uneaten lunch scraps by composting them in order to create fertilizer for the school flower garden. In another school, children make peanut butter sandwiches for the local homeless shelter once a week. Community service may provide an opportunity for outdoor experiences as well.

THE CLASSROOM

Even though it is an artificial setting, the classroom can, through careful planning and arranging, become a world for social studies learning. In any developmentally appropriate classroom, children can find water and sand, rocks and mud, woodworking tools, computers, art materials, blocks, books, other children and adults, boxes, foil, animals, and many other resources for learning. Again, keep in mind outdoor opportunities for activity and exploration.

But the careful selection of resources for social studies learning is not enough. Teachers must know how and when to present them to children. Clearly, manipulatives alone have no great educational value unless the teacher knows the materials and can instruct children in their productive use.

Anyone can present children with materials, but good teachers use those materials to lead children to meaningful activity and thinking and to the fulfillment of their educational goals. Good teachers know many things:

- What materials to select and how and when to present them to children
- When and how to interact with children as they use the materials
- How to extend children's activity and expand their thinking
- When to remove resources, add new materials, or end activities

By creating learning centers of interest, the teacher arranges the classroom to provide as many opportunities for learning as the home, community, and world do. The teacher arranges clearly defined spaces where children can find equipment, materials, and furniture grouped together for specific purposes and goals (Isbell & Exelby, 2001). Taking on the appearance of a workshop, these learning centers permit children to make choices about how and what they will learn. The learning centers enable individualization of instruction as children themselves select the materials to use, decide how to use them, and determine the purposes for their use. Centers enable children to use all of the multiple intelligences in their learning.

The idea is for children to be actively engaged in meaningful learning, either alone or with others. As children work in these centers, they learn social skills, especially cooperation and sharing, and they run head-on into the ideas, attitudes, and values of others.

Any number of centers can be located in one room. Decisions about the number and type of centers depend on the goals of the program, interests of the children, and space available.

Children select materials and decide how to use them.

Deciding on Learning Centers

Typically, every preschool and some primary classrooms should include areas for sociodramatic play, blocks, science and mathematics, art, library, manipulative play, music, writing, sand and water play, and woodworking. For the social studies curriculum, other areas are planned. These depend on the children's interests and the curriculum (see Figure 3.1). It is important to set up the classroom carefully, considering access to materials, traffic patterns, ease of transitions, and noisy/quiet spaces.

Centers seem to become less common as children move through the primary grades. Often, whole group instruction increases as children's attention spans lengthen, so center time decreases. The push to cover material included in state and local standards may seem incongruous with center-based learning. However, centers and center time remain one of the most powerful ways to engage children in active, meaningful learning even in the primary grades. Even if centers are used on a limited basis, the kinds of activities and materials described for centers should be a significant part of the social studies curriculum occurring in both large and small groups.

Depending on the curriculum or the characteristics of the community, you might want to create a post office, a gas station, a grocery store, a doctor's office, an airport, or another area to promote sociodramatic play. Or you could set up learning centers of books and pictures about children living in a different country. These areas can be rotated and changed with areas added as needed and removed when no longer in use. A country or cultural center might include artifacts or clothing from the country.

It is important to think carefully about what materials, artifacts, books, pictures, props, and equipment will make each center most effective and to have these well organized and readily available. In some cases, it might be appropriate for children to collect materials such as leaves outdoors for a particular learning center. The needs of special needs children and English language learners must be taken into account when selecting materials.

Introducing Centers

Just setting up centers does not ensure that learning will take place. You need to allow children blocks of time and the freedom to explore and experiment, and you need to be actively involved with the children as they work in the centers.

Introduce the centers by describing some of the possibilities and limitations and the rules of each one: "Here are the paints, brushes, and paper; this is how you wash the brushes." These kinds of statements give children the adult guidance necessary for them to assume responsibility and begin to be self-directing. You can also tie centers to the current theme: "You might want to paint something related to our theme."

As children use the centers, you can suggest problems for them to solve and interest them in different learning opportunities. As 4-year-olds enter the classroom, the teacher might talk with each child, discussing the possible choices available in the centers and asking him what things he might want to do that day. A group of 5-year-olds can listen to a description of the learning areas, materials, and problems and select the area in which they wish to begin working. Children in kindergarten and the

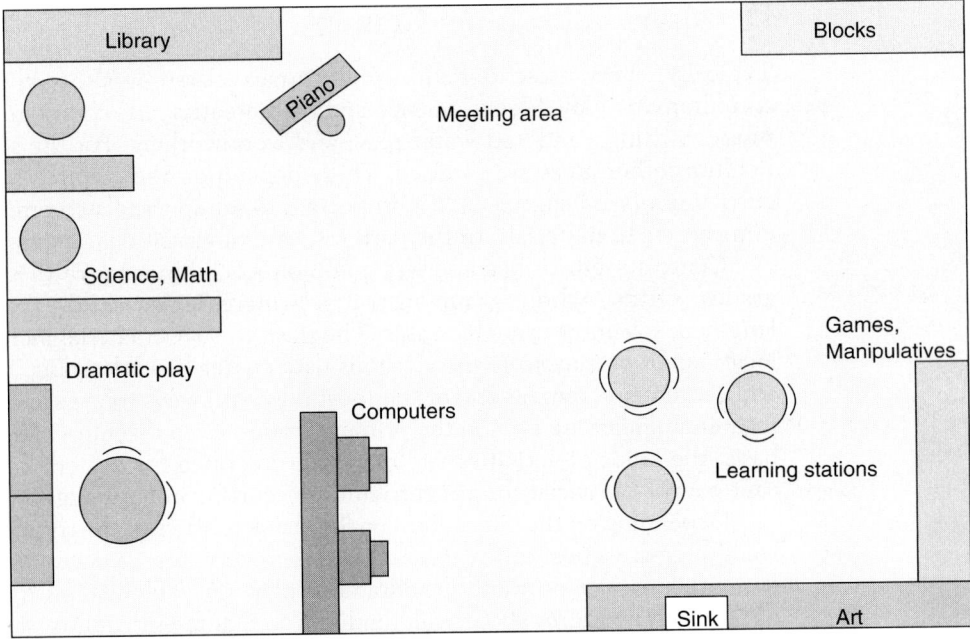

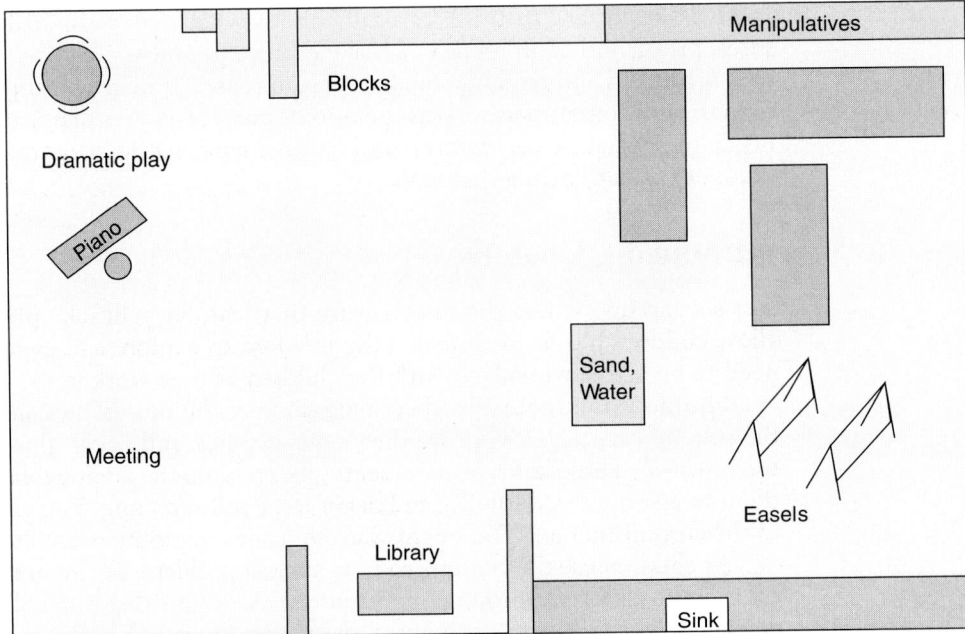

Figure 3.1 Learning centers.

primary grades can place their names on a chart, indicating the center or centers they will work in that morning. They could also keep their own record of the centers they worked in, whom they worked with, and what they completed in a Center Folder.

Types of Centers

A Place of Their Own

In open classrooms filled with interest centers, it is imperative that children have some place to call their own. Young children seem to feel more comfortable when there is a territory they are sure of. This does not mean necessarily that children need a desk of their own or even a cubicle or a locker. Discarded shoeboxes, empty ice cream cartons, or other boxes for their treasures give children the feeling of having their own territory.

A Place to Come Together

The specific physical arrangement for the area in which children gather does not matter. They might sit on risers or a special rug, but the classroom should have some space for the total group to come together to listen to poetry and stories, discuss events, and share news.

Sand and Water

Sand and water areas are useful resources for social studies learning. As children play with natural materials, they are constructing physical knowledge. Sand and water centers may not be available every day, but they should be regular centers. It is not necessary to purchase commercial sand tables: Large cardboard boxes, plastic bathtubs, or discarded plastic wading pools make excellent substitutes. Partially filled, flat cardboard containers ($12 \times 18 \times 3$ inches) can become miniature sand environments for children's explorations, such as transportation or mapmaking.

In the sand, children can construct roads, tunnels, bridges, cities, farms, airports—anything they have seen and want to re-create. A clean squirt bottle can be filled with water so that the children can keep the sand moist enough for building. Props that might be added to the sand include various sizes of containers, measuring spoons and cups, toy animals, people, shops, cars, airplanes, shells, sticks, feathers, marbles, rocks, or even live land crabs and beetles (see Figure 3.2), depending on the curriculum. Children might collect stick or rocks outdoors to add to their water or sand table.

A water center gives children the opportunity to learn more about their earth. You can easily provide water for children's use: Small plastic dishpans placed on a plastic or newspaper-covered table are adequate. Other containers might be plastic tubs or buckets, commercial water tables, or plastic wading pools. Children can cover themselves with plastic aprons, and teachers can keep an extra set of clothing handy in case children do become too wet.

Adding objects to water play gives children new ideas and materials with which to experiment. Sieves, funnels, bottles, a piece of hose, plastic spoons, cups, and dishes

> Relate children's play with sand to the social studies (Barbour, Webster, & Drosdeck, 1987):
> - ❏ Give labels to their sand creations. "This looks like a valley between two mountains." "This is a river, and this is a stream."
> - ❏ Pose problems. "What would happen if rain fell on your mountain? Do you want to try using the sprinkler?"
> - ❏ Motivate building with stories. After reading *Desert Life* (Kirk, 1970), second graders created animals' homes in the sandbox. A first-grade class created a clam flat in their box after reading *One Morning in Maine* (McCloskey, 1952).

Figure 3.2 Sand and the social studies.

are all appropriate additions. If children lose interest in water play, adding dishes, pots, pans, and doll clothes to wash renews their motivation. Adding small boats adds to a transportation theme.

Primary children use sand and water to learn more about measurement and volume, make comparisons, identify cause and effect, and problem-solve (Moriarty, 2002). These older children can also observe how things float, sink, and dissolve. Clipboards near the sand and water areas allow children to record their findings.

Blocks

Blocks are one of the most valuable learning resources in the social studies. Block building invites children to work together. Rather than relying on suggestions from the teacher, the discipline of construction itself asks for cooperative effort. Children seek each other's help, working together as they build (see Figure 3.3).

First introduced by Friedrick Froebel (1887), unit blocks were used by Caroline Pratt (1948) in the early 1930s as a primary tool for social studies learning in her New York City nursery school. Smooth, solid, and increasing in size in length only, unit blocks allow children the comfort of repeating forms and predicting results. Although initially expensive, unit blocks are indestructible and are a good investment.

A variety of blocks might be used in addition to unit blocks. Large, wooden, hollow blocks; cardboard blocks; blocks made from wood scraps that have been sanded and smoothed; and blocks made from paper milk cartons stuffed solidly with newspaper and covered with paper are all useful. Storage of blocks is easiest on open shelves with a place on the shelf for each shape and size. When blocks are stored in this manner, children can see all of the possibilities for constructing and can find the right block for the job. Symbols on each shelf, representing the shape of the block to be stored there, help children remember where to return the blocks when they have finished working with them (Hewett, 2001). Building materials such as plastic crates can be used for making constructions on the playground.

A smooth, hard surface is best for constructing. If possible, allow the buildings to stand as long as the children's interest lasts. Encourage the children to add to or rebuild them, thereby extending their original concept and using it in play. If this is

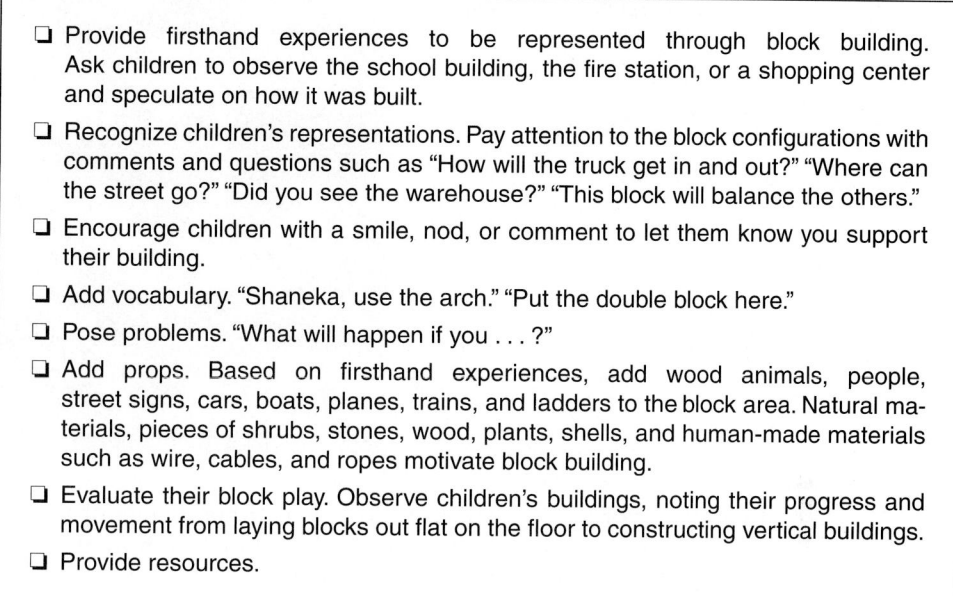

Figure 3.3 Blocks—the teacher's role.

not possible, you can set aside an area away from traffic and with a measure of privacy for block play.

Children's first block buildings are explorative. Young children begin to build by placing the blocks in rows or making lines across the floor. Later they start putting one block on top of another, knocking them down, and then beginning again. Simple construction is next, with square and rectangular buildings of one level appearing (Hewett, 2001). Older children, who have a wider background of experiences, begin to create the things they have observed in the community—the zoo, the airport, an apartment house, a mobile-home park, and the neighborhood. They begin cooperative play with plans, goals, and purposes: Their block play and its resulting structures become increasingly complex based on group effort and individual ideas.

Literature stimulates primary children to construct many kinds of things with blocks:

- Read *The Lot at the End of My Block* (Lewis & Cartwright, 2001). Then children can figure out how to build a house with blocks.
- Read *Tunnels Go Underground: A Building Block Book* (Hill, 2000), which engages children in building tunnels with blocks.
- Read *Building an Igloo* (Steitzer, 1995), and try to engineer an igloo with blocks.
- Read *Canals Are Water Roads* (Hill, 1997a), and build canals with blocks.

Children can create their own literature around block building. At the Center for Young Children at the University of Maryland, the 3-, 4-, and 5-year-olds keep block journals. Teachers take digital photos of children's block buildings and paste

Children's first block buildings are explorative.

them in children's journals. Children then either dictate or write about their block building. They describe how they balanced blocks, how they used unit blocks to build arches, and how the building would be used.

Dramatic Play

Dramatic play encourages children to take on the role of another being and use symbolic thought (see Figure 3.4). Dramatic play has been called a unifying force by which children integrate their social and physical experiences in the external

---

Seek donations for items like these:
- ❏ Used but safety-proofed kitchen utensils
- ❏ Doll and baby clothes and furniture
- ❏ An assortment of clothes for dress up: a lace curtain or panel becomes a king's gown or a queen's skirt; ordinary boots and galoshes become those of a lumberjack, an astronaut, or a fire fighter
- ❏ Tool kits, lunch boxes, briefcases, and other items representing the work of parents
- ❏ An assortment of scarves and jewelry
- ❏ All kinds of hats
- ❏ Papers, pencils, old receipt books and checkbooks, plastic credit-like cards, and notepads for writing and note taking
- ❏ Old telephones
- ❏ Books and magazines
- ❏ Paper, envelopes, and stamps (those found in mail soliciting for donations or magazine subscriptions)
- ❏ Play money, both coins and bills

Figure 3.4 Equipping the dramatic play area.

world with their internal mental and emotional processes to produce novel transformations, which children then project outward in symbolic form (Bodrova & Leong, 2003). Sociodramatic play—children acting like astronauts, mothers, fathers, doctors, or teachers—is important in the development of learning strategies and the skills involved in thinking. In the housekeeping area, children learn to (a) maintain a planned sequence of activities, (b) abstract and embody the salient features of a situation or a role, and (c) focus their attention over a period of time on the capacity for objectivity and empathy.

Keeping in mind the social studies experiences the children have had and the theme you are studying, you can add other props to encourage children to try out still different roles. A trip to the dentist's office might be followed by the addition of a mirror, a chair, and a white shirt; a trip to the airport by the addition of suitcases and a ticket desk; and a visit from the postal clerk by the addition of a shoulder bag and a hat (Vukelich, 1990).

Every area of the social sciences can be reinforced with props in the housekeeping area (see Figures 3.5 and 3.6):

- *Economics*—play money for purses and wallets, scales for weighing groceries, cash registers, blank receipt books
- *History*—sunbonnets, long skirts, ranch-hand hats
- *Geography*—road maps, dress-up clothes for traveling, wheel toys, steering wheel
- *Multicultural education*—clothing, games, or other objects used in other countries

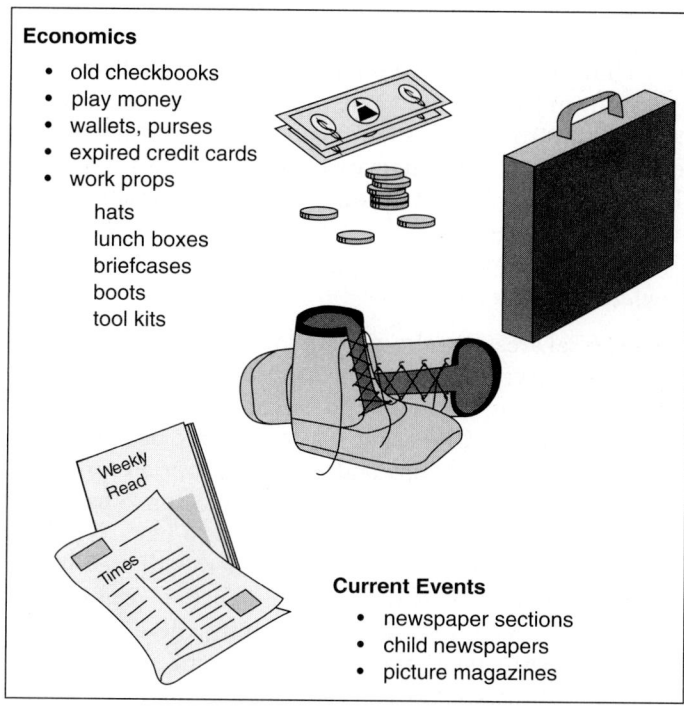

Figure 3.5 Social materials for the dramatic play area.

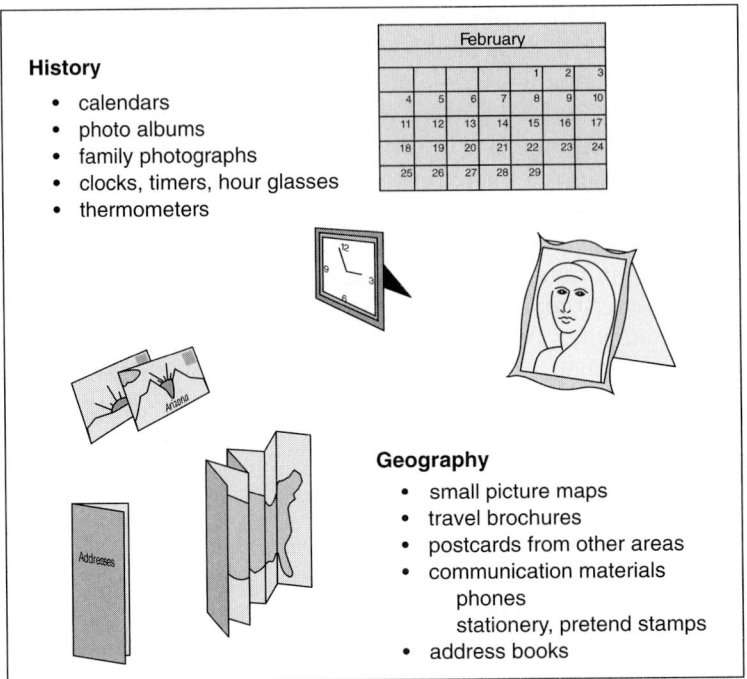

Figure 3.6 History and geography materials for the dramatic play area.

Primary children continue to enjoy dramatic play. The nature and purpose of this play differ from that of preschoolers. In the primary grades, children can make masks and costumes to act out their favorite stories, assigning parts and rehearsing their roles; or they can write their own plays, put on puppet shows, or role-play historical events or problem situations. At times, dramatic play materials may be taken out onto the playground.

Special Centers

A number of special areas are also required from time to time to foster social studies concepts. The grocery store is well known in kindergarten and first-grade classrooms. Other shops may come and go as children's interests and experiences and curricular themes change. Children could use a large packing crate with a change of signs and the addition of curtains and a few appropriate props to portray a sailing ship, a post office, a card shop, a beauty or barber shop, a hardware store, a gasoline station, a drugstore, a toy shop, a laundromat, or a bank. These kinds of shops are most useful if the children have experienced them and are interested in re-creating the experience. Social studies centers might also include props for historical characters such as Johnny Appleseed. Even if space permits, there is no need for these special centers to become permanent additions to the room; they change with the curriculum and children's interests. Consider which ones might be outdoor centers.

Library

A library area is more than a place to read books. It should be filled with color and beauty: growing plants, a dried-flower arrangement, a terrarium, prints, children's art. Here children can read by themselves or with a friend; they can curl up in a big, overstuffed chair or use a pillow on the floor.

To reinforce children's social studies experiences, you need to offer all types of books at all reading levels appropriate for children's use. Simple reference books, picture dictionaries and encyclopedias, books about various topics studied by the children—all are useful resources for children's social studies learning. Books that show the beauty of language, humor, security, suspense, and excitement are also appropriate. You want to include books that deal with history, geography, economics, civics, and cultures as appropriate to the age of the children and the topic being studied.

You may want to include a listening center with audio books so children can follow along with the words and pictures.

Keep children interested by rotating the books, selecting those relevant to children's interests or experiences. Too many books at one time can be confusing. Display the books on a table or arrange them on shelves in low-cut boxes so children can easily see the choices available. You can help children sharpen their thinking skills by providing several different books about the same topic (compare and contrast), two different versions of the same story (find similarities and differences), or two identical books (discuss and play riddles: "I see a picture of . . ." "What page am I on?").

The best-loved and most frequently read books in the library are those the children dictate or write themselves. Class booklets, in which children in the class contribute an illustration or a dictated or written story about a class trip, an experience, or a unit topic, give them the pleasure of cooperating in a group project while expressing and recording their ideas. Individually written booklets are also valuable additions to the library corner. The authors of these books grow in self-esteem as others read their books or as the teacher reads them to the class. Class scrapbooks with photos of the children on a field trip, at work, or at play are also useful library resources.

Books can be shelved in other areas of the classroom as well. In both the library area and other places in the room, some teachers separate books in plastic crates according to type. Biographies, nonfiction, fiction, concepts, and poetry are stored in separate containers. Some books are arranged in other centers. For example, Lynn Cohen, a teacher in New York, places a plastic container of books about building in the block area, pop-up books with art supplies to provide children with ideas for their constructions, or Mother Goose and baby poem books in the housekeeping area to use to "read babies to sleep."

Writing

The social studies provide a point of departure for children to write and record their experiences and ideas (see Figure 3.7). Children can share their writings with each other, the whole group, others in the library area, their parents, or another class in

> Teachers of primary-aged children can either make a journal for each child by stapling some paper together between cardboard covers or purchase a loose-leaf notebook for each child. Labeling these with children's names and storing them in a plastic bin, along with pencils, markers, and pens nearby, encourages children to record their experiences each day.
>
> Teachers of younger children, those in kindergarten and preschool, also encourage journal writing. Younger children will probably use a combination of drawing and writing, scribbling, and invented spelling to record their experiences, thoughts, or feelings.
>
> Make certain, however, that children do have something to record and are free to write in their journals during the day. Artificially setting a "journal time," when everyone in the class *must* sit and write in their journal, seems to destroy the spontaneity and the need to record only those things that are important and meaningful to children.

Figure 3.7 Journal writing.

the school (Schickedanz, 1999). If children's interest in writing lags, you might suggest that they dictate or write a story about how they think it would feel to go to the moon, what they saw on their latest field trip, how they would feel without a friend or about their friend, or some other topic. Prewriters can draw stories, pretend write, or dictate stories to the teacher, aide, or parent volunteer. Writing outdoors can connect children to nature and the world around them.

In kindergarten and the primary grades, a writing area fosters children's written expression and allows children to record their ideas about social studies learning. A shelf set aside for writing materials in the library or art area is all the space that is required. You can provide a can of sharpened pencils, crayons, or markers in a variety of colors; blank booklets (several sheets of paper stapled together); and an assortment of different sizes, shapes, and colors of paper. These supplies can be available to children who have a story to dictate, write, or draw. You might provide box dictionaries (boxes of cards with words that children can read), chart dictionaries or word walls (lists of words that might be needed during a special season or unit of study), and commercial dictionaries.

Art

Every social studies experience can be enhanced by re-creating it, giving it expression through an art activity. As children create, they share materials, sometimes work together in a group, take responsibility for cleanup, and help prepare the materials needed. They are learning and practicing social skills. The very act of creating is emotionally satisfying, for it lets children know they have power and control over materials and things. It enables them to explore and make sense of new knowledge and experiences. It is a safe, acceptable way of releasing feelings and expressing ideas.

Through art, children become acquainted with cultures and historical periods other than their own. Observing paintings from Japan, touching pottery from

Mexico, or examining a woven mat from the Philippines, children gain understanding of other cultures, places, and people. "What do you see in this painting?" "Who made this?" "How did they do it?" "Why did they make it?" "What does it mean to them?" "How is it different from what we see or use today?" are questions that might be asked.

An art center is really many different areas containing a variety of materials through which children can symbolize their knowledge and understanding as well as their values and attitudes. Every day, children need to find something with which to draw, paint, cut, paste, model, construct, sew, weave, or build. In addition to all of the materials readily available for children's use, one additional ingredient is required—experience. All of the social studies experiences—field trips, observations, information, interactions with others—stimulate children's art (Seefeldt, 1995a). Encouraging observation gives their minds more information to incorporate into their creations. As with other centers, doing art outdoors can be an enriching experience.

The products of children's artistic expression also serve as a tool for learning. By displaying all of their work in a variety of ways, children have the opportunity to reflect on their experiences and learning. These displays can serve as assessments to inform adults, school administrators, teachers, and parents about what children are learning (Seefeldt, 2002).

Another type of art experience involves viewing works of art. By sharing an object of art with children, you stimulate ideas for art while introducing them to the cultures, times, and places of others. You might share a Mexican bark painting with the children, examining how it was made, who made it, and why. Children can then make their own bark paintings on brown wrapping paper or wooden planks. Historical paintings, such as portraits of George Washington, can be effective discussion stimulators and learning tools.

Many other ideas are appropriate for children in the primary grades:

- A piece of Inca or Pueblo pottery can lead children to finding out who made it and how they lived and to making their own pottery.
- An Oriental brush painting can give children ideas about using their brushes in new ways to achieve different effects.
- Puppets can be constructed to portray the first Thanksgiving, the discovery of America, or other historic events.
- A unit on American Indian life can lead to replication of American Indian designs and sign writing.
- A model of a farm, a factory, or an airport can be constructed with blocks or boxes.
- At Halloween, a story about masks can lead to making masks.
- Costumes made of brown paper bags and decorations can be constructed for plays and creative dramatics when children act out some historic event.
- Jewelry made of ceramic clay might replicate jewelry made by Mexicans, Spaniards, or American Indians of the Southwest.
- Hats and clothing similar to those worn in another country or time can be constructed.
- Rhythm instruments such as drums, bamboo sticks, and shakers can be constructed to duplicate those used by other peoples.

Drawing and Painting. Because drawing and painting are symbolic processes, they are uniquely related to the social studies. As children draw and paint, they have the opportunity to clarify relationships among their social studies experiences and bring their own interpretation and imagination to them. Drawing and painting activities contribute to children's social skills by permitting them to communicate ideas, feelings, and experiences and to solve problems.

You can provide a variety of drawing tools. None requires much space, but the organization of the materials should remind children of their availability. A shelf, a tabletop, or even a windowsill can hold drawing materials. For ease of cleanup, each type of drawing tool should be kept in a separate container, either a clear type or one that is labeled with a symbol of the tool.

Easels, already set up with cans of paint, brushes, and large newsprint stored nearby are typical but not the only possible arrangement. If easels are not available in the classroom, any type, size, and color of paper; a can of brushes; and a six-pack of paints can serve as painting tools. Children can pick up their materials and begin to paint anywhere in the room or even in the hallway.

Commercial tempera paints are usually best suited for children's painting since they provide a smooth, bright medium thick enough not to run or drip. An assortment of brushes—wide, rounded, and fine pointed—can be provided.

Murals are often outcomes of children's social studies experiences. Children may need some introduction to the purpose of working together to create a group project. The value of having children work together to create a project enjoyed by the entire class is worth any effort needed. One approach, especially with younger children, is to divide the large brown paper used for murals, giving each child a section to paint. This permits children to work by themselves and with a group. After the class has enjoyed the mural, it can be cut apart, and the children can take home their own paintings. Older children might be able to plan or sketch the mural before painting it. You might suggest mural themes depicting your current social studies topic—transportation, the firehouse, the farm—and each child can do something connected with the theme.

Social studies experiences are enhanced when children create things.

Constructing. An assortment of odd pieces of junk such as berry baskets, toilet-paper tubes, cookie containers and other types of boxes, ribbons, string, foil pie pans, and almost anything that will be discarded fosters a wide range of creative responses to social studies concepts. Masking tape, hole punches, plastic-coated wires, and pipe cleaners also are helpful additions. Larger constructions can be done outdoors.

Once the children have joined boxes together with masking tape or wire, they can paint them with tempera with detergent or liquid starch added to allow it to adhere to a variety of surfaces; or the entire structure can be covered with a thin layer of papier-mâché and left to dry. Once it is dry, the children can paint the piece with any type of paint.

Sewing and Weaving. Sewing and weaving are important aspects of many cultures. Once children have mastered the techniques of sewing and weaving, they can create banners, flags, mats, and clothing representative of these cultures.

Large, blunt needles and brightly colored yarns are ideal for beginning stitchery experiences. You will need to show children how to thread the yarn through the eye of the needle and how to make a knot in the end of the yarn. Usually, one or two of the children catch on quickly and can help the other children with the threading and knotting tasks. The stitchery experience is much more successful if the sewing material is loosely woven. Plastic screening or berry baskets, net potato or onion bags, or burlap with a border of masking tape to stiffen it are useful materials for beginning sewers since the large needles and thick yarn slip easily through the mesh. Tightly woven material does not permit the large needle, threaded with thick yarn, to pass through it easily. Mounting the material to be stitched on an embroidery hoop or stiffening it in some other way is very helpful for young children, enabling them to hold the material more securely.

Primary-age children find an old-fashioned sewing box useful. This box may contain spools of thread, blunt scissors, buttons, fancy lace, patches, and a large sewing needle. Before using the sewing box, children should know how to use needles and scissors safely. A sewing kit allows children to make puppets, clothes for puppets and dolls, or clothing for a play or to mend other items.

Weaving is possible with a large variety of materials. First, children can begin the weaving process with strips of construction paper. Later you might provide the cut paper and let the children weave with materials they have found during a field trip or nature walk. Once children learn the over-and-under pattern of weaving, they can use it to make decorations, wall hangings, mats, or items of clothing.

Woodworking. Children have always delighted in the power and sensory pleasure of working with wood. Wood is solid, has weight, and takes up space, and real products can be created with it. A woodworking bench is not necessary for children to have experiences with wood. Any discarded stand, table, shelf, or solid wooden chair, indoors or outdoors, can become a woodworking bench with the addition of C-clamps, which hold the wood while children are working.

Tools—strong, sturdy, and real—can be mounted on a pegboard hanging on the wall or stored in a box. You can get softwood scraps from the local cabinet shop, from high school or college industrial arts programs, or from builders. As with other art materials, children progress through definite developmental levels when working with wood. The first experiences with wood are exploratory. Children pound nails into pieces of wood, not joining anything but enjoying the power and thrill of working with real materials. The next stage involves joining two pieces of wood together with no definite plan in mind; sometimes, after the pieces have been joined, children will give names to their creations. The last stage involves making plans, deciding on materials to use, and completing the construction.

Many social studies concepts are reinforced as children work with wood. Primary children could work together in committees to build a product the class can use—a rabbit hutch, a shelf, a CD-player stand, or a playhouse—or they can re-create their observations of construction workers, cabinetmakers, or builders. If involved in purchasing the wood and wood supplies, they become consumers as well as producers. Woodworking might also stimulate interest in this type of career or in finding out how things are made and who makes them; or they could use the skills they have gained working with wood to do other projects:

- Create a model of the Empire State Building with wood after reading *The Empire State Building* (Holland, 1998).
- Construct a dam after reading *Dams Give Us Power: A Building Block Book* (Hill, 1997b).

Cutting and Pasting. Even the youngest children enjoy cutting and pasting and making collages. Age-appropriate scissors that cut and an assortment of things to cut—paper, fabric, ribbons, yarns, gummed papers, tissue paper, felt, feathers—plus glue and paste give children unlimited possibilities for re-creating their experiences. Children who have not yet mastered scissors can make torn paper collages.

Collage materials are more useful when they are stored by category. Keeping all of the feathers, sticks, pebbles, shells, ribbons, upholstery scraps, and toothpicks in their own boxes enables children to select the materials needed. Returning from a trip to the zoo, one group of kindergartners went directly to the box of rough-textured upholstery scraps and began creating the animals they had seen—with the exception of one child. He ignored the upholstery scraps, picked up the box of toothpicks, and re-created, with all the intricacies of spans and wires, the bridge they had crossed on the way.

Modeling. Modeling activities are excellent for making objects, folk art, pottery, jewelry, or a character—animal or human—from a well-loved story. Preschool or primary children, without a background of experience with modeling materials, will need time to experiment with clay before actually creating objects. Teachers may also need to introduce children to techniques of working with clay—such as slipping two pieces together—for children to make objects. When children examine clay products from other cultures or times, you might ask, "How do you think they made this point?" "Feel this seam. They must have joined it here." "What tools do you think they used to make this rough part?" These kinds of questions help children see possibilities for their own modeling work.

Water-based clay can be stored in any airtight container. If it dries, you can add water, and in a day or two it will return to its original pliable texture. Storing clay in fist-sized pieces and keeping it pliable and soft encourages children to use it. Plasticine, because of its oil base, will never completely dry out; however, it is not as pliable as other materials and may be more difficult for young children to handle. A set of oilcloth-covered boards, stored next to the clay container, allows children to take a piece of clay or dough and a board and work in any area of the room (Koster, 1999).

Vicarious Materials in the Classroom

Vicarious experiences cannot replace children's concrete experiences. Learning that results from vicarious experience is often inaccurate and incomplete. Nevertheless, until children can actually walk on the moon or go to a foreign country, they can learn something about these places from others. Looking at photographs, reading, watching a movie, or visiting a website about the moon, children learn something about the moon's nature. Artifacts or reproductions of artifacts enable children to explore another culture in a hands-on manner. The wise use of audiovisual materials, bulletin boards, books, artifacts, and pictures can help children (a) clarify concrete experiences, (b) refine their perceptions of these experiences, and (c) extend their meanings. A video filmed during a trip to a bottle factory can be a useful tool for children's learning. Shown after their trip, it enables children to do several things:

- *Recall.* "Do you remember what that was used for?" "What was the purpose of this tool?" "Let's watch the movie again to find out."
- *Focus.* "When we see the video this time, be sure to look at how the bottles got into the box."
- *Clarify.* "Let's check that idea when we watch the DVD."

Then, too, concrete experiences seem to happen so quickly: The moth emerges from the cocoon, the snake sheds its skin, the lights are fixed, the telephone wires are spliced and back in their casing. Children have little opportunity to make accurate observations. Thus, vicarious materials—a book on electricity, photographs of the telephone system, a movie showing a moth emerging from a cocoon in slow motion—enrich and extend children's actual experiences.

Careful selection of materials and resources for vicarious experience is necessary. Deciding on the materials to use depends on the goals and objectives of social studies. You will want to choose whatever materials help foster the children's attainment of your goals. A computer in your classroom will enable you to put images or information at a child's fingertips. Having determined that a specific resource might aid in fostering your goals and objectives, you can ask the following questions:

- How available is the resource? Materials that require mailing time require advanced planning time. Materials that are not readily available when children demand them are not useful.
- How costly is it? Can a natural material or real experience serve the same purpose less expensively?

- How easily can it be used? Finding space for projectors or changing rooms to see a movie, especially with young children, may require more time and effort than it is worth.
- How does it fit in with the children's background of experiences? Does it fit logically and provide information on which to base future experiences?
- How will it be used to meet the needs of individual children? Not all resources are necessary for the total group; some might be selected for use with individual children or small groups.
- What accommodations will be needed for special needs children and English language learners?

Children's Literature

In today's classrooms, children's books are everywhere. Stories, narratives, and historical fiction are powerful ways for children to learn, understand, and relate to social studies. The integration of social studies and literature can provide deep understanding of social studies and improve literacy skills. For children to respond to literature in honest, personal, rich, and deep ways, the books that they find in the library, dramatic play areas, science and math corners, and throughout the room must be of the highest quality possible. Only then will children be able to identify and become involved with the major characters of books, learning about faraway people and places (National Council for History Education, 1998). Libraries are very willing to lend teachers armloads of books for a month to 6 weeks at a time. Beautifully illustrated books are available at all reading levels to meet children's interest on any social studies topic. Every group of books should include various ethnicities and both genders.

The power of children's literature depends on the responses that children bring to it. Having enjoyed listening to a story read by the teacher or another child or having read special books themselves, children can follow up on this pleasurable experience. To build on the books they have read or listened to, children might do these activities:

- Draw or paint a picture of the parts that they enjoyed most, that frightened them the most, or that were the most exciting
- Make clay models of an animal, a character, or some object in the story
- Construct something that was made in the book or that the book was about
- Act out the story with puppets or with other children

Social studies textbooks may be useful as well. Instead of ordering one text for each child, it may be more valuable to have a few copies from each of several different textbook series. When texts from various series are available, children can select the book they need and find information about a particular topic or problem of interest to them. If you use an adopted social studies text, it is best used as a supporting resource rather than the main resource.

Reference Materials

Feet propped up against the table and with a newspaper open, the 5-year-old boy clearly was trying on the role of father. Intrigued by anything that appears to be

The library area—a valuable resource for learning.

adult-like, young children find something appealing about using newspapers, magazines, and other reference materials. It makes them feel grown up. Taking advantage of this natural interest, teachers can use newspapers and magazines as social studies resources. Magazines are particularly interesting and useful because they often contain colorful pictures.

You can gradually introduce the local newspaper to young children. Besides being a useful prop in the housekeeping area, it also contains information that children can use. Certain sections of the newspaper—the picture magazine, sports or feature sections—are manageable for children, and some newspapers have a children's page.

Some newspapers or magazines are produced especially for children (see *www.scholastic.com*, for example). You can subscribe to these for individual children or obtain a few copies for use by small groups of children. The value of these newspapers depends on how they are used. It is inappropriate to give an entire group of kindergarten or primary children the same paper and make them listen to an adult read it, for any reason. If you make these papers available as they pertain to topics of interest and as incidental resources, they might be useful. In the housekeeping area or on the library table, they can be used independently.

When you have determined that the children understand what constitutes news, you can begin to present articles from newspapers or magazines to teach them to understand individual stories or items. Perhaps beginning with the news story and pictures carried in the local paper, the news chart or board can be expanded to include news of the broader community and environment. You or the children can clip a news item from the paper, tell the class about it, and put it on the board. It is best to begin with local news of interest to the children. A story about and a picture of storm damage, the new shopping center, street repairs, or a new baby animal at the zoo can arouse children's interest in looking through the newspaper.

You can bring newspapers or magazines to the classroom for children to find items to share. Primary children might be interested in analyzing the parts of a newspaper. Using several old papers, children could cut out different elements—headlines, news stories, news pictures, want ads, advertisements, weather maps, and comics.

Newspapers are not the only source of news for children. Television, radio, and the Internet are other major sources. To make television news useful for young children, you might do the following:

- Record or download a segment of a major news story to show to the children the next day. This lets them view and discuss current events that might not be available to them or that might be too long to hold their interest. A brief segment from a presidential inauguration, a space launch, or some event from this country or another would be interesting to children.
- Use a television in the preschool or primary grades so that children can watch a segment of some special news event.
- Tape short portions of other events children could listen to. The Martin Luther King, Jr., "I Have a Dream" speech is an example.

As children become interested in the news and aware of current events, they will come into contact with controversial issues as well as tragic events. Some teachers omit all controversy or news of tragedies from the classroom, believing that young children are not mature enough to handle these. Others believe it is not only impossible to protect children from these topics but unfair. Nearly every child watches a plane crash or natural disaster on TV over and over again and observes grieving families. It would be unfair and untruthful not to discuss this event with children or at least recognize that, having witnessed the event, they may need help in processing and understanding it. Either way, teachers need to approach controversial and tragic events with care and caution (Levin, 2003).

Before including a news topic for study, assure yourself that the children do have the ability to discuss and explore it. Ask yourself the following questions:

- Do these children have the mental maturity necessary to work on this topic?
- What in their backgrounds would enable them to respond to it and understand it? Is there anything in their backgrounds that might make it traumatic?
- Is the issue of real significance to the children? Is their interest high?

You also must be certain that you understand the issue, know its history, and can objectively analyze your own values and attitudes toward the issue. In addition, you will want to inform the parents of your plans to handle the topic with the children. You might ask parents to serve as resources, sharing information they know about the issue. Controversial topics can provide children with a focus for research, encouraging them to find additional information, analyze it, and reach their own conclusions. Watching television news shows and reading magazines and newspapers allow children to begin to build a concept of the importance of being informed citizens.

Visual Discovery

Pictures mounted on a bulletin board, projected from the Internet, or available for children to handle, sort, feel, or carry are a valuable social studies resource. You can use them to introduce a theme or begin a discussion, to serve as a take-off point for role-playing or dramatic play, or to give information about people, places, or things far from the child's immediate environment. Picture reading helps to develop thinking skills—to discover new information and generate hypotheses about what they see (Bower & Lobdell, 2005). For pictures to be valuable, they must be read as thoughtfully as the printed page is read. When problem solving provides the motivation, children read pictures to discover clues about landforms and climate, economic development of an area, relationships of work to environment, cultural likenesses and differences, density of populations, characteristics of historical periods, and so on.

Children do not automatically learn to use pictures to solve problems in this manner. Young children should not even be asked to read pictures until their experiential background indicates readiness. Although most young children have had these experiences, it is important that they begin with real objects and events before being asked to interpret a picture or a photograph. Pictures are symbols that stand for some object or event, and young children require many experiences in classifying, comparing, and contrasting real objects and events before they can interpret a picture representing them.

The first stage in visual discovery involves naming and describing the objects that appear. At the beginning level, ask questions that require children to name, list, or tell what they see in the picture.

The next stage in visual discovery is interpretive. Having mastered the ability to describe or name what is in the picture, children can then begin to discuss and interpret what is happening. Then they gain the ability to develop hypotheses about what is happening and why and to make predictions about what might happen. Repeated experiences, increased maturity, language development, and a background of experience in creative thinking will improve children's facility in using and interpreting pictures over time.

Teachers can ask questions to stimulate visual discovery. The questions should "spiral" from concrete to abstract (Bower & Lodbell, 2005). Beginning questions revolve around description and knowledge: "What do you see?" Next, comprehension questions—"What is happening?"—seek to elicit a response that indicates an understanding of the conditions or trends included in the picture. Higher-level questions demonstrate the use of an abstraction in a concrete situation: "What will he do?" "Why did this happen?" "Do you think he did the right thing?" These questions search for responses that demonstrate children's ability to identify elements, relationships, or organizational principles or the ability to put together elements and parts to form a whole that is not clearly identified in the picture.

Not all children will see the same thing in a picture, nor will they interpret the picture in the same way. These differences in perception can lead to small-group discussions and later to critical, analytical thinking. Visual discovery is not always easy for children; repeated experiences with picture reading are required before the process is entirely successful. You need to encourage children's development of picture-reading skills, accepting the level of skill they bring to the task and continuing to use pictures as a resource for learning. You will want to choose pictures carefully. Be sure they have a developmentally appropriate amount of detail, will be interesting to the children, and illustrate the content you are teaching. Even state coins (or enlargements thereof) can be used, particularly those that have historic or geographic significance (United States Mint, 2011). Today, teachers have an abundance of visual images to choose from on the Internet.

Bulletin Boards and Displays

Bulletin boards and displays are one way for children to organize their thoughts and reflect on a social studies experience. Bulletin boards should be created by children or enable the children to interact with the bulletin board. By arranging materials on a table or creating a bulletin board, children have the opportunity to classify information, to find some way to record their ideas and experiences, and label them (see Figures 3.8 and 3.9).

Set the stage for involving preschool and kindergarten children in constructing a display or bulletin board by asking each to make a contribution to the display.

Figure 3.8 Interactive bulletin boards.

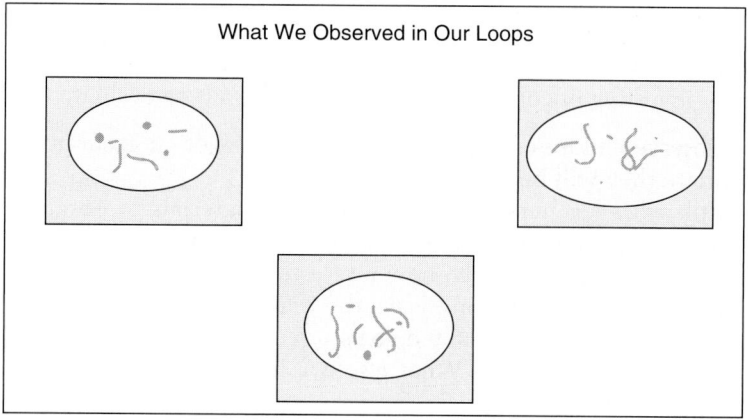

A class took yarn loops outside and observed what they found inside the loops when they placed them in different areas on the playground.

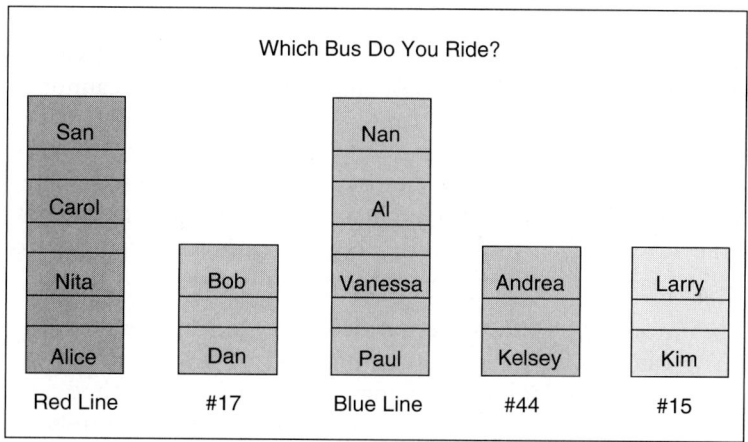

Figure 3.9 Interactive bulletin boards (*continued*).

Popular topics might include a bulletin board titled "We Are in Kindergarten." Each child draws a self-portrait for the board, which is later labeled with the child's name and other information. Other boards might be "Ways We Travel," "The Supermarket," "Weather," "Clothes We Wear," or "Our Friends." Materials collected outdoors, such as leaves, may also be used on bulletin boards.

Primary-age children may take more responsibility for the boards and displays and will be better able to begin coordinating their work as members of small groups. They can select a theme and decide what will be included and how things will be displayed. Displays and boards might be created around themes such as "Fire Fighters," "Machines in School," "Local Native American Tribes," or "Recycling in Our Neighborhood" to illustrate and explain content of interest or things that children have learned through some social studies experience or theme.

Commercial Materials

Commercial kits and materials are available for teaching social studies concepts. Before investing in commercial kits, you will want to evaluate them carefully:

- Observe children using similar materials to get an accurate idea of how appropriate they will be.
- Talk with teachers who have used the materials to obtain other information about children's reactions to them. Ask if the children were able to use the materials independently, how interested they were, whether the materials held their interest, how many ways the materials could be used, and whether they helped to accomplish stated goals.
- Answer the question "What else is available that would accomplish the same purpose for less money?"

Audiovisual Resources

Many videos about places, people, and things of interest to children are readily available. As with other resources, you will need to select them carefully and use them with a specific purpose and objective in mind. Short videos, CDs, DVDs, or portions of longer ones work best since young children cannot attend to vicarious information for long periods of time. United Streaming now makes videos and video clips available via the Internet. YouTube and TeacherTube offer rich sources of information. If the content of a particular video is of interest to the children but the narration is too complex, you might show it with the sound off, letting the children tell the story in their own words, letting the pictures tell the story, or having the children make up the narration as they view the video.

1. *Before viewing:* Preview any video you select before showing it to the children. You can then give the children a focus for viewing, asking questions, or identifying things to look for or things to support their "I thought so's." You can ask the children to predict what they will see. Before the presentation is the time to clarify unfamiliar vocabulary and prepare children for viewing.
2. *During viewing:* Encourage children to talk with one another, ask questions, or make points while the video is being shown. You may want to show it twice: the first time for viewing, the second for discussing; or once for listening and looking, and again for children to look and tell the story in their own words.
3. *After viewing:* A number of more hands-on experiences can follow a video. Children might not want or need to follow the video with any activity; on the other hand, videos often are used to stimulate discussion, ideas, or activities. Here are examples of follow-up experiences:
    - Dramatic play with props added to the play areas reflecting the theme of the video
    - Books to read about the topic covered
    - Art, music, and rhythm activities based on something seen in the video
    - Graphic organizers to identify the main points, make comparisons, or organize new information
    - Further study of the topic by observing the environment and interviewing others

Video Clips and Digital Images

Video clips and visual images are sometimes more practical than videos are. If computers are set up in the room, children can learn to use them to view digital images individually or in pairs.

An interesting way to discuss relationships or to solve problems of living with one another in a group is to use images of the children while working and playing. Some might be used to illustrate the rules that are necessary when using wheel toys, the swing, or the slide. Others could be used to discuss how to settle arguments or to illustrate cooperative use of materials. All children enjoy seeing themselves, and images will stimulate language use as well as help children see solutions to problems.

Digital cameras afford many options. When photos are taken with a digital camera, they can be projected onto a screen for viewing by the whole class. Prints of the photographs can be used in the same ways as pictures or made for each child and family. Digital photos can be used in endless ways: on charts, posters, or bulletin boards; to document children's learning; pasted in scrapbooks; or incorporated into slide shows and shared on large screens or websites for classroom, whole school, or community events. They can also be used to document children's work to be assessed by the teacher.

CDs, Recording, and Television

CDs, used with or without headphones, are also useful to reinforce children's social studies concepts. Some recordings offer children the opportunity to listen to the music of children from other countries or regions. Students might listen to folktales recorded by Native Americans, songs and music from Hawaii, the sound of African musical instruments, or the music of Appalachia. You can type a keyword such as "Appalachia" followed by ".mp3" into a search engine to pull up audio files. The value of this type of listening lies in children's responses: singing, dancing, making instruments, or recording their own folk songs.

Singing the folk songs of a culture, especially in their original language, children are transported in spirit to this culture and, in the process, feel a kinship with its people. Listening to music recorded in a particular culture serves the same purpose (Klein, Surback, & Moyer, 2003).

After the Communists overtook Hungary in the 1950s, Kodaly, a Hungarian philosopher and musician, created a national music curriculum. He believed that if the Hungarian people could sing and share the experience of their music, they would continue to be united and connected with their culture until they could once again experience freedom. During the Velvet Revolutions in Eastern Europe, as the Soviet Union was breaking up, a news program showed the Hungarian people in Freedom Square celebrating their freedom by singing the folk songs of their country. Listening to their national anthem and songs, one could only conclude that music can transmit a culture and hold people together (Seefeldt, 1993).

Reports, stories, or interviews with school personnel or parents can be recorded using audio- or videotape recorders, iPods, or MP3 players. You might capture the sights and sounds of the children. A recording of the sights and sounds of a factory, taken during a field trip, lets children review and remember the trip. Recording stories that the children love allows them to listen to them again and again. Some teachers use the recordings to leave messages for the children, such as a news item, a surprise that will happen during the day, or some directions to follow. Children can develop strong listening and observational skills through use of recorded sounds and images.

Occasionally, a television program or a news show can be useful as a resource for children. When some event will be broadcast—the visit of a king, the arrival of a new animal at the zoo, a space launch—a television could allow the children to witness the event. Young children will want to listen and watch for only a brief time, just long enough to satisfy their curiosity.

Few television shows in their entirety are appropriate for viewing by young children in school. Investing 20 or 30 minutes in the vicarious experience of a television program is not an efficient use of time. Video-sharing sites like YouTube can deliver bite-sized bits of video geared to a specific topic, enabling children to find out the meaning of a term or enjoy a segment related to their interests or created at their level.

TECHNOLOGY RESOURCES

Technology is now part of nearly every child's world (at home or elsewhere) and of nearly every early childhood and elementary program. Today's children are growing up with a different reality in terms of how they communicate and learn, a different set of tools, and different ways of accessing and connecting to their social network (Richardson, 2009). One report suggests that the fastest growing group of Internet users is 2- to 5-year-olds (NetDay News, 2005). Technology is part of the here-and-now world in which children live.

Technology can support just about every aspect of the curriculum. Numerous technology-based digital tools and resources are available for children to use for social studies learning: computers, websites and online resources, CD-ROMs, Smart Boards, tablets, and handheld game systems like Leapster and V.Smile. Small wireless laptops are now inexpensive and come with touch screens.

Technology Standards. The International Society for Technology in Education (ISTE) has developed standards that identify the knowledge and skills that students will need to be effective and productive citizens. The standards are as follows:

1. Creativity and Innovation
2. Communication and Collaboration
3. Research and Information Fluency
4. Critical Thinking, Problem Solving, and Decision Making
5. Digital Citizenship
6. Technology Operations and Concepts (ISTE, 2012).

ISTE has also identified profiles (examples) of experiences with technology for different age groups. The following examples apply to PK–2, ages 4–8.

1. Illustrate and communicate original ideas and stories using digital tools and meda-rich resources (standards 1, 2).

2. Identify, research, and collect data on an environmental issue using digital resources and propose a developmentally appropriate solution (1, 3, 4).
3. Engage in learning activities with learners from multiple cultures through email and other electronic means (2, 6).
4. In a collaborative work group, use a variety of technologies to produce a digital presentation or product in a curriculum area (1, 2, 6).
5. Find and evaluate information related to a current or historical person or event using digital resources (3).
6. Use simulations and graphical organizers to explore and depict patterns of growth, such as the life cycles of plants and animals (1, 3, 4).
7. Demonstrate safe and cooperative use of technology (5).
8. Independently apply digital tools and resources to address a variety of tasks and problems (4, 6).
9. Communicate about technology using developmentally appropriate and accurate terminology (6).
10. Demonstrate the ability to navigate in virtual environments such as electronic books, simulation software, and websites (6). (ISTE, 2012)

These may help you design developmentally appropriate technology-based experiences for young children.

The NCSS (2010) Theme 8 is called Science, Technology, and Society. It states that social studies should include "experiences that provide for the study of relationships between science, technology, and society" (p. 21). It is not enough for children to learn to use technology; they must also explore its impact, societal context, and relationship to science as well as evaluate its use and impact. Developmentally appropriate questions, knowledge, processes, and products are outlined to help teachers in planning.

Developing Comfort with Digital Tools. Children are becoming competent in the use of new technologies such as computers and cell phones just as they are learning to use more traditional tools such as the telephone and television. In fact, many young people are more competent and comfortable with technology than are their parents and teachers (Richardson, 2009). To develop and refine a skill base with a

Children are competent computer users.

variety of digital tools, they need to spend time using them in a supportive environment. For children to learn to use a standard Macintosh or Windows computer, they need time using a mouse-based interface. This includes turning the monitor on and off, learning to type with a keyboard, gaining comfort with a browser, and so on. Children can also learn to use a tablet, which has a somewhat different set of skills. Children can develop these skills in the same way they develop any other skills—through social play, exploration, and guided practice. In addition, children need to learn to evaluate Web-based information and to make choices that facilitate their learning.

Online Resources. Widespread use of the Internet has opened up a world of possibilities for children and teachers. Many online resources can enrich young children's social studies learning: simulations, virtual manipulatives, virtual field trips, websites, blogs, references materials, archival and primary source documents, photos/digital images, and works of art. These can be accessed through computers or tablets.

Online resources can provide needed information about a myriad of social studies topics. Some teachers routinely ask children to find information by accessing *www.askkids.com*, where children can search any social studies topic. The Web-based program Journey North enables children to track the migration routes of butterflies. Google Earth enables children to focus a bird's-eye view of any place on the earth. Lemonade Stand offers an economic simulation game. The National Archives provides access to primary source documents for children to see and read along with lesson plans for teachers. The list is endless. Make sure your browser is up-to-date and that you carefully choose and monitor screen content so that children do not run into inappropriate content.

Webquests are carefully structured online opportunities for students to gather information on a particular topic. Second- and third-graders have been shown to complete WebQuests successfully (Henning & Bell, 2011; Bennett & Cunningham, 2011). Preplanning, choice, and cooperative learning—in addition to appropriate content—can make webquests developmentally appropriate (Henning & Bell, 2011). Children learn technology skills, social skills, critical thinking, and research skills, and show engagement and responsibility in addition to content knowledge. Challenges teachers must plan for include difficult vocabulary words on the websites and back-up plans for technology glitches.

Podcasts are audio and/or video files that can be saved to a computer or accessed via the Internet for viewing and re-viewing. Podcasts can be professionally created, downloaded from the Internet, or created by children. Kindergarteners can use images, sounds, music, book readings, and video clips to create podcasts (Berson, 2009). Children change from passive observers to active participants, showing increasing interaction with the content over repeated use. Podcasts can be used in large groups, small groups, learning centers, individually, or at home. They can also be viewed by parents and other classrooms around the world. Viewing podcasts links children to the larger world and helps them learn content in interesting ways. Creating podcasts adds technology skills, personal interest in the subject matter, confidence, and social skills (Berson, 2009).

Online resources put children in direct contact with other people in different parts of the country and the world. Other potential tools include email, blogs, wikis, Real Simple Syndication (RSS) feeds, social bookmarking, and online photo galleries (Richardson, 2009). These tools can facilitate publication, communication, and collaboration. While building a knowledge base about others, these resources, when used with teacher guidance, can challenge children to connect to the global community, understand the lives of others more fully, and even advocate for equality of opportunity for all (Berson, 2001). By its very nature, the Web models interconnectedness and perspective consciousness (Merryfield, 2007).

Teaching Content. Technology is not the end of learning; it is only a tool, only the servant of learning (Postman, 2000). When carefully designed and selected to meet specific goals of the curriculum, technology-based resources and activities can increase achievement in vocabulary development, mathematics, and prosocial development (Hesse & Lane, 2003). By focusing on specific content, these resources give children the tools to publish their own books, practice skills, and publish online versions of their stories, drawings, and songs (Blagojevic, 2003).

Selecting Technological Tools and Resources. Technological tools and resources must be carefully and purposefully selected and evaluated just as any other resource should be. Technology must be used and evaluated in the context of developmentally appropriate curriculum goals as well as children's experiences and interests. It is also important to consider what the technology adds. For example, it does not make sense to do a KWL chart on the computer, because it needs to be posted for children to see throughout the unit; it is more practical to create it on chart paper and tape it to the wall. By contrast, when a child has a question and wants to find the answer, it may be more practical to search the Internet than to go to the library and search through various books and reference materials.

In selecting technological tools and resources, ask yourself the following:

1. Can the technology be used by individuals, pairs, small groups, or the whole group as appropriate to the lesson?
2. How can I arrange the computer area to promote child–child interactions?
3. How does the technology differ from typical active learning activities? What value is added by using the technology? How can the technology help connect information to the child's here-and-now experience?
4. Will the technology be used only for low-level tasks and rote learning? How can the technology aid in developing higher-order thinking skills such as researching, judging, evaluating, analyzing, and synthesizing information?
5. Does the program require some action on the part of the child, such as drawing, moving things, or writing? Such as searching for and evaluating information?

You will want to examine the program for accuracy of content. Additionally, examine the values that it presents. Like any book or media, some computer games, websites, or digital material can portray gender or ethnic bias or emphasize violence.

Safety

The Internet is or will be part of children's here-and-now world at younger and younger ages. Teachers can teach children about Internet safety and enhance the safety of Internet use in many ways:

- Schools and libraries are required to filter content for minors and to have a safety policy in place (Richardson, 2009); use only filtered content, and adhere to the policies.
- Plan carefully, screen and bookmark websites, and create Web quests or Web tours.
- Follow the school or state policy on publishing children's personal information (this often involves parental permission).
- Monitor children's work and screen content.
- Teach children what is acceptable and what is safe; teach appropriate use; teach appropriate responses to unacceptable, unsafe, or inappropriate sites.
- Teach about Internet predators just as you teach about street predators.
- Consider developmentally appropriate guidelines for the amount of freedom children have to surf; for preschool and primary children, teachers will want to plan, screen, and organize online information and websites for their students; primary children can begin to learn about appropriate use.

SUMMARY

The world is available for children's learning. Become an astute observer of the environment, and use all the resources you can find to foster children's learning. Children and their parents, as well as the school staff, can serve as resources for the social studies. The school building, the local community, and the classroom provide children with many opportunities for learning social studies concepts.

Fieldwork is one of the cornerstones of the social studies. You can plan several different types of field trips for the year. Children learn best through actual experiences, and these trips offer a rich resource for the social studies, as do guest speakers and community service.

The classroom should contain a quiet space for each child, hands-on materials, technology, and learning centers. The class should have centers for blocks, dramatic play, reading, writing and listening, and the arts and centers related to the current theme.

Other materials are also useful. You can select textbooks, children's literature, reference materials, audiovisual resources, technology-based programs and tools including the Internet, and pictures to foster specific concepts. Real objects aid in re-creating the natural environment and are vital to the social studies: Things for children's manipulation and experimentation are best. You can also use interactive bulletin boards and commercial materials as resources.

Technology is part of children's here-and-now world. Teachers can plan developmentally appropriate technology-based experiences that foster children's content, social, critical thinking, and technological learning.

Discussion Questions

1. Lucy Sprague Mitchell's idea was that learning begins with the children's own environment (Mitchell, 1934). She said, "The school's job is to begin with the children's own environment whatever or where ever it may be." (Mitchell, 1934, p. 16) Having read the chapter, what does this quote mean to you? What is Mitchell implying about resources?
2. Why is family included in this chapter as a resource? How can families be used effectively as resources? What are the advantages for the children?
3. Think back to field trips you went on in school. What do you remember about them? Do you remember what the teacher did before, during, and after? To what extent were they powerful learning experiences; or were they "just" fun? How can you as a teacher make fieldtrips powerful learning experiences for your students?
4. Children are using technology at younger and younger ages. What are the implications for education? What is developmentally appropriate use of technology for preschool and primary children? What is the teacher's role? How can young children be "protected" from inappropriate content and predators?
5. Why does NCSS Theme 8 emphasize the relationship between technology and society? What are some examples of those relationships? What is the value of learning about nonelectronic technology from the past? What understandings and attitudes toward technology in relation to society should young children develop? What is "digital citizenship"? (Nebel, Jamison, & Bennett, 2009)

Extend Your Knowledge

1. Walk in and around a school building. List all of the possible resources for children's social studies found within the building and the block around it.
2. Make a floor plan of a primary classroom designed for children's learning. Include as many learning centers as space allows, but plan carefully for the arrangement of each.
3. Observe an activity or work time in a preschool or kindergarten and a primary classroom. How do the activities differ in each room? List the social studies experiences the children have during this time. How many skills, attitudes, and concepts do you see children using or reflecting?
4. Make a card file or spreadsheet of children's literature that relates to history, geography, economics, civics, and cultures. Keep a list of websites that relate to history, geography, economics, civics, and cultures.
5. Begin a resource collection of your own. Include pictures and reference materials, print and digital, for your use and the children's use. Begin to collect posters, photographs, websites, and other materials you believe would be useful for teaching social studies.

Resources

Scholastic has several classroom magazines for preschool and primary children, teachers, and parents. For example, *Let's Find Out* (*www.teacher.scholastic.com*) is a 32-issue, theme-based newsletter for young children that supports the early childhood curriculum and active learning projects. With accompanying mini-books and take-home activities, these magazines are a great introduction to newspapers. They are available in Spanish and English.

Books

Professional books offer many ideas for using children's here-and-now world as their learning environment:

The Power of Projects (Helm & Beneke, 2003) describes how to plan projects based on children's here-and-now learning environment.

Early Learning Environments That Work (Isbell & Exelby, 2001) provides detailed descriptions of innovative, functional, and beautiful room arrangements.

Creating Rooms of Wonder (Seefeldt, 2002) provides teachers with suggestions for creating social studies dioramas and displaying children's work.

Social Studies Alive: Engaging Diverse Learners in the Elementary Classroom (Bower & Lobdell, 2005) provides teaching strategies, lessons, assessments, tips, and resources based on social learning and multiple intelligences.

Digital Age: Technology-based K-12 Lesson Plans for Social Studies (Bennett & Berson, 2007).

Favorite Lesson Plans: Powerful Standards-based Activities (Wilen, 2000).

Websites for Unit Plans, Lesson Plans, and Materials

www.earth.google.com
www.journeynorth.org
www.lemonadegame.com
www.archives.gov
www.nga.gov
www.c-spanclassroom.org
www.learner.org

(Select Social Studies and History, which will take you to Social Studies in Action: A Teaching Practices Library, K–12.)

Also check the national subject area groups (see Chapter 1 resource list) for online resources and activities.

CHAPTER 4

Thinking and Concept Formation

> Focus Questions
>
> After you read this chapter, you should be prepared to respond to the following questions:
>
> - How can teachers plan authentic experiences that will foster children's thinking?
> - How can teachers foster higher-level thinking processes?
> - What is concept formation, and why is it an important part of social studies?
> - How do teachers nurture concept formation?

Eighteen-month-old Rhya is playing with her toys on a rug. As she pushes blocks around, piles them up, and knocks them down, she stops to take a sip of juice from a plastic bottle her mother has given her. She drops the bottle and juice spills out on the rug.

By accident, Rhya puts her hand on the wet spot on the rug. The wetness puzzles her. She looks at her hand, at the rug, sensing a problem. She feels the rug once more. She looks at her hand, the bottle, and feels the rug again. Rhya takes her bottle, drinks from it, and then looks back at the rug. Once again, she feels the wet spot, appearing to formulate tentative solutions to the problem.

Next Rhya tests her hypothesis by deliberately spilling some juice on the rug and feeling the new wet spot. She does this again, feeling the wetness she has just created on the rug and once again feels the original spot, collecting additional data. A large smile appears on her face, and she grabs the bottle, drinking the remaining juice as if satisfied by her conclusions.

At one time, educators believed that critical thinking was possible only for older students or exceptionally bright younger children. Today, however, we know that young children like Rhya use all of the same processes involved in adult thinking. They question and sense problems (identify a wet spot on the rug), locate information (feel the rug and the wet spot), see relationships between ideas and things (spill some juice on the rug), organize and summarize information, and reach conclusions (decide that the juice caused the wet spot).

Observe children at play and you will find that they do independently question and sense problems (Figure 4.1). Children question constantly, and according to researchers, this questioning is the initial step in thinking. If the goal is to teach children to think, then teachers should encourage them to question and to identify a problem—one that is their own, not the teacher's.

Young children also locate and collect information in connection with their play. "I found a feather," squeals a delighted child. Another looks up into the tree and asks, "Which bird lost the feather?" Back in the classroom, they try to find a reference book about birds to identify the one that the feather came from. They also see relationships between ideas and things and begin to generalize: "This paint is just like mud—it slips around." By 4 years of age, children can relate an experience to something that has happened before or will occur in the future. After the

Thinking children solve problems.

```
Children sense a problem.
    Observe
    Notice
    Wonder
    Question

Children explore and investigate.
    Observe closely
    Ask questions
    Collect information
    Organize information

Children test ideas.
    Try things
    Do things differently
    Interpret collected information

Children reach conclusions.
    Discuss
    Reflect
    Express ideas through drawing, writing, movement
```

Figure 4.1 The process of inquiry.

age of 5, children begin to relate their ideas to those of others by listening and through books and other media. From a simple generalization that mud is like paint, children increase their ability to draw generalizations about the things in their world, connecting one fact or concept to others.

Play is the cornerstone not only of a child's social/emotional development but also her/his cognitive development (Isenberg & Quisenberry, 2002; Durlak, Weissberg, Taylor, Dymnicki, & Schellinger, 2009; Vygotsky, 1986). Sociodramatic and representational play have been linked with the emergence of symbolic thought (Hanline, Milton, & Phelps, 2008). The ability of the child to think symbolically in preschool is positively related to literacy and mathematical ability. When a child uses a block as a truck, or a coat hanger as a purse, the child is using symbolic thought. This type of play is an indication that the child has entered Piaget's Preoperational stage. Incorporating play activities into social studies content is valuable. The more the child uses imagination and make-believe props and situations, the more the child's ability to think in the abstract and use symbols increases.

Children begin to classify their world and organize information during infancy. They learn that some things are for sucking; other things are not. Some are food; others are not. By the time children are toddlers, they use words as a means of categorizing their world. They also infer, solve problems, and reach conclusions. These abilities are some of the highest forms of thinking. Children 4 years old and younger solve problems daily: "Sit up on the seesaw. Then we can make it go up and down." By 5 years of age, problem solving extends beyond personal experiences into the classroom, the school, and the community.

PLANNING THINKING EXPERIENCES

Teachers can foster children's thinking in the preschool and primary classroom by providing children with meaningful, integrated, and interesting experiences (National Research Council and Institute of Medicine, 2000). Effective teachers take the time and care to identify resources that families, communities, and children have to offer. These resources have the potential to provide children with firsthand, meaningful experiences that are of high interest to them.

Experiences that stem from children's here-and-now world promote thinking because they (a) are firsthand, (b) involve others, and (c) are filled with language.

Firsthand Experiences

The younger the child, the greater is the need for firsthand, sensory experiences. Through the primary grades, children must find plenty of opportunities to touch, taste, move about, take apart, and put together again (Sousa, 2000). Through these sensory experiences, children absorb information about the nature of their world and develop perceptions about heavy/light, smooth/rough, and soft/hard. Raw materials such as paints, blocks, sand, and water provide children with the opportunity to solve problems, make decisions, and think (Bodrova & Leong, 2003).

Dewey (1944) called for more "stuff" in schools and encouraged teachers to use raw materials so children could develop the ability to think. He believed that raw materials, such as wood, clay, and paints—without any predetermined end or goal for their use—push children into thinking (Bronson, 2003; Prawatt, 2000). Given blocks, sand, water, and boxes, children must figure out what to do with the materials, how they will do it, and when they have achieved their goals. They will have to monitor their own thinking and doing. When children are failing to achieve a goal, they must decide whether to adjust their actions and change their plans. When they reach their goal, which they alone have determined, they experience the joy of achievement and the satisfaction that comes from thinking (Brown, 1997).

Young children are in the process of developing a knowledge base housed in their long-term memories. The ability to retain information in the long-term memory appears early in life and increases with age (Bauer, 2006). As children encounter new experiences and events, they will draw on this knowledge base to explain and react to them. The more their knowledge base grows, the greater their ability to explain new events and experiences with more complexity and react to them more successfully (Siegler & Alibali, 2005). Therefore, teachers must provide children with a wide variety of rich experiences with which to build this foundational knowledge base.

Experiences Involving Others

Experiences to foster thinking must involve others. Throughout the day, while working in centers, arguing on the playground, or discussing a story in the classroom,

Vygotsky believed that social activity was the generator of thought.

children are expected to interact freely—talking, discussing, arguing, and negotiating. Through these naturally occurring interchanges, especially when playing, children are challenged to adjust their egocentric thought, assimilating and accommodating different points of view (Bodrova & Leong, 2003). If children are to get along at all, they must consider the ideas, thinking, and wishes of others. Through this informal give-and-take, children are forced to deal with the perspectives of others and build a foundation for understanding that there are different ways of looking at the world (Prawatt, 2000).

Vygotsky (1986) maintained that this type of social activity is the generator of thought. He believed that individual consciousness is built from outside through relations with others: "The mechanism of social behavior and the mechanism of consciousness are the same" (p. ii). Whether working with others in centers or playing outside, children have an opportunity to build this social consciousness.

Experiences Requiring Language

Experiences make the need for language real and necessary. "Children not only speak about what they are doing, their speech and action are part of one and the same complex psychological function" (Vygotsky, 1986, p. 43). Through talking, arguing, discussing, listening, reading, and writing, children clarify and expand on their experiences.

Experiences and activities give children something to talk about. When children are given the freedom to talk, their informal conversations and interactions "contribute substantially to intellectual development in general and literacy growth in particular" (Dyson, 1988, p. 535). Children converse informally as they work together on a puzzle, rotate the eggs in an incubator, or build with blocks. More formal conversations take place during group times. Teachers encourage children to tell how they completed a project, how they found their way to the nurse's office, or why they think the fish died. Plans for the day or the party next week may be discussed. As children talk, listen, and discuss shared experiences, they gain insights into one another's perceptions of the experiences—how others view the world.

Writing also is used to communicate. Children can write or dictate invitations and thank-you notes. They can write notes to another class and dictate and send letters to siblings, grandparents, and parents. Children can also e-mail other classes far away who are studying the same concepts. They then can compare their findings and ideas with those of others.

Experiences demand expression. Langer (1942) believed that humans were born with an urgent physiological need to express the meaning of their experiences in symbolic form—a need that no other living creature has. As children think about their experiences, they develop images, feelings, and ideas about them. Expression can take any number of forms. Children may draw or paint a picture about their experience, describe it in dance, tell about it in words, or dictate or write down their ideas.

Teachers can use literature and reference books to extend and expand firsthand experiences so that children have a richer mental model of their world and the vocabulary to describe it. Stories may be read aloud several times a day. The entire range of literature, from poetry and folktales to the encyclopedia, helps children sum up and clarify ideas gained through firsthand experiences (Whitehurst & Lonigan, 1998). See the Children's Literature Box for book ideas (Figure 4.2).

Where's Waldo? The Search for the Lost Things (2012) by Martin Handford. Search interesting scenes to find what Waldo has lost.

Where's Waldo? The Incredible Paper Chase (2011) by Martin Handford. Search a variety of scenes to spot pages torn from Waldo's notebook.

Are You My Mother? (1960) by P. D. Eastman. A newly hatched baby bird goes searching for its mother. Making distinctions.

A Bus for Us (2001) by Suzanne Bloom. In Spanish and English editions; making distinctions.

It's Raining Pigs & Noodles (2005) by Jack Prelutsky. A hilarious collection of humorous poetry.

The Random House Book of Poetry for Children (1983) compiled by Jack Prelutsky.

The Everything Kids' Giant Book of Jokes, Riddles, and Brain Teasers (2010) by Michael Dahl and Kathi Wagner.

Jokes By Kids: Volume 1 (2012) edited by Barbara Feldman. [Kindle Edition]

Zoolarious Animal Jokes for Kids (2012) by Rob Elliott.

National Geographic Kids Just Joking: 300 Hilarious Jokes, Tricky Tongue Twisters, and Ridiculous Riddles (2012) by National Geographic Kids.

Figure 4.2 Children's Literature Box for Thinking and Concept Formation.

FOSTERING THINKING PROCESSES

Setting the stage for thinking is necessary but not sufficient. Teachers also need to recognize and foster the processes involved in thinking: questioning and sensing problems, locating information, organizing information, interpreting, reaching conclusions, and making generalizations.

Questioning and Sensing Problems

Children are full of questions, at least when outside of school. The same type of questioning should abound in preschool–primary classrooms. This is not the old-fashioned kind of questioning in which teachers asked children to recite the "right" answers or questioned them to "test" their knowledge. Rather, thinking begins when children themselves sense a problem and pose a question to try to understand reality.

It is not always easy to think of a question. Think back to your own experiences—for example, perhaps after a professor ended a lecture by asking, "Are there any questions?" only to be met with silence. In this situation, there were no questions because no one in the class had an idea, understanding, or knowledge of the content. Without knowledge or understanding, there was nothing to question. Then, too, suppose you had a question about the lecture but felt uncomfortable asking it because everyone would recognize your ignorance and might laugh at you.

Children, as well, must have some knowledge, information, or content to sense a problem or ask a question. In a classroom filled with materials for learning—sand, water, blocks—and a teacher who uses the child's here-and-now world in the broader community as a resource for learning, questions will arise. Rooms should be arranged with centers of interest and materials within the centers juxtaposed to challenge students to ask, "Why?" "How?" "What if?"

The teacher can also stimulate questioning by asking questions of her/his own. Questions that stimulate higher-level thinking are valuable. Based on Bloom's taxonomy, questions can be categorized and developed in the following way (Bloom, 1981; Anderson & Krathol, 2001):

Higher-level thinking questions:

APPLYING questions ask children to apply information/knowledge to specific situations, in order to solve a problem. For example:
- How could _____ help _____?
- How and when could _____ be used for _____?

ANALYZING questions ask children to look for cause and effect; identify patterns; make categories. For example:
- How is _____ like _____?
- So what? Why does it matter?

CREATING questions ask children to think up new ideas and ways to do things or to create something new. For example:
- How could _____ be used for _____?
- If you did _____, what would you get?

> Teachers can model questioning techniques by frequently asking:
>
> Why? What if? How come? Explain. . . . Give reasons. . . . Prove. . . . Which? Account for. . . . Tell the meaning. . . . Why is that important? Tell why you agree. . . . Why do you disagree? Show me how. . . . Can you think of something else? What is the difference? What is the same? Why did this happen? What happened? What would happen in? Which would you rather? What would you say if someone told you . . .? How do you know?

Figure 4.3 Modeling questions.

EVALUATING questions ask children to give their own opinions on a topic. For example:
- What do you think about _____?
- Which is more important, _____ or _____?

Lower-level thinking questions:

REMEMBERING questions ask children to recall specific information, facts. For example:
- What happened first in the story?
- Where did you go over the weekend?

UNDERSTANDING questions ask children to summarize, compare, and describe ideas. For example:
- What is the main idea in _____?
- What are some examples of _____?

By gearing questions to these levels, teachers can model thinking skills and at the same time guide the children to higher-level thinking.

It is not enough to have a rich environment to stimulate questioning. A psychologically safe environment is also necessary. A child may have a question or sense a problem but may not feel free to ask it. Children's questions must be accepted and not seen as frivolous or as attempts to challenge authority. In classrooms where children are respected and teachers themselves question and ponder, children feel safe and are free to question (Figure 4.3).

Locating Information: Field Trips

Young children learn about their world and themselves through observation; nearly every social studies activity includes observing. By encouraging children to use all their senses, you can strengthen their observation skills.

Field trips are especially useful in fostering observation skills. Whether a trip is within the school building, schoolyard, or immediate community, children have opportunities to gather information through the senses (Seefeldt & Galper, 2000). You might plan different types of field trips to make children aware of the information they can gain through the senses.

A Feeling Trip

Plan a trip to discover the different textures in the school building or classroom or outside the school. Children can take large pieces of newsprint and blunt, chunky crayons with the paper removed to make rubbings of the textures they find. Placing the paper over the texture of a tree trunk, sidewalk, screen grating, or concrete block, children rub over the paper with the side of their crayon, actually feeling the differences between rough and smooth, and observe the texture that appears on the paper. Back in the classroom, children can discuss the textures they noted, observe other textures in the room with their hands and eyes, and try to incorporate roughness and smoothness into their drawings and paintings.

Children can use feeling–observation skills for collecting information on other field trips. You might ask children to feel the smoothness of the fire truck or the roughness of the truck's tires on a trip to the fire station, or to observe textures of the environment on a trip to a farm. Trips within the school building, the immediate neighborhood, or the larger community become more meaningful when children are aware of the information they can obtain through the sense of touch.

A Smelling Trip

Children could take a trip to notice how useful the sense of smell is in gathering information. Smells of the office, cafeteria, gym, outdoors, street, or different stores can be observed and discussed. On the trip, children can be helped to distinguish between observations and inferences: "What do you smell?" "Now, what do you think that smell means?" "What are the cooks making?" "You think you smell bread, but can you be sure that it is unless you see it for yourself?" Children can complete their observations and test their inferences by seeing and tasting the bread.

The sense of smell can be used to make continual observations about and gain information from the environment. As they try foods from other cultures, children can be asked to smell the food before tasting it or to use smell to identify plant life in the neighborhood.

A Looking Trip

Children can take other trips to strengthen the sense of sight. Ask them to look for different colors, shapes, and sizes they notice within the school building or even a room of the building. Encourage them to describe what they observe specifically—characterizing things as tall, thin, wide, narrow, shiny, low, bright, or tiny instead of the usual big or small.

Extend children's ability to look by providing them with inexpensive cameras. You can solicit donations from a local business or ask your school to keep a supply of inexpensive cameras available for all classes. Inexpensive digital cameras work well because you can print numerous copies of the photos and send them to children's families via e-mail.

Remember, too, that it is not necessary for each child to have her own camera because children can take turns. Show them how to look through the camera and frame what they are photographing. Using clipboards, have children take notes about what they took pictures of and why. When the photos are printed or developed, they can be mounted in scrapbooks or on charts or just left on a table for children to sort through and talk about.

A Hearing Trip

You could arrange a field trip just for listening. "What sounds do you hear in the room? In the hallway? In the cafeteria? In the gym? On the street? In the supermarket?" Take along an audio recording device to capture some of the sounds. Have the children listen for information by asking them to stand still, close their eyes, and name the things they hear. Back in the classroom, children can listen to the tape and recall the sounds they heard. They might draw pictures of the sounds they heard or tell about other things that make similar sounds. They might compile booklets of the sounds of home, school, cafeteria, or office.

Observation is a process that continues throughout the day. Teachers use every opportunity to help children locate information by observing. Look for ways to challenge children as they observe. Use questions such as "What else do you see? Is it larger than . . . ? Smaller than . . . ? How does it feel?" and statements such as "Look at this part," "Find another one just like it," "It is green just like . . . ," and "Look at the dots on it." These questions and statements help children collect information through close observation of the environment.

You can provide additional activities to check the children's observing ability and foster their observation skills. The following suggestions make good transition experiences between activities:

1. Three or four children face the class in a line. Ask the other children to observe them closely and then close their eyes. When eyes are closed, rearrange the children in the line. Then ask the other children to open their eyes and describe what has changed. As children show an increased ability to observe and describe changes, have the children in the line change or remove something they are wearing—eyeglasses, a pin, a scarf, a headband, and so on—and then ask the others to tell what is different.
2. Put a few objects on a tray. Ask the children to look closely and then close their eyes. While their eyes are closed, remove one of the objects or change the positions of the objects on the tray. Then ask children to tell what is missing or what has changed.
3. Make sounds behind a screen, using a piece of cardboard or a large box as the screen. Crumple some paper, whirl an egg beater, hit wood blocks, ring bells, and make other sounds, asking children to identify each: "What do you hear?" "What do you think made the sound?"
4. Cut up an apple, a turnip, a radish, a pear, a potato, or another white fruit or vegetable. Cut the pieces into identical sizes and shapes, removing the outer skin or coloring. Ask children to taste the cubes and describe their observations: "What does it taste like?" "How does it feel?" Children can describe what they observe through taste, touch, and sight; then ask if they can guess what they are tasting and name the fruit or vegetable. With any tasting projects, children must be

Thinking and Concept Formation

Children use all their senses as they observe things in their environment.

mature enough to be aware of the dangers of identifying unknown substances by tasting them. Without frightening them, caution children against ever trying to find out about some strange material by tasting it. Tell children always to ask an adult before tasting, smelling, or feeling something they do not know about.

Kindergarten and primary-age children will want to begin to locate information through references and resource materials. Locating information through the library and other media sources does not take the place of direct observation but is used in addition to it. When children ask, "Where does the garbage go after it is in the truck?" "Why did the orange tree die?" or "How does the telephone work?" you can reply, "I don't know, but let's find out." In this way, children can use prints, photographs, pamphlets, magazines, newspapers, maps, and other reference materials to collect information.

Organizing and Interpreting Information

Once children have collected information, they must organize it. The process of concept formation serves to organize information; children become aware of the need to classify, compare and contrast, summarize, and interpret the information, ideas, and questions that arise from their observations.

Classifying

Classification, the process of arranging information into categories, is basic to concept formation. It is used to impose order on a collection of objects or events, to identify objects or events, and to show similarities and differences, as well as interrelationships, among them. Children classify without direction from adults. They sort, group, and regroup buttons, sticks, acorns, rocks, and toys as they play with them. Given any group of objects, one of the first things children begin doing is to sort them by placing them into groups and categories.

Gelman (1998) documented that children have an impressive understanding of categories. They understand the distinction between appearance and reality, use names as a guide for making inferences, and realize that growth is an orderly, natural process. This understanding of categories is an important tool for thinking.

Children's ability to classify follows a set pattern of developmental stages:

- *Stage 1.* Children sort objects according to a single property that is perceptually obvious, such as color, size, or shape; or they may classify according to some category they cannot communicate or are not really aware of themselves. They change their categories frequently, beginning again. When asked why he put all the buttons in this pile, a child might shrug and say, "I don't know," or "All of those are like my mother's."
- *Stage 2.* True classification refers to abstracting a common property in a group of objects and finding the same property in other objects in that group. All of the red buttons and so forth are grouped together, and children can identify how they have classified the objects.
- *Stage 3.* Multiple classification refers to objects grouped on the basis of more than one common property. Multiple classification entails a recognition that any given object could belong to a number of different classes at the same time. For example, children will group all the large red buttons together.
- *Stage 4.* All/some relationships appear at this level. All/some refers to children's being able to recognize a distinction among classes on the basis of a property that belongs to all members of the class and one that belongs only to some members of a class. For instance, in a display of red squares, red triangles, and red circles, understanding all/some relationships would enable a child to recognize that all the shapes are red but that only some of them are squares, circles, or triangles.
- *Stage 5.* Class inclusion relationships refer to children's ability to form subclasses of objects or events while including all subclasses within a larger class. For instance, in a container of plastic chips, some red and some blue, there is a subclass of red chips and one of blue, both of which belong to the class of plastic chips.

By age 5, children can usually classify in terms of one characteristic, later by two. Classification by the function that is performed develops even later. Children's first experiences with classification should be completely exploratory in nature, without adult interference. Later, you might ask them why they put all the objects together, if there are any other ways they could think of to group the objects, and how they would name the groups. Children can classify people at work or play, tools used by workers, or happy or sad faces.

Comparing and Contrasting

Comparing and contrasting (the process of noting similarities and differences) are used as children classify and sort things into categories. Comparing and contrasting means that children observe details and features of things and mentally sort them into categories of likenesses and differences. Comparing and contrasting is used to form concepts and is considered basic to thinking. You can use any experience to help children see likenesses and differences among objects or events. A kitten wandering onto the playground can lead children to wonder how the kitten is like them and different from them. Determining likenesses is difficult for young children, but with help, they can see that the kitten eats, sleeps, and has two eyes and two ears. Children can compare and contrast themselves, animals they raise, jobs their parents do, pictures they see, books they read, movies they watch, or stores they visit.

Critical thinking might be part of comparing and contrasting. As children see how things are alike and different, you can ask them to state their preferences for one or the other. When they make selections about the way they like to sing a song, hear a story, or play a game, you might ask why they made the selection: "What parts of it do you like?" "How does it make you feel?" "Why do you like it?" and "Why didn't you choose something else?"

Having collected, compared, classified, and contrasted information, children need to summarize it. In connection with unit topics, lessons, or something of interest they have experienced, children can summarize their findings as follows:

- Report to the class, either by speaking, writing, or dictating to the teacher, who then reports to the others
- Draw, paint, or model something that describes their findings
- Act out a skit or a play or tell a story about the topic
- Make charts, tables, records, or graphs of their experiences

Graphing

Children can present information and convey ideas in many ways. Charts, graphs, sketches, cartoons, and pictures are useful for summarizing and presenting information in simplified form. Graphs can be used by young children, especially if the children construct them (Martin & Miller, 1999). They should be closely related to children's experiences and based on their interests.

"Emily has the most brothers in her family; see—she has more boys on our family graph than anybody else," pointed out Haley, age 4, to the visitor, demonstrating that she could interpret pictures in the form of a graph and gather useful information. When children graph their own experiences, they appear to grasp readily the relationships and information that the graphs illustrate (Polonsky, 2000).

The skill of interpreting graphs and being able to present information in the form of a graph is becoming increasingly important in our technological society. A graph condenses numerous facts and bits of information into an easy-to-see, easy-to-read pictorial form and is an efficient way of communicating information.

Several different types of graphs can be introduced to young children. The picture graph, which uses symbols or pictures instead of bars or lines, usually is introduced first. The bar graph is introduced after children have become familiar with the picture graph. Line graphs, made by drawing lines at right angles to each other, may be too abstract for the youngest children but can be introduced to primary children who have had many previous experiences with picture and bar graphs.

Children learn how to interpret graphs by making their own graphs to illustrate relationships they have experienced. You must introduce graphing with concrete materials and experiences, gradually progressing to abstractions.

For example, two pupils working together may each take a few handfuls of colored cubes, counters, or other suitable objects from a box. After counting up all

Children can create, analyze, and interpret pictorial bar graphs.

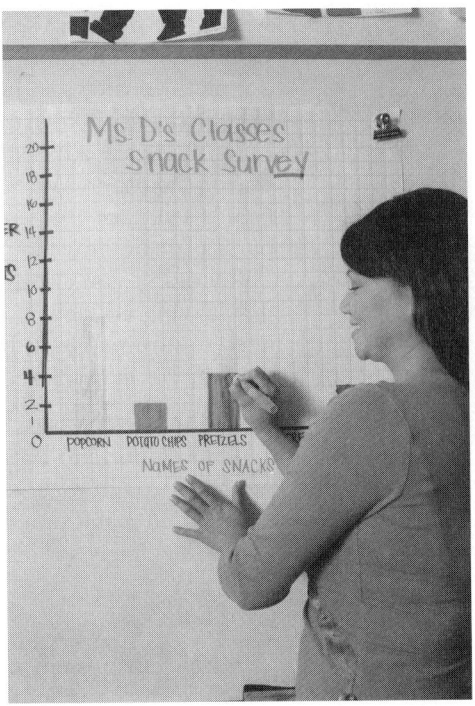

of the yellow ones taken, you could say, "Jack has five such cubes, and Keisha has two." These cubes are then placed vertically or horizontally so that the children can see how many yellow ones were collected.

Following discussion of this experience, the number of colored blocks that each child collected can be represented using colored paper squares, the same color as the blocks, pasted to another paper. Later, any kind of information—types of leaves, number of children with brown eyes, types of bottle caps, sizes of acorns found, or number of pets—can be collected and recorded. However, the teacher should not rush in moving children from graphing real objects to the use of paper.

Graphing experiences take kindergarten and primary children from the concrete to the abstract. Discussing family similarities and differences, children lined up in front of a mark on the board that represented their family type and composition. To make the children conscious of the need to record information, the teacher asked them if they could stay in their lines for a week or more so that they could talk about family size. When the children protested that they would get sleepy, hungry, or tired, the teacher asked if they could use something else in the line instead of themselves. Having rejected the use of cats, who would run away, and pianos, which were too big and expensive, the children decided on blocks, and they replaced themselves in the line with blocks. The next problem was to find a substitute for the blocks, which had to be put away. A flannel board, with felt squares representing the children, was the final abstraction.

Once children have had experience in making graphs with concrete objects, they can illustrate other experiences. Some experiences that can be illustrated graphically might arise spontaneously; you can structure others.

One class, riding buses for the first time, became nervous and anxious as the time neared to return home. Several began asking the teacher what bus they rode on, worrying that they would get on the wrong bus. The teacher quickly drew a graph on the board showing which children rode which bus. As the principal announced each bus, the teacher pointed to the graph and read the names of the children riding that bus. The children readily saw the relationship illustrated by this graph and, the next day, constructed it on a bulletin board. They consulted it for several weeks and the children were reassured that they would catch the right bus. Several of the children pointed out that bus 70 was an empty set because none of the children in their room rode on that bus.

A kindergarten class visited a farm where the farmer told them that the pony they had ridden on was 13 hands high. Using her hand, she showed them how ponies are measured. Returning to the classroom, the teacher noted the children's interest in measuring objects in their room using their hands. As the children traveled around the room measuring everything in sight, the teacher began transferring their observations to a graph. Later, the entire class constructed the graph. Each child in the class, when asked, was able to point to the trash can, the tallest thing measured in the class, and feet, the shortest thing measured.

A graph illustrating how many states each child had visited was constructed in a first-grade classroom in a city in Florida, which is heavily populated with families from every state in the nation. The teacher suggested and structured this graph to initiate a discussion of where the children had lived and to acquaint them with the states of the nation.

You might suggest graphs showing the number of children who have a birthday during each month; the number of sunny, rainy, or cloudy days in a month; who lost a tooth each month; or the number of children with the same hair color. As the children play with sand or water, you could ask them to graph how many cups each of their containers holds. Children's weight and height also lend themselves to graphical representation.

Question children about the graph. Try to probe children's understanding of the relationship between variables. Ask, "What does this mean?" "How is this related to . . . ?" You might also ask children to show which has the most, the least, more than, less than, or fewer than, and then encourage them to discuss the representations of the graph.

Seeing Relationships and Beginning to Generalize

Generalizations are relationships between two ideas or two or more concepts usually expressed as declarative, highly abstract statements such as "History is a process of change," "The earth is constantly changing," or "We are all interdependent." Generalizing is the process of seeing and making connections, connecting one idea to another based on similarities and differences.

Because generalizations are highly abstract, educators once believed that teaching them in the preschool or primary classroom was inappropriate. Today, educators recognize that, although memorizing abstract generalizations is meaningless, children can and do generalize when given concrete referents and experiences.

The child who said, "Mud and paint are the same—they both feel slippery," could not have produced or understood this generalization without experiencing both paint and mud. The child who generalized that everyone has a home could not have done so without first observing the homes of rabbits, birds, and classmates. Both children collected information from various media and then reflected on, organized, and analyzed the information. Because they have produced these generalizations based on their experience, the generalizations have real and authentic meaning for them.

"History is a process of change over time" is a very abstract generalization. However, kindergarteners who make timelines of their lives from birth to kindergarten produce generalizations such as "people change as they grow up." Third-graders studying ancient Greece and Rome may generalize that "societies change" or "civilizations were different then than they are now." These are foundational or subgeneralizations based on larger generalizations about history.

Skillful, reflective teachers encourage generalizations by asking questions that help children focus on connections: "How are these similar? Are these alike in any way? What do all people have in common?" They also plan experiences that are presented as a continuous whole instead of isolated activities. A thread of meaning should run through them, with one experience building on another so that connections will be more obvious.

A group of 4-year-old children took a walking field trip around their school to collect fall leaves. After the trip, the teacher asked the children to look through the leaves they had collected and find three different types—maple, oak, and sweet gum. The children made a graph of the three types of leaves and placed the leaves on a chart board. The teacher then read a book about trees. On a windy day, the children again went outside to watch leaves fall from trees. They talked about how the leaves twirled and swirled as they fell. Back in the classroom, the children danced like falling leaves while the teacher played the piano, matching the music to their motions. Throughout the experiences, the teacher took photographs, which, when organized on a wall chart and in a photo album, helped children reflect on their experiences and reach generalizations about trees and leaves.

A first-grade group decided to study animals, beginning with cats. They first observed their own cats and wrote stories about them. The children sorted and classified pictures of cats roaming freely in the world and those in zoos and homes. Next, the class visited a veterinarian, who described how cats and dogs grow, showed pictures to the children, and let them see the skeleton of a cat. After this experience, one group of children decided to study bones and another continued to expand its knowledge of cats by consulting books and other media. Both groups wrote stories, painted, and drew pictures. To culminate the experience, the groups presented their findings to each other. These experiences, presented as a continuous whole, gave the children the opportunity to develop conceptual relationships and generalizations between and among concepts from biology, mathematics, language, and science.

Planning continuity in field trips is another way in which teachers can foster children's ability to reach generalizations. First field trips for 3-, 4-, and 5-year-old children, who are just beginning to master relationships within their immediate environment, should be walking field trips in or around the school. Taking children away from their familiar environment may confuse them rather than clarify their thinking and enable them to make associations. By the primary grades, however, children have gained sufficient knowledge of their world, as well as the necessary cognitive maturity, to recall past experiences and relate them to new ones.

To be able to generalize, children must first have a solid understanding of the concepts to which the trips are related. Thus, some field trips and experiences should be repeated to give children the opportunity to grasp and understand the embedded concepts.

Teachers' thoughtful questions and comments help children see associations. For instance, the teacher who had the children classify leaves might have asked them, "What other leaves have points like this one?" or "How are these alike and how are they different?" During the study of cats, the teacher asked, "Can you give another example of that?" "How is this cat like the one in the zoo?" "Where else did you see this?"

Making distinctions, organizing systems, recognizing relationships, and taking perspectives are considered to be the four rules of thinking set out in the Patterns of Thinking method, also referred to as *DSRP*, by Derek Cabrera and Laura Colosi in *Thinking at Every Desk* (2009). Cabrera puts forward the idea that we teach children to be "information rich" and therefore excellent candidates for the Jeopardy game show, but we must prepare them to think in order to have true knowledge. The DSRP rules of thinking are as follows:

- **D**istinctions = identifying what something is and what it is not.
- **S**ystems = identifying the parts of something, and whether it is also a part of something else.
- **R**elationships = identifying how something is related to another.
- **P**erspectives = identifying your own point of view and also thinking about things from different points of view.

The DSRP method has been successfully used with children as young as prekindergarteners in Head Start programs. It is a program worth investigating.

Interpreting, Reflecting, and Reaching Conclusions

When you ask children about the meaning of an experience, you are asking them to interpret. Children can discuss their experiences with others, sharing their ideas about and perceptions of some event. Following a field trip, a visit from a police officer or the experience of sitting on a fire truck, children can tell each other how they felt, the part that frightened them, and generally give their interpretations of the event. When all children are encouraged to contribute, either formally or in spontaneous discussions, they begin to see how each person brings a different perspective to the same idea or experience. Through vicarious experiences, children can also use the skill of interpreting—telling about their impressions of a picture or photograph; dancing and moving to a record; drawing, painting, or illustrating in some other way their interpretation of a book or movie.

Real problems that need solving also require children's interpretations. Children must observe all the information present in the situation, understand the meaning of the events, and interpret those events to come up with a solution. In these kinds of situations, Dewey's (1933) requirement for thinking—seeing something ahead instead of something behind—is present.

You can use any problem that presents itself for children to interpret:

- Why were these blocks left out? How can we arrange things so it will not happen again?
- Why have the plants died? How can we find out, and what can we do about it?
- The bathroom toilet is always stopped up and overflows. The janitor said it is because of all of the paper towels in the toilet. What should we do?
- Too many children want to paint at the easel at the same time. How can we solve the problem?
- How many different ways can you use these materials?

You can focus children's attention on the problem to be solved by asking, "Why did it happen?" "How can we keep it from happening again?" "Where did it go?" "What should we do?" These questions might help children predict, suggest hypotheses, and evaluate their interpretations to solve the problem.

An experience is not complete unless children reflect on that experience and think about it. Young children are generally not as attuned to their own cognitive processes as older children are. Adults can help children think about their own thinking. During the preschool–primary grades, adults can introduce children to the idea that at times they will be confused and not have clear ideas. By thinking about things, however, they can reach a better sense of what to think and do.

The process of thinking about thinking might begin by helping children distinguish between understanding and not understanding things. Teachers help children think about their thinking in other ways. By organizing their ideas through graphing, classifying, or sorting materials into categories, children will be thinking about their own thinking. Other opportunities to reflect and think about their own thinking are formally planned. Teachers can do the following:

- Ask children to stop working on a problem or project—to pull away and think again about what they want to accomplish, what they have done so far to achieve this goal, and what they still have to do.
- Help children organize their ideas. Either group or individual activities enable children to do so. They may dictate or write a story, create a book or a chart, or write a poem. Journal writing, keeping a diary, or writing "My History in First Grade" are other ways for children to organize their ideas.
- Have children present their ideas to others. They might describe and discuss how they completed their project, found a solution to some problem, or put on a play. One kindergarten class became intrigued with different bears in the stories they had enjoyed. Comparing the bears in *Winnie the Pooh* (Milne,

Figure 4.4 Why did the chicken cross the road? The chicken crossed the road to smell the flowers and her children are flying in the sky. Hannah, aged 4½ years.

1991), *The Three Bears*, and *Little Bear* (Minarik, 1978), the children put on plays about the different bears. One group created a display for the room of stuffed bears and books about bears, and other children made a bulletin board and a mural illustrating what they had learned about bears.

Jokes and Riddles

Humor can be used to stimulate thinking, problem solving, and forming concepts. Children in the primary grades love absurdities illustrated in jokes such as, "My friend had a pet elephant, but then it got lost. It is somewhere in his house." The impossible image stimulates their thinking and their creativity, and they would love to brain storm places in a house where an elephant could hide. The same goes for riddles, such as the perennial "Why did the chicken cross the road?" Figures 4.4 and 4.5 are pictures of two young children's answers to this riddle. Riddles such as this also help children look at things from other points of view, as does the joke, "The

Figure 4.5 Why did the chicken cross the road? To get to her eggs. Abby aged 6 years.

other day a snail was mugged by two turtles. When the police asked him what happened, the snail replied, 'I don't know. It all happened so quickly!'" *The Laughing Classroom* (2002) by Loomans and Kohlberg is a good resource for all grade levels, as is Thompson's *One Riddle, One Answer* (2000). Jack Prelutsky's poems are also a rich source for humorous poems.

CONCEPT FORMATION

Good teaching invariably concerns itself with conceptual understanding, because concepts are the ingredients for thinking. In *Clan of the Cave Bear* (Auel, 1980), the members of the clan had no word or gesture to represent tree. With brains limited to memorization only, the clan members had to name and think about each kind of tree separately. They were unable to conceptualize or categorize trees into a singular concept or idea. Thus, they were limited in their ability to think and to solve problems.

With the ability to group things into categories or to think in terms of concepts, we are freed from focusing on each isolated fact. When children have an idea or a concept, they have knowledge about how facts and pieces of information are related and interrelated. They understand something, and because they have organized the information into a concept, it holds meaning to them.

Memorizing facts as isolated bits of data is meaningless. With enough drill and practice and perhaps a lot of reinforcement, children can memorize a great number of facts. Unfortunately, children who are taught social studies facts by rote are rather like parrots that have been taught to recite. Neither parrot nor child has any idea or concept of what has been memorized. "A teacher who tries to do this usually accomplishes nothing by empty verbalism, a parrot-like repetition of words by the child, simulating a knowledge of the corresponding concepts but actually covering up a vacuum" (Vygotsky, 1986, p. 74).

Teaching for concept formation leads to more learning because learning concepts is never complete. This incompleteness leads children and learners of any age to continue to want to learn still more in an attempt to complete their understanding. Hence, unlike a compilation of isolated facts, a store of concepts motivates a child to continue to learn more (Prawatt, 2001). For children who will be required to take standardized content tests, which often focus on factual knowledge, concepts and generalizations will make it easier for them to recall the facts.

Not only do concepts foster learning; they make it easier. Concepts are like mental filing cabinets. Children can use concepts to organize and categorize their experiences into meaningful wholes. Even the youngest children begin to understand the world by sorting the things they see, smell, taste, and hear into categories. Infants learn broad categories first—things to suck on that produce food, things to suck on that give no food; things that are painful, those that are pleasurable; faces that are familiar, those that are not.

Toddlers build broader categories of concepts (Gelman, 1998). For example, they first construct the idea of things that are dogs and not dogs. As they experience dogs and have the names of different dogs labeled for them, they begin to construct an idea.

Thus, the social studies are organized around concepts key to each process and discipline content area. As Dewey (1916) advised, the National Council for the Social Studies (1998) today advocates organizing social studies around teaching concepts, not isolated facts. By organizing social studies around key concepts or big ideas, conceptual themes, and units, children will be able to make sense of abstract ideas and facts and begin the lifelong process of acquiring knowledge.

Key Concepts

Meaningful and conducive to future learning, the concepts considered key in each social science discipline organize children's learning experiences. In *The Process of Education*, Jerome Bruner (1960) pointed out that each subject, every discipline, has its own structure. This structure is identified through concepts that are key and that define the discipline. Teachers use these key concepts, or big ideas, to organize and direct interactions with the children. When teachers think about and internalize concepts that are key to any social studies discipline, they then have a way to think about content, the way in which children understand content, and how to organize the children's experiences in the school setting.

The key concepts that relate to and connect isolated facts into a unified whole also enable teachers to organize a whole, unified, and integrated curriculum. When the focus is on big ideas, teachers not only teach facts but teach the connection between facts. The concepts and embedded facts have meaning. Thus, the wholeness of the child and of knowledge is honored.

Long before Bruner, Lucy Sprague Mitchell (1934) demonstrated how teachers bring children and social studies together by organizing their interactions with children around key ideas from geography. Before that time, the social studies curriculum had been based on isolated facts that children memorized. Mitchell called this curriculum "Pops and Caps," an abbreviation for "populations and capitals of the 48 states," which children had been forced to memorize.

Decrying this sterile and meaningless curriculum, Mitchell (1934) designed a continual, meaningful curriculum in *Young Geographers* revolving around key concepts in geography. She matched the key ideas from the field of geography with the interest, drives, orientation, and tools of children from infancy through adolescence. She observed how the infant, before walking and talking, attends to and experiences the qualities of things and how the understanding of the relationship of self to not-self develops. The tools of the infant are the use of the senses and muscles in direct exploration; the content of geography is the direct experience of the immediate environment. Mitchell specified a continuous geography curriculum for each stage of a child's life, ending with the 12-year-old who has adult interests and orientations to anything three-dimensional, the use of a wide variety of tools, and the capacity for abstract thought.

Continuing today, the social science disciplines of history, geography, economics, civics, global education, and others are organized around key concepts. This text, for example, is organized around the concepts considered key in each of the social science disciplines; it describes what is known of how children understand them, and it offers suggestions for expanding children's embryonic concepts into fully developed, complete, and accurate ideas. Using key concepts of any given discipline, teachers can nurture children's concept formation.

Concept Development

The process of learning concepts takes place from the moment of birth. Entering the world without a store of knowledge, infants cannot think because they have nothing to think about. They have not yet constructed any ideas or knowledge. Infants, however, are very efficient learners and at birth immediately begin their lifelong pursuit of constructing concepts.

Hearing, smelling, tasting, and seeing, infants start to organize and categorize their experiences, continually seeking out and responding to their environment. The initial instincts with which infants were born—seeing, grasping, sucking—become more complex, more coordinated, and eventually more purposeful. This process is called adaptation. Assimilation and accommodation are the processes that make adaptation possible (Franklin, 2000; Piaget, 1959).

Assimilation

Assimilation is the term Piaget used for "taking in." Assimilation is absorbing new material into an already-existing idea or schema. An infant sucks and has a sucking schema. Infants suck on nipples and get milk, but this same sucking gets no milk when used on fingers, toes, or mother's hair. They have to accommodate or change their sucking schema to make it fit things that are not nipples. A child was given a whole orange for the first time and bit into it as she would an apple. She had an idea or construct of apples—whole fruits that were bitten into—but no construct of fruit that needed peeling. She was *assimilating* the orange into an already existing pattern, idea, or schema for fruit. The next time she was given an orange, she peeled it, changing her pattern of thought to *accommodate* the new information gained through experience.

Children begin the lifelong process of developing concepts.

Adaptation—Accommodation

Assimilation and accommodation are not separate or independent but take place at the same time. Piaget calls this interaction *adaptation*. Through their interactions and experiences, children construct ways of thinking that are more effective in enabling them to deal with their environment. As they gain more experiences, they acquire more structures and thus can adapt to more and more complex situations.

Early Concepts

Every day, children spontaneously form and use concepts that they construct through the processes of assimilation and accommodation. These ideas or ways of thinking about the world develop without schooling, without any type of instruction. Piaget calls them *spontaneous concepts*.

These first concepts are embryonic in nature. Children's early concepts "stand in the same relationship to true concepts as the embryo to the fully formed organism" (Vygotsky, 1986, p. 58). Although inaccurate, incomplete, and vague, children's early concepts are sufficient to enable them to make simple classifications of things in their world. They recognize a man but frequently cannot distinguish among different individuals belonging to the same class.

Children's incomplete concepts are full of misconceptions (Brophy & Alleman, 2002), which sometimes get them into trouble. A 2- or 3-year-old, for example, may have a concept of car as something that has life and intent; so, a car, alive with headlights that are eyes that can see, will obviously stop when seeing the child in the street. Young children may see a toy or candy in the store that they desire and simply take it. They have no concept of purchasing, of exchanging money for goods.

As children mature, so do their concepts. Their ability to see, hear, and feel increases. They can attend to and perceive more and more of their environment and gradually recall and remember the things they have seen, heard, felt, and tasted.

NURTURING CONCEPT FORMATION

Concepts must be constructed by each individual if they are to have meaning and be useful. Teachers can nurture children's embryonic concepts by providing a rich environment and conditions that will foster the development of fully formed, accurate, and complete concepts of social studies. Such conditions of teaching must be matched to each child's development.

The Problem of the Match

"The task of teaching a subject to a child at any particular age is one of representing the structure of that subject in terms of the child's way of viewing things" (Bruner, 1966, p. 33). This is the problem of the match—of matching what we want to teach the young child with the child's prior knowledge, ways of knowing, and abilities to learn (Figure 4.6).

> **The Problem of the Match**
>
> Chapter 2 offers a number of suggestions you can use to gain a better understanding of a child and his cultural background. Additionally, you might try these techniques to uncover the child's level of concept learning.
>
> Try to get children to tell you all they know about something. Talk with a child or a small group of children and ask
>
> - What can you tell us about . . . ?
> - What can you draw or write about . . . ?
> - What can you do to show us about . . . ?
>
> Get children to dig into their past experiences by asking them to give an example of what they are saying, draw an illustration of what they mean, or act out a "for instance."
>
> Then, too, you can observe children, asking yourself,
>
> - What does the child do in this situation?
> - How does she work with the materials confronting her?
> - What does she choose to do and say in this instance?
> - What did the child choose to do and say in a previous instance?
>
> Ask children to think through their actions, guiding them with questions such as
>
> - How did you get your answer?
> - Why do you say that?
> - Why do you suppose this is so?
> - What do you think would happen if you did that?
>
> Analyze the children's responses and your observations, asking yourself,
>
> - Are the child's errors consistent?
> - Is there a pattern to them?
> - Are they logical?

Figure 4.6 Uncovering children's concepts.

In a way, matching teaching to the child is similar to the old concept of readiness, of waiting to instruct until the child is ready. Yet Bruner (1966) wrote that this concept of readiness is not what he meant: "Readiness is a mischievous half-truth. It is a half-truth largely because it turns out that one teaches readiness or provides opportunities for its nurture, one does not simply wait for it" (p. 76).

Vygotsky (1986) refers to this as teaching to the zone of proximal development. The problem is for the teacher to understand the zone of proximal development, which means to understand a child's current mental age and the level of understanding that the child reaches in solving problems with assistance. Vygotsky maintained that good teachers do not wait for this to develop but "march ahead of development and lead it." Instruction "must be aimed not so much at the ripe as at the ripening functions" (p. 104). Teachers must try to determine the lowest threshold at which instruction can begin—what the child can accomplish alone—as well as the upper threshold, which is what the child can do with help.

If this were easy to do, all children would be successful learners. Obviously, it is not. Even if teachers had all the time and assistance in the world to uncover each child's zone of proximal development and match instruction in every content area to it, they would have difficulties.

First, concepts are unique to each child, developed through personal experiences and constructed by each individual. No two people hold the same idea or concept of something. Ask a group of people to describe their concept of beauty, truth, or loyalty and no two will have exactly the same idea or express it in the same way. Beauty is an abstract concept, but even concrete concepts, such as dog and cat, are individual to each child and influenced by experience, temperament, and environment.

Then, too, children may have fairly accurate concepts but be unable to verbalize them. Children probably do have fairly accurate concepts of cooperation, family, and neighborhood—after all, they do cooperate and live in a family and a neighborhood—but are unable to tell us about these concepts. On the other hand, children may tell us all about something, like space travel or gravity, and have no concept of it whatsoever.

Still, teachers must try to discern children's understanding of concepts. If they do not have this discernment, they cannot match their instruction or the experiences they plan to the maturation level of the child, and failure will result. In missing a child's level of understanding by offering some experience the child has already mastered, teachers can turn children away from schooling. Without some challenge, children are bored and find school a useless, meaningless activity. Conversely, the greatest failure results when teachers try to introduce children to some concept beyond their capabilities and understanding. Not only do children find this instruction meaningless, but they sense their failure to achieve and feel less able or willing to take the risks involved in learning something new. When the school reinforces this sense of failure through grouping or retention practices, children know they are failures and will try to distance themselves from the source of failure—the school—in the future.

By analyzing children's responses and behaviors, teachers will have a better understanding of children's existing concepts. This understanding permits them to better match content to children, bringing the social studies and young children together with meaning.

Guidelines for Concept Formation

Another aid to matching social studies content and children's understanding is for teachers to recall the universal characteristics of children at a given age or stage. "Research on the intellectual development of the child highlights the fact that at each stage of development the child has a characteristic way of viewing the world and explaining it to himself" (Bruner, 1960, p. 33).

This is the focus of the National Association for the Education of Young Children's *Developmentally Appropriate Practices: Serving Children from Birth Through Age 8* (Bredekamp & Copple, 1997). By identifying the characteristics of children at

Stages in Concept Formation	Supportive Learning Environment	Strategies
Becoming aware	Environment provides new experiences: activities, objects, people, events, ideas	A supportive learning environment can be created with:
	Children's interest is encouraged and stimulated with enthusiasm	• Charts, graphs, Venn diagrams • KWL
	Provokes problem solving	• Plan, do review (see Ch. 1) • Projects and thematic learning (see Ch. 2)
Exploring	Provide materials and objects to observe and actively explore	• Models structures • Murals, pictures, collage
	Encourages discovery through extended play	• Blocks, construction toys • Cooking
	Encourages children to interact with materials	• Dramatic play center • Role-playing and dramatization
	Provides activities that build understanding and creation of meaning	• Stories, poetry, rhymes, songs • Maps
	Allows for mistakes	• Cooperative groups
	Motivate by asking, "What now?"	
Inquiring/Questioning	Provides opportunities to examine and investigate various situations	
	Suggests questions that children can ask	
	Helps children formulate explanations and make connections	
	Encourages interaction between children, peers, and adults	
Applying and using	Provides situations in which discoveries and ideas can be used	
	Encourages and facilitates discussion	
	Encourages experimentation	
	Shows how learning can be used in various ways	
	Provides and demonstrates ways what has been learned can be shown in a variety of ways	

Figure 4.7 Ways to nurture children's concept formation.

a given age and describing the teaching practices that match them, this book ensures instruction appropriate for children of a given age.

Guidelines for Appropriate Curriculum Content and Assessment in Programs Serving Children Ages 3 Through 8 (NAEYC, 1998) uses the broad parameters of stages in children's concept formation as a base for making decisions about appropriate curriculum content. This is a good guide for creating a learning environment that nurtures concept formation. At first, children are aware only of events, objects, people, or concepts. Next, they explore these ideas, beginning the process of figuring out the components or attributes of events, objects, people, or concepts. Inquiry is the next process of developing understanding of commonalities across events, objects, people, or concepts, and utilization is the functional level of learning, at which children can apply or make use of their understanding (see Figure 4.7).

> To learn something new, children must become aware, explore, inquire, use and apply. This process occurs over time and reflects movement from learning that is informal and incidental, spontaneous, concrete-referenced and governed by the child's own rules to learning that is more formal, refined, extended, enriched, more removed in time and space from concrete references and more reflective of conventional rule systems. (NAEYC, 1998a, p. 36)

The process continues over and over throughout life and learning.

Helping All Children Form Concepts

Children come to school with very varied experiences and knowledge bases. The teacher's job is to get to know each child and differentiate instruction as much as possible to meet each child's needs. Some children, especially the English language learners, will need more visuals and graphics. Some may need more play and hands-on experiences in order to move into the concrete development stage, when logic overrules their senses. This means that they understand that if one of two identical balls of clay is flattened, there is still the same amount of clay in each ball, although they look different. Other children might need more help to use language to express their ideas.

SUMMARY

Organizing the social studies around the skills of thinking and concept formation is essential. Thinking, a continuous process, begins when the curriculum is organized around children's experiences with the world and their play. Through play, children sense problems and begin to question. Teachers then use these questions and problems to encourage children to locate information, organize data, interpret data, and reach conclusions. The questions asked by teachers are also a powerful aid to foster thinking.

Teaching for thinking is also teaching for concept formation. Teachers identifying key ideas or concepts from each of the social science disciplines then use these to organize children's learning experiences. Knowledge of each child's level of understanding of the concepts is necessary to plan experiences that will foster children's thinking and concept formation. Differentiated instruction is necessary in many classrooms.

Discussion Questions

1. Take a social studies topic/lesson and in groups generate questions at each level of Bloom's taxonomy.
2. Discuss how a group of people can have different understandings of such concepts as friendship, family, education, and courage.
3. What examples of differentiated instruction have you seen out in the schools? What effect did it have on classroom organization?
4. Share ideas for field trips in the community where you are. How could they be included in the social studies curriculum?
5. What value do you see in using a KWL strategy in social studies ("What do you know? What you wonder? What did you learn?")? How will it affect learning?

Extend Your Knowledge

1. Observe children at play. Note and record their questions, the problems they sense, and how they solve the problems. Which of the other processes involved in thinking—locating information, organizing data, inferring, generalizing, and reaching conclusions—are observed?
2. What ideas do children have about social studies concepts? Ask children to tell you what a family is or to give a definition for *brother* or *sister*. Are children's everyday concepts spontaneous concepts or adult-like concepts? Report your findings to the class.
3. Take a concept, such as family, and design a lesson plan that takes children from awareness to complete utilization of the concept.

Resources

Every early childhood teacher should read the original writings of both Piaget and Vygotsky:

Piaget, J. (1959). *The language and thought of the child.* London: Routledge & Kegan Paul.

Vygotsky, L. (1986). *Thought and language* (Rev. ed.). Cambridge, MA: MIT Press.

The following texts offer myriad suggestions for fostering children's thinking in a variety of situations:

Sure, M. R. (2000). *Raising a thinking child workbook.* Champaign, IL: Research Press.

Cabrera, D., & Colosi, L. (2009). *Thinking at every desk: How four different thinking skills will transform your teaching, classroom, school, and district.* Ithaca: Research Institute for Thinking in Education.

Loomnas, D., & Kohlberg, K. (2002). *The laughing classroom.* Tiburon: H. J. Kramer.

Thompson, L. (2000). *One riddle, one answer.* New York, NY: Scholastic.

CHAPTER 5

Self, Others, and the Community: Social Skills

> **Focus Questions**
>
> After you read this chapter, you should be prepared to respond to the following questions:
>
> - How do the development and identity of the individual intersect with groups and institutions in society?
> - What are the main characteristics of a child's social development at ages 3–4 years, 5 years, and 6–7 years?
> - How do developmental theories explain the development of social skills?
> - What factors affect social development?
> - Why is children's sense of self (their self-concept) important to the development of social skills?
> - How do children make and keep friends?

INDIVIDUAL DEVELOPMENT AND IDENTITY AND INDIVIDUALS, GROUPS, AND INSTITUTIONS

Individual development and identity is incorporated in a discussion about self, others and the community, and social skills (NCSS, 2010), and the communities to which we belong are composed of groups and institutions, which have an effect on our development (NCSS, 2010). Therefore, let us take a quick look at NCSS Standard IV and NCSS Standard V, both of which address these concepts (see Figure 5.1). The ideas in the two standards go together because social skills are developed to enable an individual to function in the community's groups and institutions. As you read through this chapter, look for connections to both the issues of individual development and identity, and individuals, groups, and institutions.

Thumb in mouth, Jacob stands watching Taylor, Emily, and Anna build with the blocks. Taking his thumb from his mouth, he asks, "Can I play?"

"*No!* Only us can build with blocks."
Jacob sighs, then sits at a table and watches a group of children pasting pictures into scrapbooks.

"I'm the mother," Hannah informs the group playing in the housekeeping corner. She then proceeds to direct the children in their play until, one by one, they leave and find something else to do.

"Anisha, Anisha," the girls call, "come and play store with us."
Smiling and nodding, Anisha takes Bella by the hand and joins the others, saying, "Bella's going to play with us too, okay?"

SOCIAL SKILLS DEVELOP

Young children enter an early childhood classroom with a wide range of social skills. But once in the classroom, they face the daunting task of learning to relate effectively with adults and children, most of whom are strangers. Not only are new and perhaps different social skills required, but children will be asked to give up some of their individuality for the good of others and the group.

Nevertheless, children will learn necessary skills, attitudes, and values as they live. The small democracy of the early childhood program is designed to support and foster the social skills and knowledge children need to (a) participate in democracy

> **Standard IV: Individual Development and Identity**
>
> Through the Individual Development and Identity standard,
>
> - children will come to understand
>   - who they are and how they change;
>   - the ideas about growth, change, learning; self, family, and groups;
>   - how people are alike and different;
>   - when solving problems and making decisions, people bring their own abilities, talents and interests to the situation;
>   - people change over time;
>   - a person's uniqueness, development, and ways of interacting are influenced by their physical, cognitive, and social-emotional development;
>   - a person's individual identity and development are shaped by their physical and social environment;
>   - society and individual considerations influence a person's choices;
> - children will be able to
>   - discover how a person's identity develops and grows;
>   - describe their own interests, abilities, and understandings;
>   - explore gender, race, culture and physical aspects;
>   - assess how they can work with others;
>   - list people, groups, and institutions that aid development.
>
> **Standard V: Individuals, Groups, and Institutions**
>
> Through the Individual, Groups, and Institutions standard,
>
> - children will understand
>   - that people are influencd by the groups and institutions to which they belong;
>   - the meanings of community, culture, role, competition, cooperation, rules, and norms;
>   - what distinguishes one person from another;
>   - the distinctive features of individuals, groups, and institutions, and their common constituents;
>   - how their lives are affected by all social institutions;
>   - the effect of their groups' norms and rules on their lives;
> - children will be able to
>   - enquire about the influences of individuals, groups, and institutions;
>   - describe how individuals, groups, and institutions interact;
>   - talk about the tensions engendered by individuals, groups, and institutions;
>   - investigate how belonging to more than one group is part of life, and know that this can result in both cooperation and conflict;
>   - describe how institutional roles foster both change and stability;
>   - groups and institutions try to meet individual needs but can either support or hinder the common good;
>   - use surveys and interviews to get information about their schools' groups.

Figure 5.1 NCSS Standard IV: Individual Development and Identity.

and to (b) work to change and improve that democracy in the future. In the democratic society of the classroom, social skills are fostered daily as teachers plan opportunities for children to do the following:

- Interact with one another
- Lead and follow

- Select leaders
- Vote
- Resolve their own conflicts (Bronson, 2000)

Valued and respected within the democracy of an early childhood program, children, in turn, are able to respect others—both those who are similar to themselves and those who differ. The individual's rights are continually balanced with those of the group:

- Freedom of speech and thought are fostered.
- Dissenting voices, even when in the minority, are respected.
- Children are expected and taught to assume responsibility for themselves.
- Children participate, to the fullest extent possible, in the working of the group.

The entire early childhood program and curriculum are designed to foster children's social skills; but the skills that enhance children's abilities to learn, make decisions, and develop as competent, self-directed citizens are more meaningful and useful when developed within the context of the social studies (National Council for the Social Studies, 2010). Through the social studies, children

- form the foundation of a healthy self-concept, and
- develop the skills of
    - communicating,
    - sharing,
    - cooperating, and
    - participating in a social group.

Differences in the ability to relate with others depend in part on a child's level of development:

- Most 3- and 4-year-olds are moving from parallel play to beginning associative play and can manage one playmate at a time.
- Some 3- and 4-year-olds prefer solitary play and are not yet ready to relate to others.
- By age 5, children generally have developed a special friend and will be able to visit this friend on their own.
- At 6 or 7, most children can
    - take turns,
    - negotiate,
    - cooperate, and
    - form peer groups.

These skills will emerge as the result of each child's experience and environment, and the more positive the latter are, the more favorable the outcome.

Various theories address the development of a child in all three domains—physical, cognitive, and social-emotional. Some of these focus more on the development of the social child.

THEORIES OF SOCIALIZATION

Children enter the preschool and primary classroom with a wide range of social development and skills. Researchers have advanced many theories to explain why children differ in their ability to relate effectively with others.

Behavioral Theories

Behavioral theory has its roots in the philosophy of John Locke (1690), who believed that children arrived in the world as blank slates. By educating a child through a series of rewards and punishments, adults write on the slate.

Historically, behaviorists have believed that the following:

- Learning comes about because a person receives a reward or reinforcement for an action or a correct response (Skinner, 1974).
- Learning comes from having their needs satisfied—or not satisfied—by another person or environmental factors.
- When a child's behavior is followed by something pleasant or some type of reward or reinforcement, the child will repeat the behavior.
- If a child's behavior is followed by something unpleasant or ignored, the behavior will eventually disappear.

Using the idea that reinforced social behaviors will increase, teachers do the following:

1. Make certain that children's interactions with other children are positive and rewarding.
2. Arrange the room with sufficient materials to enable children to interact pleasantly, without being frustrated by lack of space or materials.
3. Praise and reinforce prosocial behaviors; thus, a child who shares or cooperates and is praised will continue to share and cooperate.

On the other hand, behaviors can be extinguished. Inappropriate or undesirable social behaviors can be eliminated simply by ignoring them, although sometimes this is a difficult task. For example, many 4-year-old children like to spit. The child who is spat on screams and cries; the adults admonish or punish the spitter. This serves the same function as attention; thus, the child spits again. When teachers ignore the spitter and focus their attention on the child who received the abuse, they open the possibility of eliminating the antisocial behavior.

Not all social behaviors are learned through a series of stimuli and responses. Behaviorists' studies have shown that children also learn social and antisocial behaviors by observing models. The models may be their teachers or parents as well as the media. By observing people, cartoon characters, or actors receiving rewards for aggressive behaviors, children will model and repeat these behaviors. Prosocial behaviors, likewise, will be modeled and imitated.

By studying the theories and practices of behaviorists, teachers can learn to do the following:

- Reinforce children's positive social skills and foster their development
- Eliminate undesired behaviors

Teachers using these techniques, however, must realize that they are controlling children externally. Children still need to develop internal controls for their behavior.

Erikson's Theory of Psychosocial Development

Erik Erikson (1963) developed a theory based on psychoanalytic theory that focused on the ego and what it means for human development. Erikson believed that each stage of life is characterized by a central issue. He saw these crises as psychosocial, or resulting from social interaction.

Erikson theorized that there are eight psychosocial stages, each of which has a positive and a negative trait:

1. Basic trust versus basic mistrust
2. Autonomy versus shame and doubt
3. Initiative versus guilt
4. Industry versus inferiority
5. Identity versus role confusion

Early childhood programs are entirely designed to foster children's self-concept and social skills

6. Intimacy versus isolation
7. Generativity versus stagnation
8. Integrity versus despair

The eight positive psychosocial strengths are characterized as follows:

- Each exists at all eight stages and is related to the others.
- Each has a critical period for development.
- There is a proper sequence to the stages.

For a child to develop in a normal pattern of behavior, the *positive attribute of the stage needs to be satisfied at the critical period before the next stage is developed*. The person's development from a trusting infant to an old man or woman with ego integrity depends on the successful integration of all the stages.

The following stages are most pertinent for early childhood educators:

- Basic trust versus mistrust (birth – 18 months; infancy)
- Autonomy versus shame (18 months – 3 years; toddler years)
- Initiative versus guilt (3 – 6 years; preschool years)
- Industry versus inferiority (6 years – puberty; elementary school years)

Basic Trust

The world is safe; the world is not safe. For basic trust to develop, infants between birth and 18 months of age must gradually develop a sense of inner goodness because they feel assured of an outer predictability. For example, they develop trust if they are fed when they are hungry; mistrust if they are not. Without this security, children develop a basic mistrust and hostility toward others and the world (Copple, 2003; Marshall, 2001). Nevertheless, if their later care is responsive and caring, they can still develop trusting relationships.

Autonomy

I am worthy; I am not worthy. Between 19 months and 3 years of age, toddlers develop a sense of autonomy. As they start to walk, they develop a desire to let go as well as a need to hold on. Children begin to develop a sense of self and pride in their achievements. If they are shamed because of their attempts at letting go and their experiments with the world, they develop a sense of shame about themselves and self-doubt as they function in the world. Caregivers need to be aware that not all cultures see the toddler's struggle for independence as a good thing and they attempt to moderate it (Rasmussen, 2009).

Initiative

I am good; I am bad. At the age of 3 or 4, a new stage, initiative, unfolds. At this stage, children can undertake and carry out their own activities and do them both individually and in cooperation with other children. If the adult world does not offer proper regulations, children may undertake more than they can achieve, thus developing a sense of guilt or failure. On the other hand, if the adult world does not

Initiative unfolds–children plan their own activities in cooperation with others.

permit them to practice developing skills, children live with a sense of failure. When young children break a rule or fail to meet expectations, they become very upset (Thompson & Virmani, 2010).

Industry

I can accomplish; I cannot accomplish. From 6 years of age until puberty, children develop a sense of industry. At this stage, they become producers of things and users of tools, not the least being reading, writing, and mathematics. Children become socially adept as they work beside and with others. One potential problem at this stage is that children may develop a sense of inadequacy in using the tools of their world or may see themselves as inferior to others. They may always compare their own abilities to those of others in areas that are important to them and lose self-confidence if they believe they are lacking (Wu, West, & Hughes, 2010). Another danger is overworking, so that the child becomes a perfectionist—a "conformist or thoughtless slave of his technique" (Erikson, 1963, p. 247).

Social–Cognitive Theories

Social–cognitive theories recognize that children are whole beings. They cannot be divided into parts for physical, intellectual, social, or emotional growth. Its supporters see social–emotional growth as parallel to, or even the same as intellectual growth.

The basic principles of social cognitive theories are as follows:

- *What happens in one area of growth or development affects other areas (Bronson, 2000):*
  - Children who cannot make friends, cooperate, or share have difficulty in a group.
  - Unable to relate with others or to make friends, these children may also have difficulty focusing on schoolwork.

- Likewise, children who have trouble learning may also have difficulty developing social skills.
- Emotional problems—perhaps anxiety, learned helplessness, or insecurities—can affect children's ability to learn and achieve.
- *A child's social behavior is considered within the context of cognitive maturity.*
  - A 3-year-old who is scribbling away on a piece of paper continues scribbling with the marker on a neighbor child.
  - The child is not punished because a 3-year-old cannot yet cognitively differentiate that others are not objects but have feelings like herself.
  - Rather, the teacher attempts to teach the child, saying, "Color on your paper," showing her the paper and saying, "Color here. Do not color on other children."

By evaluating children's social behavior in terms of cognition, teachers have a better understanding of what they can and cannot expect children to do at any given age.

- *The individual is in charge of his or her own learning.*
  - Although growth stems from the interaction of maturation and experience, the individual must construct social knowledge.
  - Stimulating children to think about social relations and offering them suggestions to enable them to construct knowledge of social skills are viewed as important.

With this framework, teachers guide children to talk about social situations or problems and help them come up with their own solutions. Instead of offering solutions to a child who grabs a toy from another ("Use your words instead of grabbing so she'll know what you want") or offering alternative solutions ("Give her a turn now"), the idea is to develop children's skill in thinking of solutions for themselves. There is no recrimination. Shaming or blaming children for behavior is not acceptable in a democratic classroom.

Spivack and Shure (1978) developed the cognitive approach to interpersonal problem solving. Inherent in this approach is the assumption that the ability to think clearly paves the way for emotional relief and healthy social adjustment:

- When children have problems relating socially, teachers ask them the following:
  - What happened
  - How they felt in the situation
  - What they did, and what other ways they could act in similar situations

In addition to the scripted learning experiences that form their program, Spivack and Shure maintained that the dialogues teachers have with children informally and in connection with ongoing events are even more important in developing children's social skills.

Cognitive–Developmental Theories

Cognitive-developmental theorists focus on intellectual processes and how children have an active role in their own development. Jean Piaget (1896–1980) was the first of these theorists, and although he is known best for his stages of cognitive development, he also wrote extensively on how, over time, children construct an understanding of what is good and bad behavior (Piaget, 1960).

Some of Piaget's key ideas are as follows:

- Preschoolers believe that that being "good" means obeying rules.
- By 8 or 9 years of age, children realize that rules exist to help people and can be changed to better fit a situation.
- Children in the lower elementary school grades believe that those who caused the most damage or harm are the "bad" people. For example, a child who breaks six glasses while helping to wash the dishes is more badly behaved than a child who breaks one glass while trying to steal cookies off a shelf.
- Older elementary children realize that intent is an important aspect in how good or bad a behavior is, and therefore the child who accidentally broke many glasses while helping is less culpable than the other who broke one glass while trying to steal.

Moral reasoning is the main focus for the cognitive-developmental theory of Lawrence Kohlberg (1927–1987). He is also a stage theorist, looking at age-related ways in which people approach moral issues. He proposed that there are three broad levels of morality, each of which has two stages (Kohlberg, 1984):

- Level 1: Preconventional morality: observed in preschool children and some elementary, middle school, and high school students.
  - Stage 1: Avoiding punishment and obeying.
  - Stage 2: Exchange of favors; right and wrong relate to themselves.
- Level II: Conventional morality: Observed in some upper elementary children, some middle school, and many high school students.
  - Stage 3: Good boy/ good girl; pleasing others.
  - Stage 4: Law and order; society has rules that should be obeyed.
- Level III: Postconventional morality: Rarely observed before college, and stage 6 is rare even among adults.
  - Stage 5: Social contract; rules guide behavior and can be changed if they are no longer appropriate.
  - Stage 6: Universal ethical principles; answer to their consciences and principles; ideal and rare.

Further research has uncovered limitations to this theory, such as the fact that females tend to consider compassion more important than justice, which tends to be the prime moral compass for males.

Vygotsky's Sociocultural Theory

Lev Vygotsky (1896–1934) was a Russian scholar whose premise is that children's development is shaped by their everyday experiences and the culture in which they live. He strongly believed that interaction with other children and adults is of prime importance to a child's development, and that a child's behaviors are influenced by noticeable cultural ways of thinking (Vygotsky, 1978, 1986). Thus it is important to take into consideration a child's family, community, and total environment in order to understand the child's social development.

Developmental Systems Theories

These theories demonstrate how a child's development is governed by numerous elements—both nature and nurture. A whole child is the product of his or her biological body, which is an assembly of living parts working in harmony and the product of her or his social and physical environment (the world in which he or she lives). Urie Bronfenbrenner (1917–2005) developed his *bioecological* model of human development to demonstrate this theory (Bronfenbrenner, 2005). He contends that the following people, social institutions, and cultural practices influence a child's development:

- The child's family, immediate and extended, and primary caregivers
- People outside the family who support children and compensate for home disadvantages
- Other elements in society that affect the child's quality of life such as the parents' workplace, level of education, salaries or wages, political systems, and friends
- The pervasive influence of culture on values, social interaction styles, and relationships
- The child's own temperament, personality, and abilities

In summary, the development of a child occurs within an environment that is communal, multidimensional, and dynamic.

FACTORS AFFECTING SOCIAL DEVELOPMENT

Children's development of social skills is affected by the nature of their family and early educational experiences (National Research Council, 2001). Whether in a nuclear, blended, or extended family; a communal arrangement; or a single-parent family, the child learns social patterns and skills within this context. Children find love and security and form attachments with people who protect and care for them.

In the family, children become socialized through interactions with parents, siblings, relatives, and neighbors; once in a school setting, they need new ways of acting, relating, and socializing. Children who have had a strong attachment to a nurturing figure and see themselves as separate from this nurturing figure are ready for a group situation. Children who have not fully developed strong attachments to other persons may have more difficulty adjusting to the complexity of the social system of the school.

The Family

Children who experience the security of loving parents or consistent adults in their lives and have strong attachments to them are better able to reach out to relate with others. According to attachment theory, children who enjoy a secure attachment relationship with their parents or family members and caregivers do the following:

- They use this relationship as a support to venture out and explore their environment (Maccoby, 1993).
- They reach out to others, return to the caregiver for support, and venture out again, going further into the world of social relationships (Ainsworth, Belhar, Waters, & Wall, 1978; Cortez, 2008).
- As they confidently wander out to test the social waters, they enlarge their social world, expand their social contacts, and are more likely to learn from experience in social interaction.

Parents who are social themselves serve as models for their children. Children may use the image of their parents interacting with others in their own attempts to make and be friends with other children or to cooperate and share. Socially competent parents may affect their children's social skill development in another way: Parents who are secure and competent offer children a model of security from which to build their own social skills.

The nature of parent–child interactions is also related to a child's development of social skills:

- Children who are raised in *democratic* families, where reasons are given along with the rules, are more likely to be socially active and open-minded. Such parents explain, "No hitting. If you ask her for the truck instead of hitting, she'll give it to you," or "We always say thank you to someone who does something for you," or "In church, we sit quietly during the sermon so others can hear. If you want to, you can write in your notebook or take a puzzle with you so you don't disturb the others." These parents are more likely to have children who cooperate, share, and initiate social activities.
- Parents who are more *authoritarian*, who demand obedient, conforming, and dependent offspring, may have children who are never really comfortable exploring the world for themselves. Often, these children fail to develop the ability to relate effectively with others throughout their life (Dorsey, 2003).

Gender differences play a role as well. In one study, fathers' negative attitudes toward child rearing predicted behavior problems in children (DeKlyen, Biernbaum, Speltz, & Greenberg, 1998). Fathers' warmth and control have also been related to better academic achievement for children, and interactions with nonpaternal men can result in more prosocial behaviors toward peers (Coley, 1998).

Role of Community

The characteristics of a community's culture also affect children's developing social skills (Wardle, 2001). Teachers who take the time to observe and know the culture and community in which children live are better able to build on its strengths or work to mediate its potential negative effects on children's social development (Cortez, 2008; Huijbregts, Leseman, & Tavecchio, 2008). This is particularly true

Self, Others, and the Community: Social Skills

of children who have been raised and socialized in a collectivist culture and who then have to adapt to the mainstream individualist culture.

Children who live in violent or unsafe communities may be fearful and withdrawn in the classroom. These children will need to find the following in the preschool–primary classrooms (Gross & Clemens, 2002; Slaby, Roedell, Arezzo, & Hendrix, 1995; Wallach, 1995):

- Meaningful relationships with caring and knowledgeable adults
- Schedules and environment that are as consistent as possible
- Structure and very clear expectations and limits
- Many opportunities to express themselves safely in play, art, and stories and storytelling

Some children and their families have been directly and deeply affected by war and terrorism. Even children with no direct contact with war, however, can be deeply affected. Children who witness violence or have been personally affected by violence will express their needs, grief, fears, apprehensions, and thoughts in different ways (Ronen, Rahav, & Rosenbaum, 2003). Some may withdraw, become irritable, or stop eating or sleeping; others may act out. It is important for teachers to take their cues from the child. Support each child as an individual while providing all children with the following (NAEYC, 2001):

- Make sure routines are kept, that children know and can depend on the structure of the day.
- Accept children's feelings and behaviors with support and acceptance.
- Find ways for children to express themselves, whether through outdoor play, running, drawing, painting, building, or telling stories.

Many children view far too much violence on TV or in games, toys, stories, and other media. In schools throughout the nation, you can observe children acting out the violence they observe—playing war or pretending to be a superhero and acting aggressively. This became more frequent after the deregulation of children's television 20 years ago. After this, teachers noticed children imitating the violent and

Children model violence they observe.

antagonistic behavior they saw frequently portrayed on television (Levin & Carlsson-Paige, 2004). Teachers can redirect children's play by providing props that suggest other themes for children to act on.

Teachers have found a number of ways to help children and their parents cope with the prevalence of violence in children's lives. Teachers and parents can discuss the problems of children's exposure to media violence and work to change the media (NAEYC, 2001). They also work with children to do the following:

- They develop the concept of real and not real by informing children about which stories, movies, and television shows are "real" and which are not. They then ask children to determine which shows or movies are factual and which are fantasy.
- They foster the development of critical viewing skills for evaluating media violence.
- They reduce television viewing.
- They ensure that children watch more prosocial television programs.

Role of the School

Once children are in a school setting, other factors affect their social development (Berk, 2001; NRC & IM, 2000). In addition to a child's parents and family, the teacher becomes an agent of socialization. Now the teacher, and perhaps the principal, sets rules, limits, and standards for behavior. Other children also become models, setting new or different standards for social behaviors.

Entrance into the school society can be difficult for young children (Seefeldt, Galper, & Denton, 1998). Upon leaving home, preschool–primary students, unsure of how to manage interactions with this new socializer and with other children, can find school a miserable experience at first. Many transition techniques have been designed and implemented to ease children's entrance into school:

- Some schools encourage parents to stay with their children for part or all of the first few days to let the children know they are not being totally deserted.
- Some schools begin by inviting a small group of children on the first day and adding another four or five each day until the total group has been integrated. This approach allows children to get used to relating to small groups and become familiar with the school and the new social situation before the entire group is present.
- Home visits by the teacher or school visits by parent and child help ease possible stress.

The dichotomy of socialization—developing a strong sense of individuality while learning to become a member of a group—is ever present in school. Children must retain their individuality, yet they must give it up by putting the welfare and interest of the group before their own. At school, they find they must share not only materials, toys, and time but also the teacher's attention. Here they learn to cooperate, see others' viewpoints, and work together for the common welfare.

The school's role during these early years is twofold:

1. First, school experiences must focus on strengthening the child's self-concept and feelings of individuality. Children who feel good about themselves can make the difficult, complex adjustments necessary for group living.
2. Having aided the child's development of self-esteem, the school then uses this strong sense of self as the basis for guiding children into positive group experiences where they can learn the skills necessary for living in a society.

In the school, the focus on social skill development is threefold, revolving around the development of the following:

1. *Self-concept.* Children's feelings about themselves are the foundation from which they learn to relate to and communicate with others.
2. *Prosocial skills.* Being able to cooperate and share are necessary for forming solid relationships with others.
3. *Making and keeping friends.* Children who relate to and communicate with others, sharing and cooperating, are those who are accepted by their peers and can make and keep friends.

SELF-CONCEPT

"I'm not big now, but I'm growing. I can ride a bike and run and jump and skip, and next year I'll learn to read, too," answers Domingo when asked to tell about himself. Domingo's answer reveals his attitude about himself—not very big but growing; an "I can do" attitude; and an attitude that says, "I will grow, I will learn, I can do it!"

Stop for a moment and think about these questions: *Who are you? What do you like about yourself? How do you relate to others?* In doing this, you are examining your *sense of self*—self-concept, self-esteem, and self-identity. Educators use these terms to denote the totality of meanings, feelings, and attitudes that children maintain about themselves.

- *Self-concept* refers to cognitive activity: children's awareness of their own characteristics and of likenesses and differences between themselves and others (Marsh, Craven, & Debus, 1998).
- *Self-esteem* refers to children's positive regard for and feelings about themselves, and this is closely related to a child's self-concept (Richman, Hope, & Mihala , 2010).
- *Self-identity* has a social connotation; it includes awareness of self and of group membership.

Whatever definition or terminology they use, scholars have long recognized the importance of feelings of self-esteem in human behavior. As a theoretical construct, the self has been an object of interest since the seventeenth century, when René Descartes (1646) first discussed the cogito, or self, as a thinking substance. Throughout the ages, prominent theorists and researchers have recognized the importance of feelings of self-esteem in human behavior. Theories of Sigmund Freud (1949), Carl Rogers (1961), Abraham Maslow (1969), and others have been directed toward understanding the conduct of human beings by examining the feelings and beliefs that individuals hold about themselves.

The theories of these scholars differ greatly. Amid the diversity, however, some assumptions are basic to all theories of self:

- Self-esteem begins to be established early in life and is modified and shaped by the children's succession of experiences with significant people in their environment.
- Self-esteem has a predictable effect on behavior.
- Self-concept is based on past behaviors and deeds (Meadow, 2010).
- Self-concept, self-esteem, or self-identity is multifaceted: Children's self-concepts about their social, academic, physical, and other facets may differ (Marsh et al., 1998).

Finally, theories of the self generally agree that an early childhood program can foster children's self-esteem and build the foundation for future relationships with others (NICHD Early Childcare Research Network, 1998). Teachers can structure the classroom and respond to children in ways that contribute to their feelings of general identity, their physical and academic self-competence.

General Identity: Names

People's names make them unique. Using children's names in the classroom fosters their sense of esteem. When you use a child's name, you are saying, "I know you and I respect you." Teachers may encourage children not only to call one another by name but also to use the names of teachers, volunteers, and assistants. In this way, children learn that each person is an important individual and that each is different from the other.

"I can't say my last name, but I can show it to you," says Michael, leading the teacher to a piece of plaid fabric, mounted and framed. "My last name begins with *Mc*, and that's my sign." First names come naturally to the children and teacher, yet you do not want to neglect children's family names. Children might, as Michael did, find out the history of their last names, the places on the map where the names originated, or what they mean.

Very young children might be encouraged to learn their parents' first names. Understanding that their mothers and fathers have their own names helps children see their parents as people in their own right. In the classroom, you might do the following:

- Use children's names in songs and substitute their names in stories, poems, and games.
- Write the children's names on objects that belong to them.
- Make up news stories using the children's names: "Susan has new shoes. They are brown."
- Purchase a stamp pad and rubber stamps with the children's names individually imprinted on each. Children just learning to read their names enjoy these stamps.

- Place two stacks of name cards on the game table for the children to play with. Children can sort through them and find their own name, all the names they can read, or any names that are alike. Depending on their age, they can classify the name cards according to boys, girls, friends, or initial or final sounds.
- Take snapshots of the children and mount them on cards with their names. As the children become familiar with the pictures and names, cut the names from the cards. Then the children can match the names with the pictures.
- Make bulletin boards using children's names. One might read, "We are in kindergarten. There are 15 children," with the children's self-portraits and names below.
- Make a name picture book. Place a photo of each child on a page. Then the child or you writes her name under the photo and a sentence about what she likes.

Non–Euro-American names can pose a challenge; however, sensitive teachers should ask the parents whether the family has "Americanized" the child's name and, if not, how to pronounce it. Always respect the name that the child wishes to be called. If the child's home language is written in a script other than the Roman alphabet, find out how it is written in the original. Share this with the children in the class. They will be fascinated to learn that more than one way exists to write words and names.

The Physical Self

Children, as physical beings, have attitudes about themselves involving their physical body. How that body moves and interacts with objects, how children think they look, the kinds of skills their bodies can do—all influence self-esteem. Self-awareness is thought to originate when infants begin to discover themselves and their environment by flinging their hands about and learning what is part of their bodies and what is not. Sensations of cold, hunger, and warmth all work together to help infants learn about body and self. During the entire sensorimotor period, children use their bodies to learn about themselves and their world.

Recognize the importance of children's physical selves to the development of self-esteem:

- Take many photos of children for scrapbooks, bulletin boards, or gifts.
- Talk about differences in skin color. The California Tomorrow project (1999) recommended obtaining paint chips and having children find chips that match their skin color. If possible, also get paints and crayons especially made to match a variety of skin tones. These paints are available from several early-childhood supply and material catalogs. They have delicious sounding names like peach and gingerbread. The children will be intrigued to explore what their skin color is called! Children can be taught that they have different skin colors because of different amounts of melanin inside their bodies.
- Provide all kinds of mirrors for children to use—full-length, hand, magnifying—and give children descriptive feedback as they look at themselves: "You have dark brown eyes." "Look at your shoulders." "Where are your eyebrows?"

- Keep records of children's height and weight. Cash-register tapes or long strips of paper that are exactly the heights of the children help them see how tall they are. Make certain you are sensitive to children who are taller or smaller than others.
- Measure other parts of the body, such as hands, feet, ears, thumbs, and noses, with arbitrary measures such as hands and feet.
- Make a graph with children's names on one axis and skin, hair, or eye color on the other.
- Discuss differences in skin, hair, and eye color. Play games that emphasize body parts—Head, Shoulders, Knees, and Toes; Looby Loo; or Simon Says.
- Provide large- and small-muscle equipment for children to climb in, through, over, and under and to manipulate with their fingers and hands.
- Make booklets or charts of things children can do. A booklet called *I Can Run* could begin with the main sentence "I can run," which then serves as the basis for other pages in the book: "I can run quickly; I can run slowly or angrily or happily," and so forth. Children can illustrate each page. Similar books could be titled *I Can Jump, I Can Bend* (or *Climb* or *Stretch* or *Hop*), and so on.

A vital part of the child's physical self is gender. As children mature, they become aware of sexual differences. This awareness is often apparent in frank discussions while using the bathroom or in detailed drawings of self. A confident and aware teacher treats discussions and questions with respect and is ready to help clear up misconceptions (Chrisman & Couchenour, 2002).

Teachers and parents must recognize the importance of sexuality and its relationship to children's positive or negative feelings about themselves (National PTA, 2002). Adults working with children should use proper names for genitals, talk frankly about the differences between boys and girls, and encourage children to take on the roles and feelings of others during sociodramatic play.

Adult attitudes toward sexuality are important to children's self-esteem. For many adults, the topic of sexuality produces guilt and anxiety as well as positive feelings. Adults who infer in subtle ways that certain behaviors are bad may create anxiety or shame in the child. Positive feelings are aided by a teacher who understands and accepts the child's sexuality.

Gendered attitudes develop during the preschool years (Gunnar, 2003). Promoting unbiased attitudes and values toward gender and gender roles requires you, the teacher, to examine your values and prejudices. Women's movements have made our nation aware of society's part in assigning rigid gender roles early in life. For example, the statement "He's all boy" reinforces behavior in boys that would not be tolerated in girls. You can help children become aware of their own sexuality without assigning them stereotyped gender roles:

- Be certain that the block, woodworking, and wheel-toy areas do not become boys' centers and the housekeeping area a girls' center.
- Dismiss or call together children with red shoes, blue socks, buckle shoes, zipper jackets, green eyes, and so forth, rather than dividing the group by boys and girls.
- Provide male and female models in a variety of job situations.
- Ask the boys to help clean up, cook, wash tables, and do other tasks often stereotyped as women's work.

- Find stories to read portraying men and women in various occupations not assigned by gender role.
- Challenge children when they make statements such as "Boys can't do that" or "That's not for girls" by giving information and facts to correct their stereotyped thinking.

Self-Efficacy/Self-Worth

Crucial to children's self-esteem is the belief that they are capable individuals who can set goals for themselves and achieve them. Children can have good concepts of self and realistic self-esteem, yet not be able to succeed in school or life because they lack the belief that they are capable (Bandura, 1997). Self-efficacy, like self-concept and self-esteem, is highly related to children's later academic and social success. Children who believe they can learn to read and write are those who can set goals for their learning and, if they fail, try again. Schools provide children with many opportunities to experiment with ideas and materials and time to gain some kind of mastery.

You can help children perceive themselves as learners and enhance their self-efficacy through activities such as the following:

- Provide toddlers and very young children with equipment they can handle by themselves. Low coat hooks and small tables and chairs permit the youngest child to achieve some sense of mastery over self and the world. Juice can be prepared in small pitchers so that 3-year-olds can fill their own glasses. In the bathroom, small fixtures and towels and soap placed within children's reach help them be in control. Children feel they are competent when they can care for their own needs.

Self-efficacious children know they can do and learn.

- Allow kindergarten and primary-grade children to continue developing a sense of mastery and self-control by encouraging them to do tasks around the classroom, such as wipe down tables, and to master mechanical things, such as the record player, the slide projector, or the filmstrip projector. Learning to use the computer also fosters children's sense of competence.
- Expand primary-grade children's understanding of the world. As children learn to read and gain information through books and other written materials, knowledge of their immediate environment, obtained through field trips and direct experiences, is expanded to knowledge of the larger community and the world.
- Provide plenty of raw materials. Raw materials force children to do the following:
  - Set a goal. "What will I do with this?"
  - Make plans to achieve their goal. "I'll tape these two pieces together."
  - Monitor their progress toward achieving their goal. "That didn't work; I'll try . . ."
  - Experience the feelings of joy and pleasure that come from achieving a goal. "I did it. I knew I could."

Assessing Self-Concept, Self-Esteem, and Self-Efficacy

As you do with any other skill, you want to assess children's growing self-esteem. Standardized tests designed to assess self-concept are available. But even if you use a standardized measure, you will still want to assess children's growth through keeping anecdotal records in the following ways:

1. *Observation.* Observing children, you can record how well they are (a) working with others, (b) entering into group play, (c) trying new activities, and (d) growing in their overall ability to relate to others.
2. *Interview.* Children enjoy talking about themselves. Questions such as "What makes you smile?" "How do you feel when . . . ?" "Who are your best friends?" "What makes you angry?" "What will you do when you grow up?" "What do you do when you can do anything you want to?" will give you insight into children's self-concepts.
3. *Self-reports.* Helping children make self-evaluations is another way of estimating self-concept. You might help children make booklets titled *Things I Learned in Kindergarten, Things I Need to Learn, My Best Subjects Are . . .* , or *I Need to Work Harder On . . . .* Other booklets or creative writing might be titled *My Three Wishes, Things I Do Not Like, My Angry Book, A Book of Me,* or *My Family.*

RELATING TO OTHERS

With a strong sense of self, children are ready to learn to live in a group. Basic to living with others is the ability to communicate.

People live in a community by virtue of the things they have in common. Communication is the way through which people come to possess things in common.

Without communication to ensure that participants have a common understanding to secure similar emotional and intellectual dispositions, there could be no community, no group with which to relate (Dewey, 1944). Certainly, the ability to communicate, verbally or nonverbally, is essential before children can learn the social skills required to live in a group. Dewey believed that social life was identical to communication.

The ability to communicate is practiced and enhanced during play situations. In addition, play develops children's social skills (Collaborative for Academic, Social, and Emotional Learning (CASEL), 2007; Isenberg & Quisenberry, 2002). Social and emotional skills are essential for school success (CASEL, 2007), and competency in these areas of development leads to better academic achievement and grades. Conflicts are common in play situations, and through resolving these conflicts, children learn self-control and the give and take that they will need later in life (Vygotsky, 1978).

Communicating

Not all communication is verbal. Like adults, young children are quick to read the meaning of touching, gestures, smiles, sounds, facial expressions, and ways of moving. "Don't be scared," one second-grader told another on the way to the engineer's room. No one had said a word about being frightened of the experience, yet one child sensed fear of a new experience in the other by reading nonverbal signals.

Communication, however, is not always easy. With limited language ability and background of experiences, young children have trouble communicating verbally. Communication also demands the ability to put one's self into the role of another. Effective communication, and hence social relationships depend on children's ability to see how another person feels and to take into account the other's needs.

Researchers have long studied how and when children learn to consider the ideas, feelings, or emotions of others. John Flavell's (1979) early work suggests that understanding the thoughts of others requires the following:

a. an understanding that there is a perspective other than one's own—that not everyone sees, thinks, or feels alike;
b. a realization that an analysis of the other's perspective might be useful;
c. the ability to carry out the analysis needed;
d. a way of keeping in mind what is learned from the analysis; and
e. knowledge of how to translate the results of analysis into effective social behavior—that is, in terms of getting along better with the person whose viewpoint is under consideration.

By age 3, children seem to understand that other people are happy at parties but can be sad at other times (Lillard & Currenton, 2003). Four-year-olds and even some 3-year-olds can participate in dramatic play in which they take on the roles of others (see Figure 5.2). Everyone familiar with young children has observed them acting like parents, doctors, teachers, horses, babies, or firefighters. This type of play is particularly valuable. It helps children to understand their world, sort out the roles they observe, and understand how they fit into the scheme of things. Dramatic play that occurs spontaneously and without interference from an adult is perhaps

> Teachers Nell Ishee and Jeanne Goldhaber have a special bin for books that lend themselves to children's playacting. In this bin, kept near the area where children act out stories, are
>
> **Assorted Versions of Traditional Folk Stories**
> "The Three Little Pigs"
> "The Three Billy Goats Gruff"
> "Stone Soup"
> "Old Mother Hubbard"
>
> **Other Books**
> *Caps for Sale* (by Esphyr Slobodkina, 1940, New York: HarperCollins)
> *The Carrot Seed* (by Ruth Krauss, 1945, New York: HarperCollins)
> *In the Night Kitchen* (by Maurice Sendak, 1970, New York: HarperCollins)
> *The Runaway Bunny* (by Margaret Wise Brown, 1942, New York: HarperCollins)

Figure 5.2 Stories for reenactment.

the best way for children to learn to see the viewpoints of others, eventually learning to take on the roles of others.

Dramatic play is a highly symbolic and cognitive, as well as social, activity (Bodrova & Leong, 2003; CASEL, 2007). By taking on the roles of others, children become less egocentric. They use language and symbols and hold images in their minds for long periods of time, acting as if the blocks were trucks, the boards were streets, or the boxes were tables. Dramatic play's involvement of other children makes it valuable in strengthening social skills, and children who have opportunities to develop social and emotional learning interact more positively with others and also have greater academic success (Weissberg, Durlak, Dymnicki, & O'Brien, 2007).

Creative dramatics offer children yet another opportunity to learn the skills involved in taking on the roles of others (Bodrova & Leong, 2003; Rowland, 2002). In creative dramatics, children act out, by themselves or with others, the role of another person, animal, or thing. In the preschool–primary classroom, creative dramatics begins with rhythmic activities: Children act like leaves or snowflakes or move like animals. Pantomime is another beginning step in creative dramatics and role-playing. Without using words, children can show the group how to do something they do at home, at the beach, in a store, or at school and let the group decide what the action represents.

With rhythmic and pantomime activities serving as a base, children can be asked to act out nursery rhymes or entire stories. Younger children need something that has parts for all. "Humpty Dumpty," "Jack and Jill," or "Little Nancy Etticoat" are excellent for beginners. One child can be Humpty Dumpty and all the others can be the king's horses and the king's men. All the children can act out the parts of either Jack or Jill while the rhyme is being read and all can become Nancy Etticoat.

Children in kindergarten or the primary grades can wait to take turns or act as the audience. The folktales "The Three Billy Goats Gruff," "Goldilocks," and "The

Three Pigs" are good beginnings for creative dramatics, but many other stories are appropriate for children to act out. Eventually, children learn the process of taking on the role of another as they mature and grow.

Children's growth in role-taking ability is related to their cognitive growth and general maturity. Direct teaching of role taking is not effective for preschool–primary children, but children can be given experiences that will provide them with opportunities to practice and develop role-playing skills. You can help children grow in taking on the roles of others by using the following strategies:

- Ask children to imagine how someone else feels, to speculate: "How do you think Roberto felt when you called him that?" "How would you feel?" "Have you ever had someone say something to you that hurt you?"
- Help children to connect their own feelings with the things they are involved in, with things that happen to them: "How did you feel when . . . ?" "Why were you angry?" "Did it make you feel good when . . . ?"
- Communicate to the children your understanding of the context of children's experiences, what children are feeling, and the reasons for it: "You feel very angry now because you didn't get to paint." "You're happy because your block building is tall and sturdy." "You feel sad because they didn't ask you to help them with the house."

Role-play is a technique that can be used to help children take on the view of another. As children role-play, they have a chance to gain insights into the feelings of others, think about alternatives for action, and explore the consequences of their actions.

Children can be given what-if problems and situations to act out. Young children have great difficulty placing themselves in unfamiliar roles or in roles of others. Their egocentricity does not allow them to see another's point of view; therefore, all what-if problems should be real and related to children's own experiences. You might say, "Nancy, what if Steve took your car while you were looking for a place to park it? Steve, you pretend to take the car; Nancy, what would you do? What other ways could you act?"

Here are some other kinds of questions you might ask children about real situations: "What if you are waiting for your turn on the slide and someone pushes ahead of you?" "What if you want to play in the housekeeping area, but children there say no, you can't come in?" "What if there is only one wagon, but two children want to ride in it?"

Effective communication demands the ability to receive and produce language. Once children have some verbal skills, communication becomes easier. Parents and teachers of young children often remark how much easier and pleasanter it is to work and live with preschool children once the children can express their needs, wants, and ideas verbally and understand the language spoken to them. Once children have language, they no longer need to hit, bite, scream, or cry to communicate with others. Once they can express ideas and communicate through language, many frustrations are eliminated. Language is a useful, safe, and effective way to communicate feelings, ideas, and thoughts.

Listening and Speaking

Listening is a major way in which children learn language. Listening skills, so essential to learning to communicate with others, are critical for all learning. Once children can listen to others, they can begin to see others' viewpoints, learn from others, and expand their world.

Most often, young children's listening experiences will result from their interactions with others, based on their activities and mutual explorations. If children are asked to listen to others, you should make certain they are comfortable, that outside distractions are kept to a minimum, and that the activity or speech is interesting to listen to.

Almost every school experience involves listening. In relation to social studies, children will listen to records, stories, and visitors to the class as well as to one another. The classroom provides occasions for individual children to speak in front of a group. When a 5-year-old loses a tooth, prepares to move to another school, or creates a lovely painting, that child will want to tell the entire group about the experience. These speaking and listening experiences gradually evolve into group discussions.

In one first-grade classroom, a teacher instituted community meetings. The goal of the community meetings was to create a community in which children lived and worked together, taking each other's perspectives and embracing diverse viewpoints. Usually the children chose the topic. One hot topic was taking turns. Another time, a group of children had a difficult time accepting the small parts they had in a play and wanted to talk about how children were given parts. Sometimes, however, the teacher selected the topic.

Group discussions are not easy for young children. Their ability to listen and attend to a topic while in a group and then offer their opinions about the topic cannot be rushed. Gradually, children will learn the process of holding and continuing a group discussion. Teachers can help children develop this ability by using statements that guide discussion:

- "Sekai, we are talking about the crane operator now. Can you save your book till later?" or something similar to keep the discussion focused on a topic.
- "Olivia, you were talking about your trip. Next, you can tell us what you did at Abby's house," to prompt children to keep track of what they were talking about.
- "Let Iman finish what she is saying; then we'll listen to you," to encourage children to listen.
- "Speak a bit louder so everyone can hear you," or "Tell us again what you saw on your trip," to help the child who is speaking hold the audience's attention.

Perhaps the most pleasant listening and speaking experiences revolve around children's literature (see Figure 5.3). Listening to a good book read by the teacher, a parent, or an older child is one of the most pleasurable experiences a child can have and one that can teach children social skills. Many social studies books are available, some beautifully illustrated, that tell children about the past, places far away, or their personal lives and experiences. It would be difficult not to find books specifically suited for any group of children.

> **Children's Literature Box for Self, Others, Community: Social Skills**
>
> *Marco Goes to School* by Roz Chast. This book, with its funny story and illustrations will help any child heading off to school for the first time feel more confident.
>
> *The New Kid* by Mavis Dukes. Carson is starting at a new school. There he meets a goofy teacher, the class rat, and some nice kids. When his stuffed moose goes missing, he may have to make some new friends.
>
> *A Splendid Friend Indeed* by Suzanne Bloom. Annoying Goose turns out to be a "splendid friend" to Bear.
>
> *Making Friends Is an Art!* by Julia Cook. Brown is the loneliest color in the pencil box. About building relationships and social cognition.
>
> *My Two Grannies* by Floella Benjamin. A charming story about a mixed-race family. The two grannies do many things very differently. Resolving differences.
>
> *Peace Week in Miss Fox's Class* by Eileen Spinelli. Miss Fox is tired of all the arguing, so she announces a "Peace Week" in the classroom.
>
> *Chester Raccoon and the Big Bad Bully* by Audrey Penn. A story about dealing with bullying at school.

Figure 5.3 Children's Literature Box for Self, Others and the Community: Social Skills.

When you read books to individual children or small groups, you have opportunities to recognize each child's ideas, talk about the illustrations, ask and answer questions, go back and read a favorite page one more time, or even skip less interesting parts and go on. Children can chime in, singing the repetitive phrases, reciting the last line, or telling their version of the ending. You can use stories to stimulate children's interest in a topic, to provide information, or to sum up a topic or a unit. Stories can be read before naptime, after lunch, during activity time, or during a regularly scheduled story time that is planned each day and occurs without fail. During this time, children, stretched out on the floor or clustered around the teacher, enjoy the group experience of listening to a story. One teacher calls this time "belly and book time" because his group of 4-year-olds usually stretch out on their stomachs.

Reading and Writing

Just as social studies provides ample opportunities for promoting children's listening and speaking skills, it also provides a medium for children's reading and writing. One first-grade class, troubled by a few children who bullied and teased the others, used a language-experience approach to help solve the problem (Froschl & Sprung, 1999). The teacher began by giving children time and space to talk about teasing and bullying. She used books such as Taro Yashima's (1995) *Crow Boy* as a discussion point. Afterward, the children wrote experience charts: "I feel welcome when . . ." and "I feel unwelcome when . . .". Together teacher and students developed classroom rules. As the children discussed the merits of various rules, the teacher listed those that the group had decided to keep.

Children can use writing and reading in connection with social studies in hundreds of ways. Children who are just learning to read and write can express their ideas through invented spelling and drawings:

- Drawings are a precursor to children's narrative composition. Children who have not fully mastered the linguistic code can express their ideas through artwork coupled with discussions and short, teacher-written messages (dictation) to augment their drawings (Coufal & Coufal, 2002).
- Practice writing as part of dramatic play. Provide crayons, receipt books, calendars, note pads, and envelopes for children's play. Watch children's play interests. If they are interested in travel play, add tickets and luggage tags. If they play store, add grocery lists, play money, and checkbooks with markers.
- Encourage children to talk about their work, and watch as their words are recorded.
- Include many opportunities to draw. Drawing is probably the single most important activity that assists both writing and reading development as well as understanding of others (Schiller, 1995; Seefeldt, 2000).

Children who are 4 and 5 years old can do the following:

- Dictate and illustrate booklets and stories about their experiences. Children might make booklets about the things they saw on a field trip to a popular clothing store, what they know about shearing sheep after watching a shearing, or what they learned during their trip to the post office.
- Tell about their paintings and drawings, watching as the teacher writes their words.
- Dictate letters to firefighters or other community workers, either asking questions or thanking them for a visit.
- Ask the teacher for labels for their buildings, gardens, or other group projects.
- Dictate and record plans for a party or other celebration.
- Dictate their thoughts, ideas, or concerns about a social situation or some other important event in their school.

Children older than age 5 can use reading and writing to do these activities:

- Write about their own experiences, to which the teacher will write a response, in an interactive journal.
- Plan and produce their own class newsletter.
- Vote for the name to be given to the hamster, the foods that will be shared at a party, or what games will be played.
- Write their own history books and read the books and writings of others about the present and past.

Sharing

Learning to communicate is, in part, learning to share. To communicate, children must share their ideas, take turns talking and listening, and share their time and interest. Learning to share is an important goal of preschool–primary education; the welfare of society depends on the willingness of its members to share.

Children do need to share resources—toys, blocks, materials, equipment—in the preschool–primary classroom. They also need to share the teacher's attention. As children mature, they begin to share in the life of the school, planting gardens, cleaning up the playground, putting on a school play, or decorating the hallway. All these activities encourage children's development of group social responsibilities, resulting in later participation in voting, government, and the concerns of the community and the world.

Everyone finds sharing a little difficult and uncomfortable at first. Each must give up some personal ideas, material, or time, sacrificing something for the good of others. Children have shared with their family and with those in the neighborhood; but once in school, they find they must participate in many other types of sharing and share on a larger scale. When children are part of very large groups, it sometimes seems as if they are called on to share constantly and are never able to have their own needs or desires fulfilled. Their ability to share is closely tied to their total development, especially their social development (McConnell, 2000). As children mature, their ability to share increases. In fact, sharing is a sign of maturity in our culture.

Researchers have identified levels in children's development of understanding what others feel, want, and know:

Level 0 (about age 3 to 7). Children are aware that other people think differently but either insist "I can't read his mind" or blithely assume that people in the same situation have the same point of view. Even 3-year-olds have some understanding of another's point of view. For instance, studies show that children as young as 18 months are aware that others' desires might differ from their own (Harris, 1989).

Level 1 (about age 6 to 8). Children realize that two people may see the same situation differently. They become increasingly interested in other people's inner, psychological life (Lillard & Currenton, 2003).

Level 2 (about age 7 to 12). Now children realize that another person can think about what they are thinking and tune in on their thought processes.

Children share resources as they work and play together.

Level 3 (about age 10 to 15). The child can now think about two different viewpoints simultaneously and sees how one influences the other. Children can step back from a two-person relationship and watch how they and another person interact from the viewpoint of a third party.

Level 4 (age 12 to 15). Children can now understand the role of society and the usefulness of social conventions.

The ability to share does depend on the development of role taking, but it also involves being able to read other people's emotions. Children have to learn the difference between joy and sadness, anger and happiness, and pain and pleasure in others.

Children seem better able to identify others' emotions in familiar rather than unfamiliar situations. For instance, children are better able to identify the happiness or unhappiness of children at a birthday party than the emotions of people at a summit meeting.

As a rule, children under the age of 4 do not understand motives or intentional acts. They assume that all behavior is intentional, even the actions of inanimate objects. Between the ages of 5 and 6, children begin to distinguish between unintended and intended acts. They gradually become able to differentiate between intentional acts and accidents. Up to the age of 7, children focus on concrete, observable characteristics; by the age of 8, they can focus on abstract traits such as emotions, personality, and abilities.

Fostering Sharing Behaviors

More sharing takes place in classrooms where there is a feeling of security, a model who shares is present, there is an abundance of materials and equipment, and sharing is taught.

Security

If children feel secure and if they have enough for themselves, they are better able to share with others. Thus, you need to establish a classroom atmosphere of security. Insecure children are not ready to accept the social techniques of sharing. With young children, small groups with high teacher or adult ratios seem to foster children's ability to share. Small groups allow the following:

- *More teacher–child interaction.* Teachers who have too many children to interact with are frustrated and short tempered and do not have time to give children the personal attention that says, "You're valued and respected" and "I care for you."
- *Increased recognition.* Children can share their ideas and thoughts more readily; they have more opportunities to take lunch money to the cafeteria, carry the flag, have their story read, play the game the way they want to, or lead the entire group in a song.
- *Feelings of social adequacy.* Young children just learning to relate to others can find handling relationships with many other children a monumental task. But with only a few others, children feel more adequate and competent in their ability to relate.

- *Consideration of the group context.* A shy, withdrawn child may feel more secure and able to reach out to others when in a quiet group of children than in an assertive, aggressive group. Likewise, highly aggressive children may find more security and social acceptance when in a more boisterous group (Stormshak et al., 1999).

Models

Children who observe models sharing appear to be better able to share, and the teacher is the best model. When the teacher is noticeably spontaneous, warm, and responsive, the children show many more sympathetic responses than they do in a group in which the teacher tends to be hard-boiled and unsympathetic to children in distress. Teachers who deliberately try to develop warm friendships with children and who respond freely and openly to children's needs have children who participate more freely in group activities. These children also have higher leadership scores and show more evidence of sharing than do children of teachers who make little or no effort to work closely with individuals or who participate as little as possible in the activities of the group. Conversely, when teachers react negatively to children's antisocial behaviors or enter into conflict with them, children appear to be more aggressive as well as more withdrawn (Birch & Ladd, 1998).

Physical Environment

Children confined in small play spaces with limited equipment and toys are more frequently observed fighting than are those in larger play spaces with an adequate number of materials. With plenty of space and equipment, sharing becomes easier.

You can arrange an environment conducive to sharing even if space is not available. Placing the equipment so that it is readily accessible to children, selecting some things to place on tables, and providing other materials on open shelves invite children to use and share the available materials rather than focus on a single piece of equipment or have to hunt for toys.

Direct Teaching

Teachers teach, and among the things they teach children are the social skills involved in sharing. You can use direct teaching in connection with children's play and social interactions. Children can be taught skills by directed doll play, by practice in solving conflicts over toys, or through direct statements made as they are playing: "We do it this way in school," or "Take two more turns and then it's Olivia's turn."

Explicit coaching may be helpful, particularly when teaching children to include others with special needs. Successful coaching techniques include the following:

- Clarify the concepts and behaviors that need to be addressed, such as the idea that hitting will not solve the problem.
- Discuss the idea and the behavior with children and ask them to think about alternative ways for relating with others.

- Practice social skills through role-play with others.
- Coach children in the use of concepts and behaviors in real situations (Gillies, 2000).
- Eliminate competitive activities or games. Children exhibit more cooperative behavior when engaging in noncompetitive games or activities (Finlinson, Austin, & Pfister, 2000).

Books are useful when teaching children prosocial behaviors. For example, after reading Aliki's (1987) *We Are Best Friends*, in which a boy makes new friends, the teacher can engage children in discussions of how they could make new friends. One second-grade teacher asked each child to write a personal letter to a friend.

Miriam Cohen's (1998) *It's George*—the story of a boy who is not appreciated by other first-graders until he becomes a hero—illustrates a number of ways to make friends.

Cooperating

Cooperating is another skill useful for living in a society. To cooperate, children must sometimes give up or share something and become less egocentric—less concerned about themselves and more concerned about the welfare of the group. Adults understand that cooperation is a necessity for the welfare of any society. Children, especially young children, need guidance and support in learning to cooperate; they must learn to balance the task of developing a strong sense of self with that of learning to become a member of a group.

Cooperative behaviors, like sharing behaviors, develop as children mature. The more social experiences children have had, the better their ability to cooperate. The same kinds of factors that influence sharing behaviors also influence children's ability to cooperate.

Reinforcement

Reinforcing cooperative behavior seems to work. Weingold and Webster (1964) asked two groups of children to work on a mural project. In one group, each child was rewarded for the group product. In the other group, children were told that only the

Cooperative behaviors develop as children mature.

child doing the best job would receive a reward. In the first group, the researchers saw an increase in friendly, cooperative behavior and peer interest. This group's product was also judged to be complete and creative. The latter group worked less on the product and demonstrated more boasting and deprecating behaviors. When Weingold and Webster reinforced cooperative behaviors in children they found that these behaviors continued, but cooperating behaviors decreased in those who were punished for not cooperating or ignored when they cooperated.

School Size

The size of the group influences the type of cooperative behavior among both teachers and children. In one study, large centers demonstrated more need for control, scheduled routines, and greater rigidity among adults. Teachers in the larger centers were less free to foster the warm, accepting relationships among children so necessary for both cooperation and sharing (Beaty, 1999).

Competition

Cooperation is the opposite of competition. In many classrooms, competition is fostered because of the belief that it is good for children and consistent with the beliefs of our society. This belief is false. Although competition is natural, teachers try to eliminate it whenever possible. Competition has been related to negative social behaviors (Finlinson, Austin, & Pfister, 2000), destroys group cooperation, and is especially damaging to young children's self-identity as a part of a group.

To encourage cooperation, you need to reduce competition by (a) playing games that do not have winners and losers, (b) remembering that children are individuals, (c) asking all children to take part in special tasks, and (d) complimenting all the children frequently.

Making and Having Friends

"What was the best thing that ever happened to you?" a counselor asked a group of teenagers with disabilities. "One time," replied one of the young women, "I had a friend."

Everyone wants and needs to have a friend. For young children, having friends and being accepted by peers are critical to development of a positive self-concept and prosocial skills and are related to academic achievement.

Children with friends have many advantages:

- They are accepted by their peers (Bost, Vaughn, Washington, Cielinski, & Bradbard, 1998).
- They seem to adjust more easily to school (Ladd, 1990; Ladd, Kochenderfer, & Coleman, 1997).
- They have fewer adjustment difficulties when teenagers (Parker & Asher, 1987).
- They are better adjusted emotionally and have fewer mental health problems (Parker & Asher, 1987).

- They seem to have higher achievement scores than do children without one or more friends (Diehl, Lemerise, Caverly, Ramsay, & Roberts, 1998).

Making friends is related to other social skills (Dunn, Cutting, & Fisher, 2002). It is hard to say which comes first—social skills or friends. Nevertheless, children who can cooperate and share and who can communicate effectively with others seem to be able to make and keep friends. Children who can cooperate seem to be better accepted by their peers, and those who argue and fight are often rejected by others (Ladd, Price, & Hart, 1988). In one study, children who communicated effectively with others were better liked. These children made it clear to whom they were talking, either by saying the other child's name, establishing eye contact, or touching the child to whom they were talking (Kemple, 1991). They also spoke to one another and were more likely than other children to give a reason for their actions. Instead of just saying, "No, I don't want to play," they explained, "No, I don't want to play house. Let's play office instead—you can be the secretary, I'll be the boss."

Teachers do play a role in helping children to make and be friends, especially by planning and implementing an inclusive classroom, because some research suggests that children with disabilities are less accepted by their peers than are other children (see Figure 5.4). Kemple (1991) suggests that teachers begin by observing children who have difficulty making friends. When observing, try to answer these questions:

1. How does the disliked child interact with others?
2. How does the child interact with individual children, small groups, or larger groups?
3. Does the child misinterpret the intentions and cues of other children?
4. Does the child resort to aggression as a means of solving problems?
5. When rejecting another, does the child give a reason or an alternative suggestion?
6. Does the child make irrelevant responses to playmates' communications?

Observing children who have trouble being a friend or making friends helps to pinpoint their problems. Once you identify why children have difficulty, you can choose from a wide variety of approaches to help them (Kemple, 1991). Teachers can use the same or similar techniques used to help children develop prosocial skills. In addition, Beaty (1999) and others suggest the following:

- Organize special play sessions, grouping children who lack social skills with those who are more competent.
- Pair an isolated child with a younger child.
- With an aggressive child, suggest and teach alternative means of resolving conflicts.
- Use role-play to help children develop alternative solutions to difficult social situations.
- Assist children who have difficulty becoming part of a group. ("Wendy, you can be cashier.")
- Provide on-the-spot guidance. ("Tell him what you want, Scott.")
- Use skits, puppet activities, or group discussions in which children are presented with a hypothetical situation (e.g., two puppets want to use the same fire truck) and are encouraged to suggest and evaluate a wide range of potential solutions.

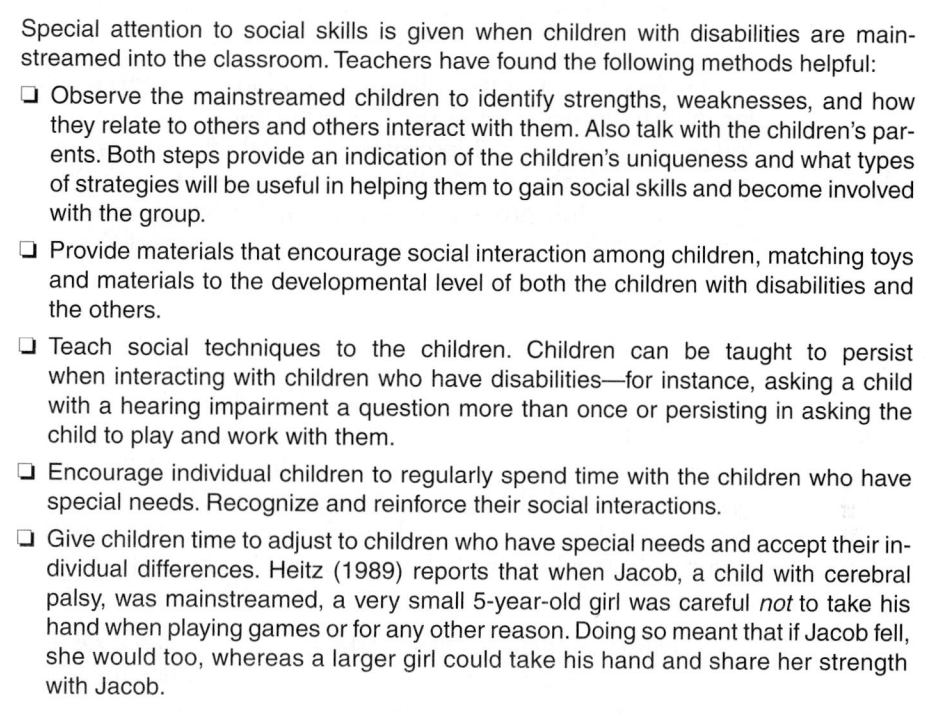

Figure 5.4 Including children with disabilities in the group.

- Steer a child who has trouble entering a social group to smaller or more accepting groups of children. Rather than suggesting that a child attempt to enter ongoing play by asking, "Can I play?" a teacher can help the child observe a group, try to figure out the theme, and then think of a role that would contribute to that theme.

You can also help children make friends by enabling them to achieve recognition and prestige in a group:

- Children feel honored and gain recognition from the group when the class makes them a get-well or a birthday book consisting of a collection of pictures and stories by the other children.
- Prestige is the reward for children who can explain to others how to make a clay dinosaur, how to find the way to the principal's office, or how to care for the hammer and saws.
- Children can make friends as the teacher encourages them to work on group projects. Singing songs and playing games together, such as "The Farmer in the Dell," "Ring Around the Rosie," and other simple games (really a remarkable accomplishment for young children) help them to feel a part of a group.
- Structuring activities that require more than one child to be successfully completed are helpful. You might arrange for children to plant and maintain a

garden, make soup or pudding, bake bread or cookies, create and put on a puppet show, construct a playhouse, paint a mural, or play board games.

Books can also be used. Reading Leo Lionni's (1991) *Swimmy*, in which a little lonely fish teaches others how to work together to scare the big fish away, can be followed by having children make a mural of Swimmy, creating a big fish from many little fish that each child draws and cuts out. E. E. McEwan's (1996) *Whose Hat?* shows adult groups, many of which provide services, and Carol Greene's (1997) *Firefighters Fight Fires* offers children a view of the daily lives of firefighters who live and work together.

Conflict Resolution

"We're sharing" was the reply when two children, scuffling over the same bike, were asked what they were doing. Teachers of young children rarely experience a day without at least one conflict in the group. Whenever young children are together, there will be fighting and arguments. Conflict is healthy and indeed necessary for children's growth and development; it is the way they balance becoming individuals with learning to become a part of a group (Levin, 1998). Children's conflicts have several sources:

- *Conflicts within themselves.* Children cry over a puzzle that is beyond their ability; they wrestle with a decision to paint or work with clay; or, making the wrong decision, they go off to sulk, with thumb in mouth, alone with their conflict.
- *Conflicts with others in the class.* Children fight with one another over toys or objects, in play, or about an idea.
- *Conflicts outside their personal worlds.* Mother and father argue over who will take the car or how much money to spend, teacher and aide disagree about the best way to discipline or reward children, and children experience the conflict that occurs in the wider world as they watch strikes, fights, and wars in the movies and on television.

Teachers can use at least two effective ways to handle conflicts that occur when children are together. The first is to validate children's feelings and help them discover ways to express their feelings through nonaggression and without hurting themselves or others (see the High/Scope model in Chapter 1). The second is to find ways to keep aggressive feelings from multiplying.

To minimize the normal conflicts in a classroom, you might do the following:

- Help children form close friendships and feel the security of friends, valuing them over possessions (Greenberg, 2006). Then they can react to frustrations with less aggression.
- Having control over toys and possessions often helps children feel they have autonomy over their lives. Give children many choices in other areas so that they do not feel so much need to control play situations (Greenberg, 2006).
- Make clear that aggressive acts are not allowed in the classroom, stopping them when and if they appear. Remember, however, that punishment can

serve as a form of frustration and may only increase a child's need to act out aggressively.
- Model for the children ways of meeting frustration without aggressive acts, and teach them conflict resolution skills.
- Establish rules, in cooperation with the children, which protect the rights of each individual.
- Remove potentially frustrating situations for the children by preparing the environment with sufficient equipment, providing tasks children can succeed in, and planning a balanced program with opportunities for choices, self-expression, and physical activity.
- Help children to deal with their feelings openly and understand that people everywhere have feelings. Bill Martin's (1969c) *David Was Mad* allows children to discuss their feelings of anger without guilt or fear of reprimand and to realize that everyone gets angry. The teacher might express personal feelings to the class—"I was really so angry that happened" or "That makes me feel so happy inside"—and then demonstrate to the class positive ways of handling those feelings. When children begin to see that everyone has feelings, they are better able to relate openly to one another and to feel at oneness with other people in the world.

Even though classrooms are arranged to minimize frustration and conflict, accept the aggression that does occur as an opportunity for teaching. When fights occur, you can intervene and, if necessary, physically separate the children, taking each child by the hand and quietly calming them down. Then, after the children have settled down, follow up with a discussion of what happened and work out a solution with the children. Rather than focusing on who started it or who said what and why—or, worse yet, asking children to say they are sorry when they really want to hit harder—explain why the fight occurred and how to handle the situation better (Levin, 2003). You might explain why one child called another a name or took a toy: "He wanted to play with the wagon and you wouldn't let him have it, so he hit you." "José, if you ask him for it, he might give it to you." "She called you a name because she wanted you to play with her and you said no." Whatever you say to the children, it is important for you not to make them feel guilty, resentful, or more frustrated, all of which can increase hostility and make peaceful settling of conflicts more difficult.

Aggressive acts are common.

Teachers need to let children handle some conflicts without interference. Because many conflicts are short, over before they have fully begun, children can handle them without help.

Redirecting children's anger or hostility gives them yet another way to deal with conflict and helps children know that they can be angry but must handle their anger in ways that will not be harmful to others. Words can help: "You really wanted to hit, spit, kick, or whatever, but you cannot hurt anyone here. Tell him how angry you are." Some teachers have found that anger can be dispelled by asking a child to run around the playground as fast as possible, pound clay, hammer nails into wood, or draw or paint a picture.

SUMMARY

Although young children bring a number of skills to the classroom—walking, talking, relating—it is the school's responsibility to ensure the continuation of skill development. The social studies teach map reading, graphing, and cardinal directions; other skills are shared responsibilities with all the school subjects.

The skills most important for the preschool–primary classroom are the social and thinking skills. The social skills of learning who you are and developing self-esteem are prerequisites to learning about others. All children's group activities are social by nature, yet teachers need to plan specific activities and experiences to foster cooperation and encourage social interactions.

Teaching children prosocial behavior involves helping them learn to relate to each other as well learn the communicative skills of listening, speaking, reading, and writing and the social skills of learning to share and cooperate. Because making and having friends are so integral to children's success in school and life, teachers also plan ways for children to accomplish this goal.

Conflicts, however, will occur. Learning how to prevent conflicts and then handling them when they arise is part of a teacher's job.

Discussion Questions

1. How do preschool and primary programs incorporate social competence into the curriculum?
2. Which theory about socialization fits best with your beliefs? Why?
3. How did your parents prepare you to have an individual identity? How have others influenced who you are? What are the implications for helping young children?
4. What would you say are the social skills that help you best work with others? How can you help children develop these skills?
5. How would you assess your "self-concept," your "self-esteem," and your "self-efficacy"? What is the meaning of each term? How does each develop in young children?
6. Discuss any experiences you have had helping a person with a disability become part of a group.

Extend Your Knowledge

1. Observe 5-, 6-, and 7-year-olds at play. What evidence of cooperation and sharing do you note? How do the ages of the children relate to any differences in their play behaviors?
2. Plan a lesson for developing social skills in a group of young children. Write a complete plan designed to foster the development of the social skill you have selected. If possible, try out your plan with a group of children.
3. Interview several teachers. How important do they consider social skills in their total program? How do they plan to foster social skills?
4. Watch four hours of children's cartoon shows and record instances of violence. Then observe children playing at home or school and record the nature and the number of instances of violence in their play. Analyze your observations, comparing the amount and degree of violence in the cartoons with that of the children's play. Did you observe similarities?

Resources

- *A World of Difference*, edited by Carol Copple (2003) and published by the National Association for the Education of Young Children, offers teachers a wealth of information on children's developing awareness of others and building inclusive classrooms.
- The Responsive Classroom movement includes social skills education in its goals: *www.responsiveclassroom.org*
- Myrna B. Shure's (2000) *Raising a Thinking Child Workbook: Teaching Young Children How to Resolve Everyday Conflicts and Get Along with Others*, published by Research Press, Champaign, IL, provides teachers with a plethora of problem-solving ideas to teach children cooperative behaviors.
- *The Peaceful Classroom in Action*, by Naomi Drew (1999), published by Jalmar Press, Torrance, California, guides teachers in developing new ways of helping children resolve conflicts, communicate, and cooperate.
- *Taking Back Childhood: Helping Your Kids Thrive in a Fast-Paced, Media-Saturated Violence-Filled World*, by Nancy Carlsson-Paige (2008), published by Hudson Street Press, New York, suggests a wide variety of ways in which teachers, parents, and caregivers can help children grow in kindness and social and emotional health with a nonviolent attitude to life.
- *Lakeshore products* is a source for washable people-colored liquid tempera paint. Available in almond, ebony, fawn, toast, peach, cinnamon, gingerbread, and chestnut (*www.lakeshorelearning.com*).

CHAPTER 6

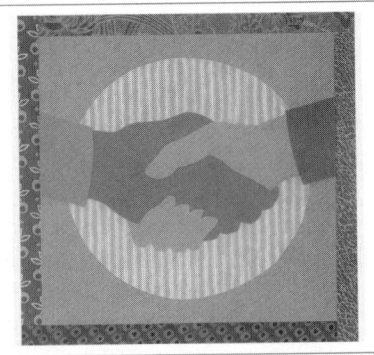

Culture, Diversity, and Values

> Focus Questions
>
> After you read this chapter, you should be prepared to respond to the following questions:
>
> - What is culture, how is it manifested, and what are its characteristics?
> - Why do you think John Dewey celebrated unity in addition to diversity?
> - Why is it important for teachers to know themselves and to examine their own attitudes and values about diversity?
> - What attitudes, values, and ideas about others do children bring to the classroom?
> - What concepts are key to teaching children to celebrate diversity?
> - Why should teaching attitudes and values be part of the social studies?
> - How are values learned?
> - Which theory of attitude and value formation holds the greatest potential for children's ability to learn the attitudes and values inherent in a democratic society?
> - Which values do you think are of primary importance in a school?

> **Standard I:**
> Through the Culture standard
>
> - children will come to understand
>   - the concept of culture;
>   - ideas about similarities, differences, values, interconnections, variety;
>   - how humans live in groups and survive;
>   - how cultures change;
>   - how cultures are passed on;
>   - how and why cultures differ;
> - children will be able to
>   - investigate the cultures of school, community, state, and religion;
>   - explain how different groups of people deal with challenges;
>   - show how groups understand experiences and facts differently;
>   - describe how groups can be both alike and different from each other and within themselves;
>   - establish how differing values help and hinder understanding among groups;
>   - appreciate the perspectives of others.

Figure 6.1 NCSS Standard I: Culture.
Based on NCSS National Curriculum Standards for Social Studies, 2010.

CULTURE

Culture is the first of the ten thematic strands developed by the National Council for the Social Studies (NCSS, 2010) that serve as a framework for K–12 social studies programs. Let us take a quick look at NCSS Standard I, Culture because it will be infused throughout the disciplines (see Figure 6.1). The importance of having culture as the first of the ten strands for social studies should not escape us. Culture is central to who we are as individuals and as a society.

What Is "Culture"?

Culture is the way of life, the total human-made environment, the values and beliefs, the symbols, the interpretations, and the viewpoint of a given social group (Banks, 2008). Culture determines the way in which each person *thinks, feels, and behaves*. The culture of a group is evident through the values, nonverbal communication, language, interpersonal relationships, dress codes, parenting, gender roles, social customs, and humor of its people (see Table 6.1). From the moment of our birth, we learn the culture of the society into which we are born through enculturation and socialization. Sharing a culture makes it possible for us to live within the group, and it is the way the group adapts to the environment in which it lives. For example, groups who live in harsh, inhospitable environments, such as deserts, have to move frequently in order to find sufficient water. Thus, they are not able to grow crops, and they live a nomadic lifestyle.

An important characteristic of culture is that it is constantly changing. American culture is markedly different today from the American culture portrayed in the movies of

Table 6.1 What is culture?

Definition	Manifestations	Characteristics
Culture is • the lifestyle • the environment created by people • the values and beliefs • the symbols and rituals • the understandings • the perspectives of a particular social group	Evidence of a culture • values • nonverbal communication • language • interpersonal relationships • dress codes • parenting • gender roles • social customs • humor	Culture is • learned • shared • an adaptation • continuously changing

only a couple of decades ago. In summary, culture is what binds us and what divides us: Understanding and accepting differences and similarities cannot begin too early in life.

When children start preschool or elementary school, they come into contact with larger numbers of children than they have before. Some of these children will be like them, and some will be different. It is important in these early years to develop an understanding of the child's own culture and to sow the seeds of cross-cultural understanding. "Social studies programs should include experiences that provide for the study of culture and cultural diversity." (NCSS, 2010, p. 14). The ensuing self-knowledge and appreciation and acceptance of others are a sound basis for the growth of democratic principles and citizenship.

The performance expectations listed in the NCSS curriculum standards (2010) call for the integration of cultural content into the curriculum. James Banks (2008, 2009) identified four approaches at ascending levels of effectiveness for achieving this integration, and he encourages teachers to move beyond the Contributions Approach and the Additive Approach levels to the Transformation and Social Action levels.

The *Contributions Approach* is the most frequently used approach, especially with young children. Its main characteristic is including ethnic heroes and holidays in the curriculum while the mainstream curriculum remains unchanged. For example, children study Hanukkah along with Christmas in December; ethnic heroes who reflect the values of the mainstream culture are included (Banks, 2009). The drawback to this approach is that the isolated information about other groups/cultures is seen as an appendage to the rest of society.

The *Additive Approach* adds units to the existing curriculum, without changing its character, to promote learning about others. For example, children study a unit on Japanese poetry that is isolated from other units of study.

The *Transformation Approach* is when the curriculum is altered to integrate multiple perspectives into concepts, skills, and ideas. For example, a unit might be organized around themes like friendship, courage, or harvest celebrations where different ways of living are explored.

The *Social Action Approach* is when the study leads students to do things that have an impact on the sociopolitical environment (Banks, 2008). Examples might include a recycling project, collecting toys for a homeless shelter, or reading to the elderly.

How do you adapt curriculum content so that it is more inclusive and reflects many different perspectives on ideas, concepts, and skills? The following are suggestions for transforming content unit themes suitable for primary grades (Dever & Falconer, 2008).

Communities

The concept of community is a common one for the social studies curriculum for young children. Expanding the topic to include diversity in their own, and other, communities would be a natural extension. The roles of community members can be included along with characteristics of their community.

By going on field trips, conducting interviews, and reading local literature, they can learn about what the town council, the mayor, the school board, and other institutions do. They could investigate farmer's markets, health clinics, and county fairs and find out about the history of these and the participants. What kind of parades does the community have? They can also find other diverse organizations and religious groups by examining the phone book (Dever, Whitaker, & Byrnes, 2001, as cited in Dever & Falconer, 2008). By exploring the beliefs and traditions of the religions found in the community, common universal themes can be tracked, such as kindness, helping others, and honesty. The parents must be reassured when children are finding out about religions that you are not promoting or teaching any one religion but are helping children gain a better understanding of the diversity of their world by learning which religions are present in their community, some of which may be followed by themselves or their peers in the classroom.

Friendship

The development of social skills is an important part of the hidden curriculum for young children (Dever & Falconer, 2008). By studying this topic, children can learn that our friends can be from different backgrounds, skin colors, religions, gender, generations, and so on (Dever et al., 2001, as cited in Dever & Falconer, 2008). Many children's books have been written on the theme of friendship, so literacy development is a natural extension. Following are examples of such books:

- *Mrs. Katz and Tush* (a friendship that crosses age, gender, and ethnicity)
- *Frog and Toad Are Friends* (acceptance of differences on several levels)
- *Amos and Boris* (friends can have different abilities but still help each other)
- *Jamaica's Find* (friendship and honesty between girls of different ethnicity)
- *The Trees of the Dancing Goats* (Christian and Jewish families become friends and share celebrations)

DIVERSITY

"I celebrate diversity every day," said a first-grade teacher. "Among the 23 children in my class, there are children from several Central American countries—two are Somali, one is from China, two are from Iran, and two are from Eastern Europe. It's a very different classroom from the first one I taught in a dozen years ago. Sure, it's a challenge to teach such a diverse group, but I love it—the diversity adds richness to my life and the curriculum. It's diversity that makes teaching so much more rewarding today than in the past."

While John Dewey (1944) might be surprised at the great diversity found in today's typical classroom, he would not be surprised that teachers find this diversity enriching and rewarding. Believing that learning can occur only through free exchange and communication with others whose views and lives differ from one's own, Dewey celebrated and honored diversity: "The intermingling in the school of youth of different races, differing religions and unlike customs creates for all a new and broader environment" (1944, p. 21).

While Dewey celebrated diversity, he also celebrated unity. The school, he pointed out, offered children a balanced environment and a common subject matter. Because it did so, education would accustom all to a "unity of outlook upon a broader horizon than is visible to the members of any group" (1944, p. 21). This assimilative force, along with an emphasis on the things that bind people together in cooperative human pursuits, would prepare children to be citizens in a democratic society and a global world. Today's standards for social studies continue to endorse Dewey's premise of celebrating unity and diversity. "During the early years of school, the exploration of the concepts of likenesses and differences" takes place (NCSS, 1998, p. 1).

A school environment that celebrates both diversity and unity is built on a foundation of deep respect for all individuals and groups (Copple, 2003; Garcia, 2003). To create a classroom that incorporates deep respect for individuals and groups means you must first understand several things:

- Your own attitudes, values, and ideas about others
- Children's attitudes, values, and ideas about others
- How attitudes toward others are learned

Attitudes and values, which direct and guide behaviors, are the foundation for celebrating diversity. But as a teacher, you need more than just an understanding of your own attitudes and the attitudes of children. You must also be familiar with concepts key to learning to celebrate diversity:

- Understanding interconnectedness and interdependency
- Knowledge of the similarities that unite people of diverse cultures, experiences, races/ethnicities, and nations
- Skills in resolving interpersonal conflict that will later serve as the base for working together with others

WHAT ARE YOUR ATTITUDES?

Celebrating diversity has much more to do with your attitudes toward and knowledge of others than with preparing and eating foods common in other cultures, hanging pictures of children from a variety of cultures on the wall, or celebrating the holidays or customs of others. These activities may be important in helping children value others, but they are the bare minimum (Banks, 2009; d'Entremont, 1997; Okagaki & Diamond, 2003).

What is critical—and far more important than these superficial attempts at valuing diversity—are your own feelings, knowledge, and attitudes toward those who differ from you. These attitudes determine how you behave toward and treat children and their parents.

Head Start programs promote the school readiness of infant to five-year-old children from low-income families by enriching their cognitive, social, and emotional development. One Head Start teacher found it very disturbing that parents sent their girls to Head Start in frilly dresses and the boys in little three-piece suits, often complete with a clip-on tie. So she told the parents "Do not dress your children like this. It's better if you send children in old clothes." After listening to the teacher tell parents over and over not to dress children in fancy clothes, a cook at the center took the teacher aside and informed her that she was demeaning the parents, their values, and their behaviors. Head Start parents, the cook explained, dressed their children the way they did because they had deep respect for Head Start and high hopes for their children's success there. They wanted their children to achieve and to respect the school and their teacher. Therefore, they dressed their children in fancy clothes.

To really respect diversity means you will need to examine your own attitudes and values toward those of different classes, cultures, or races and ethnicities (Okagaki & Diamond, 2003). Ask yourself these questions:

1. Am I constantly striving to gain more knowledge and increase my skills in human relations education?

The school environment celebrates diversity.

2. Do I approach human relationships with understanding and compassion, both in my verbal and nonverbal communication in the classroom and when relating with parents? Do I ask parents about their goals for children and really listen?
3. Is the point of view I present free from bias? Can I put aside my belief system to honestly think about the beliefs of others?
4. Do I create an atmosphere of warmth and acceptance in the classroom? Do I ask children and families to share songs and stories from their culture, putting them in the role of expert? Are signs and labels in English and in the children's home languages?
5. Do I provide freedom to create? Do I provide many opportunities for children to make choices and decisions on their level?
6. Do I encourage children to look at problems from various points of view? Do I encourage divergent thinking?

Respect starts with, and is manifested in, your behaviors. You might begin with the following actions:

- Make time for communicating with families and listen carefully to what families and children say. If you do not understand what the parent is saying, ask another question or repeat what you think the parent has said, asking, "Is this what you mean? Am I correct in understanding . . . ?"
- Develop two-way communication. Ask families to tell you what their goals are for their children, to talk about how they raise their children, and what their family preferences are. In turn, describe your goals for their children, your philosophy, and your methods of teaching.
- Observe and become a cultural ethnographer, seeking information about children's languages and cultures (Garcia, 2003; Marshall, 2003), perhaps by visiting children's homes and neighborhoods and becoming familiar with the culture and ways of the community.
- Be attentive and open to negotiation if a parent brings a concern or complaint to your attention. Keep in mind that assertive communication—when you tell the truth and care about the listener—is the most effective form of communication (National Association for the Education of Young Children, 1998b). Let the parent know you hear her. With total sincerity, repeat her statement to you: "Understandably, you are worried about . . ."
- Put the information you gathered on children's linguistic and cultural heritage in writing so it becomes as important as all the other things you write down (Garcia, 2003).
- Learn how to pronounce children's names as they are pronounced in their own family.
- Plan to work cooperatively with parents to achieve the goals of human relations education. Make your classroom a caring community of learners, and include children's families in that community.
- Open your classroom to parents, welcome them and their attitudes with respect, and establish a system of open communication.

- Include children's home languages on signs, labels, and other classroom print materials.
- Learn at least a few words in children's home languages.
- Involve children's families in the classroom.
- Model learning a child's language. One teacher asked Alberto, a child from Peru, to teach her how to roll *r*'s, putting Alberto in the role of teacher. The other children followed, consulting Alberto on ways to pronounce Spanish words.
- Find books that reflect the cultures and home languages of the children.
- Build security for language learning by snuggling up several times a day for a private read-aloud with one or two children who speak the same home language.
- Talk one-to-one with children about things that are important to them.

Figure 6.2   For children who are just learning English.

- Ask families to express their goals and objectives for their children's learning about others: "What multicultural understandings do you want your children to learn this year?" "What do you think is important for them to know in the future?" "How do you think they should be taught these things?" "What do you want them to learn about people from other lands?"
- Help families and the community explore their own attitudes and feelings about others through group discussions, meetings with resource persons, or individual conferences.
- Use both children's home languages and English in charts and other print materials in the classroom (see Figure 6.2).

Teachers can also examine their attitudes and values toward those who live far from them geographically (New, 1999a). Before teaching about another country, ask yourself what you really know and feel about the country. Because children will model you and copy your attitudes and values, ask yourself the following:

1. What have I read about each country? Did this reading present an accurate point of view? Was it current? Was it written by someone of that nationality?
2. Am I familiar with any of the country's films or filmmakers? What do I know about the art of the country?
3. What do I know about the religious customs of the country? The government? The economy? Is my current information up-to-date? Is it free from stereotypes?
4. Are my background materials relevant to the culture as a whole, or do they represent just one minute portion of the people?
5. Have I talked to anyone who is a native of the country or who has lived in the country for some length of time?

But conflicts do occur. Beliefs about child rearing and how children should be educated differ between cultural groups. For example, many families believe children should be spanked and will tell you openly, "Spank her hard if she doesn't listen." Obviously, you are not going to spank a child, yet you must respect the families' views of child rearing. Bredekamp (2003) suggests thinking about the goals of families. When parents ask you to spank their children, they are really saying they are afraid their children will not achieve in school. Instead of agreeing to spank a child, you can communicate to parents that all children will behave appropriately and learn.

Families from many cultures revere teachers as authority figures. These families often shower teachers with gifts. One school created two rules about gifts: (1) You cannot accept gifts, and (2) you cannot reject gifts. To keep these rules, the gifts of parents to teachers were used to benefit the entire school. In this way, parents' traditions of giving presents to teachers were respected, but no teacher personally accepted a gift (Bredekamp, 2003).

HOW CHILDREN LEARN ABOUT OTHERS

Once you have examined your own attitudes toward others, you need to develop an understanding of how children learn about others. Children's awareness of others begins early. By 2 years of age, children have the ability to identify ethnic distinctions and perceive similarities and differences among persons based on physical characteristics, clothing, language, and political orientation (Allport, 1952; Goodman, 1952; Ramsey, 2003).

Children do not appear to be comfortable with differences. By the age of two-and-a-half, signs of prejudice—of discomfort with physical differences—may appear (Derman-Sparks & A.B.C. Task Force, 2003). This discomfort has been related to children's thought processes. Children may respond negatively to those who differ from them because of their preoperational, egocentric thinking. Able only to see the world from their own perspective, young children may see racial or ethnic differences as something to be feared rather than celebrated. As children mature, however, and their thinking becomes more abstract and rational, they seem more accepting of others. Second-graders, for instance, recognize differences in people but have little emotional reaction about it, while younger children, 2- or 3-year-olds, often do.

Others believe that early negative ideas of others stem from the home or the culture at large. It's true; children's values and attitudes are internalized directly from parents. To survive, children must win their parents' approval by meeting their parents' expectations and by taking on their parents' attitudes and values.

Society at large also teaches children how to value diversity. Culture is, after all, a human-made part of the environment. From television, the media, churches, and other societal institutions, children learn how to value or devalue others. Perhaps because of its diversity or inherent values of democracy, our culture seems to teach children to value others. Children in our nation express greater friendliness and open-mindedness to foreign people than do children in some other nations, perhaps because of our immigrant heritage or our greater exposure to television, books, films, and travel. Research has shown that children in the United States are more

Children learn how to value, or devalue, others.

open and friendly toward foreign people than are children in 10 other nations (Lambert & Klineberg, 1967; Pellowski, 1969).

Regardless of how they are learned, ideas about others seem to have their roots in the period of early childhood (Kowalski & Lo, 2001; Teichman, 2001). Thus, learning to celebrate diversity must be part of every early childhood curriculum and program (Copple, 2003).

To begin teaching children to celebrate diversity, you should understand the following principles:

1. **The manner in which the concept of their own group is taught to children and ultimately learned by them has important psychological consequences.** The process of establishing the concept apparently produces an exaggerated and caricatured view of one's own nation and people. Thus, the stereotyping process itself appears to start in the early conceptions that children develop about their own group. Only much later, from 10 years of age on, do children start stereotyping foreign people.
2. **Early training in national contrasts appears to mark certain foreign groups as outstanding examples of peoples who are different.** The researchers noted a

strong cross-national tendency for American children, even 6-year-olds, to refer spontaneously to the same foreign groups as people who are not like them (Lambert & Klineberg, 1967).

3. **Early training in contrasts appears to leave the impression with children that foreign people are different, strange, and unfriendly.** According to the researchers, children stressed the differences of foreign people, which suggests that these children were generally suspicious in their orientation toward foreign people.
4. **Early training in national contrasts also affects children's self-conceptions.** Children in certain nations think of themselves in racial, religious, or national terms. Self-concepts of certain groups of children reflect what seem to be the culturally significant criteria used in their training to make distinctions between their own group and others.
5. **Parents and other significant people in a child's environment transfer their own emotionally toned view of other people to the child.** This happens by assigning specific attributes to members of particular groups during the period of cognitive development when the child has not fully differentiated one group from another or his own group from others.

KEY CONCEPTS

Social scientists have identified several key concepts that contribute to children's ability to celebrate diversity in the preschool–primary curriculum:

- *Interconnectedness and interdependency.* As our world becomes increasingly diverse and international contacts become common, the human experience becomes a globalized phenomenon. Today, children's learning, growth, and development are continually influenced by their interactions with others.
- *Multiculturalism.* The human experience is diverse and multicultural. Although children are quick to recognize differences in people, it is more difficult for them to recognize that people everywhere have the same needs, feelings, and concerns.
- *Conflict resolution.* Early on, children can learn to handle conflicts with others without aggression or violence (see Chapters 1 and 5). These early experiences can be extended to understanding how nations work together to settle differences without using force or violence.

ATTITUDES AND VALUES

John Dewey stated that "To value is the act of cherishing something, holding it dear and also the act of passing judgment upon the nature and amount of its value." (Dewey, 1944, p. 128) Values are a manifestation of a person's culture (Banks,

2008). Social studies educators are virtually unanimous in stressing the importance of addressing democratic values in the classroom:

> Citizens who take the office of citizen seriously are in touch with the cultural heritage of the nation. They possess the attitudes and behaviors that support fair play and cooperation. Without a conscious effort to teach these ideals, a free republic will not long endure. (NCSS, 1998, p. 2)

Nevertheless, because attitudes and values, which represent the worth or merit that people place on things, excite feelings and expression, and predispose people to behavior and action, there is less agreement about how these values, or even which ones, should be taught.

The controversy over what and how values should be taught stems from the nature of attitudes and values themselves. An opinion is a verbal expression of a belief, but values and attitudes imply an emotional liking or dislike attached to the belief. Values do not exist in and of themselves; they are not things but are reflected in specific value judgments or claims that individuals make.

Listen to and observe children or adults talking about people, society, their government, or religion. Adults yell and argue; children hit, kick, and call one another names as they defend their attitudes and values. It is clear that attitudes and values are emotionally laden, personal, and deeply ingrained.

Because values and attitudes deal with feelings and personal beliefs, many believe that children should learn them in their own homes or churches. Some claim that these institutions should have the sole responsibility for teaching values and attitudes; the school should not be responsible for teaching other people's children what to value or believe.

In a way, there can be no discussion about whether schools and teachers should be involved in teaching children attitudes and values. Even though the development of attitudes and values does occur primarily outside the classroom (CIVITAS, 2003), their transmission to young children in any early childhood program is, in fact, unavoidable.

Everything that occurs in a preschool or primary grade is bound up in and influenced by values and attitudes. Just the fact of going to school and learning to read is value bound in our cultural belief that school is good and all citizens should be literate. The social studies, however—those studies that introduce children to the different ideas, beliefs, and values of other people and cultures—are even more directly related to teaching children values and attitudes. Social studies should provide a setting for children to acquire knowledge of history and the social sciences and to be exposed to a broad variety of opinions, facilitating the formulation, reassessment, and affirmation of their beliefs (NCSS, 1998).

Prerequisite to understanding the role of attitudes and values in the social studies is knowledge of (a) how attitudes and values are learned, (b) current methods and strategies for teaching attitudes and values, and (c) which attitudes and values should be taught in schools for young children.

HOW CHILDREN LEARN VALUES

Research suggests that by age 7 children's attitudes and values—their confidence in themselves and others, or their ideas of self-worth—are fully formed. This does not mean that these attitudes and values cannot and will not change as children grow, but it does mean that, by age 7, children who say, "I can't," are likely to say, "I can't," as adults. Seven-year-olds who learn to treat others as they themselves would like to be treated are those who treat others with respect as adults.

Research also suggests that attitudes and values are learned in much the same way that knowledge and skills are gained. At least three theoretical views of attitude and value formation have been developed: (1) values and attitudes are modeled, (2) they are reinforced, and (3) they are learned.

Modeling

Young children take on the values and attitudes of those close to them. Because they love their parents and need their parents to love and care for them, young children want to be like their families in every way. Thus, they model the attitudes and values of their families (Bandura, 1997; Nucci, 2001).

Attitudes and values are learned.

Within the family, children learn the *should*s and *should not*s of social behaviors. They model the norms of the culture and their family. They learn the social conventions of how to address elders, what fork to use when, and what is sanctioned and what is not. But families also model moral behaviors of honesty, hard work, self-discipline, responsibility, and dependability (Prencipe & Helwig, 2002). The moral values and social conventions that children imitate may depend on the type of parenting strategies that families use (Berkowitz, 2000). How children learn and develop respect for others and develop concepts of right and wrong ways to care for others are influenced by the type of nurturance and support, demands, and family democratic processes that they experience (Schulze, Harwood, Schoelmerich, & Leyendecker, 2002).

Families are not the only significant group in young children's lives; teachers are also very important to young children. Children hold their teachers in high regard and have strong emotional ties to them. Because the teacher is an authority figure—one who cares for, protects, and loves them—they are likely to model the teacher's attitudes and values (DeRoach, 2001).

Teachers, like all people, are shaped and influenced by their cultural heritage, racial and ethnic identity, socialization, and socioeconomic and other factors (American Psychological Association, 2003). Teachers are encouraged, then, to examine their own attitudes and values and how they learned them. Teachers' values and attitudes may affect how they interact with children.

Perhaps one teacher's culture values and teaches children to be totally obedient and unquestioning. Another teacher may value children who work in harmony with one another and seek interdependency rather than independence. All teachers should try to understand their own attitudes and value systems and learn the origin and meaning of the attitudes and values of children from differing cultures, racial and ethnic groups, and socioeconomic classes.

Children do not live in a vacuum: "All individuals exist in social, political, historical, and economic contexts" (APA, 2003, p. 377). Children experience a variety of social contexts. This includes more than the child's family, school, or peers. It also encompasses the vast social world the child lives in and all the interactions within that society. Surrounded by shopping malls, advertisements, and media messages, children quickly learn to adopt societal values. They imitate the action figures they find in a fast-food meal and observe role models on TV and in the movies. The role models in a child's environment represent status and influence; this makes children susceptible to assuming the values and attitudes of these models.

Teachers will want to make certain that the small society in their classroom provides appropriate models. CDs, children's literature, movies, videos, DVDs, CD-ROMs, and computer software should be reviewed to make sure they offer a balance of gender and racial, ethnic, and religious groups in a variety of roles and situations. Teachers consciously provide role models who demonstrate the values inherent in a democracy:

- The dignity of each individual
- Universal participation in setting and establishing rules

- Freedom of speech and the opportunity to express ideas and feelings
- The right to feel protected and happy
- Participation in society and responsibility for others
- Cooperation and acceptance of one's role in the community

Reinforcement

Reinforcement theory is used to explain how children learn attitudes and values. Behaviorists claim that children and adults learn their attitudes through reinforcement (Skinner, 1974). Responses and behaviors that are rewarded will be repeated. The same process of conditioning is applicable to attitude and value learning. Children who behave in ways consistent with their beliefs and who are reinforced will have the belief strengthened. According to this theoretical approach, teachers should be careful to reinforce democratic attitudes and values. Beliefs incongruent with a democracy should be ignored. Eventually, they should diminish and be extinguished.

On the other hand, one only has to look at the history of Nazi Germany to understand how reinforcement can be used to negate the values and attitudes of a democratic society. In Germany, individuals and groups were rewarded for allegiance to Nazi philosophy. Children were given medals or other rewards for reporting siblings and friends who deviated from Nazi thought. Women who exemplified the physical characteristics of the Aryan race were given special privileges for bearing children of high-ranking German officials. Those children, women, and men who did not conform to Nazi thought and rules were punished or killed.

Learning

Cognitive theory is another view of attitude and value formation. Cognitive theory describes principles of cognitive growth and development and suggests that cognitive structures influence the formation of children's attitudes. This view sees humans as striving after goals. Thus, humans acquire attitudes and values consistent with these goals.

Cognitive theories of learning moral development are stage theories. Piaget and Inhelder (1969) suggested that children's attitudes and values are consistent with their thought processes.

In Piaget's first stage (ages 0–7), children obey rules because they feel obliged to. Piaget called this stage *moral realism*, or the *morality of constraint*, because children obey rules as if they were sacred and unalterable. Right and wrong are simply what authorities tell them, and they believe that everyone views things the same way. They judge the rightness or wrongness of an act on the basis of the magnitude of its consequences, the extent to which it conforms to rules, or whether or not the action is punished. If they disobey, they believe their actions will be followed by a misfortune willed by God or some inanimate object.

The next stage, called *autonomous morality*, appears around age 7 or 8. Children view rules as established but maintained through reciprocal agreement and open to modification when needed. The child's judgments of right and wrong consider intentions as well as punishments. Conforming to peer expectations, considering other people's feelings, expressing thanks, and putting oneself in the place of others guide behavior.

When formal thought develops, about the time of adolescence, children reach an understanding of right and wrong and the place of rules (Goodman, 2000). They can make new rules, understand their purpose, and understand all the consequences that arise from accepting or rejecting the attitudes, values, and rules of a society.

According to Piaget, children's learning of moral values involves maturation and interactions with others. Children's immature cognitive development, or egocentric thought, limits their ability to see things from the perspective of others, and their dependence makes them feel obliged to comply with the demands of others. Moral development requires that children give up egocentric thought as well as their feeling of being obliged to obey adults or the will of others.

Through social experiences, children are challenged to give up some of their egocentrism. Further, as children interact with peers, they find they must reciprocate and this facilitates an awareness of the internal states underlying the actions of others and contributes to the tendency to take other people's intentions into account.

Through these interactions, each person constructs individual moral values. Just as with the construction of intelligence, children come to know moral values only after experiencing, manipulating, examining, and exploring them in many ways over time. Moral values can only come from repeated encounters in which the child is an active participant in making sense of the information.

These repeated encounters should permit children to make choices. By making choices as they interact with others, children can construct a sense of right and wrong. To achieve a reliable sense of right and wrong, children must make choices; it is the task of the parents and school to make this possible. Teachers can provide children with many opportunities to choose and to experience the consequences of their choices. Initially, children might choose what they will play, with whom they will play, and when they will change their play. For children in the primary grades, choices become increasingly more complex and numerous, and the choices adults make for them decrease (Seefeldt, 1993).

Vicarious experiences—listening to stories, reading books, or listening to the voices of others—are another aspect of the cognitive theory of learning attitudes and values. By listening to and reading historical stories, myths, legends, and narratives of the lives of others, children can consider how those people and characters weighed the consequences of a variety of choices.

Some believe that the moral power of stories and histories gives children a common reference point and is a way of transmitting traditional values and wisdom to children (NCHS, 1994). Following a story, discussions take place and children gain skills in weighing right and wrong. Primary children can discuss the probable motives, hopes, fears, strengths, and weaknesses of those involved and propose their own solutions to the problems presented in narratives of the lives of others facing and solving moral dilemmas (NCHS, 1994).

WHICH THEORY?

Educators use all of these theories to teach attitudes and values. Historically, reinforcement theory was used to indoctrinate the young with certain values and attitudes. During the 1970s and 1980s, other approaches became popular. They were based on the idea that children do not learn by being indoctrinated into the values of our nation but should be taught to clarify their own attitudes and values by reflecting on the consequences of their actions and searching for consistency between their feelings and actions. Others advocated that children learn by reasoning about morals and analyzing values.

This view is still current. Experts suggest that children do need to have a variety of social experiences that engage them in disputes, conflicts, negotiations, ambiguities, and uncertainties, along with agreement, harmony, and certainties. This variety forces children to develop embryonic attempts to understand the judgments and positions of others and reconcile these ideas with those of their families, school, and others (Turiel, 2003).

Indoctrination

Some believe that attitudes and values should be indoctrinated. In fact, in many classrooms, children are exposed to stories and historical accounts exemplifying what are seen as basic American values and behaviors and then are rewarded and reinforced for expressing and behaving in ways that are consistent with these values (Brophy, 1990).

Nonetheless, indoctrination does not work. Children who experience power-assertive discipline in their homes are more likely than those experiencing indoctrination to express commitment to others or concern about good behavior (Kochanska, Padavich, & Koenig, 1996). Given unlimited amounts of time to spend in drill and practice, teachers may be able to train children to recite numerous standards. But in memorizing instead of learning, children behave like parrots—able to recite the three branches of government, explain the consequences of absence of government, or name the people representing them at the local, state, and national levels, but comprehending very little (Seefeldt, 1995b).

The ability to recite the numerous facts in the civics performance standards has little to do with becoming a productive member of a democracy. Research shows that children who have been indoctrinated in civics fail to understand the basic obligations of citizenship in a democratic society; therefore, the standards negate their very purpose (Torney, Oppenheim, & Farnen, 1975). Learning through indoctrination, children are likely to be unable to accept social responsibility as adults or participate in social criticism and are more willing to follow whoever is in power without question (Torney et al., 1975). It seems wiser and more democratic to respect young children by teaching them to value their flag, their country, and democracy in ways that are congruent with their development and learning.

Value Clarification Theory

The process of *value clarification* is based on the premise that values are something an individual chooses, prizes, and then acts upon. Then teachers plan ways for children to explore their own feelings, reactions, and values within a safe and secure environment:

- First, teachers encourage children to make choices freely. They plan many choices and child-initiated activities. They give young children information and help them uncover and then examine alternative choices. For instance, a teacher of 5-year-olds might tell them the choices they have for activity time: "Today you can build with blocks, paint at the tables or the easel, work with clay, or play in the airplane. Think about what you want to begin with." A teacher of primary children could ask them to select a book from those on a particular shelf, develop a project from three choices, or decide whether they would like to draw, construct a replica, or make a slide-tape show for a report.
- Next, teachers ask the children to weigh alternative choices thoughtfully: "If you decide to build with blocks, will you still have time to make your desert garden?" They ask primary children to weigh the consequences of actions: "Is this really important to you?" "What might happen if you use that idea?" "What other choices do you have?" "When might you use that idea?" "What would be good and bad about the idea?"
- Finally, teachers encourage children to consider what they prize and cherish: "Would other children believe that?" "Is that important to you?" "Should everyone go along with your idea?" "Did you do it yourself?" "Are you glad you feel that way?" "Have you felt this way for some time?" "Is this idea so good that everyone should feel that way?" "Who else feels that way?"

In this way, teachers help children to act on their beliefs, giving opportunities for them to express their own ideas and develop repeated behaviors or patterns in their lives.

A secure classroom atmosphere is necessary if teachers are going to lead children to develop and understand their own values and attitudes. School must be a place where children can feel psychologically safe to talk about their feelings and beliefs. Teachers need to listen to children who are expressing their beliefs and ask questions to help them clarify those beliefs. Teachers must respond nonjudgmentally to children's ideas, questions, and responses. Clarifying values dignifies children as individuals while encouraging them to deal with their feelings, attitudes, and values more consistently and maturely (Medda, 1996).

Value Analysis Theory

Through *value analysis*, teachers attempt to develop students' ability to make rational and logically defensible moral judgments by teaching the *processes of reasoning about moral or value questions* (Brophy, 1990). Value analysis is based on the idea that, although moral judgments can vary widely in the extent to which they are

Encourage children to make choices freely.

rational and logical, the goal of value education should be to help individuals learn to make rationally and logically defensible moral judgments. To achieve this goal, students are taught a set of skills essential to reasoning about moral and value questions that will help them to understand the consequences of particular values, the conflicts that may occur among two or more values, and the reasons for particular value choices.

Emphasizing thinking, value analysis is primarily a cognitive strategy. The process, which begins with identification of the problem or issue, is similar to Dewey's (1944) description of thinking and problem solving:

1. *Identify values.* In a given situation, students are asked to identify the values that people in the situation hold. The situation may be something that has happened to the children or may be a story or problem posed by them.

    A teacher read a story to the children:

    Mikey is in trouble. He was supposed to complete all his math problems and give them to his second-grade teacher before recess. Instead of working on his problems, he chose to paint. When he realized his time was gone, he asked Abby if he could copy her paper. What should Abby do?

    To guide the children in value analysis, the teacher asked, "What problem are Abby and Mikey facing?"

2. *Compare and contrast values.* Pupils can identify the similarities and differences in various people's value choices. Teachers can ask children to determine the values of the same individual in different situations or to determine the values of different individuals in the same situation.

    The teacher asked, "What does Mikey think about the problem? What does Abby think? What does Mikey's behavior tell us about what he values? What does Abby's behavior tell us about what she values?"

3. *Explore feelings.* By talking about their own feelings, identifying with the feelings of others, and experiencing situations in which new feelings are aroused, children can understand the strong emotional component of their own values and those of others.

    The teacher asked, "Why do you think Abby feels the way she does? Why does Mikey feel the way he does? How would you feel?"

4. *Analyze value judgments.* Children can provide evidence to support or refute a particular value judgment.

    The teacher asked, "What would happen if Abby helped Mikey? What if Abby refuses to help? Is there some other alternative?"

5. *Analyze value conflict.* Presented with value dilemmas, pupils can determine what the conflicts are, what alternatives are possible, the consequences of each, and what alternative might produce the best outcome and why.

    The teacher asked, "What do you think Mikey and Abby should do? Why do you think so? What do you think the outcome will be?"

6. *Test one's own values.* Testing includes four steps:
    i. Role exchange (willingness to exchange positions with the least advantaged person in the agreement),
    ii. Universal consequences (if everyone followed the course of action, would the consequences be acceptable?),
    iii. New cases (are the consequences of the action acceptable in new but similar situations?),
    iv. "Subsumption" (does the principle follow from a higher acceptable principle?).

WHICH VALUES SHOULD BE TAUGHT?

Because attitudes and values deal with the "*shoulds*"—what people should do, the standards they should live by, or the things they should value, endorse, live up, to or maintain—the question of which values to teach is controversial. One person's standards for behavior differ from another's, and conflicts arise. Each parent wants her children to learn a different set of values.

Obviously, teachers will not teach children what religion they should believe in or what political party they should vote for. Those are family preferences. No teacher can tell a child or a parent that the values he holds are wrong. On the other hand, teachers who do not raise questions about values, ask children to examine their own feelings, or promote the values inherent in our democracy may perform a disservice to our democracy by avoiding those topics. If teachers do not actively promote the values of our society, children learn nothing about tolerance and democracy; rather, they learn that they can do whatever they wish.

The values that do matter and are worthwhile and even necessary are those that are consistent with the values of equality and democracy. In schools for young children, the universal attitudes and values consistent with the rights and responsibilities of living in a democracy are those that are taught (Hayes, 2003). Stemming from the Declaration of Independence and the Bill of Rights, these attitudes and values have been described in various ways by the different commissions on the social studies.

According to CIVITAS (2003), the following dispositions of citizens are most conducive to the healthy functioning of constitutional democracy:

- Civility, including respect for others and the use of civil discourse
- Individual responsibility and the inclination to accept responsibility for one's own self and the consequences of one's own actions
- Self-discipline and adherence to the rules necessary for maintenance of the American constitutional government without requiring the imposition of external authority
- Civic-mindedness and the willingness on appropriate occasions to place the common good above personal interest
- Open-mindedness, including a healthy sense of skepticism and a recognition of the ambiguities of social and political reality
- Willingness to compromise, realizing that values and principles are sometimes in conflict, tempered by a recognition that not all principles or values are fit for compromise since some compromise may imperil democracy's continued existence
- Toleration of diversity
- Patience and persistence in the pursuit of public goals
- Compassion for others
- Generosity toward others and the community at large
- Loyalty to the republic and its values and principles

Similarly, the National Council for the Social Studies (2010) suggests that, within the context of the social studies, children learn the value of fundamental rights: life, liberty, individual dignity, equality of opportunity, justice, privacy, security, and ownership of private property. These also include valuing the basic freedoms of worship, thought, conscience, expression, inquiry, assembly, and participation in the political process.

The National Commission on Social Studies in the Schools (1989) states that civic virtue—American democratic traditions and political institutions; ideals, human values, and achievements; and the understanding and transmission of citizenship—is not just a matter of observing outward forms, transmitted from the old to the young. It is also a matter of reasoned conviction, the end result of teaching people to think for themselves.

By focusing on those values that (a) are congruent with our democracy, (b) are necessary for children to become participatory members of a democratic society, and (c) predispose children to learn, the social studies can meet the intent of the three commissions on the social studies.

Encouraging Anti-Bias Values in the Classroom

Ages 3 to 5 years old is the time to begin teaching anti-bias attitudes to children. At this stage, while still quite egocentric, children's ability to see things from another's point of view is increasing. It is most effective to integrate anti-bias teaching into children's daily activities because children 3 to 5 years old understand their world through their direct experiences. By age 3, they have begun to notice similarities and differences among people, and competent early childhood educators help children see that differences enhance our lives. The children themselves have many similarities and differences in their appearance, interests, strengths, talents, daily activities, and family practices.

Using children's personal experiences, early childhood educators can instigate and facilitate discussions about others and how people are alike and different. Children recognize differences among themselves in skin color, hair color, strengths, talents, and so on, and actual photos of the children and their families will encourage these discussions.

The learning environment can enable further exploration of the concept through play props, wall displays, and invited classroom visitors that exemplify diverse cultures—including ethnicity, class, ability, gender, and religion—helping young children experience and appreciate diversity. Suggestions for play props and materials include the following:

- Faces of many shapes and colors on bulletin boards
- Pictures of people in wheelchairs, or wearing glasses, skull caps, or veils, engaged in productive activities
- Dolls with various skin colors in the dramatic play center; this is particularly important in classrooms with homogenous groups of children who may not experience diversity in their daily lives
- Crayons and paint of various shades of flesh tones can be purchased (see Chapter 5) with such appealing names as "peach," "ebony," and "cinnamon"; help children match the colors to their individual skin colors as they are doing art projects (Dever & Falconer, 2008)

Prejudice and discrimination begin early. Children must learn that it is unacceptable for them to exclude others based on gender, ethnicity, religion, ability, or class. When this happens, early childhood educators must address the situation immediately (see Figure 6.3). Derman-Sparks and the A.B.C. Task Force (1989) suggested the following:

- *Comfort/support the child who has been under attack.* Help the upset child express his feelings to his attacker and not to accept being a victim (e.g., "I don't like it when you won't let me play with you").
- *Establish the real reason for the clash.* The discriminator may have had a reason not related to the child's identity (e.g., both children wanted to play the role of the firefighter). Help the child understand why she excluded the other child and what she could do instead (e.g., take turns being the firefighter, have two firefighters).

> Tolerance:
>
> *Fly Away Home* by Eve Bunting. Theme: Poverty
>
> This is a story about a man and his young son who are homeless and living in the airport.
>
> *Amazing Grace* by Mary Hoffman and Caroline Binch. Themes: Race and Gender: Classmates tell Grace that she cannot be Peter Pan because she is a girl and because she is Black.
>
> *We'll Paint the Octopus Red* by Stephanie Stuve-Bodeen. Theme: Disability: When baby Isaac finally arrives, Emma's dad tells her that he has Down syndrome.
>
> *And Tango Makes Three* by Justin Richardson and Peter Parnell. Theme: Sexual Orientation: This is a true story about two penguins living in the Central Park Zoo in New York City. Roy and Silo were two penguins who were a bit different.
>
> *The Trees of the Dancing Goats* by Patricia Polacco. Theme: Friendship Between People of Different Religions.
>
> *From Far Away* by Robert Munsch. Theme: Different Life Experiences: a true story about a little girl whose family has left their war-torn homeland in the Middle East, as told by the child herself.
>
> *Families in Many Cultures (Life Around the World)* by Heather Adamson
>
> *Transportation in Many Cultures* by Martha E. H. Rustad
>
> *Homes in Many Cultures (Life Around the World)* by Heather Adamson
>
> *Clothes in Many Cultures (Life Around the World)* by Heather Adamson
>
> *Children Just Like Me: A Unique Celebration of Children Around the World* by Anabel Kindersley
>
> *All Kinds of Families!* by Mary Ann Hoberman
>
> *The Family Book* by Todd Parr
>
> *A Child's Introduction to the World: Geography, Cultures, and People—From the Grand Canyon to the Great Wall of China* by Heather Alexander

Figure 6.3 Children's Literature Box for Culture.

- *Numerous occurrences* may reveal that prejudice is the reason children are being excluded. In this case, children need to learn that excluding another child is not acceptable. State explicitly that "In this classroom, it is not okay to refuse to play with someone because she wears glasses" (is Black, is a boy, etc.). Talk with the family of the child who is showing these tendencies and get their support.

Sometimes a particular family's values, as revealed through the child's behavior, do not match what is valued in the early childhood setting. For example, some parents may not allow their child to play with a child of color or a child who is known to have same-sex parents. There are two approaches you can take as a teacher. First, gently try to encourage the parents to be more accepting. Discussions can work because intolerance is frequently the result of limited experience with those who are different. Second, explain that as a teacher your role is to build a safe, nurturing early childhood environment for all the children, and changing their family values is not your main intention.

Despite the fact that children in the primary grades are increasingly able to think in the abstract, they still need a concrete point of reference for their learning.

Therefore anti-bias attitudes are best taught within the framework of children's lives and experiences. The following three instructional strategies support the creation of an anti-bias learning environment.

Cooperative Learning

Group activities should be structured to include the elements of *positive interdependence, individual accountability, promotive interaction, social skills instruction,* and *group processing.* Cooperative learning facilitates the children's awareness, acceptance, and ability to cope with their similarities and differences as each group member contributes to the task in a positive and productive way. Differences are shown to have value rather than a drawback.

Prejudice Reduction Activities

Specific activities are designed to help children learn about and value differences (Banks, 2008; Derman-Sparks & A.B.C. Task Force, 1989). Such activities emphasize and clarify the shortcomings of stereotyping and the similarities among people who are different in some way. For books that can be used to stimulate discussion, see Figure 6.3.

Conflict Resolution

Children in the primary grades are more able than younger children to take perspective. As they arbitrate conflicts and demonstrate conflict-resolution strategies, teachers develop young children's ability to take the viewpoint of others, and they help children develop the language of conflict resolution.

Teaching Peace, Understanding War

While it is necessary to teach children to celebrate diversity and learn tolerance, it is not enough. Even though they are very young, children in preschool–primary classrooms must begin the work of learning how to build a culture of peace. This work, like all their learning, begins with themselves and their here-and-now experiences.

In the typical preschool–primary classroom, opportunities to teach peace abound because fighting and conflict are a way of life for young children. Some researchers estimate that young children, with their egocentric thought, engage in a fight every few minutes (Levin, 2003).

Young children are highly affected by violence and wars. Many children have been personally involved in wars because a parent, a relative, or a neighbor is serving or has served in the military or because a relative or a family friend is experiencing war. Even for children who are not personally involved in war, far too often it is a very real part of their lives. Researchers suggest that children experience a variety of adverse effects in reaction to wars. Both boys and girls appear to exhibit more behavioral problems and higher levels of anxiety when a war is taking place, with girls in particular exhibiting higher levels of anxiety and more behavior problems (Ronen, Rahav, & Rosenbaum, 2003).

It is well known that children are exposed to violence daily through the media. Even parents who monitor their children's television viewing find they cannot shield their young children from violence in commercials for movies, upcoming TV shows, Saturday morning cartoons, computer games, or news coverage (Levin & Carlsson-Paige, 2004). Many researchers believe that the violence and fighting children witness through the media are observed and modeled (Teaching Tolerance Project, 2003). Violence marketed to children through the dolls and other toys that replicate the superheroes children view on TV or in movies further channels children into imitating violence they have seen on the screen (Carlsson-Paige & Levin, 1998; Levin & Carlsson-Paige, 2004).

Couple the amount of violence children witness with their immature thought and their need to feel powerful or in control of their lives and children's violent play is explained (Teaching Tolerance Project, 2003). By pretending to be Spider-Man, a *Star Wars* Jedi, or whatever warlike action figure is popular at the time, children feel and experience the power they do not otherwise have (Caulfield, 2002). Boys appear to exhibit more acts of empowerment when playing with war toys, while girls exhibit more acts of connectedness (Caulfield, 2002). Some observers believe war play is a natural and safe way for children to express normal aggression and, as such, is necessary. Others see war play as a way for children to handle fear of war or make sense of wars they observe in the media.

Just as children have always played war, teachers and parents have always struggled with how to respond to war play. Should teachers permit or ban war play? Should they redirect it—and how?

Early childhood educators also question whether to ban war toys from the classroom. Following are some suggestions (Levin, 2003):

- Banning war toys or play rarely works. Rather than banning violent play, try to help children work things out.
- Avoid films, books, and games that glorify violence. Provide toys and books that support peace.
- Ensure safety for all children.
- Model positive, nonviolent behavior.
- Promote creative and imaginative play rather than imitative play. Observe play and use the information you gain to help children move to more creative play. In Reggio Emilia, Italy, teachers have used children's interest in monster play to teach myths.
- Address children's needs while trying to reduce violent play.

If you think children are playing war as a means of handling their own fears, then you might try these approaches:

- Consider and talk about fears. Respect the fact that children are fearful, and give them strategies for coping, but do not embellish their fears.

- Give children accurate and appropriate information. Nothing is as bad as not knowing the truth. Know what and how much truth will help children at this time. Tell children in words they can understand.
- See that children develop mastery over themselves and their world. Put them in control as much as possible.
- Emphasize cooperative play and positive, nonviolent behaviors.

Obviously, any war play that intrudes on the rights and safety of others must be stopped. Even when war play is not out of hand, it can be redirected. Rather than focusing on the game or the war toy, teachers might concentrate on children's feelings. An openness to their own feelings and an acceptance of feelings might take away the child's urgency for making use of war games.

You cannot even think about teaching children about war, peace, or violence without first understanding children's thinking (Carlsson-Paige & Levin, 1998; Levin & Carlsson-Paige, 2003). The following strategies can help uncover children's ideas about war and peace:

- Try to take the children's point of view when you listen to them talk about war.
- Consider a child's general cognitive development and understanding.
- Think about how children will transform what they hear about war in their own unique ways.

Because of their immature sense of social morality, young children seem to accept or favor war and violence more than older children do. Girls seem less likely to become interested in war, warlike games, or aggression than boys are; boys, during interviews, referred to war more frequently. Six-year-olds demonstrate a greater hostility to others than do children of other ages, and children in the third and fourth grades rate wars as more glamorous than do children of other ages. Children's concepts of peace are somewhat less tangible than their concepts of war are. They are usually absent; when present, they are associated with interpersonal peace and absence of personal conflict.

SUMMARY

When teachers emphasize the things that bind people together and help children see the similarities among all people, regardless of culture, children learn to celebrate diversity. Your attitudes toward others and your understanding of how children form attitudes play a necessary role in developing respect toward and valuing others.

All people are dependent upon each other, and all people are similar, as evidenced in the fact that all have language; families and other social groups; systems for provision of food, shelter, clothing, government, laws, religion, and ethics; systems for explaining natural phenomena; rules regarding property; and art forms. Introducing children to the languages, art, and social systems of other peoples is one way to teach them that they are part of a larger community of people, who, though they may differ, share many of the same feelings, needs, and systems. Teachers who are trained to promote cooperative learning, value student opinions, respect the rights and opinions of others, encourage students to reflect on their experience, and play with new ideas and give students some responsibility for control over the learning process may foster many of the learning outcomes that are important in human rights education (Ramsey, 2003; Wardle, 2003).

Tolerant attitudes and values are taught in the preschool–primary classroom. Children gain attitudes and values through modeling, reinforcement, and learning and have been taught through indoctrination, programs of value clarification, and value analysis.

Each preschool–primary classroom serves as a small laboratory in which children live the values of acceptance and democracy. In an accepting and democratic classroom, teachers share control; children make choices; freedom of speech and thought are fostered; children's rights are respected, and they are not overwhelmed by the power of others; a sense of community is built; and teachers serve as models of respect for others.

Discussion Questions

1. Teaching attitudes and values means you must first understand your own belief system. As an individual, take some time to consciously scrutinize your own attitudes and values. Next, in your class, engage in a full and open discussion of values and attitudes. You might begin with one of the following topics:
    a. Competition is part of our society, and children should be taught to compete as early as possible.
    b. Every child needs two parents to develop his or her own full potential.
    c. War toys should be banned from preschools.
    d. Boys should be encouraged to play with dolls.
2. The fact that you are in college suggests that you have developed an attitude of learning to learn. How did you develop that attitude? Who was your model? When do you think this attitude developed? Did any of your experiences in early childhood education foster this attitude?

Extend Your Knowledge

1. Contact the embassies of different countries and request free materials that present current information about each country. Write to "The Embassy of _____, Washington, DC." Some of the materials will be appropriate for use with young children; others will be useful in building your own understandings of other countries.
2. Begin a resource file of children's games from around the world. Teach one game to a small group of young children, explaining the origin of the game to them. Share with your class.

3. Obtain a curriculum guide from your local school system or state department of education. Analyze the guide for stereotypic representations of other people. Share your findings.
4. Within your classroom or college, many nationalities and ethnic groups will be represented. Interview some adults from these groups, asking them what elements of their culture they want young children to understand. Share with your class.

Resources

ArtsEdge, a Kennedy Center website www.artsedge.org, offers online curriculum plans. The unit "African Art and Culture" (integrating mathematics and knowledge of Africa, its art, and its culture) offers first- through third-graders lessons in patterning, symmetry, and the language arts.

The *National Council for the Social Studies* and the *Children's Book Council* both offer a list of children's books and related literacy materials that acquaint children with people and places around the world and throughout time. Go to *www.ncss.org* and click on "Notable Books for Young People" in the curriculum resources section.

The *National Association for the Education of Young Children*'s 1996 position paper offers an excellent perspective on how teachers can learn to work effectively with cultural diversity.

Responding to linguistic and cultural diversity: Recommendations for effective early childhood education. *Young Children, 51*(2), 4–13. Available at *www.naeyc.org*

The *Children's Book Council* at *www.cbcbooks.org* offers a catalog of other multicultural books: The books listed for older children might be useful reference books as you plan to introduce young children to people of different cultures.

Following are other associations to contact for information on celebrating diversity:

Educators for Social Responsibility
www.esrnational.org

National Association for Multicultural Education
www.nameorg.org

You may also be interested in materials about tolerance:

Teaching Tolerance Project
www.tolerance.org

CHAPTER 7

Children's Study of Time, Continuity, and Change: History

> Focus Questions
>
> After you read this chapter, you should be prepared to respond to the following questions:
>
> - What does the Science, Technology, and Society standard include and why is it important?
> - Why is the study of history important and why should it begin in early childhood?
> - What concepts are key to the study of history?
> - What concepts of time do young children have? How can time concepts be taught?
> - How can concepts of change introduced to young children?
> - In what ways can children be introduced to the idea that life has continuity?
> - In what various ways can children be introduced to the past?
> - What are the methods of the historian, and how do children use them?

SCIENCE, TECHNOLOGY, AND SOCIETY

Before we begin our study of history and the other social studies disciplines, let us take a quick look at NCSS Standard VIII, Science, Technology, and Society, because it will be addressed across the disciplines (see Figure 7.1).

Standard VIII:

- builds a child's foundation for understanding and responding to an increasingly complex and technology-based world;
- addresses the relationships between science, technology, and society with a focus on
  - change over time; past, present, and future;
  - scientific discoveries and inventions;
  - impact of science and technology on societies and physical environments;
  - decision making and social choices regarding science and technology;
- ranges from prehistoric humans making the first simple tool to the computer-based present;
- is connected to and should be integrated with all disciplines and all social studies disciplines;
- raises questions such as:
  - What has been the impact of discoveries and new technologies?
  - Is new always technology better?
  - How can we manage technology for the greatest benefit?
  - How can we cope with the pace of change and feelings of technology being out of control?
  - How can we preserve our values in a technology-linked global village?

Preschool and primary **children can learn** how technologies

- form systems;
- are present in their daily lives;
- were different in the past; have evolved over time (such as cars);
- modify the physical environment (such as air conditioners);
- change the course of history (such as the wheel).

The **performance expectations** state that in the early grades children should be able to

- give examples of how science and technology have changed people's lives (such as transportation);
- give examples of how science and technology have changed the physical environment (such as dams or loss of the rain forest);
- give examples of how changes in attitudes have resulted from science and technology (such as recycling);
- give examples of laws and policies that govern science and technology (such as the Endangered Species Act);
- suggest ways to monitor science and technology in order to protect individuals, the environment, and the common good.

Figure 7.1 NCSS Standard VIII: Science, Technology, and Society.
Based on NCSS National Curriculum Standards for Social Studies, 2010.

> **National Council for Social Studies Notable Science, Technology, and Society Trade Books for Young Children**
>
> *Trains* by Lynn Curlee. The history of trains and the impact of train transportation. Illustrations, diagram, and resource information.
>
> *Soar, Elinor!* By Tami Lewis Brown. Elinor Smith, aged 17, was the youngest pilot in the United States at a time when many people thought women shouldn't fly. Bibliography.
>
> *Here Comes the Garbage Barge!* By Jonah Winter. The story of how one town solved the problem of what to do with 3,168 tons of trash. Photographs and artwork.
>
> *In the Garden with Dr. Carver* by Susan Grigsby. Tells how George Washington Carver showed poor Southern communities how to grow crops, recover their soil, and restore their health.
>
> *Neo Leo: The Ageless Ideas of Leonardo da Vinci* by Gene Barretta. da Vinci's sketches of mechanical inventions are compared to modern-day machines such as bicycles. Bibliography.
>
> *Pippo the Fool* by Tracey E. Fern. Tells how the Brunelleschi dome was created and how he had to take a chance.
>
> *One Well: The Story of Water on Earth* by Rochelle Strauss. Facts and figures demonstrate how we are all dependent on Earth's water. Notes to parents, guardians, and teachers.
>
> *Now & Ben: The Modern Inventions of Benjamin Franklin* by Gene Barretta. Shows how Franklin's inventions, though more than 200 years old, are still used today. Connects Franklin's original concepts with their modern-day counterparts.
>
> *Of Numbers and Stars: The Story of Hypatia* by D. Anne Love. Hypatia was born in ancient Egypt, when few women were educated. Her father taught her anyway, and she became a respected teacher of mathematics, astronomy, and philosophy. Bibliography, map, More About Math.
>
> *Young Thomas Edison* by Michael Dooling. Edison's mother taught him at home and nurtured his love for learning and inventions. Bibliography, websites.
>
> *Amelia to Zora: Twenty-Six Women Who Changed the World* by Cynthia Chin-Lee. A woman is highlighted for each letter of the alphabet, together with a description of her struggles and accomplishments. Bibliography.

Figure 7.2 Children's Literature Box for Science, Technology, and Society.
Based on NCSS Notable Trade Books for Young People, www.ncss.org/resources.

As you read through the following chapters on history, geography, economics, and civics, look for connections to science, technology, society. Think of the possibilities as you plan units on explorers and inventors, habitats, trade, civic responsibility, or the contributions of ancient civilizations to modern life. Figure 7.2 contains some children's literature suggestions for this area.

HISTORY

"Tell me again about when I was just a little baby," 5-year-old Kristie Marie asked her grandmother, "and you took me to the beach and I picked up a seashell and tried to eat it!" Who hasn't heard a child appeal for "just one more story about the olden days, when I was really, really little"? Young children are highly interested in their past. The stories of what they did yesterday appeal as nothing else does. Dewey (1966) recognized that teaching history to children is not difficult because children are naturally interested in people, their houses, their clothes, and other aspects of life to which they can relate.

Children's interest alone is sufficient rationale for including history in the early childhood curriculum (Barton, 2002). But history is important for other reasons as well. Human beings seek to understand themselves by understanding their past. To be able to know the past helps us to develop a historical perspective and to answer "Who am I?" "What happened in the past?" "How am I connected to the past?" (NCSS, 1998). Dewey (1966) saw other values in the study of history, which he believed was "essential to gain in power to recognize human connections and to enrich and liberate more direct and personal contacts of life by furnishing that context background and outlook" (p. 258).

Today, the study of history is considered even more critical. Theoreticians believe that without knowledge of the past transmitted through a common national memory of the study of history, children would be unable to identify with their nation and assume their civic responsibility as adults (NCHS, 1994; NCSS, 1998). Through history, children learn about a society's common memory, its core values, and what past events and decisions are part of our present circumstances. "Without history, one cannot undertake any sensible inquiry into the political, social or moral issues in society" (NCHS, 1994, p. 1).

KEY CONCEPTS

The study of history has been defined as a time-oriented study that refers to what we do know about the past. Standard II of the National Council for the Social Studies (2010) is *time*, *continuity*, and *change*. Its study should enable children to seek to understand their historical roots and to locate themselves in time. Knowing how to read and reconstruct the past allows us to develop a historical perspective and to answer questions such as "Who am I?" "What happened in the past?" "How am I connected to those in the past?" "How has the world changed and how might it change in the future?" and "Why does our personal sense of relatedness to the past change?" (NCSS, 1998).

Using this definition, teachers can introduce the following key concepts to young children:

- *Time.* The study of history is time oriented (Jantz & Seefeldt, 1999b; NAEP, 2002). As children use sequencing to establish a sense of order and time in their daily routines, they are introduced to, and become aware of, concepts of time.

- *Change.* History helps children accept the nature and inevitability of change. Through actual experiences as well as by listening to stories of the recent past and long ago, children can learn that change is constant and that human decisions have consequences (NCSS, 1998; 2010).
- *The continuity of human life.* The human connections that Dewey (1966) writes about might be thought of as the continuity in human life, which children can discover through their own experiences.
- *The past.* Children have experienced the immediate past. They can discuss and record it. Children can also handle objects and records from the more distant past and listen to stories and poetry about the past to gain an understanding of life before their time as well as differing views of the past.
- *The methods of the historian.* The goal of the study of history is not to fill children's heads with meaningless facts, but to set the foundation for historical thinking. Using the methods of the historian makes children's lives more meaningful, richer, and fuller. Using the processes of inquiry, children are taught to recognize problems and ask questions; to observe, analyze, and infer as they collect and examine evidence; and finally to reach conclusions.

The national history standards, *History for Grades K–4* (NCHS, 1994), recognize the complexity and abstractness of the concepts considered key to the study of

The study of history is time oriented.

history. Still, the authors of the standards believe that children, even in the earliest grades, can begin to build historical understandings and perspectives and to think historically. When history is presented to them in ways that are appropriate to their development, young children can do the following (NCHS, 1994):

- Gain concepts key to the study of history
- Learn to differentiate time present, time past, and time long ago
- Find history to be interesting and meaningful, particularly when it is connected to their own lives, families, and communities
- Appreciate history when its study is embedded in myths, stories, legends, and biographies
- Get a firsthand glimpse into the lives of people who lived long ago using records of the past, artifacts, letters, diaries, family records, and photograph albums
- Begin to use the methods of the historian, learning to question, study, and reach conclusions

TIME

Mark, a 6-year-old, was asked, "How long is a day?"

He replied, "It's today until you get to tomorrow!"

He was then asked, "How long is that?"

Mark replied, "Today is when you get up and you play and you eat lunch and you play some more and you go to school and you come home and it's nice outside and then it's night and you go to sleep and when you wake up it's tomorrow!" (Jantz & Seefeldt, 1999b).

Like Mark, young children do have a sense of time, but it is more intuitive than conventional (see Table 7.1). During early childhood, children can distinguish past from present and begin to describe daily events in a sequential pattern. Like Mark, young children associate chronological time with personal time as reflected by the cyclical nature of daily events (Barton, 2002; Levstik & Barton, 1997).

Development of Time Concepts

Limited to their perception of the succession and duration of time and to their ability to sequence and organize daily experiences, children's intuitive ideas of time are subjective. This subjectivity leads to errors. Five-year-olds know that waiting for 10 minutes will be harder than waiting for 5, but they also conclude that it takes less time for a fast-turning wheel to spin for 5 minutes than it does for a faucet to drip for the same amount of time (Vukelich & Thornton, 1990).

Intuitive time is distinct from operational time. Operational time involves the understanding of relations of succession and duration and is based on analogous operations in logic, which may be either qualitative or quantitative (Piaget, 1946).

Table 7.1 Time Concepts Develop

Sensorimotor Age 0–2	Preoperational Age 2–6/7	Concrete Age 6/7–10
Observes, follows routines	Ideas of time are personal and subjective	Uses clocks, watches to tell time
By 2, aware of day/night, attends to environment	Measures time with arbitrary units	Ready for instruction in time concepts
	By 5, some understanding of time units such as day	Conventional concepts will not develop until formal operational period at age 12
	Recalls past, plans for future	
	By 5, can sequence events of a day and use time words	

Not until children enter formal operations, near the beginning of adolescence, are they able to master operational time.

Perhaps because temporal sequencing requires only qualitative comparisons, such as little versus large, children as young as age 4 or 5 can demonstrate some understanding of the ability to sequence events. Four- to 6-year-olds can order actions in sequence to achieve a goal; they know that events happen in order and can sequence their day around cyclically organizing daily occurrences (Vukelich & Thornton, 1990). Four-year-olds can accurately judge temporal order at above-chance level; by age 5, children can judge the backward order of daily activities and the forward order from multiple reference points within the day and can evaluate the lengths of intervals separating daily activities. By about age 7, children can also judge the backward order of events from multiple reference points.

Children learn temporal sequencing concepts—such as before and after, tomorrow and yesterday, or those that require only that children position two points in time—more readily than quantitative temporal relations. To understand quantitative temporal relations, a child must realize that the interval between 1:00 and 2:00 is the same as that between 2:00 and 3:00. Children who understand only the sequence may not fully appreciate that the intervals are equal. Parenthetically, this same problem with equal intervals characterizes a child's initial mistakes in using linear distance.

By the time children reach kindergarten, they use terms involved in telling time with a clock. Although they have not internalized the concept of duration of an interval, such as hour and minute, they understand that these terms do have meaning. Children first begin to associate activities with the regular daily class schedule; then they associate this schedule with time by the clock. Next, concepts of hour, half hour, and quarter hour develop.

Five-year-olds begin to understand temporal units of time—such as day, date, and calendar time, formulated on the temporal or sequential order of events—and can orient themselves in time, associating time with an external event: "It is day; the sun is shining," or "It is night; the stars are out." Understanding calendar time

Young children have an intuitive rather than a conventional sense of time.

includes the ability to identify time concepts such as first, last, next, later, sooner, before, and after. By age 5, children can tell what day it is and will use general terms such as *wintertime* before they will use the general terms *today*, *before*, or *in a few days* (Ames, 1946). Children can first respond to a time word; next, they can use the word themselves; finally, they can use the time word to answer a question correctly. At ages 6, 7, and 8, children can begin to use conventional methods to orient themselves in time; then clocks, watches, and calendars start to have some meaning.

Knowledge of children's developing concepts of time leads to the idea that young children are receptive to planned instruction in time—that is, when this teaching is based on the cyclical, recurring, and sequential events of a child's day and life. Although it is inappropriate to ask young children to memorize the names of the days or months, to tell time, or to learn operational time concepts, it is appropriate for adults to give children labels for these things and to make certain their lives have routines. By experiencing routines, measuring time and its passage with arbitrary measures, children will gain initial concepts of time.

Routines that Teach Time

"I don't know what time it is, but my daddy always comes to take me home after my nap," states a 3-year-old in a child-care center. As Piaget (1965) believed, it seems desirable to help children develop time concepts based on daily routines. In school, routines and predictable procedures can help develop understandings of time as well as feelings of security.

Even though schedules in the preschool and primary classroom are flexible, there are regular routines: "After breakfast, we play outside." "Before our snack, we wash our hands." "Recess follows lunch, and outdoor play follows your nap." Children in the primary grades can chart their own routines and take more responsibility for scheduling their day according to their own desires. Even third-graders have found written day planners useful for help in organizing and using their time wisely.

Literature supplements children's firsthand experiences with routines. *Bunny Day: Telling Time from Breakfast to Bedtime* (Walton, 2002), *Get Up and Go!* (Murphy & Greenseid, 1996), *Night-Time* (Pettigrew & Kimber, 1992), and *My Grandmother's Clock* (McCaughrean, 2002) are examples of the many available books that might help young children understand the regular, timed routines of the day.

In addition to structuring regular routines and reading stories to children that deal with concepts of time, teachers should take every opportunity to convey ideas about time to children. They should give children the correct time words and phrases to connect their experiences, such as *today*, *this morning*, *next*, *a little later*, *this afternoon*, *yesterday*, and *last week*.

Measuring Time

Children may not be able to measure time conventionally until age 8 or 9. You can prepare children for measuring time with a clock by structuring experiences using arbitrary measures. This gives children meaningful experiences with concepts of duration, sequence of events, and temporal order, which will prepare them to tell time in the traditional way. Give the children some of the following equipment:

- A stopwatch is fun for children to use independently or during activities structured by the teacher. The children can use the stopwatch to see how long it takes them to put away the blocks, hang up their coats, put five pegs in a pegboard, or hop across the room. You might help them record how long they can bounce a ball, hop on one foot, or jump or run in place. Four-year-olds and younger children enjoy playing with the watch and using watches as props for their play. The accuracy of the watch is immaterial; you only want children to experience measuring time.
- Children can use an hourglass to see if they can wash the tables, pick up all the art scraps, put the doll clothes away, or get ready to go home—all before the sand empties into the other half of the glass.
- A cooking timer buzzes when the set time has ended. Children enjoy keeping track of time this way. They might use the timer to determine when the bread should be taken from the oven, when the cookies will be finished, or when the vegetables have simmered for 5 minutes. Or they might see if they can complete some task before the buzzer sounds.
- An old alarm clock is a good prop for play. Children can turn the hands, take it apart, or set the alarm. These clocks, purchased at a local thrift shop or donated to the classroom, can give the children another opportunity to take an active part in measuring time.

			Time Words Used		
Date	Center/Area	Children	Not at all	Some	Accurate

Observation—Time Words

Figure 7.3 Assessing children's time concepts.

The Passage of Time

Learning about history requires that children develop a sense of the passage of time (see Figure 7.3). "What did you do today?" you can ask the 2-year-old, as you help him into his coat before going home. The teacher of primary children asks, "Do you remember what we did for the Halloween party?" "What things should we include in our Valentine's party?" Using the children's actual experiences, these questions can help them to develop a sense of the passage of time.

Questions that might help children recall the immediate past and foster an understanding of the passage of time include the following:

- For the very young: "What did you like best about today?" "What did we have for lunch today?" "What did you like best about our walk in the rain?"
- For the kindergarten child: "How many days has it been since Karl's birthday?" "What did we have for lunch yesterday?" "What did we do last week?" "What did you like best about kindergarten this week?"
- For the primary child: "How many sunny, rainy, and snowy days did we have last month?" "How many days has it been since our Thanksgiving party?" "What can you do this year that you could not do last year?"

Nothing is more interesting to the young child than his own life. Help the child to understand the passage of time by capitalizing on this egocentrism. In the beginning of the year, you might start a history booklet for each child. Snapshots taken throughout the year, pieces of work the child has completed, paintings or stories dictated or written, records of weight and height, observations of children measuring time, and some of the interesting things said can all be recorded in a history book (see Figure 7.4). At the end of the year, the children will have individual life booklets that will give them a meaningful understanding of the passage of time.

Observation—Measuring Time			
Date	Center/Area	Children	Measuring Time (record how, why)

Figure 7.4 Evaluating children's abilities to measure time.

CHANGE

In many respects, the study of history is the study of change. Some changes represent progress; others do not. Nevertheless, change is universal. No matter where we live or how, change will be part of our lives (Brophy & Alleman, 2002). Being able to accept and adapt to change is crucial to living fully. Rather than fearing change, children can be taught to accept the inevitability of change and learn ways to adapt to the changes they experience.

Surrounding children with opportunities to experience change, the immediate environment offers many learning tools. From the school, neighborhood, nature study, and themselves, children can learn that (a) change is continuous and always present, (b) change affects their lives in different ways, and (c) change can be recorded and these records can help others to understand the things that have changed (see Figure 7.5).

In School

Whether in a child-care center, a kindergarten, or a primary classroom, things are constantly changing. The children may help rearrange the furniture for some special activity or for more efficient use of space. Painting or other redecorating of the school classrooms is a change that occurs often. Animals or plants in the classroom offer opportunities for the children to observe growth and change over time. The makeup of the class changes as children move in and others move away.

Changes also occur in the school building. Rooms are decorated for holidays; the building is readied for the demands of the changing seasons. Older primary children can study the changes that have occurred in the school building. They might be able to find pictures of the building before it was remodeled or discover records of what once stood where the school is located. How the school got its name, who

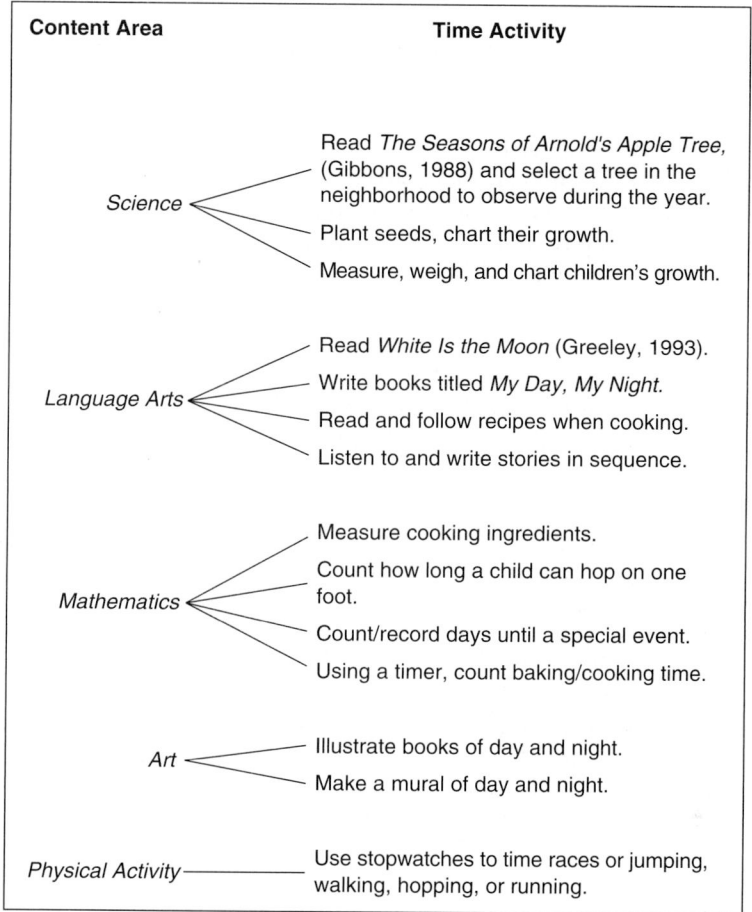

Figure 7.5 Incorporating time concepts in different content areas.

it was named for and why, how many people have been principals, and the backgrounds of the teachers in the school are all possible topics for study.

Second- or third-graders might make a timeline for their school that can help make history come alive. A good timeline might begin with the date the school was built, include its naming and dedication and any renovations or changes, and end with the present.

In the Neighborhood or Community

Leaving the school building and schoolyard helps the children recognize the many changes in their immediate neighborhood: new neighbors move in, a house goes up, a building is torn down, the street is repaired, or a park is built. You can use the changes around the school to foster children's awareness of the continuous nature of change.

The National Center for History in the Schools (1994) believes that these observations permit children to identify and compare changes in their community over time. They suggest that children should look at current photographs of the community and ask, "What things could have been here long ago?" "Why?" "What things look newer?" "Why?"

Primary children can make a record of the changes that have occurred in the neighborhood by (a) interviewing the residents to find out what changes have taken place, (b) finding records of the past in the city clerk's or newspaper office, or (c) reconstructing the past with models.

In Nature

Watching an apple tree change outside the window can provide a class with a year's activities involving the concept of change. In the fall, the children can collect and count the leaves and sort them according to size, color, and shape. They can gather apples, cut them open, eat them for a snack, and make applesauce. The class could make a booklet of the changes that occurred to the tree during the winter. The children might pose questions about the life of the tree during the winter: "Is it dead?" "Will it ever have leaves again?" "What will happen to it?" When the first buds appear in the spring, the class will conclude that the tree did not die.

This activity, although not an everyday one, can continue throughout the year as the teacher asks questions and focuses the children's attention on the tree. The outdoors yields still other changes; it may be possible for children to observe changes in caterpillars, tadpoles, or other living things.

In Children

We know that, to be effective, every learning experience we present to young children must have deep personal meaning. Accordingly, the study of time and change, of history, begins with the children themselves. Children change—they grow, learn new skills, lose teeth, get their hair cut. Children's study of history can begin with the study of children themselves. Focus on how they change:

- Celebrate their birthdays. You can make a badge or a sign for the birthday child to wear. Put a large age numeral on the badge. Let children decorate cookies or cupcakes using cream cheese frosting, raisins, nuts, or pieces of fruit. Suggest they use the same numbers of candles, fruit, or decorations as their years of age. If you have children in your class who do not celebrate birthdays, celebrate their name day or other special day.
- Have the children find out how much they weighed when they were born. Fill a bag with sand so that it weighs about the same as their birth weight. Let the children weigh the sandbag on a bathroom scale. Holding a bag of 6 or 8 pounds of sand, children gain a concept of how small they were when they were born. Weigh the children, record their current weight, and compare it to the birth

weight. This experience is not intended to measure exact weights but to give children a concrete example of how they have changed since they were born.
- Let the children taste a bit of strained baby food, perhaps some bananas or peaches; then let them taste whole bananas or peaches. Ask the children, "Why did you need to eat strained food when you were babies?" "What can you eat now that you couldn't eat when you were babies?" "How have you changed?"
- Examine items of clothing children wore when they were smaller. Some children may be able to bring diapers, baby shoes, sweaters, hats, or other items of clothing they wore in the past. Encourage the children to compare these items with similar articles of clothing they are wearing now.
- Ask them to bring in snapshots that were taken of them in the past, when they were infants, first began to walk, or learned to dress themselves. Comparing the photographs with the way they look now, children can develop the understanding that they are still the same people but have changed. Ask them, "What could you do when you were babies?" "What things couldn't you do?" "What will you be able to do in the future when you get bigger?" "How will you change?"
- Make a picture timeline of children's lives. Using photos from home and drawing pictures to fill in gaps, arrange (or have children arrange) children's pictures of their lives chronologically on long sheets of paper. Even three pictures ordered sequentially demonstrate change over time. Discuss how they have changed since they were babies.

Reading books to children can stimulate discussions about change. For example, *The Growing Story* (Kraus, 1947) motivates thinking. After reading the book, you can ask children how they are like the boy in the story: "Have you ever outgrown clothes?" "What did you do with them?"

The poem "The End" (Milne, 1955) begins, "When I was one, I was just begun; when I was two, I was barely new." Teachers can use this poem as a lead into making a mural on the theme of growing. On a large sheet of wrapping paper, print the numerals 1, 2, 3, 4, and 5. Have the children draw pictures of something they could do at each age and paste the pictures on the chart. Ask the children how they have changed. Remind them that they are the same people, even though they and the world around them have changed.

Another vehicle for developing historical understanding by documenting children's present is called CLASP—classroom lore and artifacts study project (Hakes & Eisenwine, 2003). The authors state that child-sized history happens every day in classrooms; they call this *Classroom Lore*. The class creates a documented record of daily happenings, stories, art, games, journals, student work, even weather reports. CLASP helps children record their history and learn about the past. These are captured electronically, and each child keeps a digital copy.

Timelines and narratives built around timelines with pictures and visuals are effective ways to depict change graphically over time (Brophy & Alleman, 2003). Children can create, illustrate, and sequence timelines about their own lives and experience. They can also create timelines based on the topic of study. For example,

Children can read and illustrate poems.

a unit on transportation might begin with travel by foot at the beginning of the timeline and proceed through horses, boats, wheeled vehicles, and engine-powered vehicles. Such interactive timelines get at more than just the dates and sequences; they develop broader historical understandings of the past as a process of change that impacts the present.

Children will continue to change. First- and second-graders may think about the future. You can initiate a discussion of how they will change in the future and what they will want, need, and be like when they are teenagers or adults. They could draw pictures of what they will look like when they are 14, 45, and 75. You also could ask them to write or dictate a story about their life in the first, second, or third grade with a parallel story that projects what their life will be like when they are in the fifth grade, high school, or college. Ask them, "What will you be learning?" "How will you learn it?" "What will you be like?" You can also involve children in "What I'd like to be when I grow up."

You might take a "field trip" to the upper grades or to another playground or school and let the children observe older children at work and play. Ask them to identify skills the older children are demonstrating that the younger children do not possess. Ask them how they think they will learn the skill and what other skills they will learn in the future.

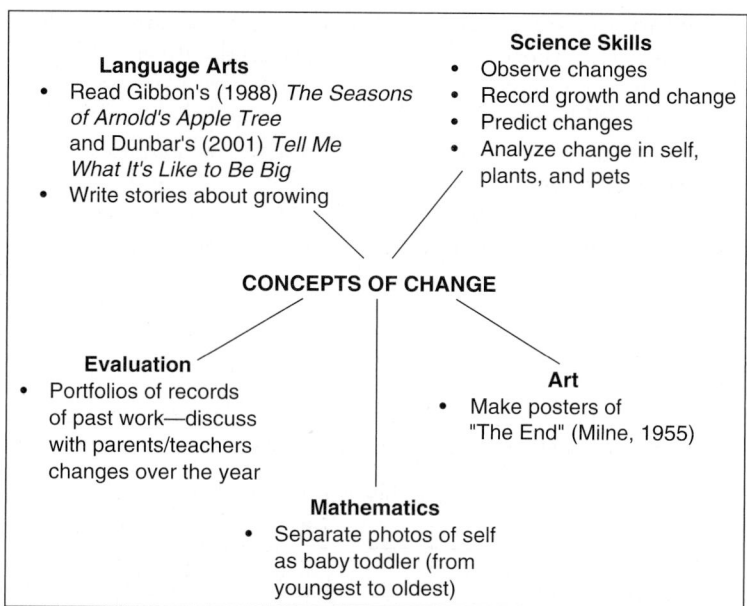

Figure 7.6   Change in the integrated curriculum.

Children experience change as they adapt to modifications in daily routine. Routines always remain stable points in the day; yet they are often changed by necessity, and these variations help children accept the inevitability of change. "Today our picnic is canceled because of the rain. What can we do instead?" "Sabrina's grandmother was coming today, but she couldn't make it, so she will come tomorrow." "Let's watch the custodian; we can have our juice later."

All of these experiences can be integrated into the curriculum to help children develop concepts of change on which to build (see Figure 7.6).

THE CONTINUITY OF HUMAN LIFE

Although life is constantly changing, there is a continuity to human experience. Exploring their family histories, children can gain a sense of this continuity. Celebrating holidays, as people have always done, also gives children the feeling of connection among human experiences (Seefeldt, 1993).

The Family

"To bring history alive, an important part of children's historical studies should be centered in people—the history of families and of people" (NCHS, 1994). Each family has something unique from the past to give to its children. You can help parents see the value of talking to their children about the parents' own past. You may need to prepare the parents for the questions their children might ask them about their past. Otherwise, some parents, faced with the struggles and problems of day-to-day living, might find such questions rude or prying.

Primary children could investigate and analyze their family. They could ask parents about their past—where they lived and what they did. Parents could share family artifacts, photos, historical documents, sites, and other records of their past with children (NCHS, 1994). In class, children could compare likenesses and differences between families' lives, activities, beliefs, traditions, family structures, institutions, and so on at various times in the past and present (Figure 7.7).

Second- and third-graders can create a history of their family. Each family has its own history. By filling in the blanks of this book, you can create a history book of your family.

My Family History

My name is _____

I am _____ years old. I live at _____

My mother's name is _____

    My mother's maiden name is _____

        She was born on _____

        in _____

        Her mother's name is _____

        Her father's name is _____

My father's name is _____

        He was born on _____

        in _____

        His mother's name is _____

        His father's name is _____

You may have a nontraditional family. If so, write about the family you live with.

This is a story of our family.

Here are our family traditions.

Figure 7.7 Family history book.

Stories and narratives of family life long ago put primary-age children in touch with the continuity of life. Reading this type of historical fiction and nonfiction can give children an understanding that, even though life changes, humans continue to share many of the same emotions and feelings. You might read children *The 18 Penny Goose* (Walker & Beier, 1998), the story of Letty, who wants to save her beloved goose, Solomon, during the Revolutionary War. *Grandma Susan Remembers* (Morris, 2002), *On the Trail of Sacagawea* (Peter, 2001), and *Full Steam Ahead* (Gibbons, 2002) tell stories of eras when life was hard and special events were communicated by word of mouth.

Intergenerational Contacts

"The continuity of all cultures depends on the living presence of at least three generations" (Mead, 1970, p. 3). In our culture, it is not easy for three generations to share one another's living presence. Older people are often separated from the young by physical and social distance. Rather than developing informal relations in the family, at church, or in the neighborhood, the ages may remain separate from one another. Thus, the connections between the young and the old are broken, and their natural ways of interacting and relating are no longer available.

Recognizing this problem, many educators are promoting intergenerational programs in school and nonschool settings to provide a space for the living presence of at least three generations. In these intergenerational programs, children, adults, and elders interact with one another, reestablishing the relationships of caring and continuity of life.

Today an estimated 100,000 older persons are involved as volunteers in schools and are working with young children. In addition to Head Start and Follow Through programs, programs exist in child-care centers, preschools, elementary and high schools, libraries, parks, recreation centers, museums, 4-H clubs, and many other community agencies. Sponsored by private organizations and federal agencies, these programs often have the primary goal of reestablishing links between young and old.

The programs build on the love and affection the young and old in our country have for one another. Researchers have found that children do have a feeling of affection for older persons, calling elders "friendly, good, rich and wonderful" (Seefeldt & Warman, 1990). Children believed it would be fun to play checkers, cards, and other games with older persons. But at the same time, the children saw old people as sick, tired, sad, bossy, wrinkled, crippled, and ugly. Further, they indicated that they themselves would never grow old. They feared and dreaded their own eventual aging and death. It is important to note that the children in this study reported few contacts with older people either inside or outside the family unit.

The American Association for Health Education (1999) has recommended the infusion of positive concepts of aging in the K–12 curriculum. Literature that shows positive images of the elderly and interactive activities such as interviewing elders are enjoyable for children and affect their attitudes toward the elderly in positive ways (Hembacher & Cruise, 2006).

Perhaps if children had contact with older people who were healthy, happy, active, and fulfilled, they would not classify the old as tired and sick, nor would they dread their own aging. If children could share the love of an older person and do things with elders that were of interest in their own schools, it might be more difficult for them to accept the stereotypical ideas of age and aging (Seefeldt & Galper, 2000).

Older people also report enjoying the company of children. In one study, they said that children would be fun to do things with and would make good friends for older people. They thought children were very interested in learning new things and were "the hope of the future" (Seefeldt & Warman, 1990).

Intergenerational programs in the school can provide a way for children and elders to enjoy one another's company, to learn from one another, to share feelings of affection, and to function as a concrete example of life's continuity. You can invite older neighbors, people on the school staff, or children's grandparents or older relatives to visit the class frequently. Just letting your community—churches, civic organizations, senior-citizens organizations, and other groups—know you would like elders to work with children in your school puts you into contact with volunteers.

Once the children and the older volunteers are comfortable with one another, the older persons might do the following:

- Read stories to one or two of the children at a time, holding them close.
- Take part in a birthday party for a child. The volunteers can tell the children how many candles their own cakes need or recall some of their early birthdays.

Connections between young and old are valuable learning experiences.

- Play with the children, helping them informally with their activities.
- Help the children prepare a special treat—making peanut butter or baking cookies.
- Talk with the children about the olden days and the things they liked to do when they were children.
- Sing, listen to music, or learn to play musical instruments.

For the children, the benefits of intergenerational contact are great. They sense the continuity of life, learn about the past, and have the attention of one more adult. The rewards are just as important for the elders (Glanz, 1991).

Holiday Celebrations and Traditions

Celebrating holidays and traditions helps children see the rich cultural heritage of their past and the continuity of life (Vygotsky, 1986). Holiday celebrations with young children can be pure fun and relaxation; at the same time, they can impart historical knowledge in an accurate and authentic manner. Holidays can serve as occasions for projects that will acquaint pupils with social studies concepts and information. They are occasions for teaching students about important ideas and customs that coexist with one another in our country and in the world (NCSS, 1998).

On the other hand, when poorly planned or thought out, holiday celebrations are disasters serving only to indoctrinate children and perpetuate myths and stereotypes. When the social studies curriculum revolves around the celebration of holidays or when the focus is on a "tourist curriculum" (Derman-Sparks & A.B.C. Task Force, 2003), children visit a culture by participating in a few activities and then go home to their regular classroom life, which leads to cultural stereotypes and trivialization—all those people do is dance, wear special clothes, and eat.

Holiday celebrations planned around the children's activities and experiences can be meaningful and enjoyable when they do the following:

- The routines of the regular school day are preserved. Any dramatic change in routine is upsetting to young children. Missing a nap or changing lunchtime might be disastrous for preschoolers. Eliminating work time for primary children is unnecessary; instead of reading from a basal text or doing the usual work, primary children might research library books about the holidays or solve puzzles with holiday words. Work time might include special materials associated with the holiday—orange and black paper and paint for Halloween or scrap papers in pink, red, and white, plus glitter, for Valentine's Day.
- Parents or other members of the community are involved to ensure sensitivity to the culture of the children. Involving parents or members of the community in planning the holiday celebration ensures, at least in part, that the culture and ethnic diversity of the children, their families, and the community will be respected. Some celebrations, such as Halloween, Valentine's Day, Christmas, or others, may be offensive to parents from differing ethnic groups or religious backgrounds and must be adjusted, handled with sensitivity, or expanded to become more inclusive (e.g., a Christmas party becomes a winter party). Parents

can add meaning to the celebrations by telling stories of their celebrations in another country or the history and meaning of specific holidays.
- The children are fully involved in planning the celebration. Children grow as they assume responsibility for their own lives. Planning holiday celebrations is an ideal opportunity for them to assume this responsibility. Young children have simple wants and are pleased when they can plan their own activities. They usually plan for very simple, manageable celebrations. "Let's play Simon Says and make cupcakes," and "We'll sing 'Flag of America' and listen to the story of Daniel Boone again," were suggested as party activities in one first-grade class.
- The activities are kept simple and low-key. Celebration of major holidays such as Christmas, Halloween, and Valentine's Day may result in tears of frustration and fatigue if children are overexcited and stimulated. A simple snack, perhaps something the children have planned and prepared themselves, can be added. Games familiar to the children can be played, with some variation added. Rather than playing Simon Says at Halloween, the children can play Witch Says. Doggie, Doggie, Who Has Your Bone? might become Steven, Steven, Who Has Your Valentine?
- A few key concepts are selected for development. Focusing on only one or two of the main ideas of the holiday, you can plan relevant activities. National and state standards can provide guidance for selecting concepts. A discussion of some of the key concepts inherent in major holidays follows.

Columbus Day

By concentrating on the ideas of courage, vision, discovery, and inquiry that characterize Columbus and other explorers, young children can commemorate Columbus Day with integrity. Kindergarten children could explore their school, neighborhood, or community with the goal of finding something that is new to them. First- and second-graders might make a dream for their own lives or draw or write about a vision they have for their own future. They could go on a scavenger hunt, acting as explorers themselves. They could also define the word *courage* and read about others who have used courage to make discoveries or do things for people.

Some teachers have celebrated the day by focusing on sailing ships, on different forms of water travel, or on floating and sinking. One teacher, who wanted to make the point that Columbus did not discover America because one cannot discover a place already inhabited by many peoples, brought items to the class that Native Americans gave to Columbus. Over a number of weeks, the children tasted chocolate, peeled and cooked potatoes, and shelled ears of popcorn, which were later popped and eaten. Another teacher focused the day around spices, asking children to find out where spices grow (geography) and why Columbus was searching for new spices. They then cooked apple slices with and without spices and determined which they liked the best.

Halloween

Halloween is truly a children's holiday because it gives children a number of opportunities to be in control. First, by dressing up as a character, children become in charge, bigger than life. Just the fact of seeing other children dressed as monsters and being able to control their own fears gives children a great deal of satisfaction. The best part of Halloween is being in control of adults, who, "fearful" of a trick, will on demand give children a treat.

Regardless, very young children may find the holiday frightening. They may be unable to understand that they and others who dress up stay the same person, even though their appearance has changed. For children younger than age 4, activities should be low-key; depending on the group of children, you may not want to include masks. Since this is a time of pretending to be frightened, one teacher used Halloween to discuss fears. In this kindergarten, the children listed their fears, found stories that included the theme of being frightened, interviewed adults to find out what they were afraid of, and dictated a class report about the nature of fear.

Halloween can also foster a sense of community in young children. One second-grade class went to the school parade as "101 Dalmations." The teacher showed the children how to make construction-paper ears. Then each child painted spots on a large white T-shirt. In another class in the same school, children dressed in orange, jack-o'-lantern, plastic trash bags. Stuffing the bags and attaching them at the neck and legs required partners to work together. Dressed as pumpkins, the class went to the school parade as "The Pumpkin Patch."

Halloween can be integrated with literature or history when children are encouraged to choose characters they have studied or want to learn about. As with all holidays, Halloween must be treated with care regarding family's beliefs and children's sensitivity to sugar.

Thanksgiving

Thanksgiving is a time for people to be together and share their thankfulness. It also parallels fall harvest festivals in many other countries. Children can draw pictures or generate lists of things for which they are thankful. Children can thank the people in the school or in their homes and community who help them. Thank-you notes or booklets might be appropriate. The children might prepare cookies, roast some nuts, or make applesauce or some other gift to share with another class in the school or to give to others as a symbol of their thankfulness. They might compare Thanksgiving with harvest festivals in other countries.

The typical celebration of Thanksgiving often includes a great many stereotypes about Native Americans. Derman-Sparks and A.B.C. Task Force (2003) proposed that, rather than perpetuating the myths about native peoples, Thanksgiving be a time for appreciating Native American peoples as they were and as they are, focusing on their lives and customs:

- Start by asking children what they know about Native Americans and what they want to know.
- Teach something about the daily life, past and/or present, of a specific Native American group and involve children in activities such as eating corn or squash.
- For children in kindergarten and the primary grades, compare the differences between daily life and ceremonial activities, compare the past with the present, and compare folktales of different Native American peoples.

Hanukkah

A happy holiday in the Jewish religion, Hanukkah is also a time to gather with friends and family. Meaningful observances of the holiday can be planned by parents or experts. Children enjoy hearing the story of the Maccabees, lighting the menorah candles, playing with a dreidel, and eating potato pancakes as they relive the traditions of Jewish families. Because Hanukkah falls close to Christmas, teachers must be cautious about distorting its meaning. Hanukkah does not have the same significance to Judaism that Christmas has to Christianity. Other, more important Jewish holidays might be observed—Rosh Hashanah and Yom Kippur in the fall and Passover in the spring.

Christmas

Christmas is often overdone and loses any real significance. Celebrations in preschools or the primary grades often reinforce the commercialism that has become deeply connected with observance of the holiday. The celebration of Christmas in non–religiously affiliated schools and centers can also contribute to the development of ethnocentrism in majority children and isolate those of minority faiths.

Celebrations of Christmas could be associated with charity and compassion and with peace on earth and good will toward others. Try the following:

- Limit Christmas activities to 2 or 3 days.
- Emphasize the giving aspects of the holiday rather than getting presents.
- Ask parents to communicate their beliefs to children.
- Become aware of the important celebrations of other religions.
- Maintain professional judgment in the face of pressures of the holiday season.

Other Winter Holidays

Depending on the children in your class, you might consider changing the Christmas celebration into a winter celebration; or you might incorporate celebrations of Christmas with December holidays from several cultural groups. Depending on the culture of the children, you might celebrate Kwanzaa (an African American holiday) or the winter solstice (a Native American tradition) as well as Hanukkah. Another festival of lights to consider is Diwali, a Hindu festival.

National Days

Lincoln's and Washington's birthdays might stimulate interest in our nation. You can focus on ecological concepts and the things we must all do to protect our land. Try to find factual narratives about Lincoln and Washington to read to the children. You can use national days to encourage children's interest in the flag or the Pledge of Allegiance, or you might take the class to visit some historical spot in their city dedicated to great people of the past.

The historic struggle for freedom, self-determination, justice, and peace is an appropriate theme for national days. To explore our nation's quest for freedom, children in kindergarten and the primary grades might listen to historically accurate stories about colonial America, the American Revolution, or the Civil War. They could also explore the ideas of freedom and justice within their own group, school, and neighborhood. Martin Luther King Jr. Day provides an excellent opportunity for children to become acquainted with the life of an important Black leader and his contribution to our nation.

Valentine's Day

Today, Valentine's Day is a day of love. In one school, Valentine's Day was just one of the days observed during the school's Month of Love celebration, which took place throughout February. Children discussed the concept of love. Groups wrote stories about love and read what others had written about the subject. One class of second-graders collected all the U.S. LOVE stamps they could find. Then in small groups, they designed their own LOVE stamps and forwarded these designs to the post office for consideration.

Best of all, however, were the songs of love the children learned. Each group within the school selected their favorite song of love to present to the entire student body. During lunchtime, individual tables of children selected a favorite song of love and then stood and sang it.

Valentine's Day also lends itself to a study of the mail system. Pictures drawn by younger children and placed in envelopes addressed to themselves are received with wonder and great joy and stimulate a great deal of discussion among the children, their parents, and teachers.

Children can send letters through the mail to a friend, their parents, other relatives, or neighbors. Teachers in the kindergarten or primary grades can read books about Benjamin Franklin's life before and during the study of the post office. Second-graders can easily trace the history of the post office and speculate on how we would communicate without it. A field trip to the local post office might be appropriate.

Other forms of mail might be explored as well. Perhaps children can find a greeting card website and send free cards to one another, or they could e-mail each other Valentine's greetings.

Other Holidays

Lesser known holidays can also receive attention in preschool and primary classrooms. Earth Day, a time to care for the earth, to clean the classroom, plant something on the playground, or do something for the community, can be a meaningful day for young children. United Nations Day, with its focus on what the United Nations is, how it functions, and what it represents, can be informative as well as enjoyable.

Cultural Universals

The units developed by Alleman and Brophy (2001, 2002, 2003) on cultural universals such as food, clothing, shelter, holidays, and transportation include many

Transportation is a cultural universal to which children can relate.

connections to history, change and continuity, science, and technology. For example, a transportation unit might include the following topics (Brophy & Alleman, 2005b):

- Transportation as a universal human need and its functions
- Modes of transportation in different times and places
- Its evolution over time and the impact of inventions
- How changes in transportation have made the world smaller
- The fundamental importance of the wheel
- The impact of building highways through farms
- School bus routes and maintenance

THE PAST

Children are intensely interested in both the immediate and the distant past. And although dates have little or no meaning, children as young as 5 years old are able to recognize the difference between past and present and have demonstrated the ability to order events chronologically, using photographs and pictures, with broad distinctions such as "long ago" and "close to now" (Barton, 2002; Barton & Levstik, 1996).

Helping children understand and explore the past does not mean you must teach them a true historic sense of time. In helping children gain a concept of the past, adults must shuttle back and forth with children from the present to the past as they react to the ever-present urge to understand what has gone before. This dipping into the past without concern for a logical development of chronology from the past to the present does not violate basic principles of learning. To wait until they can handle true chronology is to deprive children of one of the most important learnings of early childhood.

Even though the past is untouchable and far away, vicarious experiences with the past are possible for young children. Many resources are available to help young children understand the past, and some are discussed in this section.

People

Parents, grandparents, the school staff, and neighbors are all resources for helping children understand the past. You can invite these people to the school to tell the children about the olden days. The grandmother who tells children how her grandmother taught her to crochet and then shows the children how to crochet a simple chain or the grandfather who tells his story of marching out of northern Korea at the end of the Korean War both give children a vicarious sense of the past.

Primary-age children can make a family tree or a timeline of their family history for the past two generations; or they can portray their families and their histories in the form of a narrative.

Children's own lives lead to the study of the immediate past. The drama recorded in timelines of a child's own history is also enjoyed. One teacher posted large calendars in a hallway on which the events of each day, week, and month were recorded. The children referred to these calendars frequently, recalling their immediate past, and telling one another their interpretation of the days, weeks, and months that had passed. In the process of telling their own narrative of the past, these children developed the realization that history is the story of people, recorded by people like themselves, and that they were "right now making the future" (National Commission on Social Studies in the Schools, 1989, p. xi).

Primary-age children can create a narrative of their own lives. Choosing a genre, they can write the story of their own lives.

Primary Sources

Primary sources are things created during a particular time period. Primary sources may include documents, diaries, newspapers, songs, recipes, games, artifacts—anything created and used by the people at that time. The Declaration of Independence is a primary source document, as is the *Diary of Ann Frank*. They are valuable resources when studying the past, because they indicate the lives, issues, and concerns of people in the past as they occurred at the time.

Obviously, the use of primary source documents will depend on children's reading levels. Bennett and Cunningham (2011) describe a Virtual Trip to Washington, DC: a webquest in which third-graders study the Declaration of Independence, the U. S. Constitution, and the Star Spangled Banner using primary and secondary sources.

The use of primary sources is not limited by reading level, however. Artifacts—objects from the past—and historical photos provide concrete ventures into the past for readers, on-readers, and ELL students.

Artifacts

"What is it?" "What is it made of?" "How does it feel?" No document, picture, movie, or computer program can compare to real objects (artifacts)—things that children can see, hear, touch, smell, or taste for themselves. Real objects help children understand the past and life far from them and help them see significant relationships within their own neighborhood. Objects might be obtained from families, thrift stores or yard sales, local museums, commercial companies (Morris, 2000), or historical societies. Any object you can use to foster social studies knowledge is appropriate. Some examples follow:

- *Old tools.* "Who used them? How were they used? For what purpose? What tools do we use today?"
- *Clothing.* "Who wore this? Why? Who made it? What is it like?"
- *Models.* "How is this car (train, boat) like a real one? How is it different?"
- *Furniture.* "How was it made? When was it used? Who made it?"
- *Toys.* "How were they used? Who used them? How were they made?"
- *Plants.* "How is this plant like the ones we know? How is it different? Where does it grow? What does it need to live?"
- *Foods.* "Taste them. Where were they grown? Who grew them? How did they get here?"

Objects from the past stimulate thinking and language.

Objects alone stimulate children's language and thinking without adult questioning or interference. A spinning wheel, a model ship, an old-fashioned coffee mill, a cornhusk doll, or a photograph from the past provides sufficient motivation for children to begin asking questions and seeking information.

Children can compare hand eggbeaters, wooden cookie cutters, rolling pins, and kettles from the past with the newer versions. Children are fascinated by the differences when beating an egg with an old-fashioned hand eggbeater compared with an electric mixer.

Children are interested in toys and models that depict things from the past. Cars, boats, and planes, modeled after those no longer in use, give children an opportunity to make comparisons between the things they know and use today and things from the past. Scrapbooks of old-fashioned cars, trains, or toys might interest children of kindergarten age; primary children might classify models according to use or age and could make charts sequencing the models from the oldest to the newest.

Even though objects stimulate play and discussion, you could help extend and clarify children's ideas through questioning: "Why do you think the train was made like this?" "Who do you think used this?" "How do you know it was used a long time ago?" "How is it just like the one we use today?" "How is it different?"

Some objects from the past, like quilts, can lead to a unit or project. Primary-age children could make their own quilts. You could read *Sewing Quilts* (Turner & Allen, 1994) and teach children how to design a block, put the blocks together, and then to quilt. Quilts can be made from cloth or paper. You could also read *The Name Quilt* (Root, 2003). *The Quilt-Block History of Pioneer Days: With Projects Kids Can Make* (Cobb & Ellis, 1997) is another valuable resource. Other antiques that cannot be handled by the children can still be shared in the classroom. Parents and friends often have interesting and valuable items from the past that they are willing to demonstrate to the class. Teachers may want to create object boxes or resource kits of various kinds on various topics (Morris, 2000).

Almost every community has some type of museum to preserve the traces of the past. The local library, fire station, or church may house relics that children can observe. If only large museums are available in the community, you might select one room or section for the children to visit. Children also enjoy visiting older homes and buildings that have been renovated and restored.

Photographs and Visual Discovery

Historical photographs can be used to spark curiosity, develop empathy, and teach critical thinking skills as well as content (McCormick & Hubbard, 2011). Young children are able to develop the historical thinking elements of empathy and construction of historical accounts (Fallace, Biscoe, & Perry, 2007). Photographs help make concepts and time periods more concrete.

- *Old photographs.* With old photographs of their school, neighborhood, or community, or of their families, their parents, and even themselves, children can compare and contrast past and present. You might ask, "What is the same? Do you wear the same kind of clothing? What is different today?"

- *Works of art.* Works of art can also be used to show people and their environments in different times and places in order to stimulate thinking about past and present and teach about historical persons and events as well. There are many paintings and portraits of George Washington that illustrate his roles as farmer, general, family man, and president. The series *Come Look With Me* (Blizzard, 1990) selects works of art for children ages 5–10 with background information and discussion questions that encourage deep observation.
- *Pictures and digital images.* When objects are not available, pictures can be used. Pictures can also be used for activities such as comparing then and now, sorting, or sequencing.

The process of visual discovery (Bower & Lobdell, 2005) described in Chapter 3 can be used to guide children through thinking about and learning from photographs. In a first-grade example, the teacher began by waving a "magic wand." She told the students they were now "history detectives who would be looking for clues in a set of pictures to figure out what going to school before the Civil Rights Movement might have been like" (McCormick & Hubbard, 2011, p. 87). They analyzed the picture details through questioning. Then they listed similarities and differences in the pictures. Then they drew some conclusions such as the African-American children were poor based on their clothing. They also concluded they would rather be in the White classrooms with books, desks, and pictures on the walls. Finally, the teacher asked, "How would you feel if you were told you could not go to that classroom because of the color of your skin?" (McCormick & Hubbard, 2011, p. 88). The teacher had motivated the children to learn more.

Graphic organizers are helpful tools for supporting the inquiry process when using photographs and pictures (McCormick & Hubbard, 2011). Children can use them in many ways: to record, compare, identify multiple perspectives, and so on.

Narratives and the Arts

History becomes especially accessible and interesting to children when approached through stories, myths, legends, and biographies (see Table 7.2) that capture children's imaginations and immerse them in times and cultures of the recent and long-ago past (NCHS, 1994). One study found that the use of narrative historical fiction increased children's ability to understand history as a process of change—of people's choices and the consequences of those choices (Castle & Smith, 2003). Well-chosen biographies and engaging accounts of the past—such as *When I Was Young in the Mountains* (Rylant, 1992) or *Tell Me a Story Mama* (Johnson, 1989)—can bring a meaningful awareness of the past to even the youngest of children.

Some educators believe that books used to promote awareness of the historic past should be factual and truthful (Brophy, 1990). These educators claim that if myths or fictionalized accounts of the past are used to teach historic time, then children might learn to distrust teachers, who, after all, are supposed to be truthful (Brophy, 1990). Others disagree and recommend the use of all kinds of narratives to teach children history (Egan, 1997; Levstik, 2002). Narratives are inherently causal and explanatory in nature, familiar to young children—who have experienced

Table 7.2 Stories, Myths, Legends, and Biographies

Story	Something that recounts the details of an occurrence; an account; an anecdote; may or may not be true	*Where the Wild Things Are* (fiction) Newspaper story (nonfiction)
Myth	An old narrative that includes beliefs of a people or explanations of a practice or natural phenomenon; may be written down or transmitted orally	Native American stories of how the earth was created
Legend	A story that has come down from the past; may or may not be true; may be written or oral	Johnny Appleseed, Paul Bunyan
Biography	A written history of a person	*Clemente!* By Willie Perdomo
Autobiography	A written history of a person written by that person	*I Know Why the Caged Bird Sings* by Maya Angelou

them in daily interactions as well as in stories, which make up the bulk of their early contact with text—and appeal to them not only because of the story structure but because children can follow the sequence of events.

Focusing on the human aspect of narratives—feelings, emotions, ambition—teachers can foster primary children's understanding of the past. One primary teacher led children through an inquiry project on why Christopher Columbus was famous. Children were asked to consider two questions: How does the past influence the present, and how does the present influence our understanding of the past? These ideas were brought together through the concept of fame (Levstik, 1991).

Integrating drama through skits, plays, reader's theater, and role-play can be an engaging way to involve children in the narratives of history, increasing both learning and enjoyment (Otten, Stigler, Woodward, & Staley, 2004). Art, dance, and music play an equally engaging role. For examples of children's literature related to history see Figure 7.8.

METHODS OF THE HISTORIAN

Right from the start, children can begin developing the skills of the historian. To do so, they must be engaged in developing inquiry skills. Children learn to question and find out about their current and more distant past. Real historical understanding requires that students engage in historical reasoning, think about cause–effect relationships, analyze records of the past, and reach conclusions (VanSledright, 2002). Children can participate in investigations using multiple sources to answer questions such as "What did they eat at the first Thanksgiving?" (James, 2008).

Throughout their early educational experiences, children can be encouraged to do the following:

- *Generate questions and identify problems.* Begin with the natural curiosity of children by recording their questions on chart paper or a KWL chart. This serves

> **National Council for Social Studies Notable History Trade Books for Young People**
>
> *I Am Rosa Parks* by Rosa Parks with Jim Haskins. Rosa Parks tells her story.
>
> *Off Like the Wind! The First Ride of the Pony Express* by Michael P. Spradin. Describes the challenges, including a buffalo stampede, involved in making the first delivery of mail to Sacramento, CA. Map, timeline.
>
> *Peter Kent's City Across Time: From the Stone Age to the Distant Future* by Peter Kent. Illustrates a city's history and archeology over time, including artifacts buried but visible through an ant farm-like window.
>
> *Stable* by Ted Lewin. Shows a past in which horses were used for everything.
>
> *Our Grandparents: A Global Album* by Maya Ajmera, Sheila Kinkade, and Cynthia Pon. Photos from around the world show grandparents teaching children about the past and participating in family traditions. Map, activities.
>
> *The Firehouse Light* by Janet Nolan. Gives the history of firefighting, including a light bulb that has been burning for 109 years in a fire station. Activities.
>
> *Black Elk's Vision: A Lakota Story* by S. D. Nelson. Describes the life of Black Elk, a Lakota medicine man, through pictures, quotes, and drawings. Timeline, primary sources.
>
> *Clemente!* by Willie Perdomo. Tells the story of Roberto Clemente, the first Latin American baseball player, known for his charity work in Latin America. Timeline.
>
> *Climbing Lincoln's Steps: The African American Journey* by Suzanne Slade. Describes historic events on the steps of the Lincoln Memorial from Martin Luther King, Jr. to Barack Obama. Timeline.

Figure 7.8 Children's Literature Box for History.
Based on NCSS Notable Trade Books for Young People, www.ncss.org/resources.

as a basis for further inquiry. Children must be able to identify their own problems; at the least, they must perceive the problem as their own. When you determine the problem and present it to the children for solving, it becomes an exercise for them rather than a problem. Questions of problems that arise spontaneously in the classroom, school, home, or immediate community are real to the children. Learning to question—to ask, "What's happening here?" "Why?" "Who said so?"—fosters children's sense of inquiry.

- *Gather information.* To solve a problem, children must gather information. They might examine traces of the past to solve historical problems. Children as young as 3 can conduct surveys. Primary-age children might interview older people, their parents, or those who work in their school to find out what and how those people felt about a current or historical event. Kindergarten and primary children can also examine books, documents, photographs, and artifacts; watch videos; or visit museums. Primary children can begin to learn skills related to Internet research.
- *Observe the data.* Having gathered the necessary information, children need to observe carefully. You can foster children's skills in learning to observe by asking them to describe what they see, feel, taste, touch, and hear throughout the

day. Kindergarten and primary children can begin to record their observations, simply but systematically.
- *Analyze the information.* Once children have gathered and observed the information, they can analyze it and make inferences from it. What did most of the people interviewed think about why Johnny Appleseed was a hero? What do authors say about how people lived or what school was like long ago? Having gathered data from the past, historians consider them and make inferences about life—what it was like, how people lived, what they did, and what they believed in.

  Children can learn to make sense of information—and make connections to mathematics and science—by creating charts and graphs. Beginning in pre-K, children can learn to sort objects by attributes and display information in several graphic forms (Sheffield, Karp, & Brown, 2010). Primary children can ask questions and seek answers, representing their data in frequency tables, bar graphs, circle graphs, and picture graphs.
- *Draw conclusions.* Just as historians do, children reach conclusions about the past based on the available data. They may reach conclusions that are incomplete because (a) the traces of the past may be incomplete, (b) there is no one to interpret their discoveries of the past, or (c) their inferences are less than accurate. A group of children, after a visit to George Washington's home at Mount Vernon, might conclude that people in those days were very short because the beds were so small. They might look at a class bar graph and conclude that most children in the class have a pet. When encouraging problem-solving skills in children, you need not be as concerned about their reaching the correct conclusion as about their ability to use the historian's method of solving problems. You can assess children's historical thinking and understanding through observation, projects, or interviewing (Figure 7.9).

It is also important to involve children in "being historians" through hands-on experiences and activities such as archeological digs in the sand table.

Interview and record children's responses to the following questions:
1. Tell about something you like or remember that happened a long time ago, something that happened to you this week, and something you think will happen when you are older.
2. What has changed since you first came to school? What have you learned? What can you do now that you could not do then? What will you learn?

Analyze children's responses for
- completeness
- accuracy
- number of details

Figure 7.9 Evaluate children's understanding of history.

SUMMARY

Children do have a sense of the past. They are interested in studying their personal history. From these beginnings, you can foster concepts of history through the regular activities of the preschool–primary classroom. Focusing on the key concepts of time, change, the continuity of life, the past, and the methods of the historian, children can begin to develop an understanding of history. Scientific and technological change can be integrated.

It is true, however, that children's experiences in history must be as concrete as possible and vitally relevant to the child. Learning about their own pasts, experiencing the passage of time, interacting with older volunteers, studying the immediate past (what we did today), and using the methods of the historian must all be based on children's activities and experiences.

Discussion Questions

1. Why is NCSS Standard 8, Science, Technology, and Society, important? What are the connections to history, economics, geography, and civics? To science, math, literature, and the arts? How can you help children begin to understand these connections? What kinds of experiences can you create for them?
2. What is the "inquiry approach to history"? How do teachers use an inquiry approach? Why is it important for young children? What connections do you see between the development of thinking in Chapter 4 and this chapter? What are the implications for planning developmentally appropriate inquiry experiences? How is inquiry related to the methods of the historian?
3. What are primary sources? What are the various ways you can use them with children? What are some important considerations when planning to use them with children?
4. History is a process of change. What are the implications of this statement for teaching history to young children?
5. If you had to write a statement of developmentally appropriate practice for teaching history to young children, what would you include?
6. Holiday celebrations are important, but they can be done poorly. Why are holiday celebrations important? In what ways are they sometimes done inappropriately? How can be you include them in the curriculum appropriately?
7. Select one book from each of the Children's Literature Boxes. What standard (NCSS, NAEYC, or local/state) might this book be used to teach? What would a lesson or unit plan that used this book to teach this standard look like?

Extend Your Knowledge

1. Start personal history books for children in the class. You might ask the children to bring baby pictures to include in their books and compare them with current photographs. Other items you could include are a graph of each child's

height and weight and a discussion of the things each likes or does not like to do. Leave several blank pages in the book to fill with the same information at the end of the year. Children can then discuss the changes that have occurred in themselves during the school year.
2. Invite older persons to the class to discuss the things they remember about life when they were young boys or girls. Ask each one to bring a childhood photograph or an object that they used as a child.
3. Create a timeline of your life with pictures and significant events; or begin your own family history book by starting a family tree tracing your heritage.
4. Have the class make a history book of their school. They can find out when the school was built, what was on the land before it was built, whom the school was named for, and how many people have been principals of the school.

Resources

To initiate an intergenerational program in your school, you might first locate organizations that sponsor intergenerational programs. Contact the following:

Administration on Aging
www.aoa.gov

American Association of Retired Persons
www.aarp.org

To obtain information about teaching history to young children:

National Council for History Education
www.nche.net

To obtain information about the national standards for teaching history in kindergarten through Grade 4, contact the following organization:

National Center for History in the Schools
www.sscnet.ucla.edu/nchs

To obtain information on family history in the classroom, contact:

National Endowment for the Humanities
Go to www.neh.gov and search for "family history."

To obtain information about presidents and access to the presidential libraries, contact:

The Presidential Timeline of the Twentieth Century
www.presidentialtimeline.org

Books from the National Council for the Social Studies
www.socialstudies.org/bookstore

Making a Difference: Revitalizing Elementary Social Studies by M. E. McGuire and B. Cole, 2010.

Teaching Women's History through Literature: Standards-based Lessons for grades K-12 by L. Bennett and M. J. Berson, 2007.

Come Look with Me series by G. S. Blizzard includes works of art and discussion questions for children.

CHAPTER 8

People, Places, and Environments: Geography

> **Focus Questions**
>
> After you read this chapter, you should be prepared to respond to the following questions:
>
> - What are the skills of the geographer that children can develop in the preschool–primary grades?
> - What concepts are considered key to the study of geography? What topics are included under each key concept?
> - How do children develop concepts of direction and location, and how do teachers foster these concepts? What mapping skills can young children develop and how?
> - How would you best introduce children to concepts of relationships within places?
> - How would you best introduce concepts of spatial interactions?
> - How would you best introduce concepts related to regions?

GEOGRAPHY SKILLS FOR YOUNG CHILDREN

While taking a walk to mail letters, a group of first-graders stops to watch a squirrel hiding acorns under a tree stump. Two children spot a nest of leaves high in a tree and wonder if this is the squirrel's home. Cars pass by and stop at the intersection. Some children see a picture of a blue heron on the license plate of one of the cars and talk about the blue heron they saw at the beach. After crossing the street when the light turns green, each child places a letter in the mailbox.

Although they did not know it, these first-graders were experiencing and learning geography. But this learning did not involve memorizing countries and their capitals or locating them on a map. Like geographers everywhere, children learn as they observe, experience, and develop beginning understandings of the nature of their world and their place in it (Schoenfeldt, 2001). Through these early explorations of their world, children, like geographers, begin to answer the two major questions of geography: Where are things, and how did they get there? (Geography Education Standards Project, 1994). And like geographers everywhere and at every age, children, as they explore the earth they live on, develop and use the skills that "will allow the student to better understand the world around him or her and will couple social studies to the continual process of the student's trying to determine just where he or she is in the world" (NCSS, 1998, p. 44).

The national geography standards, *Geography for Life* (Geography Education Standards Project, 1994), list five skills that children begin developing during their preschool and primary years:

1. *Asking geographic questions.* Questioning comes naturally to young children. Toddlers, driven by their innate curiosity about the world, ask, "What's this?" "What's that?" By 2 years of age, the why questions begin. Why questions extend beyond just asking, "Why?" to asking, "Why is it this way?" Three- and 4-year-olds want to know "Why is the sky blue?" "Why did you do that?" "Why do I have to do this?" By the time children are in the primary grades, they ask actual geographic questions: "What caused the lake?" "What made this hill?" Later, they ask speculation questions: "Does corn always grow in this field?"
2. *Acquiring geographic information.* Locating, collecting, and processing information from a variety of primary and secondary sources, including maps, forms another set of skills. Lucy Sprague Mitchell (1934) said these skills begin right from the start, unofficially at birth. Watch as an infant flails his arms in space as if attempting to determine where self begins and ends. Watch as she stares at a mobile with a questioning frown as if trying to make sense of its movement. By the time children are toddlers, they can collect information, process it, and make differentiations such as "this is a chair; this is a sofa." In the preschool and primary grades, children consult their here-and-now world as well as secondary sources, books, authorities, pictures, and maps as they build their geographic skills.
3. *Organizing geographic information.* Although humans begin to organize and process information through their senses from the moment of birth or even before, not until children are in the preschool and primary grades do they begin

Like geographers, children learn as they observe and experience.

to develop the skills of organizing geographic information. Activities that support the organization of information include preparing maps and displays, telling and writing stories, and constructing graphs.

4. *Analyzing geographic information.* In the preschool and primary grades, children learn to use maps to locate themselves in space and learn to interpret graphs. Preschool–primary students use many kinds of observations, reference books, the Internet, and literature to study geographic relationships.

5. *Answering geographic questions.* Reaching conclusions, the final stage in the thinking/problem-solving process, completes the geographic skills to be developed in the preschool and primary grades. Children can present their findings to the group, write a story, paint a mural, or construct a replica of a place to demonstrate how they draw conclusions and make generalizations.

KEY CONCEPTS

Planning to teach geography begins with a study of children's immediate physical environment and their ability and opportunity to observe, speculate about, analyze, and evaluate that environment. Both the environment and children's explorations within it are complex and complicated. To help teachers organize the possibilities for children's geographic learning within an environment, the national geography standards, *Geography for Life* (Geography Education Standards Project, 1994) and the National Council for the Social Studies (1998) have identified major themes and concepts key to the study of geography. Believing that the study of geography is more than just place geography, the project designers call for integrating place geography with the study of human–environment relationships by structuring geographical studies around five main themes:

1. *The earth is the place where we live.* It is covered with land and water and is a part of the solar system. The physical characteristics—landforms, water bodies, climate, soils, natural vegetation, and animal life—and the human ideas and actions that have shaped their character are included in the concept of place. As children develop concepts of the earth as the place they live, they can also be introduced to the concepts, attitudes, and values inherent in learning to care for their earth.
2. *Direction and location.* From birth, children start orienting themselves in space. By age 4 children have an intuitive sense of space and are able to construct representations of space (Barry-Davis, 1999). Although they do not develop a complete sense of direction until after the age of 11 or 12, they experience concepts of direction through their own movement early in life. Being able to orient oneself in space also means being able to locate oneself in space. The ideas of distance and measurement are included in these concepts. Maps are vital tools for locating oneself in space. Children begin developing mapping skills by making and using maps before reading them.
3. *Relationships within places.* Humans interact with the earth. People adapt and modify the natural environment in ways that reveal their cultural values. Human population density is spread unevenly across the earth. People live in different communities and interact with others by means of travel, communication, and the use of products and ideas that come from beyond their immediate environment.
4. *Spatial interactions.* There are patterns of movement of people, products, and information. Again, people are scattered unevenly over the earth. How do they get from one place to another? What are the patterns of movement of people, products, and information?
5. *Regions.* Regions are convenient and manageable units on which to build knowledge of the world and study current events. Children live in a region; its geographic description affects how they live.

As you can imagine, there are infinite opportunities to integrate geography with science, math, the other social studies disciplines, and literature.

THE EARTH IS THE PLACE WHERE WE LIVE

"All stones have been made by builders out of the earth and the earth is broken stone." "Mountains made themselves so we can ski." These explanations of the nature of the earth were given in reply to questions posed by Piaget (1965, p. 207), and they aptly demonstrate young children's thinking about the nature of the earth. Piaget has labeled this stage of thinking *artificialism*, the idea that children view things on the earth as for their own use, made for purposes (usually theirs), and

Table 8.1 Geography Skills

Sensorimotor Ages 0–2	Preoperational Ages 2–6/7	Concrete Ages 6/7–10
Attends to qualities of things: self, earth, sky Moves in space	Moves on earth Orients self in a given space (e.g., in a room) Represents world in buildings and drawings Draws rough maps, can find treasures with rough map Begins orientation to distance	8+, some difficulty with left and right Some confusion about relating directions 12+, fully understands cardinal directions

either made by themselves or by others—the mountains made themselves, the builders made the stones (Table 8.1).

In attempting to determine where children obtained this line of thought, Piaget ruled out religious education or educational experiences of any nature. He hypothesized that artificialism might stem from never having considered the question before; or from children's belief that powerful people, like parents, can make things happen (like crushing stone into earth).

Keeping in mind young children's thinking, you can help children build more accurate concepts of the earth by providing them with concrete, direct experiences structured around their immediate environment. In planning earth-study experiences, you need to ask yourself, "What have these children learned through their own experiences about the way the world functions?" "What have they learned about the natural phenomena—the action of earth forces, how water runs down a hill, the effects of the growth of plants and animals?" You can use the answers to plan experiences for children based on an identified key concept of geography: knowledge of the earth.

Our Environment

We are alive, and we live on the earth. What a simple idea—unless you are a young child who believes that everything that moves is alive and that even some things that do not move, like poison, which could intend to kill you, are also alive (Piaget, 1965). To young children, cars, boats, clouds, rivers and all sorts of things that move have life and consciousness.

As children are experiencing their environment, you can ask questions to help them sort living things from nonliving things. Ask them whether the objects or materials they are playing with are living or not living. Based on their answers, you can ask other questions or offer suggestions. Try to extend children's thinking by asking, "Do you think it's alive?" "Why do you think it's living?" "How can you tell?" "Are you living?" "What other things do you know that are alive?" "What things are not alive?"

After a walk outside, you could set up a table, a bulletin board, or a chart sectioned into living things and nonliving things (Figure 8.1). Children could place objects or pictures representing things they have seen on their walks into the appropriate

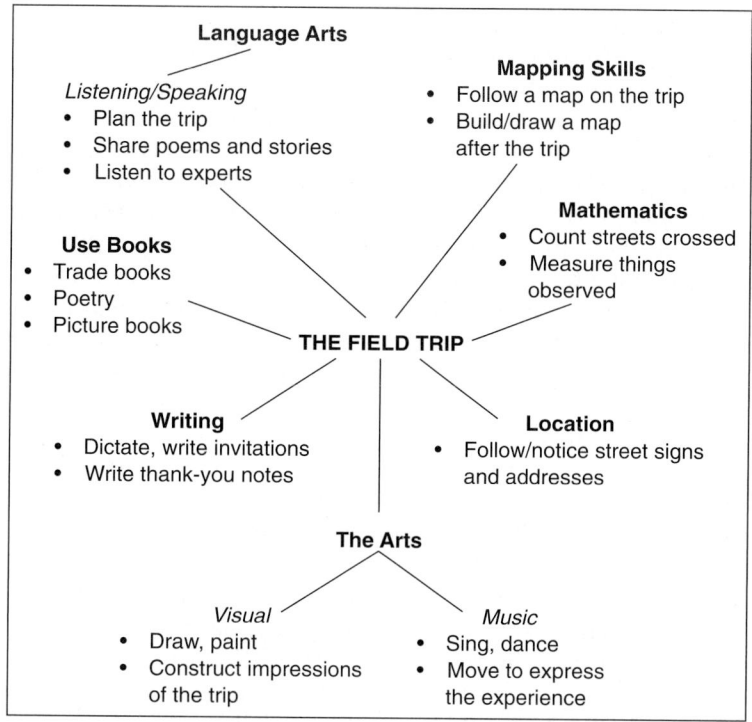

Figure 8.1 Geography—the integrative power of a field trip.

sections. Rocks, sand, and pictures of houses might be placed in the nonliving section, and pictures or pieces of plants and trees and pictures of animals and birds in the living section. You might also help children make booklets or scrapbooks of living and nonliving things. You can help children move toward the generalization that living things require food and water while nonliving things do not.

Other experiences can foster the concept that we live on the surface of the earth. When playing outdoors, children can classify things that live on the earth. You could use this activity to initiate a discussion of living and nonliving things. Having children sort pictures or objects can serve as an assessment.

The purpose of these experiences with living and nonliving things is to increase children's awareness of the world around them. Talking with children about living and nonliving things, you can gain an understanding of their thought processes, which is necessary for planning and assessing the teaching–learning process.

Land and Water

By experiencing their immediate environment, children can begin to make distinctions between the different surfaces covering their earth and the relationships between these surfaces and how they live. Children need time to play with, experiment with, and explore the nature of sand, water, and dirt—inside and outside—to learn the nature of the surfaces covering the earth. All this messing around with sand and dirt and playing with mud and water helps children construct the physical knowledge of the earth on which they live—knowledge that is necessary for later formal thinking about the earth (NRC & IM, 2000).

Children's exploration with water, sand, and mud can help them discover that these substances take on the shape of the container they are in and practice the idea that the amount of material remains the same, even when poured into containers of different shapes. On a graph or in some other form, primary-age children can count and record the number of cups of sand, water, or dirt it takes to fill a large container. Ask them to pour a filled cup into another container and to predict whether the amount of water has stayed the same. They can test their hypothesis by pouring the material back into the first container.

Remember that these experiences are exploratory and must be concrete. Abstract concepts of the nature of land and water, such as evaporation, must be taught in concrete ways. Even so, children's understanding may remain partial. Research suggests that even after instruction involving firsthand experiences, 7- and 8-year-old children believe that water that has evaporated from a dish has somehow soaked into the dish. After all, sponges and towels soak up water, so why not a dish (Landry & Forman, 1999)?

Within the school and/or immediate neighborhood, children can find different land surfaces. The playground may be grassy, paved with concrete or blacktop, or contain sand areas. Children can feel the different surfaces and classify them as hard, soft, rough, or smooth and discuss the purpose and use of each. Ask, "Why is the street hard? What would happen if you fell on it?" "Have you ever fallen on the sidewalk? What happened?" "Ride your bike on the blacktop, on the grass, and then on the sand. Where is it easier to ride? Why?" Some of the surfaces may have been made by humans; others occur naturally. Kindergarten and primary-age children may be able to classify the surfaces.

Trips taken in the wider community allow children to observe that the earth is covered with water as well as land. One second-grade class in Boston took an overnight trip with their parents and their teacher, who had been with them since they entered school as 4- and 5-year-olds, to a lake resort to swim in the lake, climb the mountains surrounding it, and actually experience different landforms for themselves.

Even with field trips, children will not be able to actually experience all the earth's surfaces: "The schools' task is to furnish source materials" (Mitchell, 1934, p. 31). Vicarious experiences with photographs, pictures, or digital images and reference or audiovisual materials may be used to help children develop an awareness of the different types of earth surfaces.

Choose both factual reference books and children's literature to extend children's knowledge of the surfaces that cover the earth. Begin by selecting books about the children's own neighborhoods and communities. Depending on where you are located, you might find the following books useful: *It Could Still Be a Tree* (Fowler, 2001), *Rivers and Streams* (Vaughan, 1998), and *Mountains and Volcanoes* (Taylor, 2002). Use other books to take children to places they may not have experienced. *One Morning in Maine* (McCloskey, 1952) and *Blueberries for Sal* (McCloskey, 1976) give children a feel for the earth and water of Maine. Older primary children enjoy

> **NCSS Notable Geography Trade Books for Young Children**
>
> *Our World of Water: Children and Water around the World* by Beatrice Hollyer. The importance of water is described in six countries. Photographs.
>
> *The Most Fantastic Atlas of the Whole Wide World* by the Brainwaves. Each continent on foldout pages plus the Earth's structure, climate, and people.
>
> *Follow That Map! A First Book of Mapping Skills* by Scot Ritchie. Geography concepts and mapping skills in the backyard, neighborhood, city, world, and space. Create Your Own Map.
>
> *National Geographic Wild Animal Atlas*. Connects animals to geographic regions and continuents. Large pages, photos, maps.
>
> *Walden Then & Now: An Alphabetical Tour of Henry Thoreau's Pond* by Michael McCurdy. This alphabet book is set at Walden Pond and shows Thoreau's love for his pond. Wood engravings complement each letter.
>
> *Mama Miti: Wangari Maathai and the Trees of Kenya* by Donna Jo Napoli. Describes the efforts of one woman to spearhead reforestation efforts in Kenya by providing women with tree seedlings. Textile and oil collages. Internet sources.
>
> *Hands of the Rain Forest: The Emberá People of Panama* by Rachel Crandell. Cultural traditions and survival practices of rain forest inhabitants.
>
> *Rain School* by James Rumford. Young children in Chad must build their school, then watch the rain wash it away. Map.
>
> *One World, One Day by* Barbara Kerley. Photographs of children around the world living their daily lives show that we have much in common, no matter where we live.
>
> *Keep On! The Story of Matthew Henson, Co-Discoverer of the North Pole* by Deborah Hopkinson. Captivating account of Henson's adventures to the North Pole. Timeline, websites, books, quotes.
>
> *Heart O'Hara* by Elvira Woodruff. When a family is forced to immigrate to America, a young girl's collection of small treasures preserves memories of her Irish homeland.

Figure 8.2 Children's Literature Box for Geography.
Based on NCSS Notable Trade Books for Young People, www.ncss.org/resources.

reading or listening to *Black Cowboy, Wild Horses: A True Story* (Lester & Pinkney, 1998), a story of the Wild West that depicts its sweeping plains. *Seven Brave Women* (Hearne, 1997) tells the story of how women came to and then created America, showing farms, forests, oceans, and plains. *Beneath the Stone: A Mexican Zapotec Tale* (Wolf, 1994) follows a 6-year-old and his family through their life in a mountain valley village (see Figure 8.2).

Depending on children's firsthand experiences with land and water and the books they have read, they could do some of the following activities, which can also serve as assessments:

- Make a two-part mural labeled "On Land, On Water" and include pictures of things that live on land or in the water, placed appropriately.

Field trips give children experiences with different environments.

- Classify a group of pictures of land surfaces—hills, mountains, valleys, deserts—as land and another group of pictures of water surfaces—streams, waterfalls, lakes, oceans—as water. Children can sort the two groups of pictures into appropriately labeled box lids.
- Discuss and draw pictures of the kinds of activities that take place on land and in water, making a booklet or a chart for the classroom. Swimming, fishing, and boating are classified as water activities; camping, playing ball, and gardening are classified as land activities.
- Observe the pictures on state quarters that depict surfaces, e.g., Colorado mountains, Nebraska or North Dakota plains, and Nevada desert (United States Mint, 2011) and sort the quarters according to surfaces.

The study of earth's surfaces can be integrated with the study of habitats in science.

Caring for Our Earth

It is particularly worrisome that many children are disconnected from what we call nature. We ourselves are part of nature, having evolved along with the other animals and plants. We ought to take more heed of our habitats, knowing that their loss is a primary cause of species extinction (Rivkin, 1995), and of climate, knowing that climate change is a primary cause of global warming.

All individuals, beginning with children, must learn to care for the place we live in—our earth. Each individual must be concerned about the chain of life; the welfare of birds, insects, grass, and trees; and the conditions of the air, water, and land.

As with any area of study, learning to care for the earth (a) is an ongoing process; (b) involves multiple disciplines; (c) must be age appropriate; (d) must be related to children's firsthand, everyday experiences; and (e) must include concepts as well as attitudes and values. You can begin by encouraging children to learn to observe their environment, providing experiences that enable them to develop an understanding of interdependency, aesthetic awareness, and social consciousness—all parts of environmental education.

Observation Skills

Observational skills, like any skills, must be taught. We need to concentrate on allowing children to explore, to experience the marvels of nature themselves (Mitchell, 2000). Encouraging children to become totally familiar with their environment is accomplished, in part, by teaching them to observe. As children observe and experience their environment, conceptual learning follows. Teach children that they can really observe by looking. Preschool children can examine their eyes. Ask, "How many eyes do you have?" "What color are they?" "What parts of your eye can you see when you look in the mirror?" Give children the names for eyebrows, eyelashes, pupils, and eyelids.

You can relate children's learning about their eyes to the environment, discussing the nature of the eyes of fish, mammals, birds, and reptiles. Primary children can conduct an entire study of eyes, observing the eyes of insects, reptiles, and mammals and doing library or Internet research.

Next, ask children to use their eyes to identify the things they can see inside and outside their classroom. Encourage them to note colors, shapes, and sizes. Ask them to look again, focusing on a specific detail in the environment. Primary-age children can also explore what happens when they look through things, such as windows, magnifying lenses, and prisms, and what happens when they look into objects such as mirrors.

As they observe, children use other senses. Observation experiences encourage children to use the senses of hearing, smell, and touch as they explore their environment. They might discuss and chart the meanings of different sounds and smells. You can see the many connections to science.

Field trips within the school building, on the playground, and in the neighborhood focus children's attention on the natural environment. For example, in a field trip around an inner-city block, first-graders noted more than 40 different types of plants growing between cracks in the sidewalks, in the street, and even between bricks of the row houses. It seemed impossible to imagine, when first looking at the cement and brick city, that so many plants could survive. The children not only observed their immediate environment but went on to classify the plants, noting their likenesses and differences and identifying the conditions that supported this life. To help them focus their observations, the teacher gave the children cardboard paper-towel tubes to look through.

Another teacher asked second-graders to look up and observe the sky. A flock of birds happened to catch the children's attention. Back in the classroom, the children identified the birds they had seen and planned ways they could provide for birds in their school. One group made birdhouses from empty milk cartons and hung them on trees around the schoolyard, and another located a large discarded plastic garbage-can lid and made a birdbath. All the children took part in spreading peanut butter on pinecones and rolling them in birdseed to make feeders for their school and homes.

Next, the children observed and recorded the birds that were attracted to their school and homes. The children found that some of the birds they observed had migrated miles to nest in the area. They marked the birds' migration paths on a map.

After interest in birds subsided, the teacher again took the children outside to observe, but this time she asked them to observe life on the ground. Turning over rocks, the children observed a variety of worm and insect life. Their observations led to their discovery of a number of different insects, worms, and grubs. The children consulted books and found that worms are necessary to human life because they enrich the soil and that other insects are useful in cleaning up the environment. Leaving an apple core in a corner of the playground, the class observed which insects ate the core and how many days it took before the core was completely gone. Observational skills can be assessed through children's comments, questions, recordkeeping, and related projects.

Observations logically lead to other thinking processes. You can ask children to make inferences, predict outcomes, and suggest hypotheses: "Why do you think it's like this?" "What made the grass die?" "What would happen if … ?" "How can we find out?" Such questions can help children see connections between their observations and protection of the environment. During these experiences, you can point out the interrelatedness of land, water, air, plants, and animals.

Still, questions should be used cautiously. Judith Dighe (1993) reminded us that some children can quickly be turned off by the "What's its name?" approach: "Surprising to me, the what-do-you-think … ? questions that teachers have been taught to ask can fall flat too" (p. 59). Asking, "What do you think made that hole in the acorn?" has "the effect of stopping a child's investigation when my intent was just the opposite" (p. 59). Dighe suggested that when children are observing and exploring their environment, it is best to take your cues from them—listen, watch, share interest, and delight first, and then ask questions that will help children further their own investigations.

Interdependency

The concept that one form of life is dependent on another is basic to learning to care for our earth and stems from the biological and physical sciences. Through observations, children become aware of the chain of life around them and of their influence on that life. You can instill a reverence for life by being cautious about picking wildflowers, tearing branches from trees, or removing a toad to place it in a jar in the classroom. Your caution lets children know that the environment deserves respect.

Keeping a variety of living things in the classroom helps foster the concept of interdependency. The care of living things demonstrates to the children the precarious balance found in nature. Reptiles cannot live without insects; insects without plants; plants without sun, water, or soil. The reptiles themselves may become food for other living things. Keeping an aquarium in balance is sometimes difficult in a classroom, yet it teaches the importance of balance in maintaining life in one type of environment. You can stress children's interdependence with other living things. To live, children depend on and need to protect plants, animals, land, air, and water. *The Lorax* by Dr. Seuss (1971) provides an engaging example of interdependence.

Aesthetic Awareness

Interwoven with the skills and concepts of environmental education is an aesthetic appreciation of the natural environment. As children learn to appreciate the beauty surrounding them, they become more aware of the chain of life and thus more concerned about protecting their environment.

Aesthetic education is subtle: a classroom that is ordered; contains prints of famous paintings, growing plants, and other living things; and is decorated with the work of the children leads them to appreciate the beauty of the environment. Dewey (1900b) wrote, "If the eye is constantly greeted by harmonious objects, having elegance of form and color, a standard of taste naturally grows" (p. 307). You can point out the delicate beauty in the construction of a spiderweb; the strong veins of a maple leaf; the smooth, shiny, purple elegance of an eggplant; or the intricate parts and patterns of a wildflower. At times you may want to display a single perfect flower, a sculpture, a wood carving, or another object of beauty. In observing the beauty of the environment, encourage children to use all their senses: to look at the object from different perspectives; to notice shapes, sizes, smells, textures, and colors; to look for patterns in nature; and to share with one another the interesting things they find in their environment.

Social Consciousness

Living in a democracy calls for the development of a strong social consciousness, which is basic to learning to care for our earth. It requires each individual to assume responsibility for environmental protection. If children have developed an awareness of the beauty of the natural environment and understand the concept of interdependence, then the development of a social consciousness—assuming individual responsibility for the common good—is the next step in environmental education.

The development of children's social consciousness, especially for the protection of the environment, may be a controversial goal. Parents and the community must be involved in formulating the objectives of an environmental education program. You will want their input into the kinds of activities you will provide to foster these goals. Some people believe that protecting the environment without concern for progress will destroy society; others, with vested interests in industry or production, might object for reasons specific to their interests. At the same time, awareness of global warming is increasing. Most people would now agree that "reduce, reuse, recycle" is a worthy goal, and it is one that is included in many state standards of learning.

Developing respect for the dignity and worth of life and sharing responsibility for the care of private and public property are part of developing social consciousness. Caring for their immediate environment leads children to concern for the wider environment.

To foster social consciousness, introduce the three *R*s of being a good environmentalist into the classroom: recycle, reduce, and reuse.

Recycle Young children do not understand how goods get to a store. Thus, they will have difficulty understanding the concepts involved in recycling. Regardless, even the youngest children can be taught the habit and importance of recycling. They can learn to recycle glass bottles, jars, paper, and aluminum foil used in pie plates, frozen meal trays, and cans. Set up boxes to enable children to sort their trash and arrange for them to take the containers to a recycling center. Parents can be involved and asked to purchase recycled notebook paper, stationery, and greeting cards.

Reduce All of us, even the youngest, can begin to learn to reduce our use of materials—to cut down on what we consume. Children can do the following things:

- They can learn to reduce their use of water. They can be taught to brush their teeth by first wetting their brush and then turning off the water and to use water cooled in the refrigerator instead of letting water run from the faucet to cool off. Teach children to remember to conserve water by saying, "Presto on! Presto off!"
- They can ask themselves if they really need a paper bag to carry a book home and if presents need fancy wrapping paper.
- They can conduct a waste audit. First- and second-graders can conduct an inventory of the amount of waste in their classroom or school. They might focus on the cafeteria and observe the food placed in trash cans after lunch or focus on their room alone, determining how much paper, electricity, water, or paint is being wasted; or, they might conduct a waste audit in their own homes. After the audits, they can report their findings to the class.
- They can get into the habit of using string bags, canvas totes, or backpacks rather than paper or plastic bags to carry things.
- They can look for things to buy that are not wrapped in elaborate, unnecessary packaging. Even though they love individual pudding snacks or fruit juice containers, they might find other ways to have individual snacks that conserve packaging.
- They can use a lunchbox instead of brown paper bags.
- They can learn to reduce the amount of art materials used.

Reuse. Children can be taught to reuse whatever possible.

- They can learn how broken toys and other items can be fixed.
- They can save plastic bags to use again. If the bags are dirty, turn them inside out, rinse them, and hang them up to dry. A caution: Do not reuse plastic bags with printing or pictures on them, such as bread bags, in this way. The dye in the printing can contaminate food.
- They can wash off aluminum foil, let it dry, and put it away.
- They can think of ways to use empty containers or other trash.
- They can cut up brown paper bags to use for wrapping packages, mailing, drawing, or painting.

Children learn respect for the earth by reusing and recycling.

- They can use computer paper for other projects.
- They can give books, toys, and materials that they no longer use to someone else who can use them.
- They can use old greeting cards, catalogs, and magazines in their collages and other artwork.
- They can reuse empty milk cartons as plant containers.

One second-grade teacher initiated a unit on recycling. She first asked the children to predict the amount of material they would find in the trash cans from the school's office, their own room, and the work room, where the copying machines and art and classroom supplies were kept. After the children charted their predictions, they collected the trash cans and sorted the trash into materials that really were trash and needed to be discarded, those that could be recycled, and those that could be reused. The final activity was following the trash collected in their own room on its path to the landfill. The group met with representatives from the sanitation department, mapped and followed the route of their trash, and observed a landfill. They speculated about what would happen to the trash when this specific landfill was full.

The children then formed groups to find out where and how materials could be recycled or reused. After identifying how materials could be recycled, one group canvassed the entire school and gained the cooperation of all to institute a recycling program. Another group made toys from recycled materials, including rhythm instruments, a kaleidoscope, and milk-carton dollhouse furniture.

Following the interest of the children, the teacher broadened the unit to include concern for the wider environment. The children picked up trash around their school and learned how it was disposed. Awareness of waste processing can also be followed by making or decorating trash cans for the playground and posters for the school about recycling, reducing, and reusing.

A Nearly Round Sphere in a Solar System

How can young children, or any of us (except perhaps astronauts), discover through personal experiences that the earth is round and is part of the solar system? These two concepts can only be taught through vicarious experiences. Children do, however, appear to have the concept of a spherical earth (Takahashi, 2000). Perhaps children, as we all do, learn about the roundness of the earth through photographs and books.

One useful book to inform children about the spherical nature of the earth is *Looking Down* (Jenkins, 1995), a wordless picture book that illustrates the perspective of astronauts viewing the earth from space. *Earth from Above for Young Readers* (Arthus-Bertrand & Burleigh, 2002), for older children, could be read to younger children, who will enjoy the photographs and illustrations of the earth.

Most classrooms for young children have at least one globe. Recognizing that children under 7 or 8 years of age are cognitively unable to fully understand the globe, teachers use it instead to enable children to become aware that the earth is round and can be represented as a sphere.

Our Sun Is a Star (Martin, 1969b) presents a simple yet accurate account of the earth as part of the solar system. Primary children can read the book themselves, and 4- and 5-year-olds enjoy the beauty of the illustrations and the text when it is read to them. Again, there are strong connections to science.

Movement in Space

A complete and accurate understanding of the rotation of the earth on its axis and its revolution around the sun is not possible for young children. Yet beginning, concrete experiences with the consequences of the earth's movement are possible and can form the foundation for later, more advanced understandings.

One effect of the earth's rotation is the appearance of night and day. Talk with the children about their day and night experiences. Ask if they can remember what they did at night after they went to sleep. Just as young children may believe moving things are alive, they believe that dreams really happened. They will not believe an adult who tells them, "It was just a dream." Nevertheless, discussing night and day dreams and constructing murals or booklets of "Our Dreams" let children express their feelings about dreams.

You can encourage children to talk about what night looks like, how it feels, and how it differs from day. Ask, "How is the sky at night different from the sky during the day?" Children can draw two different pictures—"My Room at Night" and "My Room by Day"—or they can make night and day collages. Using a T-Chart or two different pieces of construction paper, one black and one white, they can cut pictures from magazines and paste them onto the appropriate place.

Day and night can also be represented in a circular format. Prepare construction paper circles by cutting a large half-circle out of black construction paper and another half-circle the same size out of white paper. Tape the two together to represent the two halves of our 24-hour day. Children can use white tempera to paint nighttime phenomena on the dark side and colored tempera to draw daytime phenomena on the light side. These can be used to assess children's understanding of day and night.

Playing with shadows can help children understand the earth's daily rotation. Some children may be able to figure out for themselves that the changes in a shadow's position, size, and shape are related to the time of day the shadow is made; other children are content to play. Some may want to know why there is no shadow at all at a particular time of day, or why the shadow is directly in front of the school building at one time of day and is off in another direction at another time. Other children may not relate the position of a shadow to the position of the sun at all. Children will absorb different depths of understanding from their experiences, and they need to be able to set their own pace with shadow play. You will want to respect children's individuality, for they are engaging in research as they explore and experiment with their shadows.

You cannot plan just when children will be able to experiment with shadows but will have to take advantage of the weather conditions as they occur. You might want to explore shadows on sunny, cloudy, and windy days as well as at different times of the day and year. Children can do the following:

- Find out what kinds of shadows they can make with their bodies.
- Make shadows with different objects—umbrellas, boxes, or different kinds of toys.
- Mark the shadows of a landmark—the school building, a tree, or a fence—at different times of the day. Discuss how the shadows differ, and talk about the effects of the earth's rotation around the sun. Draw around shadows at different times of the day and compare the drawings.
- Play shadow tag.
- Play Simon Says with shadows: "Simon says: touch your shadow; stand with your shadow in front of you; hide in your shadow; step on someone's shadow."

At the child care center in Reggio Emilia, Italy, children's spontaneous play with shadows on a sunny day turned into an extensive exploration of the properties and magic of *l'ombrars*. Teachers used this natural response to the environment as the building block for a long-term investigation of shadows.

As children played with shadows, the teacher captured the event through photographs. The sharing of the photographs stimulated many more days of play with shadows. Children used a variety of objects to create shadow images, and the teacher followed their lead, providing other props, asking some questions, and suggesting experiments: "How many ways can you make a shadow of a pear?"

After each experience, the teacher asked the children to draw their understanding of the experience or answer the question, "How are shadows created?" with a drawing. Finally, the teacher added a provocation, placing a sticker "sun" on each child's paper and asking them to draw themselves and their shadow in relation to this sun. These products served as assessments of the children's understanding.

Climate Conditions

Observing and recording climate conditions is the first step in understanding the revolution of the earth around the sun and the effects of this revolution on people.

Many of these experiences will occur incidentally as children work or play; you can structure others.

You can use seasonal changes in weather to focus children's attention on the climate. Whether it is sunny and warm, cool and rainy, or cold and snowy, children can observe how weather changes throughout the year and draw conclusions about its effects on people's lives. Children can do the following:

1. Stand in the sun and then in the shade. What is different?
2. Stand in the wind and in a protected spot on the playground. What is different?
3. Discuss and examine different clothing worn in different weather conditions. Why are boots, hats, wool clothing, sun hats, snowsuits, or shorts worn?
4. Explore the nature of the wind. Go outside and blow soap bubbles: Give each child a paper cup half filled with soapy water, a straw to blow into the cup, or a pipe cleaner to swish through and make bubbles with.
5. Fly a kite.
6. Make pinwheels and take them outside to play with in the wind.
7. Take a walk in the wind. Walk with your back against it. How did it feel? Walk facing the wind; walk with the direction of the wind. Which way was it easiest to walk?
8. Watch cloud formations and play "Do you see what I see?" Then go inside, make cloud pictures, and read a poem about clouds.
9. Wash some doll clothes or dress-up clothing. Dry them in the shade, the sun, or the wind. Where do they dry the quickest? Why?
10. Take a walk in a light rain. What happens to the surfaces of the playground in the rain? Write your own class book of rain as did students in a first-grade class in Nevada, who wrote *Rain Song* (Evans, 1995).
11. Catch snowflakes on a piece of dark construction paper.
12. Read Tomie dePaola's (1975) *The Cloud Book*, the story of the 10 most common clouds identified in myth and story. Go outside, identify the clouds in the sky, and predict what the weather will be like. Then ask children to write their own myths or stories.

Kindergarten and primary children can begin long-term recording of weather conditions in the form of a timeline with symbols for sunny, cloudy, cold, or warm days and other seasonal weather conditions. Children can also make charts or booklets of "Things We Do in Winter," "Clothes We Wear in Summer," or "Foods We Eat in Summer" to focus attention on how the seasons affect people and their activities. Again, children's comments, questions, and products can serve as assessments.

DIRECTION AND LOCATION

Directionality is a projection of a sense of body-sidedness (laterality) into objective space. As the child projects his body-sidedness into space, he is constructing for himself the coordinates of left-right, up-down, and front-back. Thus, through body movement, the child builds directional orientation.

Human development takes place in space. By the time infants are a month or two old, they are exploring space around them by visual and tactile means. When children begin to walk, their investigations become more active and widespread. By 2 years of age, a child constructs what Piaget (1965) terms *sensorimotor space*—not the abstract representation of space an adult creates but something bound up with the individual's sense of self and with motor activities.

The initial concepts of space that develop from children's actions and direct experience of moving in space provide the basis for the subsequent formation of representational space. The child's discovery of space and of directionality within space will not be completed until the beginning of adolescence (Marzoff & DeLoache, 1994).

Children with physical disabilities that limit their mobility have a special need to experience space. Children who cannot move for themselves still need to experience space, direction, and location. One teacher took the time to position children with physical disabilities around tables in a circle to play games that other children experience. She believed that these children, even though restricted to a table, needed to experience playing Looby Loo, Farmer in the Dell, and the other games that help children orient themselves in space. She also planned field trips into the community so the children could use maps, follow directions, and experience themselves in a larger space. Using two vans and a volunteer for each child, the group visited fast-food restaurants, doughnut shops, supermarkets, and the gas station—places often visited by children, but not always available to children with severe physical disabilities.

Through moving in space, children gain concepts of directionality.

Movement Exploration

A geography curriculum designed to help children orient themselves in space is a program of movement exploration. Movement exploration begins with the children becoming aware of their bodies and the things their bodies can do in space (Sanders, 2002). Children are made aware of the following:

1. Body awareness—the shape of the body in space, where the different body parts are, how the body moves and rests, the body's behavior when combined with other bodies, how the voice is a part of the body.
2. Force and time—being limp, energetic, light, fluid, staccato, slow, or quick.
3. Space—where the body is in a room; the body's level: high (erect posture or in the air), middle (crawling or stooping), or low (on the floor); the body's direction (forward, backward, or sideways); body size (bigness or smallness); the body's path through space; and extensions of the body parts into space.
4. Locomotion—movement through space at various levels and speeds: lowest (wriggling, rolling, or scooting), middle (crawling, crouching, or using four limbs—ape walk), or highest (walking, running, skipping, galloping, sliding, leaping, hopping, and jumping); slow, medium, fast.
5. Weight—relationship of body to the ground, ways to manage body weight in motion and in relation to others, body collapse, body momentum.
6. Working with others—collaborating with others to solve problems, develop trust, explore strength and sensitivity, and feel a sense of belonging.
7. Isolations—how individual body parts (head, shoulders, arms, hands, elbows, wrists, neck, back, upper torso, ribs, hips, legs, knees, ankles, feet) can move (swinging, jerking, twisting, shaking, lifting, tensing, relaxing, becoming fluid, pressing, gliding, floating, flicking, slashing, punching, dabbing).
8. Repetitions—getting to know a movement and how it feels when repeated often; being able to repeat a shape or action.

The teacher acts as a guide and offers children a challenge or a problem to solve. You might say, "Show how many different ways you can walk," "Make your body very tall; very small," or "How many different ways can you move across the room?" Children select their own level of participation and creativity as they respond. The teacher can take anecdotal notes on children's responses as an assessment of understanding. You can comment to help them analyze their movements and become aware of (a) their relationship to the physical environment, (b) their bodies and what they can do, and (c) the components of movement—speed, direction, and force.

To increase and clarify the concepts of directionality stemming from movement exploration, have children write booklets or construct charts. These can be called "I Can Move" and can illustrate in writing and pictures the ways in which children move: fast or slow; high, low, or sideways; with their hands touching the floor; on one or two feet; hop, skip, or slide; move with someone else; and so forth. These can serve as assessments.

Directional Terms

You can introduce games to help children develop concepts of up and down and other terms suggesting directionality. Ask a child to stand by any object in the room. Now ask another child to name a different object in the room. The first child must identify body position in relation to the named object—for example, in back of the desk, on the side of the workbench, in front of the window. Kindergarten children can begin this game. The more experienced children may be able to respond by saying, "The teacher's desk is on my right side" using directional terms. Preschool children may begin more simply by placing a teddy bear "in front of the desk." Anecdotal notes serve as an assessments.

Up and Down

To learn concepts of up and down, children can sing "The Noble Duke of York," acting it out as they sing and pretending to be mountain climbers, rain, snow, falling leaves, airplanes, kites, or floating dandelion seeds. Teachers can play other games to check children's growth in understanding directions by having individuals place a truck, a doll, or a block in positions that the teacher or another child suggests. You can say to a child, "Place Raggedy Ann on top, over, under, to the side of, behind, next to, or to the right of the sand table," using terms the children need to learn.

Left and Right

Concepts of left and right develop very gradually. A study in England revealed that even 8- and 9-year-old children could not accurately identify left and right in many cases. Learning the concept of left and right occurs as children move in space, grow, and mature. These concepts will develop with time and with many experiences of moving and exploring space (Roberts & Aman, 1993).

You can use the terms *left* and *right* incidentally but always in connection with a real situation. You could ask the children to put the double blocks to the left of the cars when picking up blocks, to hold the bike with the left foot while reaching for something else, to park the wagon on the right, or to walk on the left side of the street on a field trip. Children can experience other left and right situations while playing Simon Says, Hokey Pokey, Looby Loo, or Follow the Leader. You will want to introduce children to the concept and allow them opportunities to experience it.

Cardinal Directions

Children as old as 12 years of age do not appear to have a complete grasp of cardinal directions. Frank Lord (1941) demonstrated that many children are not aware of cardinal directions until they have nearly reached adulthood. Children in our culture, with its abundant signs and guideposts, appear to have no pressing practical need to become direction-conscious; many of them, indeed, do not develop this awareness. Yet the ability to orient oneself and to acquire a sense of direction is essential. To foster this ability, activities with cardinal directions should be informal and used as they apply to the actual experiences of young children.

One study, however, has demonstrated that direct teaching of cardinal directions to children in grades 1, 2, and 3 can be successful. Howe's (1969) study consisted of taking children outdoors around 8:45 a.m. to observe the position of the sun and telling them that this was the eastern part of the sky. The same process, conducted from a new location, was repeated as weather conditions permitted. After the children mastered the concept that the sun was in the part of the sky called the east, Howe proceeded to the second step, asking children in what part of the sky the sun appeared in the morning.

Steps 3 and 4 helped children acquire an association between the noon sun and the southern part of the sky. Leaving the school in advance of the usual 11:30 a.m. lunchtime, Howe established an association between south and east by asking the children where the sun had been in the morning. The fifth and sixth steps associated the later afternoon sun with the western part of the sky; this direction, in turn, was associated with the others by reviewing where the sun was at noon and in the morning.

Howe next introduced a shadow stick, and the children developed more complex skills. This apparatus was constructed of a square foot of board, with a 30-inch stick, not more than an inch wide, rising from the center of the board and perpendicular to it. The children took the shadow stick on field trips when they left the playground and used it to find the cardinal directions wherever they were.

At the end of 10 weeks, Howe tested the children. More than 50 percent of the first-graders could answer correctly all the questions pertaining to cardinal directions; 75 percent of the second- and third-graders were successful in answering all the questions. Howe concluded that young children, if taken outdoors, can be taught cardinal directions in relation to the sun and that this teaching would later lead to the elimination of confusion over cardinal directions that many of us still have.

Relative Position

For developing concepts of relative position, second- or third-grade children can play a game called Who Is at My Side. Ask one child to stand before the group, facing away from the children. Ask another child to stand to the left or right of the first child. Give directions to the child standing on the side: "Stand in front of the child who is 'It'; stand in back; stand facing; stand to the left." All the children can take turns with this game and the teacher can take anecdotal notes on their responses.

After children are familiar with the game, ask a group of three to stand in front of the class with their backs to the others. Ask the middle child to tell who is standing on the left or right. Then the other two children can each tell where the middle child is in relation to them.

Location

Concepts of location begin to develop as infants explore and attend to the qualities of things in their environment, including their own bodies and visual and tactile senses. From age 14 months to 3 years, children can distinguish between objects that are near and can be grasped and those farther away, and can begin to distinguish the space boundaries of their immediate environment, such as the bedroom or the yard.

Initially, infants work out their own location and then go on to discern the whereabouts of other objects in their environment. With increasing visual skills and mobility, children expand their space boundaries. The greater the children's opportunities to roam about, the greater their ability to keep track of position and location.

By the early preschool years, children have an understanding of the spatial relationships between objects. Children express these concepts as they build with blocks, play with sand and water, and construct with other materials. Throughout the preschool and primary grades, children's concepts of location continue to develop and are refined through their direct exploration of their immediate neighborhood and community.

Many concepts of location can be developed through children's experiences in the school and community. Activities that foster concepts of location include the following:

- Ask the children to locate their classroom while on the playground or in front of the school building. Can they locate the office and the lunchroom? After walking around the building to another place, can they locate their room again?
- Take the children for a walk inside the school to find the signs that indicate location. Some schools may even have a map by the office door showing the school's floor plan. Other signs might include the exit and entrance and signs over the stairs.
- Take the children outside to find street signs that indicate location: the sign that names the street where the school is located or the address of the school. Walk around the school with the children and ask them to tell how they would locate it if there were no street signs or addresses.
- Use the children's addresses to teach concepts of location. Ask them to draw a picture for or write a letter to their parents. Then either dictate or write the children's addresses on their envelopes and mail them. Make a bulletin board of "Our Neighborhood"; the children can exhibit drawings of their houses and label them with their addresses.
- Make a class address book listing children's names, addresses, and phone numbers.
- Role-play a visitor game. Have a child pretend to be new to the area. The other children will help the visitor locate a street or a specific point in the classroom, school, or neighborhood.

Concepts of location are, in part, concepts of direction because being able to orient oneself in space means locating oneself in space. Concepts of location also include understanding distance.

Distance and Measurement

Watching children at play, you can see them use their hands, feet, or sticks to measure off boundaries and distances. The concept of distance is important to the study of geography as well as for day-to-day living. It seems crucial, however, that experiences with the measurement of distance be informal, arbitrary, incidental, and based on actual experiences; children who cannot conserve quantities cannot understand measurement.

Piaget (1952) concluded that "there could be no more striking evidence that measurement is impossible without conservation of the quantities to be measured, for the very good reason that quantities that are not conserved cannot be composed" (p. 225).

The Nuffield Mathematics Project (1969) suggested that teachers begin to introduce concepts of distance as children play by building on the vocabulary that children use in their play. Children all use the word "big"; the teacher can expand the children's meaning of "big" by using words such as "near," "far," "high," "low," "deep," "wide," "tall," "long," "up," and "down."

Recognizing the importance of play, the Nuffield Project recommended that teachers use all the play situations they can to refine children's vocabulary. In addition, it is helpful to ask children to think of the largest, the deepest, the nearest, and the farthest thing they know. You can play a riddle game with the class: "I am thinking of something nearer than … ; I am thinking of something farther than … but not as far as …".

Children can use arbitrary measures—hands, feet, lengths of string or ribbon—as well as standard measures—rulers, yardsticks—to measure from one side of the room to the other, all the way around the desk, or to the top of the bookshelf. Preschool children play with rulers, tape measures, and yardsticks at the woodworking bench to simulate carpenter play but do not use them as actual measuring tools.

Here are some other materials children might use for measuring:

- They can use trundle wheels to measure around the playground or the length of the hall, the room, or the school building. At least two children can use the wheel: one to push it and the other or several others to record the clicks.
- Bamboo sticks or broom handles are useful measuring sticks.
- Although preschool children will not use odometers as measuring tools, they can use one on a field trip to see that distance is measured in this way, too.

Distance and measurement can easily be integrated with math and age-appropriate mathematical standards.

Maps and Globes

Maps are used to help people position themselves on the earth. Because maps are abstractions of reality, the skills needed to read and use them do not develop completely until children reach the age of 11 or 12. The ability to use maps requires an understanding of the following concepts:

- The map is a representation. It is a small picture of a much larger place from a bird's-eye view.
- Symbols have meaning.
- The map is a way to orient oneself in space, which requires an understanding of location and direction.

For children to conceptualize the total relationship of a map to the objects it represents or to infer information based on those relationships, they need a cognitive maturity not possible during the preschool–primary years. Maturity, however, is not enough. Without a foundation of spontaneous, playful, and exploratory experiences

Children learn that maps represent space and location.

with maps, children, no matter how mature cognitively, will not be successful map readers or users.

Introducing Maps

When planning to introduce maps and map-reading concepts to young children, you might want to (a) survey the children to find out what their concepts are, (b) remember that all mapping must be done in connection with the children's own experiences, and (c) identify a few key concepts from the numerous skills involved in map reading.

Survey the Children. Showing the children a map of their city or town, you ask, "What is this used for?" "Have you ever seen one before?" "What do maps tell you?" "What do you know about maps?" "What are these lines for?" "What does this blue part stand for?" Other clues for questions arise as the children discuss their experiences with maps. Answers such as "It shows you where you live" or "There's the ocean" give you an idea of the children's knowledge of maps and can direct lesson plans toward extending this knowledge.

Young children seem to have a personal understanding of maps. Researchers have found that, without any hesitation or need for prompting, children as young as age 3 interpreted aerial photographs and maps in geographical terms. They identified roads and decoded other environmental features. Although the children could not explain perspective, scale, or how the photos and maps were constructed, they did understand the concept of map.

Research has not yet demonstrated the exact developmental sequence of children's understanding of maps. Experiences with maps in the preschool–primary classroom should be based on children's actual experiences and used to acquaint children with maps and map reading in order to build a foundation they can use later, when they have the maturity to think more abstractly (Gouteux, 2001; Miller, 1985; Mosenthal & Kirsch, 1991). Teachers can assess children's understanding of maps and mapping and provide activities that build on their current knowledge.

Use Firsthand Experiences.   Mitchell (1934) wrote, "I'm afraid of words with no images" (p. 18). Already an abstraction, maps must be introduced to children in relation to their actual experiences. Many concrete opportunities present themselves for introducing maps. A field trip to visit a neighbor or buy a flower at the local nursery can find children consulting a map, while the arrival of a new student can have children locating the newcomer's neighborhood on a large map.

Three- and 4-year-olds can play with small picture maps in the housekeeping/dramatic play area and with wheel toys, cars, and trucks on a map rug. Board games such as Candy Land, Cherry Tree, Chutes, and Ladders involve basic mapping concepts.

Five-year-olds begin to use maps in connection with their experiences. Using personal knowledge, they can follow a map as they walk on a field trip or find a hidden treasure on the playground. The children enjoy a map showing the school, where they live, and the routes they follow to school.

Over the age of 5, children use maps as they build with blocks and will make maps of their school and room. By the primary grades, maps are a regular part of classroom activities, with children locating their homes and places far away from them on maps, globes, or GoogleEarth.

One third-grade classroom mapped e-mail friends. Using their families' e-mail addresses, children sent out e-mails requesting responses. They wanted to see how many different places e-mails came from and would place a pin on the map location of each e-mail they received in return. They found that their families had friends all around the world.

In one study, children in the primary grades said they liked maps, but when questioned, they did not really grasp the concept of maps. Using constructivist theories, cooperative learning, and other cognitive strategies, however, these second-graders were able to develop an understanding of maps and the ability to use them in their everyday lives (Whiteside, 2000).

Children of all ages need to draw and write about their observations with maps. Researchers find that children who are encouraged to represent their experiences through drawing and writing gain a better understanding of mapping concepts. By creating their own journal pages and drawings, children are able to depict their ways of seeing and understanding, constructing, or reconstructing the phenomena through their own lens of experiences (Shepardson & Britsch, 2000).

Develop Concepts.   Key concepts can help you plan for teaching map reading to young children. Before children can fully comprehend maps, they must understand representation, symbolization, perspective, and scale.

The concept that one object can represent another is not new to young children. They have looked at pictures representing cars, trees, or animals and have seen photographs representing themselves. To fully understand maps, children must be able to understand that a map represents something else—a place.

MAPPING OF THE	GRADE	MATERIAL	
Classroom	* 2–3	Blocks	From the concrete to the abstract
School	K–3	Boxes	
Playground	K–3	Dollhouses	
House	K–3	Sticks	
Route to school	K–3	Paper	
Immediate neighborhood	1–3		
Wider community	1–3	Drawing materials	

*Years of age (child care or preschool)

Figure 8.3 Continuum of mapping experiences.

The idea that a map represents a place can be taught to children as they make their own maps. "Young children make maps before they read them" (Mitchell, 1934, p. 91). It may be that the children have already begun making 3-D maps as they work with blocks—laying out streets, shopping centers, and airports.

Blocks and other three-dimensional building objects, which give children a semiconcrete experience, are useful in map construction and in fostering the understanding that maps do represent some other thing. Using blocks, you and the children can work together to make a map of their room or playground. When using blocks to map the playground, classroom, or nearby neighborhood, you can help the children orient their building in the correct direction. Children can construct "cardboard cities" of their neighborhood using various sizes and shapes of cereal and crackers boxes and milk cartons (Figure 8.3).

After children have become familiar with the idea of using blocks to represent a place that is familiar to them, they can transfer their map-making activities to paper. A walk around the block is an excellent time to draw a simple map of the area to consult during future walks (Figures 8.4A and B).

Rearranging furniture in a classroom provides additional opportunities for making maps. During informal work time, one teacher began to arrange different pieces of construction paper on a larger sheet. Curious children were asked to help "find a way to arrange the furniture." Telling them that this was a floor plan map of their room and that the red paper represented the piano, the blue paper the bookshelf, and the yellow paper the tables, the teacher and children moved the pieces around until they were satisfied with the arrangement. Later, the teacher and the children used this room map to place the furniture. Stimulated by this activity, the children made similar maps of their bedrooms, their houses, and their routes to school.

After traveling to someplace in the city or community, children often represent their trip by building the visited places with their blocks. To foster mapping concepts, Mitchell (1934) often added strips of blue oilcloth and long brown paper to the supplies of blocks. The children used these to lay out streets and to represent water as they constructed with the blocks, further extending their concept of representation.

One teacher in New York City created a floor map of Manhattan for children to use with their blocks. This map, about 10 by 20 feet, was constructed using brown wrapping paper and colored construction paper and was covered with clear plastic. Using their personal experiences and ideas as a guide, the children erected buildings representing the Empire State Building and the Wall Street area.

264 Chapter 8

Figure 8.4A Map of route to school by a 4-year-old.

Figure 8.4B Map of route to school by a 6-year-old.

Children can also make maps from large pieces of linoleum, varnished wrapping paper, or canvas. When such maps are placed on the floor, 3- to 8-year-olds build small-scale buildings, bridges, and lighthouses on them, working out their own ideas of scale, direction, location, perspective, and orientation.

Mitchell (1934) called this type of map a *tool-map*. Tool-maps are not accurate maps. They are "rough maps which are not an end in themselves, but a means to better play and better thinking" (p. 28). Tool-maps, which can be made by the teacher or the children themselves, force children to actively work out relationships and organize their thinking.

All map play and map making designed to foster the development of the idea of representation should stem from children's own experiences and be on a continuum from the concrete to the abstract.

Using incidental experiences and the children's interests expands children's understandings of the concept of representation with maps. Children who are moving to another city or state or who have entered the class from another state can be shown on a map where they have come from or where they will be moving. In multicultural classrooms, children can use maps to locate their family's country of origin (Brophy & Alleman, 2005). You can help children route visits to grandparents, vacations, and other trips, showing them on a road map where they will travel. News stories of interest to the children can also create occasions for you to use a map or a globe to show the children where the event has taken place.

Play with maps may also foster children's understanding that maps represent places. You can put road maps near the bikes, in the housekeeping area, or near the wheel toys and blocks, encouraging children to use a map to "take a trip." Some commercial table-block games come equipped with maps for arranging trees, houses, buildings, and cars, giving children another experience in the representational nature of maps.

A map, itself a symbol for a place, uses other symbols. Colors symbolize land and water, lines symbolize roads and railroad tracks, and other symbols are used for houses, churches, or schools. Children are already familiar with some symbols—letters for the sounds in their names, traffic signs—and can learn how other symbols are used in maps.

While constructing their own maps, children will often want to portray trees, playground equipment, cars, and other things in the environment. You can present these symbols in pictorial form during their initial experiences. As their understanding of symbolization increases, you can introduce more abstract symbols.

To help children see the use of symbolization in maps, you might pin a small picture or cutout figure of each child to a map of the country to show each child's birthplace. Later, you can substitute a thumbtack or a pin in place of the picture.

Color is used in a variety of ways on maps to symbolize different types of data. Young children can understand that the blue areas on the map generally represent water and other areas—brown, green, or some other color—symbolize land.

You might introduce primary children to the use of a map's key and teach them how to use a map's legend. They might make their own maps, using colors to represent land and water and lines to represent railroad tracks, highways, or boundaries.

Children create their own maps.

Primary children can add map titles, legends, and compass roses. *Mapping Penny's World* (Leedy, 2000) is a helpful picture book that children enjoy.

The assessment of children's maps should not focus on their accuracy, but on children's understanding of the concepts (Figure 8.5).

The concept that a map pictures a place as if you were looking at it from above is often difficult for young children to grasp. You must foster their understanding of a bird's-eye view.

Perspective is a most difficult concept for young children, but you can introduce it. Children may not develop a complete understanding of looking down on the top of an object, yet you can expose them to the idea of a bird's-eye view. Living in New York City gave Mitchell (1934) the opportunity to take her kindergartners to the top of a tall building to look down on the city. Following this trip, children's drawings indicated that they had gained the idea of perspective.

You can provide other experiences, such as taking the children to various elevations to view the neighborhood or carefully standing on chairs to look down on something placed on the floor in the classroom. Photos depicting the same area from different points of view can help children gain experience with this concept as can books such as *Me on the Map* (Sweeney, 1996).

A block activity you might introduce in the primary grades involves asking children to select one block and trace around it on a piece of paper. Next, ask the children to see how many blocks of the same size and shape they can fit onto the form on the paper, piling one block on top of the other. This activity demonstrates to

> Assessing children's map skills is a continuous activity done on an individual and group basis using observations and structured interviews with individual children.
>
> **Map Skills**
>
> How often, and where, do children play with maps?   Date   Date   Date
> - Housekeeping area
> - Blocks
> - With wheeled toys
> - Other
>
> How often do children   Dates
> - Refer to maps as if they were taking a trip?
> - Talk about something on a map?
> - Consult a map as they are building/painting?
> - Try to locate a place?
> - Refer to scale (e.g., "This is much smaller.")?
> - Talk about perspective (e.g., "It's like a bird looking down.")?
> - Draw, paint, or build maps?
>
> Which children use maps?   Names
>
> Which children do not use maps?   Names

Figure 8.5 Assessing children's mapping skills.

them that, no matter how high they build, the shape of the block on top remains the same as the shape drawn on their paper. This shape, which shows only the top of the block, represents the way that maps show only the tops of areas. Experiences such as these may not fully develop the concept of perspective in young children, yet they will form a foundation on which you can build future learning (Figure 8.6).

Some computer programs and Internet sites for children give them the opportunity to manipulate graphical perspective of objects and areas. Google Earth (*earth.google.com*) is a 3-D computer model of the earth. It enables the viewer to "fly" around the earth, exploring geography and places. One teacher has described his use of Google Earth with primary children (Britt & LaFontaine, 2009). First, he reviewed basic map skills and vocabulary. Then he led the children on a tour of the school, using a map for each child. Back in the classroom, he modeled on the board how to draw a map of the school by hand. Then he introduced Google Earth and used the search feature to "fly" to the school. On the second day, the teacher paired a map of the town with a Google Earth view. Children used these resources to write directions

---

| Name _____ | Date _____ |

You will need a small map to show the child and paper and markers or crayons.

Show the child the map and ask: <u>Correct</u>   <u>Incorrect</u>
    What is this?
    What do we use it for?
    Point to various symbols and ask:
      • What do these lines (street, highway) mean?
      • What does this blue (river, lake, ocean) mean?
      • What does this bell (school) mean?
    Why is the map so small?

Give the child a piece of paper and markers and ask the child to draw a map of how he would go from the school to his home.
Judge the map:
    The child's map demonstrated: <u>Yes</u>   <u>No</u>
      • Understanding of scale
      • Perspective
      • Use of symbols
      • Knowledge of place

Figure 8.6 Individual evaluation of children's mapping skills.

from school to a local restaurant. On the third and fourth days, he taught landforms by combining Google Earth with hands-on activities. They used maps, photographs, and Google Earth to investigate regions such as the African plains, the Rocky Mountains, the Amazon River, the Sahara Desert, and their own local region. Children made written observations and created Play-Doh models of each landform. For the final assessment, each child was given a list of landforms. The teacher "flew" to a region using Google Earth and the children had to identify each landform.

While you need to adjust these activities to the children in your classroom, note that the teacher tied the use of the technology to concrete objects and experiences throughout the unit. He also made extensive use of questioning to promote thinking about the concepts. Such technological tools, when coupled with the concrete and careful questioning, can help children do the following:

- Develop spatial knowledge
- Develop a deeper understanding of the earth
- Understand that a globe is a model of the earth
- Describe and locate places and geographic features such as countries, continents, bodies of water, landforms, and even their own town and school (Britt & LaFontaine, 2009)

Maps reduce the size of an actual place. Children can be introduced to the idea that a map is like the original place except it is much smaller. Making maps small makes it easier for people to think about the place and to hold the map.

You can plan simple experiences with scale for young children. It will be some years before they can interpret the scale of distance on a map, yet they can understand the concept of scale—a map shows a real area made smaller (Liben & Downs, 1993). Comparing the children's floor plans, block maps, or maps they use to find where they were born, you can continually point out that each is a map—just like the thing it represents, only smaller.

Photos of the children and pictures of familiar things are useful in demonstrating the concept of scale: "This is a picture of you. It's just like you, only you're much bigger and this picture is very small." You can use model cars, boats, doll furniture, and dolls in the same manner, pointing out that there is a difference between the real object and the toy: "The toy is smaller; it's not real; it's a scale model." When Karl rushed into the classroom with a map of his bedroom, he told the other children, "It shows my bedroom just like it is, only this is much smaller." The teacher realized that Karl was beginning to grasp the concept of scale.

RELATIONSHIPS WITHIN PLACES

Geographers study how humans and environments are related, what advantages and disadvantages are present for human settlement, and how people modify and adapt to the environment. They try to find out why people live where they do, what the potentials are of this place or that, and how much of what is where.

The basic concept for children is that people impact their environment, and the environment impacts people. Young children can be introduced to the idea that humans have taken control of their environment but, at the same time, are also controlled by their environment. For example, to introduce children to the idea that they can control the nature of their world, they might do the following:

- They can look at the way in which they control their own environment. Children in kindergarten and the primary grades could work with you to arrange and rearrange their room or the playground. Where should the new shelf be placed? If it is placed against the wall, how will children be able to reach it? Will placing it at an angle disrupt the flow of traffic to and from the bathrooms?
- They can take trips into the neighborhood to observe others changing the nature of their physical world. Children can observe people creating hills, ponds, and flat surfaces to build roads or make room for new buildings.
- They can control the environment around their school, perhaps planting a garden, flowers, or shrubs or taking part in building a sand area.
- They can visit a private farm or a farm maintained by the city parks to acquaint children with farm life. At the farm, children can be introduced to the idea that people use soil, water, and sun to grow crops. They build fences to keep animals secured and use ponds or streams for their water (Fromboluti & Seefeldt, 1999).

- They can observe how others have shaped their environment. Children in the primary grades might visit a bonsai garden or a reservoir, take a trip through a tunnel that goes under water or through a mountain, or observe a house being built on a hillside.

Humans respond to the environment. In the primary grades, children may begin to explore why people settled where they did or how they used the resources of the land. Preschool and primary children can do the following activities:

- They can take a trip over a river and talk about why people built bridges over the water.
- They can observe the weather and identify what they can and cannot do outside (e.g., if it is raining, we cannot have outdoor recess).
- They can go for a walk in the woods or go camping. It is easy to understand why we wear long pants and shoes where there are rocks and brambles on the ground and to realize the importance to early settlers of being near water when you no longer have the convenience of a faucet (Fromboluti & Seefeldt, 1999).
- They can take a nature walk through a park or a wildlife reserve to learn about local plants and wildlife and how natural features change over time.
- They can find out the name of the city they live in or the name of the city nearest to them. Third-graders can take a trip to a nearby city and speculate on why people settled in an area.
- They can relate what they are learning about the needs of living things (water, food, air, shelter) to where people did and did not settle.

SPATIAL INTERACTIONS

Regardless of where we live, we interact with others far from us. A part of the study of geography is understanding that people interact with others far from them. We depend on other places for food, clothes, and even items like pencils and paper. We share information with each other using phones, newspapers, computers, radio, and television to bridge the distances. People live in places different from where we live. People move from place to place. Children can do the following:

- They can take a trip to the local supermarket to observe the food delivery system. Children can chart the types of trucks used to deliver the goods and find out where the goods came from, who grew the produce, and how many different types of preparation were required—picking, packing, canning—before the food got to the supermarket.
- They can make a graph of the transportation systems they have traveled on. They might graph the boats, buses, trains, or cars they have been in.
- They can find out how many different ways they can move on the surface of the earth. They might walk, run, hop, skip, jump, crawl; use a bike, a wagon, roller skates; and so forth.
- They can explore how animals move on, through, or above the earth or in the water.

- They can study the school's communication system, noting all of the machines used in the school for this purpose.
- They can use the mail system, writing and sending letters to one another or to their parents.

The booklet *Early Childhood: Where Learning Begins, Geography* (Fromboluti & Seefeldt, 1999) lists other ways of fostering the idea of spatial interaction:

- Give children opportunities to travel by or read about travel by car, bus, bicycle, or on foot. Whenever possible, take other forms of transportation, such as airplanes, trains, subways, ferries, barges, and horses and carriages. If not possible, read books that include such travel.
- Use a map to look at various routes you can take when you try different methods of transportation.
- Watch travel videos and movies.
- Primary children can play a license plate game, looking at as many different states' plates as they can and noting what each plate tells about the specific state. Children might focus on the plates of parked cars.
- Let primary children walk around the school building and identify where things come from. They might even look at labels in their own clothing to determine where their clothes came from. At lunch, talk about where the foods were grown. Where is the nearest dairy? Where did the bananas and oranges come from? How did they get to the school? This presents many opportunities for integration with economics.
- Have primary children chart their family history by asking relatives where they came from. They could find these places on a map and make a chart of them or make their own chart, mapping their own birthplace. They could discuss how and why they or their ancestors left this place or stayed.
- Interview older people to find out what the neighborhood was like when they were young. Specifically, ask about how they traveled, how they communicated with people far away, the foods they ate, the clothes they wore, and the schools they attended. How have things changed since the older people were children?

REGIONS

A region is an area that includes a number of places—all of which have something in common. Geographers categorize regions in a number of basic ways, two of which are physical and cultural. Physical regions are defined by a particular type of climate, landform, or vegetation. A cultural region has a cultural and historical continuity that separates it from other adjacent or distinct regions. In these areas, people may speak the same language, observe the same holidays, practice similar religions, and share political identity.

Physical Regions

All children live in a community of some kind. You can take the class on trips into a neighboring community to acquaint them with its characteristics. As children

Trips acquaint children with the concept of physical regions.

walk through the community, you can ask, "Why do people live near one another?" and "What do you think makes a neighborhood?" Back in the classroom, they could list all the things they found in the neighborhood. You can also use photographs and the visual discovery process.

Primary children might be asked to differentiate how geographic areas in their community are alike and different. The students might take a trip to a park, a shopping center, or an industrial area and chart changes within these areas over the year. Students can interview people living or working in the regions to find out how the changes affect their lives. Photos and Google Earth can be used to observe characteristics of different regions vicariously.

Integrating the study of regions with the study of habitats in science helps children see the connections between a region and how life is affected by the environment.

Cultural Regions

Culture is transmitted through language, art, music, and games (see Chapters 6 and 11). Children of all ages can be introduced to the songs, rhymes, arts, and oral traditions of their culture and the culture of others. Preschoolers enjoy learning nursery rhymes, role-playing them, and even creating new endings for the rhymes. Involve parents in learning rhymes by asking them what rhymes, folktales, and sayings they were taught as children. The parents could visit the class and teach them to the entire group to expose children to a variety of cultural traditions.

Primary-age children, who glory in learning new words, enjoy learning words of another language as well as songs and simple poems in other languages. They can learn how other cultures play familiar games and compare them to the games they play themselves. For example, hopscotch is played in nearly every culture in the world. Teach children how to play hopscotch. Then teach them how to play Vietnamese hopscotch. For this hopscotch, two children wrap arms around each other's backs and hop together from square to square. If either touches a line, both are out of the game and another couple takes a turn. Ask children to interview their grandparents, parents, and other relatives to find out how they played hopscotch. As a group, review the many ways to play hopscotch, make a chart of similarities and differences, speculate why hopscotch differs among cultures, and vote on your favorite way to play hopscotch.

Cultural regions are defined by art, music, literature, and social organization. Primary children can do the following:

- Look at the art of many cultures.
- Listen to stories and folktales from other nations and compare them to the folktales and poetry of our country. For example, the common theme of the physically weak triumphing over a bully, found in the Norwegian folktale "The Three Billy Goats Gruff" and the Mexican tale "Borrequita and the Coyote" (Aardema, 1991), illustrates that people, regardless of where they live or what culture they come from, share many of the same feelings. Versions of the Cinderella story occur in several cultures.
- Read and discuss the book *People* by Peter Spier (1980). This beautifully illustrated book shows how people are all different, yet are the same in some ways. The illustrations can be used to explore regions and human–environment interactions as well.

SUMMARY

You can help preschool–primary children develop basic geography concepts by keeping in mind that children learn by doing. They can experience the earth on which they live, learning the names and qualities of its land and water surfaces. They can experience the rhythms of day and night and of changing seasons.

Through movement exploration and other physical activities, children begin to understand the concept of direction. Learning their addresses, taking field trips, and locating themselves and objects in space, children learn the concept of location. They can explore the nature of geographical regions through field trips and vicarious experiences such as movies and technology.

Knowing how people interact, even though they are separated in space, helps children develop the concept of spatial interactions. Moreover, children are introduced to the idea of mapping their world as they draw and build their own maps.

When you teach young children geography concepts, it is important to keep in mind the directives of Mitchell (1934): Children learn by doing, through action, and with concrete experiences.

Discussion Questions

1. You may think of geography as memorizing states and capitals. Geography is so much more. Describe how and why geography is more than memorizing states and capitals. Include the concepts that are foundational for young children.

2. Brainstorm ways to integrate geography with science, math, literature, and the other social studies disciplines.
3. How could you use Google Earth to teach each of the five themes of geography: location, place, region, movement, and human–environment interaction?
4. How can a teacher help to make abstract concepts of geography concrete?
5. Geography involves learning skills, concepts, specific knowledge, and attitudes. Give examples of each.
6. Why is movement important to the learning of geography? How can you use it to teach geography? Why are observational skills important? How can you teach them to young children?
7. Given what we know (and do not know) about how young children develop mapping skills, describe developmentally appropriate practices for teaching mapping skills.
8. Select one of the books from the Children's Literature Box. What standard (NCSS, NAEYC, or local/state) might this book be used to teach? What would a lesson or unit plan that used this book to teach this standard look like?

Extend Your Knowledge

1. Interview a group of 5-, 6-, and 7-year-old children to determine their concepts of land and water. You might ask them to observe a dish with a small amount of water placed in the sun early in the day and again at the end of the day. Ask them what happened to the water. You might do the same with things that float and sink, dissolve, or change form.
2. Working with a small group of children, ask them to construct a map of their classroom with blocks. How do the children indicate understandings of the basic concepts of mapping: representation, symbolization, perspective, and scale?
3. Strengthen your own concepts of geography by reviewing the national geography standards. Which of these standards do you understand? Which could you learn more about?
4. Take a walk around a school's neighborhood. What land forms do you observe? What are the physical characteristics of the area that make it unique? Design a learning experience for primary children based on your findings.

Resources

The National Geographic Society offers many free and inexpensive materials that can be used by teachers to plan social studies experiences as well as materials that children can use. The National Geographic Research and Exploration office of the National Geographic Society can be contacted for copies of *Geography for Life: National Geography Standards* (1994) or you can view the standards online with lesson plans.

www.nationalgeographic.com/xpeditions/standards

The U.S. Department of Education publishes *Early Childhood: Where Learning Begins, Geography* (1999) by Carol Sue Fromboluti and Carol Seefeldt. For a copy, write to U.S. Department of Education, Washington, DC 20208-5520.

Population Connection produces outstanding materials and creates activities for K–12 that help students understand not only population but the various geographic, human, and resource issues affecting an interdependent earth. The activities are linked to social studies standards as well as those for science, math, and literacy.
www.populationconnection.org

Google Earth is a website that enables children to locate and look at places anywhere in the world. The website includes tips and ideas for teachers.
www.earth.google.com, www.GElessons.com, www.googlelittrips.com (integrates Google Earth and literature)

Flat Stanley by Jeff Brown. This book is used to teach children about traveling and letter writing. The official website of the Flat Stanley Project is www.flat-stanley.com. Flat Stanley is also a customized placemark on Google Earth, enabling children to "fly" to various locations based on clues.

Geography from A to Z: Picture Glossary by Jack Knowlton. Uses the conventional globe and the Google Earth virtual globe to connect the real world with geography vocabulary.

The United States Mint website includes lesson plans that can be used for geography as well as the other social studies disciplines.
www.usmint.gov/kids/teachers

Project Wet International. Focus on water education.
www.projectwet.org

GeoLiteracy is a K–8 package of 85 lessons developed by the Arizona Geographic Alliance that teaches geography while practicing reading and writing skills.
alliance.la.asu.edu/geoliteracy

CHAPTER 9

Production, Consumption, and Decision Making: Economics

> **Focus Questions**
>
> After you read this chapter, you should be prepared to respond to the following questions:
>
> - Why is economic literacy important? What is involved in economic literacy?
> - How do children's economic concepts develop?
> - What concepts are key to the study of economics?
> - Why is introducing children to the concept of scarcity important, even in the preschool–primary grades? What economic decisions can young children make?
> - How can you introduce young children to concepts of consumer and producer? What kinds of concrete experiences can you provide?
> - How do you prepare children today for careers tomorrow?

"I'll clean your car for 4 dollars," 6-year-old Sabrina told her grandmother, adding, "When I get 20 more dollars, then I'll have enough dollars to buy a Nintendo Wii."

"Here," said 4-year-old Paul to the clerk, placing a handful of change on the counter. "I'm buying this book for Mark's birthday party."

ECONOMIC LITERACY

Young children are aware of economic concepts because they experience them daily. While children are not ready to reason abstractly about economic issues until they reach the age of 10 or 11, they encounter economic concepts daily and express a high level of interest in them (Seefeldt & Galper, 2000). Since economic illiteracy is widespread, it is important to begin introducing economic concepts early.

Children enter the preschool–primary classroom knowing, at some level, that their wants often exceed their resources, that it takes money to make purchases, and that they can offer some service or product to get money. In preschool and primary classrooms, teachers plan to build and extend children's informal knowledge of economics. They do so not only because children are interested in money and what it can buy for them, but because teachers know that economic literacy is essential for citizens of a democracy (Seefeldt & Galper, 2000).

According to the National Council for the Social Studies (1998) and the National Council on Economic Education (1997), it is critical that all children be economically literate in order to function in today's and tomorrow's global economy. "When students understand economic concepts they're better able to make sense of their world and better prepared for their adult roles as consumers, producers and voters" (Meszaros & Engstrom, 1998, p. 7).

NCSS Standard VII. Production, Distribution, and Consumption, focuses on the unequal distribution of resources, the systems of production and exchange that are designed to improve economic well-being, and the dynamics of economic decision making (NCSS, 2010). Questions for children in the early grades to explore include the following:

- What questions are important to ask about wants, needs, goods, and services?
- Why can't people have everything they want?
- How are goods made, delivered, and used?
- How do people decide what to produce and what services to provide?
- How do we make choices about scarce resources?
- How does the availability of resources influence economic decision making?

Children in the early grades should be able to:

- Ask and find answers to questions about the production, distribution, and consumption of goods and services in the school and community
- Analyze the differences between needs and wants
- Evaluate how the decisions that people make are influenced by the trade-offs of different options
- Examine and evaluate different methods for allocating scarce goods and services in the school and community
- Assess how consumers will react to rising and falling prices for goods and services (NCSS, 2010).

The National Council on Economic Education recommends that, by age 12, children should have developed several kinds of economic knowledge in order to become competent citizens (NCEE, 2002). The association suggests that all children need to be able to do the following:

- Maintain sound personal finances
- Understand and appreciate the contribution of the many groups of workers who produce goods and services
- Interest themselves in the economic system and understand how it operates
- Think critically about economic problems, assume responsibility for them, understand basic economics concepts, make sound economic decisions, and reason logically about key issues that affect their lives
- Be ready to participate in economic production by preparing for future careers

If all people had everything they wanted, then knowledge of economic concepts would not be critical. But today there are major differences between what people need and what they can have. Thus, an accurate and workable image of the social system in general, and the economic system in particular, is increasingly essential to human survival. The concept of scarcity—the difference between the unlimited wants of people and the limited goods, services, and materials available—is a major concern of economic education.

DEVELOPMENT OF ECONOMIC CONCEPTS

Economics is the study of how goods and services are produced and distributed and the activities of people who produce, save, spend, pay taxes, and perform personal services to satisfy their wants for food and shelter, their desire for new conveniences and comforts, and their collective wants for things such as education and national defense.

Children experience economic concepts daily. They observe parents exchanging money for goods, and they themselves participate in paying for some purchases. They receive money as gifts, sometimes saving it in a bank, or they may even participate in opening bank accounts. Advertising convinces children early in life that they need more than they can have, and children make decisions between the things they really need and those they only want.

In their play, children reveal some understanding of economic concepts. They use economic scripts as they play store, pretending to see and purchase goods; they pretend to use money to obtain services. Nevertheless, like their geography and history concepts, children's economic concepts are far from fully developed. Not until after age 9 do children fully understand the value of money and comprehend the idea of credit or profit.

Following Piagetian theory, children's stages of economic understandings have been identified as (a) the unreflective and preoperational level exemplified by a highly literal reasoning based on the physical characteristics of objects or processes, (b) the transitional or emerging reasoning level exemplified by higher-

Children reveal economic concepts through play.

order reasoning and similar to Piaget's concrete operational stage, and (c) the reflective level of economic reasoning.

Researchers have found that 3-year-olds can distinguish between money and other objects but are unable to differentiate between types of coins. Three-year-olds often think that a nickel is worth more than a dime because it is physically larger. Until around 4½ years of age, children are generally unaware that money is needed to purchase things. Three-year-olds may take candy or toys from a store, totally unaware of the fact that money is exchanged for goods (Berti & Bombi, 1988). Children under age 4, however, often "know that you can buy things in stores and recognize money and pretend to pay for things. They know the difference between 'yours' and 'mine' and identify adult activities as 'work'" (Berti & Bombi, 1988, p. 175).

Between ages 4 and 5, children still cannot distinguish between coins and believe that the larger the coin is physically, the more it is worth. However, they are aware that you need money to buy things. Children who are 4 to 5 years old develop play scripts of pretending to ask for and get goods, give and receive money, and go to work, suggesting that children of this age do have concepts of economic exchanges. They still do not understand the function of money in buying and selling but believe that any type of coin is suitable for any type of purchase. No concept of production is present. At age 4 or 5, children believe that shopkeepers get their goods from some other shop, which gives them away without asking for money. These children do not understand that shopkeepers are customers as well (Berti & Bombi, 1988). When asked where milk came from, Josh, a student in Head Start, said, "From the store."

Even though they understand that people go to work to get money, children do not understand the relationship between work and pay. To them, a person works and also gets money rather than gets money *because* she works. When 5-year-old Danny's mother told him she did not have enough money to buy the toy he wanted, he suggested they go to the "money store" to "buy" some more money.

By age 6, children are progressing into concrete operations and have a clearer understanding of money; they can distinguish between and name the various denominations of coins and know which coins will buy more things. They still cling to the idea that the larger and perhaps more elaborate the coin, the more it is worth. First-grader David's father, who traveled a great deal, brought David coins and bills from other countries. David was fascinated with the size, shapes, and colors of the money and was convinced that the coins of other countries were worth "much, much more" than American nickels, dimes, quarters, and bills because "they're so large and so pretty."

Children of this age also continue to believe that the shopkeeper gives customers money but are moving toward the idea that there is a manufacturer who produces goods for which the shopkeeper has to pay. Economic experts suggest that a best practice in economics education involves engaging children in literature, factual and fictional (VanFossen, 2003). Because children are in the concrete stage of thinking, reading books about money such as *Bunny Money* (Wells, 2001), *The Story of Money* (Maestro & Maestro, 1995), *My Rows and Piles of Coins* (Mollet & Lewis, 1999), and *Follow the Money* (Leedy, 2002) can give primary-aged children additional insights into the function of money (also see Figure 9.1).

Around 6 or 7 years of age, children know that, although you do not have to have the exact money to pay for a purchase, you do need enough. They are also moving toward some clarity of employer–employee relationships but are far from any clear understanding of customer and producer concepts (Table 9.1). They can begin to distinguish between needs and wants.

Seven-year-olds can compare coins and understand the value of money. They know that manufacturers are paid, as are employees, and that numerous persons and activities are necessary for the production and exchange of goods and money. Children no longer consider work as going someplace to get money but begin to make a connection between the activity and the benefits (Berti & Bombi, 1988). They now have some idea of production and selling and can describe a few paid occupations that they can actually observe and with which they have direct experience, such as a police officer or a bus driver. They also now seem to understand that people are paid differently for different jobs, but they say that police officers make much more money than doctors or shopkeepers do. Seven- and 8-year-olds can begin to distinguish between natural and human resources.

Between ages 7 and 10, pre-economic ideas are replaced by more accurate and conventional ideas. Nevertheless, not until the period of formal operations, ages 12 and older, are children able to understand that the price of goods is based on the costs of production, which include the cost of labor. They do not understand that the materials necessary for production are not old or broken things, and they still confuse making something with mending something.

> **National Council for the Social Studies Notable Economics Tradebooks for Young Children**
>
> *Joha Makes a Wish: A Middle Eastern Tale* adapted by Eric A. Kimmel. Joha's wishing stick brings him nothing but trouble.
>
> *The Little Red Hen and the Passover Matzah* by Leslie Kimmelman. In this version of a favorite folktale, an industrious hen finds the meaning of Passover despite her lazy friends. Recipe.
>
> *The Life of Rice: From Seedling to Supper* by Richard Sobol. Chronicling the significant role of rice in the cultural and economic lives of the people of Thailand. Photographs, rice facts, rice holidays.
>
> *Farm* by Elisha Cooper. Shows the seasonal activities of farm life, from planting to harvesting, including children's chores.
>
> *Give a Goat* by Jan West Schrock. A fifth-grade class reads a story about Beatrice, a girl in Uganda who was not able to go to school until her family was given a goat, so they could earn money from its milk. The fifth-graders decide how they can help families in need.
>
> *Desperate Journey* by Jim Murphy. The trials of a girl and her family's day-to-day life in 1848, working on the Erie Canal. Historical information.
>
> *Going Fishing* by Bruce McMillan. In Iceland, Friorik and his two grandpas fish, contributing to the country's main export. Encyclopedic entries about Atlantic Cod and Lumpfish, photographs.
>
> *Lunch Money* by Andrew Clements. A sixth-grade boy starts a comic book business at school and learns about economics and friendship.
>
> *Hard Hat Area* by Susan L. Roth. Tells the story of Kristen, a young ironworker, at a skyscraper construction site.
>
> *Miss Bridie Chose a Shovel* by Leslie Connor. A young immigrant girl takes a shovel on her voyage to America in 1856. The shovel provides subsistence, shelter, and safety. Woodcuts.

Figure 9.1 Children's Literature Box for Economics.
Based on NCSS Notable Trade Books for Young People, www.ncss.org/resources.

Table 9.1 Economics Concept Development

Sensorimotor, Age 0–2	*Preoperational, Age 2–6*	*Concrete, Age 6/7–10*
Observes and attends to shape and size of coins Observes shopping, consuming, and purchasing	Plays store, demonstrating initial concepts of consuming and purchasing Counts more or less Recognizes coins/money Knows money is necessary to make purchases Knows that adults "work" Distinguishes between yours and mine	Can compare coins, knows relative value of coins Understands that people work to make money Distinguishes needs and wants Some understanding of employer–employee relationship Some understanding of production and selling Can name several jobs Distinguishes natural and human resources

KEY CONCEPTS

Using knowledge of children's awareness of economic concepts and their direct experiences, teachers can introduce preschool–primary children to essential economic principles. By organizing children's experiences around economic key concepts recommended by *Economics America* (NCEE, 2002) and the National Council for the Social Studies (1998), teachers can introduce children to these main ideas:

- Scarcity: the wants of people everywhere are unlimited, but resources are limited
- The necessity of decisions regarding the use of resources
- The function of production and consumption, the concepts of trade and barter, and the idea that money is exchanged for goods and services
- Jobs and careers: educating children for future career choices and roles

SCARCITY AND DECISION MAKING

Basic to all economic understanding is the concept of scarcity. In every society—classroom, family, neighborhood, state, nation—people have a wide variety of wants and desires. Everyone always seems to need more food, clothing, things, and services than are available or affordable. The concept that everyone wants more goods and services than they can have can be introduced through experiences at school. Later, these experiences can be related to the children's families and neighborhoods.

Wants and Needs

"Daddy, I want a …" Every young child has wants and needs. Learning how to distinguish between wants and needs and how to conserve time, goods, and services may help children develop concepts of scarcity and set the stage for economic decision making.

A good place to start is with the basic needs of living things. People need food, air, water, clothing, and shelter in order to live. People may want cars and toys, but they can live without them. Illustrated bulletin boards and picture-sort activities of needs and wants can help children distinguish between the two. Basic needs of living things can be easily integrated with geography and science.

Involve children's families. Families also have many needs and wants and limited resources to obtain them. Ask the children to name all of the things their families need to live such as shelter, food, and clothing. Since these needs are cultural universals (Brophy & Alleman, 2002, 2005a, 2006, 2007), they can be used to understand needs, wants, and scarcity as well as to extend children's knowledge and understanding of others, both close to them and far away in space and time.

Experiences studying universal human needs include the following:

- Ask children to draw a picture of the home they are living in. Classify these pictures according to type of home. Discuss the need for homes. Discuss

similarities and differences in homes. Do the same with foods or clothing. Use the book *People* (Spier, 1980) to look at homes around the world.
- Read carefully selected stories about the homes of others. For example, reading selections of *Buffalo Hunt* (Freedman, 1995) could lead to a discussion of why the Plains Indians required portable housing (Brophy & Alleman, 2002).
- Primary children could study other forms of shelter. They could branch out to study why some people live in homes built on stilts or in tropical huts.
- *Uncle Willie and the Soup Kitchen* (DiSalvo-Ryan, 1997) is about an uncle who volunteers in a soup kitchen. Primary children could use this book to develop consciousness of the problem of homelessness (Brophy & Alleman, 2002).
- Draw pictures and/or make booklets called "Things My Family Needs" and "Things My Family Wants." Primary children can write as well as draw their ideas.
- Have children discuss the foods they like to eat, why people eat food, what foods they would like to try, what foods they eat only on special occasions, and where foods come from (Alleman & Brophy, 2001).

Families also need clothing. Children can discuss the types of clothing they need for the different seasons in contrast to the clothing they would like to have. A lost-and-found box reinforces the idea of the importance of not having to replace clothing. What does it mean to the children if they lose an item of clothing?

Families also want things. Some want different kinds of recreational activities; other families want pets or better housing, clothing, or cars. Charts and booklets of "Things My Family Wants" and "Things My Family Needs" help children clarify and distinguish needs from wants.

Time is another commodity that must be used wisely. Incidental experiences help children realize that they must make choices about the way they use their time. "If we clean up now, we can have time to . . ." Children should make plans for how they want to use their time. Even 4-year-olds can identify how they would like to begin their day and can list the things they think they will try to accomplish during the morning. When children make plans, they should be able to experience not having enough time to do all of the things they have planned. Recognizing the consequences of decisions is an important learning experience.

Many activities can help children begin to understand that they cannot have everything they want.

1. Ask the children to pretend they can have anything they wish. Ask them to draw, tell, or dictate three wishes. Which of the things they have wished for do they think they will get? Which do they think they will not get? Why can't they have everything they wish for?
2. Make a booklet or folder called "I Wanted, I Want, I Will Want." Encourage children to discuss the things they have wanted in the past, whether they got them, why they wanted them, and if they want them now. Draw or write about these things under the title "I Wanted." Ask them about things they want now and the things they think they will want in the future. Do the children think they will be able to have all of these things?

3. Make dream cloud pictures and have children illustrate things they want in the clouds as their dreams. Again, encourage discussion of the things the children say they want and those things they believe are realistic to have.
4. Tell folktales and stories about wanting things, such as "Cinderella," "King Midas," and "The Rabbit Who Wanted Wings" and discuss the stories. Were the people or animals wise to want the things they did? Why or why not? What things did they really need?

To make these activities meaningful for 4- and 5-year-old children, you might cut collections of pictures from catalogs or magazines so that the children can select pictures of the things that illustrate their ideas and paste them into scrapbooks or on a wall chart for the room. Kindergarten children can draw their own pictures, and children in the primary grades can be encouraged to both illustrate and write their responses.

Many classroom experiences can be used to introduce the concept of scarcity (enough/not enough). What things does the class as a group want? Which things do they need? Do we have enough supplies? If supplies and materials are limited by shrinking budgets, that conservation is a necessity. Scraps can be saved for later use, brushes no longer useful at the easel may be washed and used outdoors for water paint, or junk can be collected for sculpture projects.

The class might obtain some funding from the PTA or the petty cash fund or conduct a fundraising activity. Deciding how to spend this money can be a group project. Make a list of pictures of all the things the children suggest. After the list is made, instruct each child to place a check by the things he or she thinks the class should try to get. Then purchase the item with the most checks. You can then discuss use of the item, how long it will last, how many ways it can be used, and how many children can use it at the same time.

The needs and wants of the school give the children other experiences with the concept of scarcity. First, materialism and commercialism can be eliminated in the classroom. In "Buying More Can Give Children Less," Carol Holst (1999) suggests that teachers can make their classrooms places where children can experience the joy of their own imaginations. By reducing commercial materials and consumerism in classrooms, teachers model the need to use raw and available materials instead of commercial ones. By living with the idea that we might want more than we can have, children are more likely to develop concepts of scarcity.

Kindergarten and primary children can take a walk though the school to identify the things the school needs, or they can interview the principal to find out what he or she considers important for the school to have. What things do the children think are possible for the school to obtain? What things are just dreams?

The playground can be explored with the children naming all of the play equipment they would like to have. Later, in class, the list can be narrowed down to items that the children think are realistic additions, and efforts can be made to obtain them.

Experiences with the concept of scarcity can also arise from the subject of energy conservation (or integrated with the geography topics of reduce, reuse, recycle). The following suggested activities may help children become more aware of energy waste and to think of alternatives to waste:

- Make a list of energy-saving habits, such as turning off lights and appliances not in use, riding a bike or walking instead of using a car, and limiting water use.
- Find something at home or in the classroom to recycle or repair, such as a toy or a shelf.
- Work on a recycling project, such as collecting aluminum or newspapers from parents or others in the community.
- Using the book *Allowance Kit, Junior!: A Money System for Little Kids* (Searls, 1997), primary children can create budgets for themselves.

Decision Making

The ability to make wise decisions is an integral part of the study of scarcity. People cannot have everything they want—and sometimes not even everything they need. People must make decisions about which things they need and which they want and choices among the things they want. Children can find many opportunities for making choices within the classroom. Children, who have had little opportunity to make decisions about their lives—which families they will have, the school or church they will go to, the neighborhood they will live in, or the clothes or food they use—need classrooms that are replete with opportunities to make choices and to experience the consequences of their choices. Teachers of young children seek to give them the widest possible freedom to choose what to play with, how to play, and how to make things with a minimum of restrictive control.

It is also important for young children to be able to make decisions and experience their results in a secure classroom environment. According to Dewey (1944), there is no way to learn other than to experience the consequences of an action, yet children must have the right to make mistakes without the loss of self-esteem. As children experience the initial frustration of having made a poor decision, they can learn how to live with the consequences of that decision and ways to decide more wisely next time.

Children can make decisions about which materials to use and how to use them; what to sing, play, or dance; where to plant the seeds; which group of children they want to work with; and even what things they want to learn. Other experiences with decision making include the following:

1. Read a poem such as "The Animal Store" by Rachel Field. The children can act out the roles of pet-store owner, the children purchasing pets, and all of the pets that might be found in the store. Discuss what they would buy if they had fifty dollars to spend. Let the children make murals or pictures of the things they would buy.
2. Have children circle items that they would like to have in toy or other catalogs. Question the children: "Pick out the one toy you want. How did you decide on that toy?" For older children: "You each have 10 dollars to spend. Shopping in

this catalog, decide on a purchase. Why did you choose that instead of something else?"
3. Let the children decide what items to buy for a class project or party. Discuss what they want in relation to what is available and how much money they have to buy it.
4. Read *Alexander, Who Used to Be Rich Last Sunday* (Viorst, 1978). Discuss why Alexander had nothing left in his pockets but bus tokens at the end of a week when he started out with a dollar. Primary children could make a pretend budget for Alexander.

Children in second or third grade may be ready to participate in discussions about decisions that affect the community. Perhaps a new highway is being built or the school system must eliminate jobs. Your students may be interested enough in some of these issues to speculate on how they would respond if they were adults. Ask, "Would you suggest that school-board members cut music, art, or other special areas?" "Do you think they should combine classes and eliminate teachers' jobs?" "Should money be spent on the new highway or a new school building?"

Even though resources are scarce and choices must be made to provide for ever-expanding human needs, you can help children understand that most decisions do not involve a choice between all or nothing. They do, however, require trade-offs among desirable alternatives or goals—that is, providing a little less of one thing to provide a little more of another.

One way to make such economic concepts more concrete is through process drama (Barnes, Johnson, & Neff, 2010). In process drama, the teacher draws children into a different time period through their imaginations (to travel back to the olden days), and the children role-play scenarios as if they lived during that period. A "drama frame" serves as the scenario. In one first-grade class, the drama frames included the following:

- Long Ago (living life in a different era)
- Specific Jobs (role-playing jobs from the earlier era and getting "paid" and "taxed")
- Taxation (the "King" is lobbied by the "workers" for lower taxes)
- Limited Resources (the "workers" explore costs, living expenses, and limited resources using the "money" they earned)
- Petitioning (small groups brainstorm why the "King" should reduce their taxes)
- Priorities (the "King" listens to the "petitioners" and explains the kingdom's expenses)
- Immigration (some decide to immigrate via a bear hunt chant and determine needs and wants in their new homeland)
- Government (the "immigrants" design a government and determine what laws they need)
- Budgeting (small groups apportion their "tax dollars") (Barnes, Johnson, & Neff, 2010).

Children are producers.

Process drama helps to make economic—and integrated historical, geographical, and civics—concepts more concrete through imagination, role playing, and problem solving.

PRODUCTION AND CONSUMPTION

Closely related to the concept of scarcity is the concept of production. The function of production, to some extent, is to try to meet the unlimited wants of consumers. In a democratic society, people choose the goods and services they consume and produce, although advertising and consumer demand influence both. The concept of distribution, how goods get from one place to another, is related to production and consumption. The concept of exchange of money is related to economic production as well: Consumers use money to purchase goods and services. Children can develop concepts of (a) being a consumer, (b) the function of money, (c) the differences between goods and services, and (d) production and distribution.

Consumers

Even before children can walk or talk, they consume goods, use services, and express their wants and needs. As they mature, they begin to choose what they buy. Their values influence the decisions they make; they will evaluate alternatives and select the best buy for their money as well as act on their rights and responsibilities as consumers.

Throughout the school year, you can help children clarify their likes and dislikes. They might discuss and identify the stories they like or dislike, decide on materials they like, and explain why they did not select the alternative materials. Making lists, booklets, charts, or murals depicting favorite things at school, at home, or in the neighborhood will help children clarify their preferences. You can remind children to be honest and make decisions based on their likes rather than those of their parents, peers, or teacher.

Playing store is another way in which children make concepts of consumer and producer real to them. Taking on the role of clerk and purchaser, children gain insights into the roles of consumer and producer. Researchers have found that children's store play begins simply, gradually building in complexity and becoming closer to reality:

Stage 1. The very young child uses imitative play, often with a mother or a father, and uses imaginary goods. Usually the child has no concern about purchasing or exchanging money.

Stage 2. This is the beginning of creative play. Children improvise play materials, use buttons for money, and play at purchasing items.

Stage 3. Children appear to desire more representative goods; empty cartons, canned goods, and play money are useful at this stage.

Stage 4. Children construct the store and goods, build counters, cut money out of paper, make signs, and take part in purchasing and in exchanging money.

Stage 5. A continuation of free play leads to more involved projects and teacher-contrived explorations of children's interests. Children use signs, prices,

Playing store teaches many economic concepts.

graphs, and scales and hold sales with reduced merchandise or actually sell small boxes of raisins or things they have actually produced, such as cookies baked by the class, plants grown from seeds, or greeting cards they have drawn.

As with other play, children need time to develop complex responses and to become involved in store play. To obtain the full potential from shop play, children need the opportunity to progress from the imitative stage to the creative and complex stage. Thus, shop play should continue through the primary grades with increasingly sophisticated processes and materials rather than stop at kindergarten or first grade. For example, primary children can produce cookies and distribute them to consumers in another classroom.

The best way to learn to become a wise consumer is to practice consuming. You need to provide as many opportunities as possible for children to make choices about purchases. In deciding on materials to purchase for the class or themselves, children need to consider the following: "How long will it last?" "How many ways can it be used?" "Is it something I really need or just want?" "If I spend my money for this, will I have any left for other things?"

As consumers who watch 3 to 5 hours of television daily, children should be aware of advertising's influence on their decision making. Children do not distinguish between programs and advertisements and cannot understand that a commercial's intent is to sell something. Even worse, the advertisements are aimed at breaking down the resistance of rational adults.

Based on strong psychological research and theory, advertisements do affect consumer behavior. Teachers can begin introducing children to the idea that advertisements are designed to influence the purchase of goods and services. Children can begin to analyze advertisements. The language arts activity of writing advertisements about real or pretend products helps children to see how words are selected to influence purchases and to realize that commercials are written by people. If children do not have writing skills, the commercials can be dictated or orally presented to the class by a committee.

Children can send for an advertised cereal-box toy and, on its receipt, compare the toy with its ad. Ask, "Does the toy do what the advertisement promised?" "What else could you have bought for the same amount of money?" "Would another purchase better fill your needs or wants?" "How does the toy received differ from the advertised one?"

Primary children can also analyze ads for other toys. Ask the children to watch a particular ad on television, arrange to have it shown to the class, or bring in an ad from a current paper or magazine. Read the ad and then compare the claims with the product. The children can, if it is convenient, take a trip to the toy store, or the product can be made available in class. Have the children determine if the ad distorted the product. Typical questions include "Did the doll really move the way it did on television or the way the ad said it would?" "Did the car really move as fast as it appeared to in the television ad?" "Did any parts of the ad make you think something different about this toy? Which parts?" "Were all parts of the ad true?"

At times, certain advertising slogans become popular and can serve as another vehicle for analysis of ads. Any slogan that is popular can be tested by kindergarten or primary children: "Will this candy mint make your mouth feel fresher than another?" "Does this soap really clean the clothes better than another?" "Does this towel absorb better than another?" "Which soap makes your hands softer?" "Let's try it for ourselves."

To be truly effective, consumer education must involve parents. Let the parents know about the activities the children are involved in at school. Tell parents that the activities will help children (a) weigh their purchases in terms of their goals, values, and resources; (b) make selections from the alternatives; and (c) accept the consequences and responsibilities that arise from their decisions. Inform parents about things they can do to reinforce children's abilities to analyze ads and make wise purchases. Parents can include children in their decisions about food purchases: "Would you like this box of cookies? It contains more cookies than this other box, but the cookies in this other box are made with real chocolate." Parents can also include children in discussions about larger purchases: "We need a new carpet and a new washing machine; how can we decide which to buy?" You can invite parents to school to tell the children about their experiences as consumers, how they make decisions for purchases, or about the time an advertisement lured them into making a foolish purchase and how they felt about it.

Consumers have rights and responsibilities. Their rights are to choose which goods and services they will buy, obtain accurate information about goods and services, shop in safe places, and be able to register complaints and seek redress of grievances. Consumers also need to respect the property and rights of others when shopping. You could take a shopping trip with the children to observe good and bad shopping manners. Children can make a list of all the things they think are improper shopping behaviors: running in the store, opening packages, or crowding at the checkout line. Ask them to add a list of proper shopping behaviors. Children might be able to role-play both good and bad behaviors.

Consuming Services

Children see the exchange of money when their parents purchase goods and materials, but they may never witness the exchange of money for services. The doctor and dentist are paid by credit card or a check through the mail; the teacher, librarian, police officer, and postal employee are paid indirectly through taxes. You can focus children's attention on the services their families use by making charts titled "Goods Our Families Consume" and "Services Our Families Use."

Other children can investigate the services that are supported by their parents' taxes and the taxes of others. Ask, "Who pays for the school?" "Does the teacher get paid?" "Where does the money come from?" "What would happen if no one paid for the school building, the services of the janitor or teachers, or materials and supplies?"

You might arrange trips into the community to observe other services paid for by taxes. Children can observe police officers, firefighters, street cleaners, health workers, and other people whose services are paid for by tax money. On another

Children learn that we consume services as well as goods.

trip, children can identify public property used by everyone—streets, parks, hydrants, fireboxes, street signs, lights, and sidewalks. Ask children to speculate about what would happen if people had to build their own streets or parks or buy their own fire trucks. Bulletin boards, booklets, or murals labeled "Things Families Buy Together" and "Things Families Buy for Themselves" will reinforce and clarify the concept of using public services.

Production and Distribution of Goods and Provision of Services

Although everyone is a consumer of goods and services, not all are producers. Interwoven with the concepts of scarcity, wants and needs, and consumers' responsible use of money is the concept of producer. Children can begin to develop the concept of producer by understanding the work they do at home and at school and the work their parents do (Figure 9.2).

Goods that children can produce at school include gifts for parents, greeting cards, books, garden products, and cookies. Ask, "What things do you produce at home?" "What do your parents produce? Food? Clothing? Furniture?" "How are

Work at School		Work at Home	
Goods	Services	Goods	Services
	Our Parents Produce		
	Goods	Services	

Figure 9.2 Children's chart of their work.

these goods distributed to the place where the consumer buys them?" "What services do you produce at school?" "What services do you produce at home?"

The concept of specialization—job diversification—arises from the identification of producers. Within the school building itself there are many specializations. There may be a building engineer, a nurse, or a lunchroom worker; there are teachers, a secretary, and a principal. Children can interview these different workers, finding out about their particular jobs—what they produce and how. Ask the children what would happen if each teacher was responsible for heating the school, cleaning the room, preparing the meals, repairing the windows, and answering the phone.

Children can experiment with diversity of jobs within the classroom. One day, instead of preparing materials for the children, let them prepare their own paints, salt dough, and so forth. Discuss what happened. Ask the children which way was easier and more efficient. On another day, ask each child to prepare a snack instead of the teacher preparing for everyone. Children might time their preparation and cleanup and compare it to the time it takes when these jobs are divided and conducted by a few for the entire group.

The study of producers leads to a study of the resources used in the production and distribution of goods. Production depends on people but also on natural resources, tools, machinery, and money. Distribution is closely linked to transportation. In the classroom, children can see that different materials are needed to produce a painting or to construct a playhouse. Children can make a list of the materials needed to make cookies or valentines and determine how and where the raw materials can from and how the items were produced. Children can make a chart of all of the tools within the classroom, and they can take a trip through the school to identify the tools used by producers in the building. You can initiate a discussion of the tools used at home or by parents at work or the tools, machines, and materials needed to keep the community functioning. Children can study maps and transportation to identify the routes of natural resources to production facilities to stores.

Teachers can develop units of study that follow things children are interested in from raw materials, to production, to distribution, to consumption. The beautiful picture book, *Pelle's New Suit* (Beskow, 1972), can serve as the organizer for a unit on production. The book illustrates the production process, costs, goods and services, and jobs. It follows a young boy named Pelle through

- shearing his lamb,
- pulling weeds for Granny as she cards the wool,
- tending his other grandmother's cows as she spins the yarn,
- running errands for the painter to earn money for blue dye,
- dying his wool,
- caring for his little sister while his mother weaves the cloth,
- raking the tailor's hay, and
- thanking his lamb for the new suit.

In a third-grade class, children studied chocolate in a similar manner including the concept of distribution—the many ways that raw materials and goods are transported.

In one first-grade class the children decided to study stuffed animals (Rogovin, 2011). Through questioning, research, concrete activities, children's literature, and interviews they studied the economics (plus geography and science) of the stuffed animals they brought from home. The questions included the following:

- Where are our stuffed animals made?
- What are our stuffed animals made of?
- How do people make stuffed animals?
- And, eventually, why is China the source of stuffed animals?

They could easily have added the question of how the stuffed animals got from China to their local town.

At the end of the unit they produced a play acted by themselves and their stuffed animals that indicated what they had learned about the production process as well as their concern for the workers in China. They learned economic concepts through concrete activities focused on items of interest to them.

JOBS AND CAREERS

Everyone needs a career—something that gives purpose and direction to life, something that is significant to the individual and useful to society at the same time. Without a career, whether it is making a house into a home or being a doctor or a construction worker, humans lack purpose or direction in life and are aimless, capricious, and in danger of becoming parasites (Dewey, 1944). Recognizing the critical need for each child to become a productive member of society, schools begin education for careers in the preschool and primary grades.

The idea of beginning career education in the preschool–primary classroom, of asking young children who are barely able to comprehend concepts of yesterday, today, or tomorrow to plan for a vague and distant future, might seem inappropriate. Intent on living each day fully and on developing skills, knowledge, and attitudes required for life in the present, young children have little real concern for the future. Yet the preschool–primary class is the ideal place to begin education for a career; during these early years, children's knowledge of jobs, attitudes, values, and essential skills are formed. This knowledge, attitudes, values, and skills will remain with the children and serve to direct their entire lives. Career education becomes much more a function of attitude, value, and skill development than an artificial addition to the curriculum.

Jobs

Children are interested in what the adults in their world do at home, school, and in the community. They are exposed to many different jobs in their daily life. Children often say, "I want to be a … when I grow up." The study of jobs helps children learn job specification and diversification: Adults do different things, each having a purpose tied to goods or services.

At home, children can identify their parents' jobs and talk with them about their work. In school, they can take a walk around the building, looking for all of the jobs that people do, and interview some of the workers doing them. In the community, children see doctors, police officers, grocery store clerks, and so on; the class can generate a list. They can also generate lists of producers (e.g., farmers) and those involved with distribution (e.g., truck drivers). The various jobs can be studied in many ways:

- Having a guest talk about their job. Firefighters are often willing to visit schools.
- Conducting interviews with parents or school workers.
- Using books, photographs, and children's literature. The *World of Work Series* (2009) uses pictures and simple text to describe various jobs.
- Discussing the nature and purpose of each job.
- Determining whether each job produces a good or provides a service and charting the results.
- Including jobs in the play area using tools, hats, clothing, and other artifacts (e.g., a wagon for a distributor).
- Matching tools and vehicles to jobs.
- Talking with children about what they want to be when they grow up.
- Writing stories about people doing their jobs.
- Drawing pictures of the jobs the children do at home, such as making their bed or feeding the cat.

The study of jobs helps children understand that many jobs are necessary to make a community work and that they will be—and already are at home and in school—a part of that process. It lays the foundation for a career.

Attitudes and Values

Toward Self

Children must grow with a strong sense of self that will give them the confidence to shape their own destinies. Whether fostering career education or fulfilling the general goal of all education, you will want to plan for children to achieve all the self-confidence they need to go on growing and developing into socially responsible and constructive members of society.

Self-confidence is acquired as children are given jobs to fulfill in the classroom. Real responsibilities for preparing materials, cleaning up, and caring for pets, plants, and equipment help children feel successful, competent, and sure of their abilities to contribute to the welfare of the group and, later, to become productive members of society.

Toward Work

Attitudes toward future work are developed through responsibilities in the classroom and awareness of jobs, careers, and workers. Children need to be aware of the choices they have and the things they can do.

Children can interview the workers in the school building, neighborhood, or community to determine their attitudes toward work. Children can ask the following:

- What do you like about your job? Why?
- What do you dislike about it? Why?
- How did you decide to do it?
- What preparation did you need?
- Do you feel proud of your work? Why?
- Have you ever thought about changing jobs?

Help children think about the questions they will ask, perhaps listing them on a chart for reference. Children can compare the interview responses, exploring the different job choices available as well as discovering how people feel about their jobs.

Children can begin to speculate about the future. You might ask, "What kinds of jobs do you think you might have when you grow up?" Remind them that they might be able to do several things, such as being a student, a parent, an engineer, or an interior designer. By asking children to think about the future, you increase their awareness of career choices and opportunities.

Toward Sex Roles

The question "What do you want to be when you grow up?" continues to be answered on the basis of sex. Despite the ever-increasing numbers of women who have entered the workforce, the occupational awareness, exploration, and decisions of boys and girls tend to remain stereotypical (Derman-Sparks & A.B.C. Task Force, 2003). Sex differences in attitudes toward careers and career aspirations begin during early childhood and persist into adolescence (Chrisman & Couchenour, 2003). Boys know what their fathers do more often than girls do and are able to identify twice as many career options as girls can.

The American Association of University Women (2000) suggested creating awareness of the role of women in the workforce by taking trips into the community. The focal point of the trips is to observe people working. Younger children may take trips a few blocks from the school building. You will want to emphasize the nonstereotypic jobs and workers the children observe on the trip. Older children can extend trips over a larger area. They can explore their city, suburb, or rural area by bus, car, or train. Children of all ages can photograph their observations. You will need to guide the children skillfully: Seek out the unusual, challenge the stereotypes that are present, and point out the options that exist in career choices for all people, both men and women.

Discussions follow each trip, or children can make a mural or booklet of jobs they have seen, jobs their parents hold, or jobs in one store. The emphasis should always be on people in the variety of roles in which they actually function rather than on the stereotypes found in books, the press, and other media.

Other experiences may be vicarious. Selecting books, photos, posters, and pictures showing women in a wide range of career options, both traditional and nontraditional, is important. Challenging children's stereotypical thinking is also recommended. When children announce, "You can't play here; only men can build houses," or "You're the girl; you have to make the dinner," teachers can challenge them: "Remember when we went to the construction site? There were three women builders," or "Men can make dinner as well as girls can. At the fast-food restaurant, we saw only men making waffles."

Essential Skills

To succeed in an unknown future, children will be required to have essential skills. These include the hard skills—basic mathematics, reading, the ability to make decisions, and the ability to use computers—as well as the soft skills—the ability to work in groups and make effective oral and written presentations.

The essential skills of reading, writing, communicating, and learning to learn are basic to all education, including career education. But if these skills are taught in isolation from the rest of children's lives, they will have no meaning (Helm & Beneke, 2003). An integrated approach to the curriculum is essential. As Dewey (1900a) suggested, teachers can relate mathematics to career education as children observe carpenters using measuring devices. Then teachers can help children construct their own playhouse using measurements. Following a trip to the gas station to see what attendants and mechanics do, children can read to find out where gasoline comes from, how it is produced and refined, how it gets to the gas station, and perhaps how world politics are involved (see Chapter 11). The same can be done with any product that catches the children's interest.

The skills involved in solving problems and making wise decisions are equally essential. You can incorporate decision making into the curriculum by telling children, "Do it your way," "You decide," and "It's up to you" as appropriate.

Skills in relating to people are essential to career education. Children who cannot relate to others will have a difficult time succeeding in a career. Schools afford children the opportunity to learn to work with others and to develop firm interpersonal relationships.

With knowledge of jobs, attitudes of respect for self, work, and others, and the development of essential skills, children are prepared to find their places in a rapidly changing society where occupations appear and disappear. Children who have developed (a) respect for the dignity of people and the worth of occupations, (b) knowledge and understanding of the opportunities available, and (c) willingness to gain skills and an openness to learning throughout life are those who have been educated for careers.

SUMMARY

The major economics concepts appropriate for preschool–primary children are ideas about scarcity, decision making, and the function of production, distribution, and consumption as well as jobs and future career choices and roles. You introduce these concepts through children's experiences, both incidental and structured.

Every day, children experience the concept of scarcity. They must make choices. They must conserve materials and energy. They must consider their needs and wants in relation to available resources, and they need to make responsible decisions and learn to live with the consequences of their decisions.

As consumers, children develop an understanding of the producer concept. Some produce services, others goods. Goods must be distributed to consumers. Money is required to pay for both services and goods. The diversity of producers' work leads children into a study of different kinds of jobs as well as the resources that producers use in their jobs.

Even though their working lives are far in the future, preschool and primary children are not too young to learn basic attitudes toward self and work that will prepare them to make wise decisions about future career choices. The skills of identifying jobs, decision making, relating to others, and learning basic skills are part of career education.

Although research supports introducing young children to economic concepts, it is important to ground your teaching of concepts in children's concrete, everyday experiences through an integrated, whole curriculum. If children are to gain necessary awareness of and develop initial economic concepts, they must be involved in experiencing, doing, and acting for themselves.

Discussion Questions

1. Why is it important to teach economics to young children?
2. Developmentally, what can children learn about economics? What concepts can they begin to understand?
3. Some of the vocabulary of economics seems difficult for young children. Select some of these terms and identify synonyms or other words or phrases that might help clarify the meaning (e.g., producers + makers).
4. Define scarcity. What does this mean to young children? How can they relate to it in their lives? What subtopics are included under the concept of scarcity? How can you teach it in concrete ways?
5. Many economic concepts involve distinctions between two terms—for example, producers-consumers; production-distribution; needs-wants; natural resources-human resources. How can you help children understand these distinctions? What activities and experiences can you provide?
6. Why is it important to prepare young children for careers in the future? What elements of career development should be included in the classroom? What experiences can you provide?
7. As in all subject areas, it is essential to make learning active and concrete. What are some ways you make economics learning active and concrete?
8. How can you integrate economics with the other social studies disciplines: history, geography, and civics? With other disciplines: science, math, literature, and the arts? What connections do you see?

9. Select one of the books from the Children's Literature Box. What standard (NCSS, NAEYC, or local/state) might this book be used to teach? What would a lesson or unit plan that used this book to teach this standard look like?

Extend Your Knowledge

1. With a small group of children, visit a supermarket or a neighborhood store. What things are the children interested in that you could use to build economic concepts? List how you could extend these interests in the classroom.
2. Select one concept from economics. Interview a group of children to determine their understanding of that concept. What experiences could you plan that might build more accurate, complete understandings of the concept?
3. Interview a 5-year-old child, a 6-year-old child, and a 7-year-old child. Ask each child what he wants to be when he grows up and why, and what he (or she) thinks he will have to learn or do to achieve his career choice.
4. Nearly every state in our nation mandates some form of economics education in elementary or secondary schools. Write, call, or search the Internet to locate information about your state's guidelines for economics teaching. Even though some of the plans and guidelines may be designed for older children, review them and identify concepts, activities, or plans that could be adapted for younger preschool and primary-grade children.

Resources

The Foundation for Teaching Economics is a nonprofit organization providing leadership in economic education for educators and young people selected for their leadership potential. The foundation welcomes inquiries, comments, and suggestions.
www.fte.org

The National Council on Economic Education is the leading source for materials and information dealing with economic literacy in the K–12 environment. Their website includes a large list of lesson plans for the teaching of economics to K–12 children.
www.ncee.net

Many universities have centers for economic education that provide economic education programs, workshops, materials, and lesson plans. A Google search will give you several good websites to explore.

Economic Simulations

There are many simulations appropriate for children. For example, Lemonade Stand is an electronic simulation for learning economics. See one version at www.lemonadegame.com. Do a Google search on "lemonade stand" for other versions as well as a search for economics simulations.

Curricula

The Alleman and Brophy (2001, 2002, 2003) units on cultural universals all integrate economics concepts.

Books

The following books offer parents and teachers ideas for teaching economics to young children:

    Bodnar, J. (1993). *Kiplinger's money-smart kids.* Washington, DC: Kiplinger Books.
    Bodnar, J. (1996). *Mom, can I have that?* Washington, DC: Kiplinger Books.
    Estess, P., & Barocas, I. (1994). *Kids, money, and values.* Newark, NJ: Gateway.
    Modu, E. (1996). *The lemonade stand.* Newark, NJ: Gateway.

World of Work Series (2009). Ann Arbor, MI: Cherry Hill Press. A series of books that describe what it is like to work in different places: bank, factory, park, restaurant, school, hospital, grocery, farm. Includes photographs and questions for children.

CHAPTER 10

Developing Citizenship: Civics and Government

> **Focus Questions**
>
> After you have read this chapter, you should be prepared to respond to the following questions:
>
> - Why is civics important for young children and what are the key concepts?
> - What democratic values are included in the formal curriculum and modeled in the informal classroom?
> - What political concepts can young children understand and how can they be taught?
> - What intellectual skills and participatory skills are important for children to practice?

A group of kindergarten children sits on the rug surrounding the teacher. She asks a question, and many voices begin to answer at once with great enthusiasm. The teacher holds up her hand to stop the talking and says, "We need to talk one at a time so we can hear each other. Raise your hand if you would like to talk, so everyone will get a chance to share and to listen." In this one sentence, the teacher is demonstrating several democratic and governance principles: rights and responsibilities, the individual versus the common good, rules and laws, participation, fairness, multiple perspectives, power and authority, and the role of authority figures to maintain order and ensure that basic needs and wants are met.

Even while the Founding Fathers struggled to create the Constitution and Bills of Rights that would guide the new nation, they recognized that a free society would rely ultimately on the knowledge, skills, values, and involvement of its citizens. Therefore, civics education is essential to the preservation and improvement of a democratic society (Center for Civic Education, 1994). Schools fulfill this mission through the formal curriculum (instruction in understanding the rights and responsibilities of citizens in a democracy) and informal experiences (interactions in the classroom and participation in class and school governance that mirror the values and principles of the democracy). For young children, the informal experience of participating in a classroom consciously organized to model democratic values provides an essential foundation for increasingly complex civic understanding and participation.

KEY CONCEPTS

Two of the National Council for the Social Studies standards (2010) relate to civics. Standard X, Civic Ideals and Practices, states that "Social studies programs should include experiences that provide for the study of the ideals, principles and practices of citizenship in a democratic republic" (p. 23). Children are exposed to questions and issues such as: What is civic participation, and how can I be involved? How has the meaning of citizenship evolved? What is the balance between rights and responsibilities? What is the role of a citizen in the community, nation, and world? How can I make a difference? For young children, civic ideals and practices are experienced through activities such as helping to set classroom expectations, examining experiences in relation to ideals, conducting service projects, participating in class meetings, and considering how to balance the needs of the individual and the group. They also experience views of citizenship in other times and places through stories and drama. For example, a traditional history-oriented unit on Johnny Appleseed can become more civics-oriented if children are asked to think about what difference he made, how, and why.

NCSS Standard VI—Power, Authority and Governance—states that "Social studies programs should include experiences that provide for the study of how people create, interact with, and change structures of power, authority and governance" (NCSS, 2010, p. 19). Children are exposed to questions and issues such as: What is power? What forms does power take? Who holds it? How is it gained, used, and justified? What is legitimate authority? How are governments created, structured, changed, and maintained? How can we keep governments responsive to citizens' needs and interests? How can individual rights be protected within the context of majority rule? Young children explore their developing sense of fairness, rules, and order through relationships with others. They develop an awareness of rights and responsibilities in specific contexts. They develop notions of power and authority as they interact with their teachers.

The Center for Civic Education published the National Standards for Civics and Government in 1994. The K–4 standards provide more detail of what children should know and be able to do related to government, democratic principles, the Constitution, world affairs, and citizenship. In addition to content knowledge, they emphasize the acquisition of intellectual skills such as critical thinking within a democracy and participatory skills.

DEMOCRATIC VALUES

In preschool and primary programs, children are not just preparing to become members of a democratic society but actually *are* citizens of a democracy (Dewey, 1944). Daily, they contribute to building and fostering a democratic society and receive the benefits of belonging to this society.

Through every experience in the program, young children learn that they are worthy, valued, and respected. They know that their individual needs and wants will be met and that their freedom of speech, pursuit of happiness, and other rights will be protected. At the same time, however, they are learning to expand their concerns and give up some of their egocentrism. As members of a democratic community, children develop a sense of shared concern, recognizing that their interests overlap with the interests of others and that their welfare is inextricably entwined with the welfare of others (Boyle-Baise, 2003). They learn to balance their individual needs with the common good.

Children learn that they are worthy, valued, and respected.

The teacher establishes and maintains the basic principles of democracy in the classroom. The ways in which the teacher establishes control, deals with individual children and their interactions with one another, and teaches all students send a powerful message to children about the values of a democracy. Although there is no one right or wrong way for a teacher to do this, when observing a democratic classroom, one immediately becomes aware of how teachers actively support individual worth and dignity while protecting and nurturing the welfare of the total group. In a democratic group, certain tenets are consistently followed:

1. *Teachers share control.* They do not give orders and expect children to blindly follow their directions. Rather than emphasizing only the task or the skill to be learned, teachers focus on how children are feeling, reacting, and interacting with one another as well (Bredekamp & Copple, 1997). For example:

   A second-grade group was working in the computer room with the computer teacher. One child had difficulty with the program and did not seem to know what to do with the computer or how to solve the math problems. His neighbor turned to him and began to help. "Stop talking now!" said the teacher firmly, writing both children's names in a box on the board, which meant each child might later lose some favored activity or reward. "It's not time for social talk; it's time to do your math." The teacher ignored both the fact that one child had no clue about what to do or how to use the computer to practice this particular math skill and the fact that the other child was offering to help.

2. *Children make decisions.* Being able to make wise decisions is required of participants in a democratic society (Longstreet, 2003). Instead of prescribing the work to be done, how it will be done, and under what time constraints, the teacher lets children make choices about what they will learn, how, and with whom. Cookbook approaches—filling in the blanks and following prescribed lesson plans—are replaced by centers of interest, learning stations, and open-ended materials for learning. Rather than solo learning, group work is fostered (New, 1999a). For example:

   "Here are some plastic containers," said a teacher to the first graders, who had been grouped into committees. She gave each group a box of different-sized and different-shaped clear plastic containers. "Your group's task is to decide which container holds the most sand and which the least. You may use the scale, the tape measure, or any other materials in the sand or water tables. Report to me when you have reached a decision."

3. *Discipline is firm and consistent but does not revolve around force, coercion, embarrassment, or threat.* Already believing that rules come from authority and that being good means following orders, children need to participate in setting and following rules and begin the long process of separating intent from action. For example:

   Jennifer, a rambunctious 5-year-old, always seemed to be the cause of some trouble with the other kindergarten children. She jumped from one group to another, often upsetting what the others were doing. She never seemed to sit still or simply walk from one place to another but jiggled, jumped, and ran around—a perpetual-motion machine in action. One day, as she darted across the room, she knocked down Sean. The teacher took her aside and repeated the process of identifying and labeling for Jennifer her actions and their results: "You are a very active girl. You need to move about a great deal. When you do so, you can hurt others. How can we arrange for you to move around without disturbing the other children?"

4. *Freedom of thought and speech are fostered.* Children are expected to have opinions and express them. This expectation governs every area of the curriculum (Greenberg, 1992). Instead of giving children sheets of paper on which to color or patterns to trace around for art activities, teachers ask them to express their own ideas, thoughts, and feelings in drawings, paintings, or constructions. They are asked to discuss, write, and express what they know and feel in language arts and to make choices about how they will learn math and science skills. For example:

> A kindergarten teacher, picking up on the children's interest in dinosaurs, asked them to draw their favorite dinosaur. Clifford drew a large scribble, added some legs and horns, and called it a monster dinosaur. Judy laughed at him, saying, "That's not a dinosaur. That's not real; that's just a scribble."
>
> The teacher said, "Judy, this is the way Clifford draws a dinosaur. It's his pretend monster dinosaur. Your dinosaur is a picture of a stegosaurus, Roberta's is a green dinosaur, and Alice didn't draw a dinosaur at all but drew the forest in which they might have lived." This teacher demonstrated for the children that, although they have different ideas and express them in different ways, each individual's expression is valid.

5. *Children are never overwhelmed by the power of others.* Teachers are not power figures in the classroom, and they do not permit children to govern through power assertions, bullying, or threats. For example:

> In a kindergarten, two boys had gained control of the class. They threatened the others with physical violence, took smaller children's milk money, and had on more than one occasion overwhelmed children in the bathrooms, taking their pants off. As a result, the other children refused to go to the bathroom and began giving the two their money and following their demands. Knowing these behaviors could not be permitted to continue, the teacher began a behavior-management program with the class and the two boys. She taught the other children how to ignore the boys and some skills for coping with them. At the same time, she began rewarding the two boys for cooperative behavior. She channeled their need for power in constructive ways by asking them to lead a song, take charge of the blocks, and become monitors. The behavioral techniques did not completely solve the problem, but they gave the teacher and the other children a way to regain control without being overwhelmed by emotions. As a result, she was then able to work with the boys on the cause of their behaviors.

6. *A sense of community is built.* A classroom is a group of individuals, and the teacher develops this group into a community by helping them share goals. Even young children can begin to see that they are a part of, and share in the

common goals of, their family, their own group of friends, the class, and the school. Not only are children encouraged to see themselves within the context of the total group, but small groups within the total group are fostered (New, 1999a). For example:

> Common shared experiences lead to common goals. A trip to the zoo leads to deciding on group rules for the trip, which questions will be answered, and which exhibits will be visited. After such a trip, one second-grade teacher arranged for the whole group to complete a mural of their experiences. Knowing that a sense of community develops as children work together, the teacher then divided up the group by their interest in birds, reptiles, fish, and mammals and had each group complete a project and then report to the total group. Throughout the process, the teacher helped the children recognize both their own identity and the needs of the group.

7. *Teachers model respect for others (DeRoach, 2001).* A teacher who cares about and respects each child in the group and each adult who works with the children serves as a model for the children. Teachers model and encourage mutual respect, and they let the children know in a number of explicit ways that each is respected and cared for. For example:

> "Let me know when you want me to help you with your math." "You be the judge." "It's up to you whether you want to keep this in your book report or not," a second-grade teacher was heard saying to the children. A teacher of 4-year-olds fostered the idea that it is all right not to be competent in everything. Talking privately to a child who could not walk the balance beam, she said, "It's okay not to be able to balance—you'll be able to do so as you grow. You do know how to dress yourself, draw, and sing." Overhearing one child laughing at another's sandwich of shrimp and catsup, a kindergarten teacher said, "When you laugh at Sallie's lunch, it upsets her. It's okay if you don't like it, or even if you'd like to try it, but you may not make fun of what other people like."

8. *Teachers elicit respectful, caring behaviors from the children.* Teachers are powerful models for children. They not only model respectful, caring behavior, but they explain what they are doing and find other ways to demonstrate respect. For example:

> Kathy, a 5-year-old with spina bifida, was mainstreamed in the kindergarten. The teacher not only modeled caring behaviors for the children but was explicit in gaining their respect for Kathy. At times, the teacher casually asked a child to help Kathy with her coat or chair or to reach something. Other times, she paired Kathy with a partner for necessary help. To enable Kathy to be a responsible member of the group, the teacher found a carpenter's apron with lots of pockets that could be filled with toys and materials. This permitted Kathy to assume some responsibility in cleaning up. At the same time, the teacher provided the same kind of apron for the other children. Thus, even though Kathy was different, all the children could take advantage of cleaning up with a pocket apron.

Children's ideas should move continually toward conventional knowledge. However, Slekar (2009) warns against citizenship education as political indoctrination

Goals to Move Toward	Goals to Move Away From
Knowing that rules and laws are established by people	Perceiving rules as coming from "on high"
Realizing that rules and laws are always changing	Thinking of rules as unchanging
Understanding that people have control over their own lives	Perceiving people as powerless before the law
Being empathetic, socially responsible, and considerate of others	Being egocentric, self-centered, and indifferent to others

Figure 10.1   Children's developing ideas about civic participation.

and focuses instead on civic education for genuine democracy. Children should be moving away from the following goals (Figure 10.1):

- Perceiving rules as coming from "on high"
- Thinking of rules as unchanging
- Perceiving people as powerless before the law
- Being egocentric, self-centered, and indifferent to others

They should be moving toward these goals:

- Knowing that rules and laws are established by people
- Realizing that rules and laws are always changing
- Understanding that they have control over their own lives
- Being empathetic, socially responsible, and considerate of others

Civic Participation

The ability to be responsible for oneself and to participate fully in the welfare of the group is an asset in any society; but in a democratic society, it is a requirement for citizenship (Morgan & Streb, 2001). *The National Standards for Civics and Government* (Center for Civic Education, 1994) indicate that, by the end of fourth grade, children should have developed the following participation skills:

- Influencing decisions by working with others
- Clearly articulating interests and making them known to decision makers
- Building coalitions, negotiating, compromising, and seeking consensus
- Managing conflicts

The disposition to work for the common good and participate in joint efforts begins early in life. For children under the age of 7 or 8, participation begins when they assume responsibility for themselves. Rooms for 3- and 4-year-olds are arranged not only to permit but to promote children's responsibility for their own dressing, toileting, and washing. These very young children may begin to assume responsibility for others and the group by joining in small groups for discussions, activities, stories, or songs. With adult assistance, 3- and 4-year-olds can participate in setting tables, serving food, cleaning up after play and work, or caring for plants and animals that belong to the group.

Early on, children learn to participate in enabling children with special needs to function fully in the group (Copple, 2003). As described earlier, the children casually and regularly helped Kathy by helping her put on her coat, carrying things for her, and waiting patiently for her as they played.

Primary children participate in other types of group activities. They can plan together and divide responsibilities. By sharing ideas, children in the primary grades can solve problems and make plans for their own learning. Children who are given responsibilities that they can fulfill within the group are learning to participate in a democratic society.

Learning to live and participate within a group means setting rules and following them (CIVITAS, 2003). Children should take part in establishing rules in the class. They can contribute to the rules for woodworking, block building, use of the bathrooms and water tables, and so forth. Other rules are made for the children. All must participate in a fire drill; and because there is little opportunity for them to contribute to the rules of the drill, they can use this occasion to discuss why it is important to follow certain rules, why rules are made, who makes them, and how they are made. Children can also become aware of other rules they must follow: the traffic laws, rules for riding the bus, and rules at home. These questions might be discussed: "What would happen if no one followed the rules?" "Do you think everyone should obey traffic rules?" "Why?"

Experiencing rules and discussing their purposes can help children realize that rules are made to protect them and others. Children should also realize that they have the responsibility to follow the rules, to make rules that are needed for living within a group, to change rules that no longer function to protect them and others, and to adjust the rules to fit changing situations (Nolte, Harris, & Harris, 1998). Involving children in creating classroom rules increases ownership of the rules and engages them in democratic processes and responsibilities (Figure 10.2). Class meetings are an effective way to model and practice democratic values in an authentic way to clarify rules, resolve interpersonal conflicts, and do collective problem solving (Angell, 2004; Arends, 2012).

Participation in creating classroom rules increases ownership and demonstrates democratic processes. Steps include the following:

- The class generates a long list of classroom rules.
- The class discusses which ones are most important and why.
- The children vote or agree on 5 or 6 rules.
- The teacher carefully guides discussion so that all rules on the final list are appropriate.
- The rules are then posted.
- Each child signs the posted rules.

Figure 10.2 Creating classroom rules

The values of participating in a democratic society extend to the wider community as well as to the classroom. Even very young children can be introduced to the idea of serving others. "I don't want to go," a 6-year-old said when asked if he wanted to go visit the elders in a nearby nursing home. "But I'm going! You see," he said, "sometimes it's good to do things for other people. I don't like it, but I'm going because the old people like to see little kids."

Serving others is part of being a productive member of a society. Even though a primary developmental task of young children is to feel secure and safe and to know that adults and their community will protect and serve them, young children can be introduced to the concept of serving others. Research shows that active participation in service learning in social studies classrooms improves learning and attitudes toward civic involvement for diverse students at different grade levels (Wade & Yarbrough, 2007).

Within the family, children are taught to care for siblings or pets and help their parents. Two-year-olds are able to fold diapers and entertain the baby. Three- and four-year-olds assume more of their own care by putting their toys away and setting the table. They can also accompany their parents when visiting or bringing food to elderly or ill family members or neighbors.

Once in primary grades, children are taught to serve their peers as well. Some learning occurs as children model their teachers, who demonstrate how to care for other children. At times, children may be asked to care for others directly: "Ask Cassidy to join you," or "Hold Bryan's hand while we're on the trip."

Children may also learn to serve the adults who care for them: "Help Ms. Jones [the aide] set the tables," or "Ms. Jones needs two helpers to mix paints." "Who will sweep up the sawdust, wash the clay off the tables, or pick up the scraps on the floor?" teachers ask, adding, "We want to help Ms. Smith, the custodian, so she won't have as much work to do." At other times children may cook something for the lunchroom workers or present a painting or a thank-you note to the director or principal of the school.

Knowledge of the community is necessary to expand children's service of others in the broader community. Children can interview community workers to find out how they can help with their jobs. Firefighters, police officers, and other community helpers are more than willing to involve children in serving the community. During a visit to a first-grade class, one firefighter told the children that they could help by asking their parents to check their smoke alarms each Halloween. By doing so, they would help keep their family safe, which would help firefighters do their jobs. Several parents reported to the teacher how grateful they were for this instruction; when they checked their smoke detectors, they found out that the batteries were dead.

Primary-age children, like the 6-year-old who articulated his good feelings about doing something for others, can serve others in their community. Depending on the community, neighbors who need help, or the agencies and associations serving others, children can be involved in many ways. For example, one primary group took on the task of picking up trash from an elderly neighbor's yard next to the school. Another group made name tags from old greeting cards for a community

Community service teaches civic responsibility.

organization. Others have written get-well letters, read their favorite stories on tape to give to hospitalized children, and selected books to give to Ukrainian children learning to speak English. One school made peanut butter sandwiches for the homeless once a week.

Five-year-olds in one community wrote joke books and distributed them to children in waiting rooms of nearby medical facilities and doctors' offices. Parents and children waiting to see the health-care provider found the books relaxing, and the 5-year-old helpers learned that the process of helping others gives the helper a lasting sense of pride and satisfaction.

These days, service projects may extend beyond the local community to those in need around the globe. You may recall that the unit on stuffed animals in Chapter 9 resulted in concerns for Chinese factory workers.

Service projects are most effective when they grow out of the experiences and concerns of the children. Most units can be planned and implemented with possibilities for service and/or action in mind. For example, a unit on "reduce, reuse, recycle" clearly has implications for civic participation, responsibility, and action. A unit on community helpers or being healthy may have resulted in the books for doctors' offices described earlier. Asking children questions such as "How could you make a difference?" will model service-oriented thinking and might result in some actions (see Figure 10.3).

National Council for Social Studies Notable Civics Trade Books for Young Children

My Senator and Me: A Dog's-Eye View of Washington, D.C. by Senator Edward M. Kennedy. Role of a senator as seen from a pet's perspective. Follows Senator Kennedy through a typical day on Capitol Hill. Biography of Senator Kennedy, and an explanation of how a bill becomes a law.

The Cupcake Thief by Ellen Jackson. A student accuses another of stealing his cupcake, so they must go to Student Court. Examples and definitions of using student courts to resolve disputes.

She Sang Promise: The Story of Betty Mae Jumper, Seminole Tribal Leader by Jan Godown Annino. Betty Mae Jumper, one of the first women to be elected leader of the Seminole Tribe, started the first Seminole newspaper and was an advisor to President Richard Nixon. Timeline.

The Impossible Patriotism Project by Linda Skeers. Caleb can't come up with an idea for his patriotism project for Parents' Night. He is disappointed that his dad won't be present, until he learns the reason.

Boycott Blues: How Rosa Parks Inspired a Nation by Andrea Davis Pinkney. Recalls the bus boycott in Montgomery and the Supreme Court ruling to end segregation. Suggestions for further reading.

Prize by Isabel Pin. Introduces the Nobel Peace Prize and various ways to make a difference in the world.

31 Ways to Change the World: We Are What We Do by Candlewick Press. Top 31 ideas by children in Great Britain on ways to change the world. Helps children think about the little ways they can make a difference.

The Taxing Case of the Cows: A True Story about Suffrage by Iris Van Rynbach and Pegi Deitz Shea. Recounts the story of two sisters whose cows were confiscated during the struggle against taxation without representation. Illustrates actions against women that fueled the suffrage movement. Bibliography.

Nelson Mandela: Long Walk to Freedom abridged by Chris van Wyk. A first-person account of Mandela's life, growing up in Soweto, working as a lawyer, and building a new South Africa. Timeline.

A New Nation by Betsy Maestro. Thirteen colonies declare their independence from England, and forge a new nation. Timeline, Founders' quotations.

Margaret Chase Smith: A Woman for President by Lynn Plourde. Story of Senator Margaret Chase Smith, who ran for president in 1964. Timeline of key events in historical context.

Brought Them Together by Herb Shoveller. True story about service learning that recounts how Jimmy learned in school about the unsafe drinking water in Uganda and decided to do something.

Figure 10.3 Children's Literature Box for Civics.
Based on NCSS Notable Trade Books for Young People, www.ncss.org/resources.

Henning and Bell (2010) describe a WebQuest entitled "Community Services of DeKalb" in which second-graders connected to their community. In small groups, children conducted research on preselected, local community service agencies and completed a worksheet that guided their investigation. They wrote three questions they wanted to ask about the agency. Then a guest speaker came from each agency, and the children posed their questions. Following the speakers, the children did a concept map of community services and the teacher clarified misconceptions. The class chose one organization they wanted to help: a local historic home. They participated in a clean-up day and raised $260. Henning and Bell state that three things made the WebQuest developmentally appropriate: choice, cooperative learning, and preplanning. Although the planning took some time, they conclude that it was worth it, given the student's engagement, critical thinking, and opportunity to do something for their community.

Young Citizens of the World (2009) provides a curriculum framework for linking democratic knowledge with civic action. Integrating with the other social studies disciplines, the model calls for children to:

- Become informed about ideas, events, or issues by, for example, acting as detectives to find information and provide evidence; sorting concepts into examples and nonexamples; or asking questions and developing hypotheses
- Think it through by, for example, acting out scenarios through drama; or interpreting visual representations
- Take action by, for example, using deliberation strategies; discussing two sides of an issue; drawing conclusions; and considering actions they could take (Boyle-Baise, Bernes-Kinkead, Coake, Loudermilk, Lukasik, & Podany, 2011).

The foundation for democratic citizenship is laid within the democracy of the preschool–primary classroom. Political awareness grows from this base.

POLITICAL CONCEPTS

Political concepts, typically based on children's own experiences, are introduced to children informally. Most children are acquainted with rules, have been exposed to authority figures at home and in school, and perhaps know some symbols of democracy such as the flag, songs, the president, or the Pledge of Allegiance. You can use this knowledge to introduce political concepts. In addition, knowledge of the voting process can be developed through life in the political groups of the family, the classroom, and the community.

When teachers follow the principles of a democratic society, children experience political concepts every day. They understand that some people are in authority and know that these people make and enforce rules in their homes, schools, and communities. The child's peer group, family, school, and community relations initially expose them to the core of politics, which is power and its use. Children directly experience rules and limitations as givens and behavior as good or bad depending on whether it conforms to the rules.

Children understand authority through their experiences at home and in school, and they see the president as a symbol of the government. Thus, children begin to understand that there are "official" people long before they can distinguish their positions and roles. They can also begin to understand that people in authority are responsible for making sure that needs and wants are met, that order is maintained, and that conflicts are managed and resolved.

Research

Research tells us about children's developing political thinking. Even very young children are aware of politics beyond their classroom. Researchers note that children have become increasingly more politically aware and can talk about many topics from the field of political science, even though their range of knowledge about any one topic is narrow. Gary Allen (1997) found that, in conversation, first-graders could recall political knowledge from a news story. Allen also found that first- through third-graders' knowledge of the presidency and elections became more elaborate during an election year.

In another study, 6-year-olds were found to be aware of and to endorse democracy and free speech (Helwig, 1998). Even though these children were relatively young, they recognized that freedom of speech is an important part of human activity that must be secured against general intrusion by any form of government. The study concluded that children can consider basic issues of rights and justice and that these can and should be introduced into the curriculum during early childhood.

Even 4-year-olds can identify and accurately label pictures of political symbols, such as the flag and the president and his wife. Connell (1971) noted that the political concepts of children before the age of 5 are made up of bits and pieces of information collected from home, school, and the media. These concepts typically reflect young children's lack of ability to synthesize information as well as their lack of cognitive development. Their political concepts are "full of political figures, cartoon characters, familiar figures of fact and legend that jostle each other with splendid promiscuity" (p. 11). At age 5, children seem to have concepts that reflect their personal knowledge of political symbols, such as the flag, pictures, songs, and stories.

Around the age of 5 or 6, children understand that the world has two groups of people—special and nonspecial—with those in power being considered special. The special people in power are also viewed with benevolence. Children see authority figures as benevolent people who will care for each of them personally. This perception is a result of children's cognitive ability and/or their emotional needs for safety and security.

The visit of Hillary Clinton as former First Lady to a kindergarten classroom exemplified children's beginning awareness of politics and political symbols. To prepare for the visit, the teacher asked the children to tell what the president does and what the First Lady does. They responded that the president "gives money to good guys and puts bad guys in jail," "takes care of us," and "works for us." They said that the First Lady "shares with people," "likes to farm," and "takes care of children."

In their study of children's political understanding, Robert Hess and Judith Torney (1967) found that young children's involvement with politics begins early with strong emotional attachment to the president. Children seem to think of the president personally—as someone who would help them if they telephoned him or went to him in person with a request.

By age 7, children's political concepts, partially as a result of changes in their cognitive abilities, also seem to change. Concepts are now more accurate, and a political consciousness develops. Children can construct a simple idea of government and the political world. They seem to have a store of ideas but continue to draw randomly from it. They do not yet distinguish among levels of government; when asked what political figures such as mayors, congresspersons, and presidents do, they say that all those people do the same thing.

Connell (1971) concluded that children, even by age 7, do not reproduce the communications that reach them from the adult world; they work them over, detach them from their original context, and assemble them into a general concept of what government is all about. However inaccurate and incomplete children's political concepts are, they form the base for children's later development.

From the research on children's political learning, the following conclusions can be drawn:

1. Concepts of politics begin in early childhood, and the process of development is continual.
2. Basic attachments and identifications are among the first political concepts acquired.
3. Children view political authority figures as positive, benevolent, and personal.
4. Feelings and affection develop before knowledge.
5. Not until late childhood can children distinguish between different political roles and synthesize basic factual information.

With experiential understandings of rules, authority and power, rights and responsibilities, and citizenship, children will be able to learn increasingly detailed, differentiated, and abstract information regarding the structures, documents, and processes that define and guide the government in a democracy.

Voting

In a democracy, decisions are made in many ways, including negotiating, consensus building, and voting. The right to vote and make choices for ourselves, however, is one of the most valued rights and responsibilities of living in a democracy. The habits and procedures involved in voting can be an appropriate part of children's early educational experiences (Figure 10.4).

When we vote, we accept that the will of the majority is followed. Young children, because of their egocentric thinking, may not understand completely the concept of winning and losing; nevertheless, they can start the process of learning to vote. Children who have made many choices for themselves and experienced the

> Children gradually learn the concepts of voting and majority rule. Teachers can use these first steps:
> - Ask children to make choices and explain the reasons for their choices.
> - Let children experience the consequences of their choices. One 5-year-old was observed putting blocks away while the rest of the class watched a video clip. When asked why he wasn't watching the clip, he said, "I decided to keep building. Now I have to clean up and miss the video. It's logical consequences."
> - Graph children's choices so children can talk about them.
> - Give children two choices, with all children getting their choice. (Decide to make chocolate or vanilla pudding; then graph how many children made chocolate and how many made vanilla.)

Figure 10.4 Learning to vote.

consequences of those choices can gradually learn to accept the consequences of the vote.

To begin, voting experiences can be structured so that each child will have his or her way. For example, children can vote to make either gelatin or pudding, with each group being allowed to make what it chooses; or, the class may be divided for games, those voting for Simon Says playing in one area of the room and those for Looby Loo in another area (Seefeldt & Galper, 2000).

You also could read the poem "The King's Breakfast" from *Now We Are Six* (Milne, 1955) and try butter or marmalade on pieces of bread. After tasting both, the group votes on whether the king was wise. Chart how many children voted for marmalade—like the king—and how many for butter.

The right to vote is one of the most valued rights of living in a democracy.

> In November, send a note to children's families:
>
> Part of our curriculum is teaching children to make wise choices. We ask children to vote and make decisions about many things in the classroom. You can help us build children's understanding of the voting process by taking them with you when you go to vote.
>
> When you go to vote, talk to the people outside the polling places and let your children examine the buttons and materials that are handed out. Inside, have the children examine the sample ballot and the voting machine. If you can, take your child into the booth when you vote. Explain that you are voting and making choices about who will represent you in our government.

Figure 10.5 Families vote!

After several experiences with voting, the entire class may follow the will of the majority. The class could vote and follow the will of the majority in deciding on any of the following issues:

- Rules for cleanup time
- Specific equipment they want to purchase for their class or school
- How to take turns for a specific task
- Who will lead the group for the day
- What service project to do

Children in the primary grades can begin developing ideas of local, state, and national elections. When elections take place, ask families to take their children with them as they vote (Figure 10.5). In the classroom, try to make the idea of voting as concrete as possible:

- Find books about voting, cooperation, and democracy. One class read *A Picture Book of Benjamin Franklin* (Adler & Wallner, 1991). Primary-age children can talk about the themes of the book: equality and cooperation.
- Create a voting box for the class so children can role-play voting.
- Allow children to vote on topics that are meaningful to them.

These ideas are introductions to voting, not actual involvement in a national or local vote. Still, they can be the foundation for building the concept that although not everyone holds the same opinions, everyone has a voice.

Symbols of Democratic Government

Children understand that symbols stand for things (e.g., their first word, *Mama*, stands for the person who is their mother), and children's minds are full of developing symbol systems (such as letters, numbers, and melodies). Using a variety of symbols including pictures and visuals, stories and songs, and movement can help children begin to understand abstract political concepts in concrete terms.

The President

Children see the president of the United States as a primary symbol of the country. Learning about past presidents through stories, songs, drama, and visual discovery is motivating for most children and builds a foundation for basic concepts of both government and history.

The Flag

The flag serves as a visual symbol. Children as young as 6 years old seem to recognize the importance of flags. Under age 6 or so children know that a flag designates a place or country, but they are not aware that flags carry explicit symbolic meaning (Helwig & Prencipe, 1999). Hess and Torney (1967) found that children see the flag as something belonging to a class of objects, such as chairs, but may not necessarily connect it with a particular country until later. Experiences with flags can help develop a sense of ownership ("That is the flag of my country," "This is the flag that I made"), which is the foundation for pride and loyalty (i.e., patriotism).

You can help children develop a concept of the flag when you do the following:

- Encourage children to design flags for the classroom. They can design flags that mean time to come in, time to clean up, or story time; or, they can design a class flag, deciding on its design, color, and meaning.
- Post various flags around the classroom or pin them on a world map, including those from children's native countries. Ask children where else they see the flag. Have them construct a booklet called "I See the Flag," drawing pictures and stories of the flags they see in their school, neighborhood, and community.
- Read stories about Betsy Ross and the history of the flag. A book for older children is *The Flag We Love* (Ryan, 1996). Children of all ages enjoy Nancy Caudill's (1995) *Did You Carry the Flag Today, Charley?*
- Start primary children on a research project about the U.S. flag. They can find out why the flag is sometimes called the "Stars and Stripes" and how and why the flag changed over the years. In their research they can find out why the flag first had 13 stars, then 20, and finally 50.
- Help primary children research other flags. These can include the flag of their school, their county, their state, other states, or their native countries.
- Sing songs or read poems and stories about the flag that may be meaningful to young children. "This Land Is Your Land," "Yankee Doodle," and "Flag of America" are examples of songs that children can enjoy and understand.
- Ask the Veterans of Foreign Wars, American Legion, or other patriotic groups to demonstrate the proper ways of handling and caring for the flag.
- Arrange for the children to participate in displaying the flag.

The Pledge of Allegiance

Although the Pledge of Allegiance is a common national symbol in elementary schools, teachers must be careful about requiring children to recite it under the assumption that recitation leads to understanding.

Written in 1892 by Francis Bellamy, associate editor of the magazine *The Youth's Companion* and vice president of the Society for Christian Socialists, the Pledge of Allegiance was created to celebrate the 400th anniversary of America's discovery. Since then, the debate over whether students should be required to recite the pledge in school has been ongoing (Seefeldt, 1989).

From 1937 to 1943, there was constant litigation with rulings both upholding and rejecting the constitutionality of requiring students to salute the flag and recite the Pledge of Allegiance. In 1940, the U.S. Supreme Court ruled that a state could require all children to salute the flag. The Court reversed itself in 1943 and held that the flag salute required by state law violated the religious beliefs of Jehovah's Witnesses and could not be compelled.

This holding remains today. No one, whether child or adult, may be compelled to salute the flag. Requiring children to recite the pledge is therefore a violation of fundamental constitutional rights and freedoms. Totalitarian countries impose political orthodoxy upon their citizens by mandating displays of allegiance; the United States does not.

Recital of the pledge may be opposed for other reasons as well. For most children, the ritual of the pledge is a meaningless one, done without thought. As such, it does not foster love of democratic attitudes and values. As with other political concepts, children construct their own knowledge of the pledge by putting together things they know with the unknown in splendid capriciousness. Thus, they recite, "one nation on the windowsill," "with liberty and jelly for all," and "I pledge allegiance to the flag, of the United States of American, and to the Publix [the name of a Southern food-store chain] for which it stands …".

Further, children have no clear idea of what the pledge is. "It's like a song, I guess," explains a 7-year-old. "No, I think it's a prayer," said another child. Asked what they think about when they say the pledge, many children confess, "I think about going out to play" or "about sitting down" (Seefeldt, 1989). Because the pledge holds little meaning, reciting it is an act more of indoctrination than of learning.

Ritual acts of indoctrination do not promote ownership; rather, they have the opposite effect. In fact, frequent participation in such rituals has been associated with lower scores on knowledge of civics and less support for democratic values. Rather than using the pledge as a form of nonsensical indoctrination, children should be introduced to its meaning:

- Reserve saying the pledge for special days—Earth Day; Lincoln's, Washington's, or Martin Luther King, Jr.'s birthday; Flag Day or other holidays—so that children learn that it has a special meaning and importance.
- Invite members of a scout troop to class to demonstrate their flag ceremony and recite the Pledge of Allegiance. The scouts might explain the meaning of their actions and tell what the flag means to them.

OWNERSHIP AND PRIDE

Ownership of and responsibility for democracy involves much more than daily recitation of the pledge or even recitation of the pledge on special occasions. Children must first learn who they are and how they fit into their own immediate community. Only after children develop individually in relation to family, school, neighborhood, and community can they begin to gain an understanding of their democracy.

School and Community

Explorations into the school community are a first step. Children develop pride in being members of the school community. They share in caring for the school, keeping it clean, decorating its halls with artwork, and participating in events such as assemblies or parties. Children can also observe the work of the many people who serve the school. They see the diversity of jobs, the variety of people, and the need for mutual cooperation.

With this base of understanding, children can then take neighborhood field trips and explore the larger community. Here, too, they observe how people are interdependent and begin to see that they and their school are small parts of a larger world.

Nation

You cannot take children on a field trip through the nation, but you can give them experiences that will enable them to begin to comprehend its size, magnificence, and diversity. Some of these experiences will necessarily be vicarious; but many can be concrete, with each planned to help children develop knowledge of their country. Integrating civics and government with children's study of history and geography can help as well.

The pleasurable, sensory experience of eating is one way to acquaint children with their country. When children eat oranges from Florida, they can locate Florida on a map and learn something about why oranges grow in Florida and not in Illinois; or, they could eat avocados from California, peaches from Georgia, potatoes from Maine, cherries from Michigan, or pineapples from Hawaii. It is also fun for children to plant the seeds from the foods. Then they can make comparisons between distant places and their own community.

The best resources are the children themselves. They can find out where they were born and where their parents and grandparents were born and lived. Primary children can locate these places on a map, or they can bring photos or props illustrating life in different areas of the United States or different countries around the world.

SUMMARY

Each preschool–primary classroom serves as a small laboratory in which children live the values of democracy. In a democratic classroom, teachers share control; children make choices; freedom of speech and thought are fostered; children's rights are respected, and they are not overwhelmed by the power of others; a sense of community is built; and teachers serve as models of respect for others. Through their interactions with others within a democracy and its symbols, children will learn political values, especially those of the rule of law, participation in a democracy, ownership, and responsibility.

Discussion Questions

1. Discuss "civic education as political indoctrination" versus "civic education for genuine democracy." What does each term mean? Why is it important to educate children for genuine democracy? How is that different from indoctrination? In what ways does indoctrination turn children off to civics?
2. What are the elements of a democratic classroom? What experiences are important for young children? How do these experiences teach them civics?
3. This chapter includes two NCSS standards. What are they? What are the key concepts of each one? What connections, if any, do you see between the two?
4. How can you prepare children for civic participation and community service? What experiences are important?
5. What can you teach children about political symbols? How can you help them begin to sense the meaning of the symbols?
6. Why are ownership and pride important in civic education?
7. What connections to you see between civics and the other disciplines? What opportunities are there for integration?
8. Select one of the books from the Children's Literature Box. What standard (NCSS, NAEYC, or local/state) might this book be used to teach? What would a lesson or unit plan that used this book to teach this standard look like?

Extend Your Knowledge

1. Observe in a classroom. Record any observations of teachers' modeling of democratic values. What instances can you find of teachers sharing control with children, respecting each child, encouraging children to speak freely and have opinions, and fostering children's willingness to participate in the workings of the group?
2. Research the flag of the United States. What did you learn that you did not know before? Research a flag from another country. What do the symbols mean? What do the colors stand for? What does this tell you about that country, its history, and its values?
3. Interview young children about a particular political concept, such as voting or the president. What basic understandings do they have? What misconceptions?
4. Hold a class meeting to discuss classroom rules. What do the children understand about rules? What suggestions did they have? How did they participate? What social skills were evident? What social skills need development?

Resources

The **Center for Civic Education** and CIVITAS (www.civiced.org) offer a variety of teaching resources and aids:

- *The National Standards for Civics and Government*
- *CIVITAS: A Framework for Civic Education*
- *American Legacy: The U.S. Constitution and Other Essential Documents of American Democracy*
- *Comparative Lessons in Democracy*
- *Morality of Democratic Citizenship*

You can order *The Constitution Papers* (available on CD-ROM), a complete research tool on the U.S. Constitution, dozens of state constitutions, historical documents, and selected speeches from American history for your own use.

The *Social Science Education Consortium* offers materials such as *C Is for Citizenship: Children's Literature and Civic Understanding* by Laurel R. Singleton (1997, Boulder, CO). These can be ordered through the National Council for Social Studies.
www.ncss.org

For a discussion of how to develop learning communities and conduct class meetings, see *Learning to Teach* by Richard I. Arends.

CiviConnections is a program developed by the National Council for Social Studies that integrates local history with community service learning.
www.ncss.org

The *Census Bureau* has activities for children.
www.census.gov

CHAPTER 11

Global Connections

> Focus Questions
>
> After you read this chapter, you should be prepared to respond to the following questions:
>
> - What are key concepts about global connections?
> - What is meant by interdependency? What are the major commonalities among the peoples of the world?
> - What are some examples of resources for learning about others?
> - What is global education, and what are its benefits?

Global Connections: Social studies programs should include experiences that provide for the study of global connections and interdependence. (NCSS, 2010, p. 22)

The ninth strand in the NCSS curriculum standards (2010), Global Connections, is typically integrated into units and courses about geography, history, economics, and culture (Figure 11.1). In this text, we have decided to bring it to your attention by giving it a place of its own. In today's global world, about which we

> **Standard IX:**
> Through the Global Connections standard
>
> - children will come to understand
>   - connections between peoples world-wide can be based on cultural exchange, politics, trade, economics, or travel;
>   - our everyday way of life is affected by these global connections;
>   - some global issues have existed for many years, but others, such as almost instant communication and advancing technology, are recent developments;
>   - global connections influence, and are influenced by, how different cultures meet their needs;
>   - global change has been more rapid during the past decade or so;
> - children will be able to
>   - examine global developments, patterns, and connections using maps and other sources of information;
>   - explore the connections to people around the world;
>   - recognize instances of regional, state-wide, and community-based global connections;
>   - report on cases of conflict and cooperation world-wide;
>   - examine how global connections are affected by technology;
>   - understand that the wants and needs of people in one part of the world may clash with those in another part of the world;
>   - study problems experienced by people living in other lands;
>   - describe how understanding and misunderstanding can result from art, books, music, and movies produced by other cultures.

Figure 11.1   NCSS Standard VIII: Global Connections.
Based on NCSS National Curriculum Standards for Social Studies, 2010.

hear so much in the media and politics, this standard takes on a whole new perspective. The young children we teach now will be the citizens and change agents of the future. We cannot imagine what the world will be like 40 years from now, but one thing is guaranteed: These children will be the adults contending with those future issues.

Social studies in the early childhood years have traditionally focused on the immediate life and environment of the young child; however, it is possible to help children explore global connections by relating those connections to their own experiences and lives. Worldwide events affect young children through the media and, for some, through personal experience. Many hear about wars and other conflicts overseas on a daily basis, and television brings images of how children live around the world. Many of the images children see are negative, and as teachers we need to help them interpret them—turn them into a positive experience by suggesting plans for responsive actions. There are also many wonders and common understandings that the world offers. These, too, should be shown to our children so that they grow in appreciation of the planet and global society in which they are destined to live.

KEY CONCEPTS

- *Interconnectedness and interdependency.* We need to live with others, and others need to live with us. Young children will not be able to understand how our nation relies on other nations for trade and commerce, and they certainly will not understand the political and cultural interdependency of all nations. Regardless, teachers can foster in young children a basis for the concept that every part of the world is interdependent.
- *Similarities.* Humans have many things in common. All societies have in common basic needs, group rules and organization, and art forms. All of these can be investigated, focusing on those in America and comparing them to those found in other countries.
- *Resources for learning about others.* Children's knowledge about others can be based on their own backgrounds and experiences. Other people in the community are equally rich sources of information. The Internet is a useful, if vicarious, information source, as are children's books and other literature and media.
- *Global education.* Children's natural interest in toys can be a springboard for investigating the life of children in other countries. This can lead to further investigation into the lives and perspectives of others. Peace education can introduce the children to the idea of helping others.

INTERCONNECTEDNESS AND INTERDEPENDENCY

Interdependency begins early for humans because infants depend on their parents for care. Parents, to be parents at all, depend on their infants. Within the context of the home, children experience the idea of interdependency and interconnectedness. Once in the preschool–primary classroom, young learners can examine and explore their connectedness with and interdependency on others in a variety of ways (NCSS, 2010). These might include the following:

- Live pets, which require food, care, and attention, give children concrete experiences with the interdependence of living things.
- Each child can tell the class something he or she can do well or likes to do for the class. These statements can be recorded in a booklet or on an experience chart.
- A pictorial chart, showing ways in which children can help one another, can be an ongoing project, with pictures added as new ways of helping are developed.
- Children can be involved in activities that require working together, such as setting a table, cooking simple foods, caring for a garden, or building a piece of large equipment. Each child can be responsible for a specific part of the group project.

Experiencing interdependency, however, is not enough. Teachers need to help children construct ideas of both dependency and interdependency. Some teachers begin by using the word *dependent*. For example, as children care for pets, teachers say, "The guinea pig is dependent on you. It cannot live without you."; or, when working together on a cooking project, caring for a garden, or constructing a large piece of equipment, teachers remind children of how dependent they are on each other: "We're depending on you, Jose, to stir the eggs." "Hold that wood still; we'll depend on you so we can hammer the nail here."

When children are familiar with the concept of dependency, they can be introduced to the idea of interdependency—that they are dependent on others and that others are dependent on them. Immediate classroom activities and events demonstrate this idea to the children. As children return toys and materials to their proper places, leave the easels ready for the next painters, pick up coats that have fallen from hooks, or help one another button painting smocks, describe what the children are doing: "Thanks, we're dependent on you to . . . and you're dependent on others to do the same."

For children in the primary grades, class activities such as small-group work and class meetings (Vance & Weaver, 2002), in which issues and ideas are openly discussed, can foster children's awareness of their interconnectedness as well as teach them the skills necessary to live and work with others. During group meetings, problems can be solved, children recognized for their contributions to the group, and explicit feedback given on how children are working together as a group.

Trips through the school to observe the interdependency among faculty and staff can foster children's ideas of the concept. A trip to the office or the cafeteria to identify workers and their tasks acquaints children with the idea of how connected one individual is to many others.

Literature and factual books can clarify or expand children's ideas of dependency and interdependency. *Frog, Duck, and Rabbit* (Gretz, 1992), a story about how

Live pets give children concrete experiences with interdependence.

three animals work together to construct a costume, and *The Chocolate Train* (Kornfeld, 2002), about chocolate making, are examples of books that can contribute to children's understanding of interdependency.

How our lifestyle is dependent on products from other parts of the world is an interesting concept for primary grades. Ask the children to examine the packets and boxes of things they use in the home and in the supermarket to find the country of origin. Other things we use that originate or are made overseas, such as oil, cars, and clothes, can be discussed, and the teacher can find more information from the companies, at the public library, and from the embassies of countries such as Brazil, Japan, and China. A world map to identify the countries of origin will reinforce the concept of global connections (see the Resources section at the end of this chapter).

Teachers can encourage America's children to think globally by illustrating how they are individuals who are also members of the whole human race, and that this connection to all humankind supersedes all other cultural aspects.

Similarities

A focus on similarities rather than differences is recommended for several reasons. First, children can already identify differences and are more likely to concentrate on them rather than on how people everywhere are similar. Further, children begin stereotyping other groups by expressing distrust or fear of those who are different.

Focusing on similarities is not simplistic ("We have different-colored skins, but we're all alike"). Rather, it is complicated and complex and emphasizes the fact that humans everywhere share in the human experience (Brophy & Alleman, 2002). This shared human experience and cultural diversity can be woven into all aspects of the curriculum. The emphasis on social and emotional development can be expanded to incorporate the enhancement of children's cultural identity and their awareness, concerns, and respect for other people (Ramsey, 2003).

By illustrating that, regardless of group membership or geography, people are bound together by their similarities, the content of the social studies unites people (Brophy & Alleman, 2002). Children who understand similarities among people are less likely to fear, distrust, and stereotype others. Around the world, in all societies, people share the following commonalities:

- Art forms
- Group rules
- Social organization
- Basic needs
- Language
- Celebrations

Art Forms

Children who are encouraged to create their own poetry, paintings, dance, literature, or handicrafts can readily understand and appreciate the art of other countries

All cultures have music and art.

(Seefeldt, 2000). Art from other nations can help children discover people's common heritage. Children can do many of the following activities:

- Visit museums to observe the art of many cultures. You can display art from all over the world in the classroom.
- If you have artifacts from other countries, or if the children's families do, set up a museum in your own classroom. A map of the world with colored tacks to show all the places from which they came will fascinate the children.
- Exchange their paintings, drawings, or creative writing with a school in some other land.
- Invite foreign visitors to tell folktales from their nations. You can compare the folktales with those of the United States.
- Listen to poetry from other lands—perhaps some haiku from Japan—and dictate their own poetry.
- Listen to music and folk songs from other lands. These are readily available on CDs and DVDs from the local library or any book and music store.

Figure 11.2 suggests how technology can help. Children can reflect their own cultural and racial identity in their own artwork. One primary group of children from El Salvador was taught how to weave. The children first talked with their grandparents, who remembered weaving and told them how it was done. Then they studied pictures of woven mats and went to visit a textile museum displaying weavings from Central America. Back in the classroom, they designed rugs and wall hangings using crayons and markers. The designs were then transferred into line

> Use technology to show children that their own art forms are both similar to and different from art forms in other countries:
> - Set up a class e-mail exchange with a class in another country.
> - Using digital photography, exchange e-mailed artwork. You might choose a theme, such as *Clothing We Like, Special Food, Butterflies We Know, What We Do in Winter,* and so on. Both classes draw, paint, or construct their ideas about the theme and exchange their artwork through e-mails or a web site.
> - Find web resources about art from other times and places. Compare this art to the work the children create.
> - In a discussion, compare artwork from other places and times with children's current work.

Figure 11.2 Using technology to unite children.

drawings on larger sheets of paper, which were placed in back of a loom. An art teacher demonstrated how to execute the design through weaving.

Using paint, crayons, and clay in multicultural skin tones allows children to create pictures and forms of themselves and others in their classroom and school (see Chapter 5 for a paint source). The natural skin tones of washable paint, crayons, colored pencils, markers, and modeling clay, which can be applied and blended or mixed easily, allow children to express pride in themselves, their families, and their community through their own artistic expression.

Group Rules

As children begin to realize that rules are necessary to live together effectively, they can understand how groups function more successfully when the rights of each group member are recognized. Children can do the following:

- Establish their own rules for using playground equipment, allowing people into the housekeeping area, or walking to the cafeteria.
- Use the rules of the school—e.g., walk in the hall, remain quiet while waiting for the bus—to illustrate the rules of a larger community. You can also help them compare classroom rules with their rules at home.
- Explore the rules of the community, such as the traffic rules. Do all communities have such rules? Why?
- Determine what rules the nation has, and compare them to the laws of other lands.

Social Organization

Although the composition of families and social groups varies dramatically from place to place, all human beings live in some type of group or social organization.

To comprehend the similarities among social groups, children in primary grades can do the following activities:

- Graph their own families' composition to show how many different kinds of family units are represented in their classroom. You will want to discuss with the children how these family units are the same.
- Exchange letters with a family in some other nation to learn how it is like a family in this country.
- Invite visitors from other countries to tell about their families, the things family members do together, and how they share work or celebrate holidays.
- Read books and watch DVDs about the lives of families in other countries. Focus on the similarities in routines, such as bedtime rituals. *Lala Salama: An African Lullaby* by Hannah Heritage Bozylinsky (1993) is a delightful book. It is written in Swahili and English and tells how a small Maasai boy says "Good night!" (Lala salama!) to the animals around his home and to his family.

Basic Needs

Borrowing concepts from the field of economics, you can teach children that people the world over have the same basic needs for food, shelter, and clothing (Brophy & Alleman, 2002, 2005a, 2007). Children might be able to do the following:

- Examine different shelters from around the world. Ask children, "How are they just like our homes?" "How are they different?" "How many different kinds of homes do we live in?" "How are they alike?"
- Compare the clothing of other nations. Ask, "How is it just like the clothing we wear?" "What things do we use that they do not?" One kindergartner, after comparing shoes from seven different countries, said, "The shoes are different, but everybody has feet."

A unit on bread illustrates how people of different cultures, while having the same basic needs, meet those needs in different ways. After reading the book *Bread, Bread, Bread* by Ann Morris (1989), teachers asked children what kind of bread they ate at home. The names of the different breads were listed and discussed. Samples were brought to school, compared, and tasted. Children made bread and wrote stories about breads, learning that bread is a food that most people have in common, even though the types may differ.

Language

People everywhere communicate both verbally and nonverbally. Verbal communication may involve many languages; nonverbal communication is useful when the verbal communication of others is not understood. Children can learn that both verbal and nonverbal communication skills are involved when they try to express feelings, ideas, attitudes, and knowledge. Following are some suggestions:

1. Give children many opportunities to communicate in the classroom on a one-to-one basis or in large or small groups. Methods might include using a telephone

or audio cassette recorder or dictating to the teacher. Draw children's attention to their use of nonverbal communication and extend the concept by introducing American Indian sign language or the sign language used to communicate with the deaf (American Sign Language [ASL]), role-playing, or dramatizations.
2. Read children the story *Children of the World Say Good Morning* (Martin, 1969d), and teach children to say "good morning" in some language other than English. Read *What Is Your Language?* (Leventhal & Wellington, 1998), in which a small child from New York City packs his bags and travels around the world, asking, "What is your language?" and learning to say "yes" and "no" in 10 languages. This simple book introduces children to the idea that they are part of a worldwide community.
3. Expose children to someone who is speaking another language; you or a visitor might teach the children a few phrases in the language. You could teach a few simple songs and let the children listen to music from other countries. The following two Internet sources can help you with more information on other languages:
   - Say Hello to the World Project at www.ipl.org
   - I love Languages at www.ilovelanguages.com
4. Remember that different accents and dialects are also types of linguistic diversity. Model Standard American English (SAE), but do not correct any child who uses a different dialect.
5. Children in the primary grades enjoy and benefit from having a pen pal. Even kindergarteners can learn about others by exchanging pictures and dictated letters with other young children who live far from them, perhaps using e-mail or the Internet.

The written language in stories, poetry, nonfiction books, and other forms of literature is a way of bridging the gap between what children know about others and what they do not. Such books can provide accurate, authentic information about the similarities and differences among people everywhere. They can help teachers open communication and foster environments of understanding and respect. Each year the National Council for the Social Studies and the Children's Book Council offers a list of multicultural books (Figure 11.3).

An element common to communication is that people everywhere have feelings. Children learn to express their feelings positively in the classroom, without hurting others; they learn to recognize that all people have the same feelings. When reading stories about people from other lands, such as *The Story of Ping* (Flack, 1977), you can ask the children, "How do you think the boy felt when he fell into the water?" "How would you have felt?" "Has anything like that ever happened to you?"

One teacher, after reading Aliki's (1987) *The Two of Them*, asked children to talk about love. The children talked about love they receive from adults, how a cat loves her kittens, and so forth. In another lesson, a teacher used two guinea pigs of different colors to demonstrate how things can be alike but different, which led to a discussion of how people can love others who may be different from them and can be friends with others of a different skin color.

> *Is There Really a Human Race?* by Jamie Lee Curtis and Laura Cornell. Teaches children to enjoy life's journey, be kind to all, and be true to themselves. It was adopted as a UNICEF book.
>
> *Got Geography!* (2006), poems selected by Lee Bennett Hopkins. These poems show that geography is more than maps and globes; it is an adventure.
>
> *Children of the World: How We Live, Learn, and Play in Poems, Drawings, and Photographs* by Anthony Asael and Stephanie Rabemiafara.
>
> *Children Just Like Me: A Unique Celebration of Children Around the World* by Anabel Kindersley and Barnabas Kindersley, available at www.amazon.com/Barnabas-Kindersley/e/B00287R9C0/ref=ntt_athr_dp_pel_2. Sponsored by UNICEF.
>
> *Children Just Like Me: Celebrations!* by Anabel Kindersley and Barnabas Kindersley. Describes celebrations and festivals around the world.
>
> *Wake up, World! A Day in the Life of Children Around the World* by Beatrice Holliger.
>
> *Let's Eat: What Children Eat Around the World* by Beatrice Hollyer.
>
> *Celebrate!: Connections Among Cultures* by Jan Reynolds.
>
> *Global Art: Activities, Projects, and Inventions from Around the World* by MaryAnn F. Kohl and Jean Potter.
>
> *What Does It Mean to Be Global?* by Rana DiOrio. A conversation starter to teach children about exploring, appreciating, and respecting other children's traditions, religions, and values the world over.
>
> *Mama Miti: Wangari Maathai and the Trees of Kenya* by Donna Jo Napoli. The story of the Nobel Prize winner who worked with the women of Kenya to reforest their country.

Figure 11.3 Children's Literature Box for Global Connections.

Some children have lived in other parts of the world. Reading *A Country Far Away* (Gray & Dupasquier, 1988) will open up discussion about the lives of children in other countries. The book compares the life of two boys, one in a Western country and the other in Africa. Pictures of the boys' lives are shown together on each page, providing excellent opportunities to discuss the similarities and differences.

Other classroom experiences give children opportunities to clarify their feelings toward other people and understand the feelings of others. You can ask the children, "How did you feel when you hit him?" "How do you think he felt?" "How did it feel when they asked you to play with them?" "How did you feel when they called you a name?" You can also help children perceive the feelings of others: "What do you think she was telling you when she screamed at you?" "How do you think she felt?"

Celebrations

Many cultures celebrate seasonal changes in fall, winter, spring, and summer; or such changes as the rainy season and the dry season. These usually have become formal traditions. This is a "big idea" that children love exploring, especially around the month of December. The following are excellent sources to learn more information about world religions and celebrations/festivals:

- The Earth Calendar at www.earthcalendar.net
- Holidays at www.holidays.net
- Virtual Religion Index at virtualreligion.net/vri

Trade

Our interconnectedness and interdependence with other countries can easily be illustrated by examining the places in which our clothes, cars, and other commodities have been manufactured. In addition, a trip to a supermarket's produce and international foods section would provide excellent examples of how our diet is influenced by foods from other countries. A class exploration of the adventures of a banana would provide opportunities to examine maps of sea and air routes and also climate information.

Technology

The advent of more advanced airplanes, telephone systems, and the Internet have greatly enhanced worldwide communication. As a child, one of the authors was raised in Hong Kong. Trips back to the United Kingdom to visit grandparents, aunts, and uncles were rare, happening every 4 years, because of high costs and slow travel. It took 3–4 weeks by sea, and 36–48 hours by plane. After being sent back to England to attend boarding school at the age of 11, contact with parents was not easy. Phone calls were expensive and had to be booked in advance; therefore, they happened on Christmas day only and lasted for only 6–10 minutes. Letters sent by mail could take up to 3 weeks to arrive. This is unimaginable today in these times of instant e-mail and text messages, long-distance calls around the world, and rapid jet flights.

RESOURCES FOR LEARNING ABOUT OTHERS

The most effective resources available for children's development of international concepts are the children themselves. Their heritage and backgrounds of experience provide a base from which you can build their knowledge. Teachers, along with children and their families, can explore children's ethnic heritage in class by making charts of the different nationalities represented, discussing the customs of different families, and participating in these customs.

Equally effective resources are people who have lived in or visited other countries or who are citizens of other nations. As visitors to the class, they can illustrate how people everywhere are similar yet do things in different ways. The mere presence of resource persons, however, does not guarantee the development of positive attitudes and understandings. To ensure a positive experience for both the visitor and the children, you need to:

- Know something about the person to make sure that he has more than a cursory knowledge of the country and can talk to children.
- Brief the visitor about the class, and help plan the presentation. Young children become restless when asked only to listen. The visitor might be asked to include some concrete materials or props in the discussion to attract the children.
- Be certain that the children have sufficient understanding of the country. Visitors from Mumbai or Rio de Janeiro are frequently appalled when children want to know whether they have refrigerators or cars.
- Prepare the children for possible differences in appearance or language before the visitor comes. Discuss with them how to behave in the presence of a guest. Plan with them about ways to make the guest comfortable: "Who will take her coat? Where will she sit? How will we listen, ask questions, and thank her?"
- Have globes and maps available so children can locate the country.
- Use online resources to learn about others.

You can use other experiences to help children recognize cultural similarities. You might suggest specific television shows that offer children insight into other people's cultures, or you might bring in newspaper and magazine articles that clarify children's concepts of others. Reference books, travel posters, photographs, and videos are also useful to compare people's similarities.

Analyze these materials to make certain they do the following:

- Reflect the many groups in our nation and world
- Do not omit, distort, or present insensitive pictures of a group of people
- Reflect our pluralistic society

Holiday activities can introduce children to pleasant and interesting aspects of other people's customs. Young children enjoy a Japanese Kite Day as they marvel at the Japanese custom of giving children a day off from school to fly kites. An egg tree

Online resources let children reach out to others far from them.

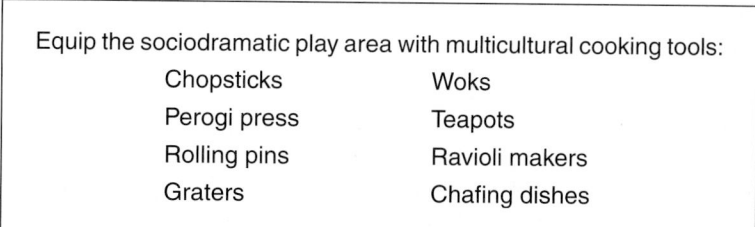

Figure 11.4 Playing with multicultural props.

for an Easter/spring celebration helps children understand and appreciate Slovakian celebrations. Baking and eating hot-cross buns may help children feel close to children in Great Britain.

Tasting other foods from various cultures is useful. Discuss why people prepare the foods the way they do, and find the countries on the map to help children develop an awareness of other people's customs and similarities.

Museums, historical societies, and embassies all offer children concrete experiences with other cultures. Each community will have some type of museum where children can view artifacts from other lands and compare their similarities.

Toys and play are universals in childhood and can be a natural basis for a global education curriculum (see Figure 11.4). Teachers can use toys and play to connect children from all parts of the world. You can provide children with toys made in various countries, such as puzzles from Holland, blocks from Switzerland, dolls from Korea, or games originating in Africa. Children over age 6 or 7 can be introduced to games that children in other nations play. But teachers need to interact sensitively with children. They may point out that the differences in the dress of dolls reflect clothes that people wear rather than being costumes or that steering wheels on cars in other countries are on the *other* side of the car rather than the *wrong* side.

Kindergarten children can play with puppets and use them to retell stories. The variations in familiar folktales—such as the various ways people around the world tell the story "The Three Billy Goats Gruff" and the role of the troll—can be compared and acted out with puppets. First-graders can compare toy catalogs from other nations or draw and write their own, and second-graders might put on a toy fair in the school library.

GLOBAL EDUCATION

The term *global education* is used more frequently nowadays in schools. It focuses on how people in other countries live their lives and examines the similarities and differences. An important part of this curriculum is encouraging children to look beyond their own cultural perspectives and understand how the daily lives, beliefs, and understandings of peoples in other countries are shaped by their culture. It has been found that such a program does lead to a more open-minded attitude towards the people of the countries studied (Meyer, Sherman, & MacKinster,

2006). Merryfield (1997, as cited in Meyer et al., 2006, p. 349) outlined eight elements of global education:

- Human beliefs and values
- Global systems
- Global issues and problems
- Cross-cultural understanding
- Awareness of human choices
- Global history
- Acquisition of indigenous knowledge
- Development of analytical, evaluative, and participatory skills

These all fit with the Global Connections strand for social studies.

Peace education also fits in with this concept. It has moved on from merely being a call for the end of war (Baker, Martin, & Pence, 2008). Peace education now focuses on counteracting poverty, prejudice, and discrimination as well as violence and war (UNESCO, 1945). The aim is to humanize education and optimize human development to bring about a kinder, more accepting world.

Even young children can be encouraged to participate in social action (Banks, 2008). They can donate toys, books, and clothes to overseas charities for children in poverty-stricken areas of the world, if you help them select a specific cause and country. They can locate the places on the map, and the charity will send literature with information about the recipients. Of course, this activity has to be addressed with sensitivity where young children are concerned since they are exposed to images of poor, hungry, and destitute children on the television. Knowing that they can help in a practical way will ease the horrors of those images for them.

SUMMARY

The world in which young children live is becoming increasingly global. Including aspects of global connections in social studies will expose them to big ideas and prepare them for the future.

The big idea of global interconnectedness and interdependency can be introduced through experiencing dependency. We are dependent on others for help and friendship. Class pets and plants will not survive without care. The next step is to examine ways in which that dependency is mutual, leading to the concept of interdependency. We help each other in groups, in school, and at work. We depend on other countries for such goods as oil, food, and materials. Those countries in turn depend on the United States for products and services.

People around the world are more similar than different. We all have basic needs, art forms, group rules, social organization, and language. Teachers can introduce each of these commonalities to the children. There are many activities that will help children explore these ideas, and the necessary information can be obtained through museums, the community, embassies, and the local library.

Global education encourages children to inquire beyond their own cultural perspectives and understand the world of other peoples, investigating similarities and differences. Human beliefs and values, global issues and problems, cross-cultural understanding, and becoming aware of human choices are all concepts included in global education.

Peace education focuses on making the world a better place in which to live. This can lead to social action projects, empowering the children while helping others.

Discussion Questions

1. Can you identify the interdependencies in your life? Create a concept map of them. How can you begin to teach children about the meaning of interdependency?
2. What are the origins of some of the everyday foods and their ingredients that you see in the stores? How many countries of origin can you identify? What are the implications for the world in which young children will grow up?
3. To which other countries have you travelled? What were some of the best experiences you had? What were some of the worst? What did this teach you about other countries? How can you use what you have learned to teach children about other countries?

Extend Your Knowledge

1. Interview a group of primary grade children and ask them if they know where some of the goods we use every day come from—for example, gas for the car, bananas, sneakers.
2. Listen to music and folk songs from other countries. How many American folk songs do you know? Teach some of them to a group of children.

Resources

- Maps of the world showing air routes, ports, food and commodity sources, etc.: *www.mapsofworld.com/world-maps*
- Airline route maps: *www.airlineroutemaps.com*
- Celebrations of Light: a lower elementary thematic lesson on holiday celebrations: *www.learner.org*
- The Earth Calendar at *www.earthcalendar.net*
- Holidays at *www.holidays.net*
- Virtual Religion Index at *virtualreligion.net/vri*
- Say Hello to the World Project at *www.ipl.org*
- I Love Languages at *www.ilovelanguages.com*
- National Geographic Society Education *www.nationalgeographic.com/education*
- National Council for Social Studies Notable Trade Books for Young People including books on global connections at *www.ncss.org/resources*

References

Aardema, V. (1991). *Borrequita and the coyote.* New York: Dragonfly.
Adler, D. A., & Wallner, J. W. (1991). *A picture book of Benjamin Franklin.* New York: Holiday House.
Ainsworth, M. D., Belhar, M., Waters, E., & Wall, S. (1978). *Patterns of attachment.* Hillsdale, NJ: Erlbaum.
Aliki. (1987). *We are best friends.* New York: Morrow.
Alleman, J., & Brophy, J. (2001). *Social studies excursions, K–3, book one: Powerful units on food, clothing, and shelter.* Portsmouth, NH: Heinemann.
Alleman, J., & Brophy, J. (2002). *Social studies excursions, K–3, book two: Powerful units on communication, transportation, and family living.* Portsmouth, NH: Heinemann.
Alleman, J., & Brophy, J. (2003). *Social studies excursions, K–3, book three: Powerful units on childhood, money, and government.* Portsmouth, NH: Heinemann.
Allen, G. L. (1997). Children's political knowledge and memory for political news stories. *Child Study Journal, 27,* 163–177.
Allport, G. (1952). *The nature of prejudice.* New York: Doubleday Anchor.
American Association for Health Education. (1999). *Mission statement and resolution.* Reston, VA: Author.
American Association of University Women. (2000). *A license for bias.* Washington, DC: Author.
American Psychological Association. (2003). *Guidelines on multicultural education, training, research, practice, and organizational change for psychologists.* Washington, DC: Author.
Ames, L. (1946). The development of the sense of time in the young child. *Journal of Genetic Psychology, 18,* 97–125.

Anderson, C. B., & Metzger, S. A. (2011). Slavery, the Civil War, and African American representation in U. S. history: An analysis of four states' academic standards. *Theory and Research in Social Education, 39*, 393–415.

Anderson, L. W., & Krathwol, D. R. (Eds.). (2001). *A taxonomy for learning, teaching, and assessing: A revision of Bloom's taxonomy of educational objectives.* Boston, MA: Allyn and Bacon.

Anderson, S. R. (1998). The trouble with testing. *Young Children, 53*, 25–30.

Angell, A. V. (2004). Making peace in elementary classrooms: A case for class meetings. *Theory and Research in Social Education, 32*, 98–104.

Arends, R. I. (2012). *Learning to teach* (9th ed.). Boston: McGraw-Hill.

Arthus-Bertrand, Y., & Burleigh, R. (2002). *Earth from above for young readers.* New York: Abrams.

Auel, J. (1980). *The clan of the cave bear.* New York: Bantam.

Baker, M., Martin, D., & Pence, H. (2008) Supporting peace education in teacher education programs. *Childhood Education, 85*, 20–25.

Bandura, A. (1997). *Self-efficacy: The exercise of control.* New York: Freeman.

Banks, J. A. (2008). *An introduction to multicultural education* (4th ed.). Needham Heights, MA: Allyn & Bacon.

Banks, J. A. (2009). *Teaching strategies for ethnic studies* (8th ed.). Boston: Allyn & Bacon.

Barnes, M. K., Johnson, E. C., & Neff, L. (2010). Learning through process drama in the first grade. *Social Studies and the Young Learner, 22*(4), 19–24.

Barry-Davis, J. (1999). Intuitive understanding of time and space at the age of four. *Dissertation Abstracts International, 60*(6-A), 0419–4209.

Barton, K. C. (2002). "Oh, that's a tricky piece !" Children, mediated action, and the tools of historical time. *Elementary School Journal, 103*, 161–186.

Barton, K., & Levstik, L. (1996). "Back when God was around and everything": Elementary children's understanding of historical time. *American Educational Research Journal, 33*, 419–454.

Bauer, P. J. (2006). Event memory. In W. Damon, R. M. Lerner (Series Eds.), D. Kuhn, & R. Siegler (Vol. Eds.), *Handbook of child psychology, Vol. 1: Cognition, perception and language* (6th ed.). New York: Wiley.

Beaty, J. J. (1999). *Prosocial guidance for the preschool child.* Upper Saddle River, NJ: Merrill/Prentice Hall.

Bennett, L., & Berson, M. J. (Eds.). (2007). *Digital age: Technology based K-12 lesson plans for social studies.* National Council for Social Studies: Silver Spring, MD.

Bennett, L., & Cunningham, W. (2011). Founding documents and national symbols: A third grade webquest. *Social Studies and the Young Learner, 23*(4), 13–16.

Berk, L. E. (2001). *Development through the lifespan.* Boston: Allyn & Bacon.

Berkowitz, M. W. (2000). Early character development and education. *Early Education and Development, 11*, 55–72.

Berson, I. R. (2009). Here's what we have to say! Podcasting in the early childhood classroom. *Social Studies and the Young Learner, 21*(4), 8–11.

Berson, M. J. (2001). Promoting civic action through online resources: An emphasis on global child advocacy. *International Journal of Social Education, 15*, 31–45.

Berti, A. E., & Bombi, A. S. (1988). *The child's construction of economics.* Cambridge, UK: Cambridge University Press.

Beskow, E. (1972). *Pelle's new suit.* New York: Scholastic Book Services.

Birch, S. H., & Ladd, G. W. (1998). Children's interpersonal behaviors and the teacher–child relationship. *Developmental Psychology, 34*, 934–946.

Blagojevic, B. (2003). Funding technology: Does it make a difference? *Young Children, 58*, 28–34.

Blizzard, G. S. (1990). *Come look with me: Enjoying art with children.* Charlottesville, VA: Thomasson-Grant.

Bloom, B. (1963). *Stability and change in human characteristics.* New York: Wiley.

Bloom, B. (1981). *All our children learning.* New York, NY: McGraw-Hill.

Bodrova, E., & Leong, D. J. (2003). Chopsticks and counting chips: Do play and foundational skills need to compete for teacher's attention in an early childhood program? *Young Children, 58*(3), 10–17.

Bost, K. K., Vaughn, B. E., Washington, W. N., Ceilinski, K. L., & Bradbard, M. R. (1998). Social competence, social support, and attachment: Demarcation of construct domains, measurement, and paths of influence for preschool children attending Head Start. *Child Development, 69*, 192–219.

Bower, B., & Lobdell, J. (2005). *Social studies alive: Engaging diverse learners in the elementary classroom* (Revised ed.). Palo Alto, CA: Teachers' Curriculum Institute.

Boyle-Baise, M. (2003). Doing democracy in social studies methods. *Theory and Research in Social Education, 31*, 50–70.

Boyle-Baise, M., Bernes-Kinkead, D., Coake, W., Loudermilk, L., Lukasik, D., & Podany, W. (2011). Citizenship as a verb: Teaching students to become informed, think it through, and take action. *Social Studies and the Young Learner, 24*(1), 5–9.

Boyle-Baise, M., Hsu, M.-C., Johnson, S., Serriere, S. C., & Stewart, D. (2008). Putting reading first: Teaching social studies in elementary classrooms. *Theory and Research in Social Education, 36*, 233–255.

Boyle-Baise, M., & Zevin, J. (2009). *Young citizens of the world: Teaching elementary social studies through civic engagement.* New York: Rutledge.

Bozylinsky, H. H. (1993). *Lala salama: An African lullaby.* New York: Putnam and Gosset Group.

Bredekamp, S. (1998). *Tools for teaching developmentally appropriate practice: The leading edge in early childhood education.* Cincinnati, OH: Resources for Instruction and Staff Excellence.

Bredekamp, S. (2003). Resolving contradictions between cultural practices. In C. Copple (Ed.), *A world of difference* (pp. 59–61). Washington, DC: National Association for the Education of Young Children.

Bredekamp, S., & Copple, C. (1997). *Developmentally appropriate practice in early childhood programs serving children from birth through age 8.* Washington, DC: National Association for the Education of Young Children.

Bredekamp, S., & Copple, C. (2009). *Developmentally appropriate practice in early childhood programs serving children from birth through age 8* (3rd ed.). Washington, DC: National Association for the Education of Young Children.

Bredekamp, S., & Rosegrant, T. (1992). *Reaching potentials: Vol. 1. Appropriate curriculum and assessment for young children.* Washington, DC: National Association for the Education of Young Children.

Bredekamp, S., & Rosegrant, T. (1995). *Reaching potentials: Vol. 2. Transforming early childhood and assessment.* Washington, DC: National Association for the Education of Young Children.

Britt, J., & LaFontaine, G. (2009). Google earth: A virtual globe for elementary geography. *Social Studies and the Young Learner, 21*(4), 20–23.

Bronfenbrenner, U. (2005). *Making human beings human; Bioecological perspectives on human development.* Thousand Oaks, CA: Sage.

Bronson, M. B. (2000). Recognizing and supporting the development of self-regulation in young children. *Young Children, 55,* 32–37.

Bronson, M. B. (2003). NAEYC resources in focus: Choosing play materials for primary school children. *Young Children, 58,* 24–25.

Brophy, J. (1990). Teaching social studies for understanding and higher-order applications. *Elementary School Journal, 90,* 351–419.

Brophy, J., & Alleman, J. (2002). Learning and teaching about cultural universals in primary grade social studies. *Elementary School Journal, 103,* 99–114.

Brophy, J., & Alleman, J. (2003). History is alive: Teaching young children about changes over time. *Social Studies, 94,* 107–110.

Brophy, J., & Alleman, J. (2005a). *Children's thinking about cultural universals.* Mahwah, NJ: Erlbaum.

Brophy, J., & Alleman, J. (2005b). Primary grade students' knowledge and thinking about transportation. *Theory and Research in Social Education, 33,* 218–243.

Brophy, J., & Alleman, J. (2005c). Primary-grade students' knowledge and thinking about families. *Journal of Social Studies Research, 29*(1), 18–22.

Brophy, J., & Alleman, J. (2006). A reconceptualized rationale for elementary social studies. *Theory and Research in Social Education, 34,* 428–454.

Brophy, J., & Alleman, J. (2007). *Powerful social studies for elementary students* (2nd ed.). Belmont, CA: Thomson Wadsworth.

Brophy, J., Alleman, J., & O'Mahony, C. (2003). Primary-grade students' knowledge and thinking about food production and the origins of common foods. *Theory and Research in Social Education, 31,* 10–50.

Brown, A. (1997). Transforming schools into communities of thinking and learning about serious matters. *American Psychologist, 52*(4).

Brown, J. (1964). *Flat Stanley.* New York: Harper & Row.

Bruner, J. (1960). *The process of education.* Cambridge, MA: Harvard University Press.

Bruner, J. (1966). *Toward a theory of instruction.* Cambridge, MA: Harvard University Press.

California Tomorrow. (1999). *A place to begin: Working with parents on issues of diversity.* Oakland, CA: Author.

Carlsson-Paige, N., & Levin, D. (1998). *Before push comes to shove: Building conflict resolution skills with children.* New York: Redleaf.

Castle, S. (2002). *Learning centers.* Working document. Fairfax, VA: George Mason University.

Castle, S., & Smith, L. P. (2003). *The effects of a context-based backward design curriculum revision on student learning in social studies.* Paper presented at the annual meeting of the American Educational Research Association, Chicago.

Caudill, N. (1995). *Did you carry the flag today, Charley?* New York: Holt.

Caulfield, M. J. (2002). The influence of war play on cooperation and affective meaning in preschoolers' pretend play. *Dissertation Abstracts International, 62*(11-A), 3683.

Center for Civic Education. (1994). *National standards for civics and government.* Calabasas, CA: Author.

Chrisman, K., & Couchenour, D. (2002). *Healthy sexuality development: A guide for early childhood educators and families.* Washington, DC: National Association for the Education of Young Children.

Chrisman, K., & Couchenour, D. (2003). Developing concepts of gender roles. In C. Copple (Ed.), *A world of difference* (pp. 116–117). Washington, DC: National Association for the Education of Young Children.

CIVITAS. (2003). *A summary of CIVITAS: A framework for civic education.* Calabasas, CA: Center for Civic Education.

Cobb, M., & Ellis, D. (1997). *The quilt-block history of pioneer days: With projects kids can make.* New York: Millbrook.

Cohen, M. (1998). *It's George.* New York: Yearling Books.

Coley, R. L. (1998). Children's socialization experiences and functioning in single-mother households: The importance of fathers and other men. *Child Development, 69,* 219–230.

Colker, L. (2002). Introduction. *Young Children, 57,* 10–12.

Collaborative for Academic, Social, and Emotional Learning (CASEL). (2007). *CASEL briefs: Background on social and emotional learning (SEL).* Chicago: University of Illinois at Chicago.

Connell, R. (1971). *The child's construction of politics.* Melbourne, Australia: University Press.

Copple, C. (2003). *A world of difference.* Washington, DC: National Association for the Education of Young Children.

Cortez, M. (2008). Trying to fit in a different world: Acculturation of Latino families with young children in the United States. *International Journal of Early Childhood, 40,* 97–100.

Coufal, K., & Coufal, D. C. (2002). Colorful wishes: The fusion of drawing, narratives, and social studies. *Communication Disorders Quarterly, 23,* 109–121.

CTB/McGraw-Hill. (2002). *Pre-K standards.* New York: McGraw-Hill.

DeGaetano, Y., Williams, L. R., & Volk, D. (1998). *Kaleidoscope: A multicultural approach for the primary school classroom.* Upper Saddle River, NJ: Merrill/Prentice Hall.

DeKlyen, M., Biernbaum, S., Speltz, M. L., & Greenberg, M. T. (1998). Fathers and preschool behavior problems. *Child Development, 34*, 264–275.

d'Entremont, L. (1997). A few words about diversity and rigidity: One director's perspective. *Young Children, 53*, 72–73.

dePaola, T. (1975). *The cloud book.* New York: Holiday House.

Derman-Sparks, L. (2003). Developing antibias, multicultural curriculum. In C. Copple (Ed.), *A world of difference* (pp. 171–173). Washington, DC: National Association for the Education of Young Children.

Derman-Sparks, L., & A.B.C. Task Force. (1989). *Anti-bias curriculum: Tools for empowering young children.* Washington, DC: National Association for the Education of Young Children.

Derman-Sparks, L., & A.B.C. Task Force. (2003). Expanding awareness of gender roles. In C. Copple (Ed.), *A world of difference* (pp. 118–119). Washington, DC: National Association for the Education of Young Children.

DeRoach, E. F. (2001). *Educating hearts and minds: A comprehensive character education framework* (2nd ed.). New York: Corwin.

Descartes, R. (1646/1951). The passions of the soul. In *The philosophical works of Descartes.* New York: Dover.

Dever, M. T., & Falconer, R. C. (2008). *Foundations and change in early childhood education.* Hoboken, NJ: Wiley.

Dever, M. T., Whitaker, M. L., & Byrnes, D. A. (2001, September/October). The 4th R: Teaching ABOUT religion in the public schools. *The Social Studies, 92*(5), 220–229.

Dewey, J. (1900a). *The school and society.* Chicago: University of Chicago Press.

Dewey, J. (1900b). *Art as experience.* New York: Minton Barth.

Dewey, J. (1902). *The child and the curriculum.* Chicago: University of Chicago Press.

Dewey, J. (1916). *The school and society.* Chicago: University of Chicago Press.

Dewey, J. (1933). *How we think.* Boston: Heath.

Dewey, J. (1944). *Democracy and education.* New York: Free Press.

Dewey, J. (1966). *Lectures on the philosophy of education.* New York: Archambault/Random House.

Diamond, K. E., & Stacey, S. (2003). The other children at preschool: Experiences of typically developing children. In C. Copple (Ed.), *A world of difference* (pp. 135–139). Washington, DC: National Association for the Education of Young Children.

Diehl, D. S., Lemerise, E. A., Caverly, S. L., Ramsay, S., & Roberts, J. (1998). Peer relations and school adjustment in ungraded primary children. *Educational Psychology, 90*, 506–515.

Dighe, J. (1993). Children and the earth. *Young Children, 48*, 58–63.

DiSalvo-Ryan, D. (1997). *Uncle Willie and the soup kitchen.* New York: Demco Media.

Dorsey, S. (2003). The relation of social capital to child psychosocial adjustment difficulties: The role of positive parenting and neighborhood dangerousness. *Journal of Psychopathology and Behavioral Assessment, 25*, 11–23.

Dr. Seuss. (1971). *The Lorax*. New York: Random House.

Dunn, J., Cutting, A. L., & Fisher, N. (2002). Old friends, new friends: Predictors of children's perspectives on their friends at school. *Child Development, 73*, 621–635.

Durlak, J. A., Weissberg, R. P., Taylor, R. D., Dymnicki, A. B., & Schellinger, K. (2009). *The impact of enhancing students' social and emotional learning: A meta-analysis of school-based universal interventions*. Manuscript submitted for publication.

Dyson, A. H. (1988). The value of time off tasks: Young children's spontaneous talk and deliberate text. *Harvard Educational Review, 57*, 534–564.

Egan, K. (1997). The arts as the basics of education. *Childhood Education, 73*, 346–349.

Erikson, E. (1963). *Childhood and society*. New York: Norton.

Evans, L. (1995). *Rain song*. New York: Houghton Mifflin.

Fallace, T. D., Biscoe, A. D., & Perry, J. L. (2007). Second graders thinking historically: Theory into practice. *Journal of Social Studies Research, 31*(1), 44–53.

Finlinson, A. R., Austin, A. M., & Pfister, R. (2000). Cooperative games and children's positive behaviors. *Early Child Development and Care, 164*, 29–40.

Flack, M. (1977). *The story of Ping*. New York: Viking.

Flavell, J. H. (1979). Metacognition and cognitive monitoring. *American Psychologist, 34*, 906–911.

Fowler, A. (2001). *It could still be a tree*. New York: Dial.

Franklin, M. B. (2000). Meanings of play in the developmental interaction tradition. In N. Nager & E. K. Shapiro (Eds.), *Revisiting a progressive pedagogy* (pp. 11–47). Albany: State University of New York Press.

Freedman, R. (1995). *Buffalo hunt*. New York: Holiday House.

Freeman, E. B., & Hatch, J. A. (1989). What schools expect young children to know and do: An analysis of kindergarten report cards. *Elementary School Journal, 89*, 595–607.

Freud, S. (1949). *An outline of psychoanalysis*. New York: Norton.

Froebel, F. (1887). *The education of man* (W. Hailman, Trans.). New York: Appleton.

Fromboluti, C. S., & Seefeldt, C. (1999). *Early childhood: Where learning begins: Geography*. Washington, DC: U.S. Department of Education.

Froschl, M., & Sprung, B. (1999). On purpose: Addressing teasing and bullying in early childhood. *Young Children, 54*, 70–72.

Gandini, L. (1997). Foundations of the Reggio Emilia approach. In J. Hendrick (Ed.), *First steps toward teaching the Reggio way* (pp. 14–25). Upper Saddle River, NJ: Prentice Hall.

Garcia, E. (2003). Respecting children's home language and culture. In C. Copple (Ed.), *A world of difference* (p. 3). Washington, DC: National Association for the Education of Young Children.

Gelman, S. (1998). Categories in young children's thinking. *Young Children, 53*, 20–27.

Geography Education Standards Project. (1994). *Geography for life*. Washington, DC: Author.

Gibbons, F. (2002). *Full steam ahead.* Honesdale, PA: Boyds Mills.
Gillies, R. M. (2000). The maintenance of cooperative and helping behaviours in cooperative groups. *British Journal of Educational Psychology, 70,* 97–111.
Glanz, D. (1991). Intergenerational proximity, propinquity, and social contact: An analysis of two Israeli university-based programs. *Educational Gerontology, 17,* 465–476.
Glassman, M. (2001). Dewey and Vygotsky: Society, experience, and inquiry in educational practice. *Educational Researcher, 30,* 3–15.
Goodman, J. F. (2000). Moral education in early childhood: The limits of constructivism. *Early Education and Development, 11,* 37–54.
Goodman, M. (1952). *Race awareness in young children.* Reading, MA: Addison-Wesley.
Gorter-Reu, M. S., & Anderson, J. M. (1998). Home kits, home visits, and more! *Young Children, 54,* 71–80.
Gouteux, S. (2001). Reorientation in a small-scale environment by 3-, 4-, and 5-year-old children. *Cognitive Development, 16,* 853–869.
Gray, N., & Dupasquier, P. (1988). *A country far away.* New York: Orchard Books.
Greenberg, P. (1992). Practices pertaining to respect, rights, responsibilities, and roots in any classroom. *Young Children, 47,* 10–17.
Greenberg, P. (2006) "It's mine!": Helping the child who takes things from others. *Early Childhood Today, 21*(1), 16–17.
Greene, C. (1997). *Firefighters fight fires.* New York: Children's World.
Greene, R. W. (2001). *The explosive child.* New York: HarperCollins.
Gretz, S. (1992). *Frog, duck, and rabbit.* New York: Simon & Schuster.
Gronlund, G. (1998). Portfolios as an assessment tool: Is collection of work enough? *Young Children, 53,* 4–11.
Gross, T., & Clemens, S. G. (2002). Painting a tragedy: Young children process the events of September 11. *Young Children, 57,* 44–46.
Gunnar, M. R. (2003). Gendered social worlds in preschool. *Social Development, 12*(1), 91–106.
Hakes, J. A., & Eisenwine, M. J. (2003). An electronic CLASP: Connecting children and social studies. *Social Studies, 94,* 90–93.
Hanline, M. F., Milton, S., & Phelps, P. C. (2008). A longitudinal study exploring the relationship of representational levels of three aspects of preschool sociodramatic play and early academic skills. *Journal of Research in Childhood Education, 23,* 19–28.
Harris, P. L. (1989). *Children and emotions.* Oxford, UK: Blackwell.
Hayes, G. (2003). Whose values do we teach? *Delta Kappa Gamma Bulletin, 63,* 55–57.
Hearne, B. (1977). *Seven brave women.* New York: Greenwillow.
Helm, J. H., & Beneke, S. (2003). *The power of projects.* New York: Teachers College Press.
Helm, J. H., & Katz, L. (2001a). *Young investigators.* New York: Teachers College Press.

Helm, J. H., & Katz, L. (2001b). *Young investigators: The project approach in the early years.* Washington, DC: National Association for the Education of Young Children.

Helwig, C. C. (1998). Children's conceptions of fair government and freedom of speech. *Child Development, 69,* 518–521.

Helwig, C. C., & Prencipe, A. (1999). Children's judgments of flags and flag-burning. *Child Development, 70,* 132–143.

Hembacher, D., & Cruise, M. J. (2006). The effects of a second-grade social studies curriculum infused with positive aging concepts on children's attitudes toward aging. *Theory and Research in Social Education, 34,* 58–97.

Hendrick, J. (2004). Reggio Emilia and American schools: Telling them apart and putting them together—Can we do it? In J. Hendrick (Ed.), *Next steps toward teaching the Reggio way: Accepting the challenge to change* (2nd ed., pp. 234–239). Upper Saddle River, NJ: Pearson Education.

Henning, M. B., & Bell, D. (2011). Second graders connect to their community with a WebQuest. *Social Studies and the Young Learner, 24*(1), 10–13.

Hess, R., & Torney, J. (1967). *The development of political attitudes in children.* New York: Anchor.

Hesse, P., & Lane, F. (2003). Media literacy starts young: An integrated curriculum. *Young Children, 58,* 20–27.

Hewett, K. (2001). Blocks as a tool for learning: A historical and contemporary perspective. *Young Children, 56,* 6–12.

Hidi, S. (1990). Interest and its contribution as a mental resource for learning. *Review of Educational Research, 80,* 549–573.

Hill, L. S. (1997a). *Canals are water roads.* New York: Carolrhoda.

Hill, L. S. (1997b). *Dams give us power: A building block book.* New York: Carolrhoda.

Hill, L. S. (2000). *Tunnels go underground: A building block book.* New York: Carolrhoda.

Hill, P. S. (1923). *A conduct curriculum for the kindergarten and first grade* (pp. x–xix). New York: Scribner.

Hoisington, C. (2002). Using photographs to support children's science inquiry. *Young Children, 57,* 26–30.

Holland, G. (1998). *The Empire State Building.* New York: Raintree/Steck Vaughn.

Holst, C. B. (1999). Buying more can give children less. *Young Children, 54,* 19–23.

Howe, G. (1969). The teaching of directions in space. In W. Herman (Ed.), *Current research in elementary school social studies* (pp. 31–43). Upper Saddle River, NJ: Merrill/Prentice Hall.

Huijbregts, S. K., Leseman, P. P. M., & Tavecchio, L. W. C. (2008). Cultural diversity in center-based childcare: Childrearing beliefs of professional caregivers from different cultural communities in the Netherlands. *Early Childhood Research Quarterly, 23,* 233–244.

Hunt, J. McV. (1961). *Intelligence and experience.* New York: Ronald.

International Society for Technology in Education (ISTE). (2012). *ISTE.NETS: The standards for learning, leading, and teaching in the digital age.* Retrieved from www.iste.org/standards on November 12, 2012.

Isbell, R., & Exelby, B. (2001). *Early learning environments that work.* Beltsville, MD: Gryphon House.

Isenberg, J., & Quisenberry, N. (2002). *Play: Essential for all children.* [Position paper]. Olney, MD: Association for Childhood Education International. Retrieved from www.acei.org/playpaper.htm

James, J. H. (2008). Teachers as protectors: Making sense of preservice teachers' resistance to interpretation in elementary history teaching. *Theory and Research in Social Education, 36*(3), 172–205.

Jantz, R. K., & Seefeldt, C. (1999a). Social studies for young children. In C. Seefeldt (Ed.), *The early childhood curriculum* (3rd ed., pp. 159–200). New York: Teachers College Press.

Jantz, R. K., & Seefeldt, C. (1999b). Early childhood social studies. In C. Seefeldt (Ed.), *The early childhood curriculum: Current findings in theory and practice* (pp. 159–179). New York: Teachers College Press.

Jenkins, S. (1995). *Looking down.* New York: Houghton Mifflin.

Johnson, A. (1989). *Tell me a story Mama.* New York: Orchard Books.

Kemple, K. M. (1991). Preschool children's peer acceptance and social interaction. *Young Children, 46,* 47–56.

Klein, A., Surback, E., & Moyer, J. (2003). Teaching across cultures in an international seminar. *Childhood Education, 79,* 340–346.

Knowlton, J. (1988). *Geography from A to Z: Picture glossary.* New York: Crowell.

Kochanska, G., Padavich, D. L., & Koenig, A. L. (1996). Children's narratives about hypothetical moral dilemmas and objective measures of their conscience: Mutual relations and socialization antecedents. *Child Development, 67,* 1420–1436.

Kohlberg, L. (1984). *The psychology of moral development: The nature and validity of moral stages.* San Francisco: Harper and Row.

Kornfeld, J. (2002). *The chocolate train.* New York: Simon & Schuster.

Koster, J. B. (1999). Clay for little fingers. *Young Children, 54,* 18–22.

Kowalski, K., & Lo, Y. F. (2001). The influence of perceptual features, ethnic labels, and sociocultural information in the development of ethnic/racial bias in young children. *Journal of Cross-Cultural Psychology, 32,* 444–455.

Kraus, R. (1947). *The growing story.* New York: Harper.

Ladd, G. W. (1990). Having friends, keeping friends, making friends, and being liked by peers in the classroom: Predictors of children's early school adjustment. *Child Development, 61,* 1081–1100.

Ladd, G. W., Kochenderfer, B. J., & Coleman, C. C. (1997). Classroom peer acceptance, friendship, and victimization: Distinct relational systems that contribute uniquely to children's school adjustment? *Child Development, 68,* 1181–1198.

Ladd, G. W., Price, J. M., & Hart, C. H. (1988). Predicting preschoolers' peer status from their playground behaviors. *Child Development, 59,* 986–992.

Lambert, W., & Klineberg, O. (1967). *Children's views of foreign peoples: A cross cultural study.* New York: Appleton-Century-Crofts.

Landry, C. E., & Forman, G. E. (1999). Research on early science education. In C. Seefeldt (Ed.), *The early childhood curriculum: Current findings in theory and practice* (pp. 133–178). New York: Teachers College Press.

Langer, S. (1942). *Philosophy in a new key*. Cambridge, MA: Harvard University Press.

Leedy, L. (2000). *Mapping Penny's world*. New York: Henry Holt.

Leedy, L. (2002). *Follow the money*. New York: Holiday House.

Lester, J., & Pinkney, J. (1998). *Black cowboy, wild horses: A true story*. New York: Dial.

Leventhal, D., & Wellington, M. (1998). *What is your language?* New York: Puffin.

Levin, D. E. (1998). *Teaching young children in violent times: Building a peaceable classroom*. Washington, DC: National Association for the Education of Young Children.

Levin, D. E. (2003). *Teaching young children in violent times: Building a peaceable classroom* (2nd ed.). Cambridge, MA: Educators for Social Responsibility; Washington, DC: National Association for the Education of Young Children.

Levin, D. E., & Carlsson-Paige, N. (2004). *The war play dilemma: What every parent and teacher needs to know*. New York: Teachers College Press.

Levstik, L. (1991). Narrative constructions: Cultural frames for history. *Social Studies, 86*, 848–853.

Levstik, L. (2002). Introduction: Social studies. *Elementary School Journal, 103*, 93–98.

Levstik, L., & Barton, K. (1997). "Any history is someone's history": Listening to multiple voices from the past. *Social Education, 61*, 48–51.

Lewis, K., & Cartwright, R. (2001). *The lot at the end of my block*. New York: Hyperion.

Liben, L. S., & Downs, R. M. (1993). Understanding person-space-map relations: Cartographic and developmental perspective. *Child Development, 29*, 739–752.

Lillard, A., & Currenton, S. (2003). Do young children understand what others feel, want, and know? In C. Copple (Ed.), *A world of difference* (pp. 46–41). Washington, DC: National Association for the Education of Young Children.

Lionni, L. (1991). *Swimmy*. New York: Scholastic.

Locke, J. (1690/1964). *An essay concerning human understanding*. New York: Meridian.

Longstreet, W. S. (2003). Early postmodernism in social education—Revisiting "decision making: The heart of social studies instruction." *Social Studies, 94*(1), 11–15.

Lord, F. (1941). A study of spatial orientation of children. *Journal of Educational Research, 34*, 481–505.

Maccoby, E. E. (1993). The role of parents in the socialization of children: An historical overview. *Developmental Psychology, 28*, 1008–1017.

Maestro, B. C., & Maestro, G. (1995). *The story of money*. New York: Mulberry.

Marschark, M., Lang, H. G., & Albertin, J. A. (2001). *Educating deaf students: From research to practice*. Oxford, UK: Oxford University Press.

Marsh, H. W., Craven, R., & Debus, R. (1998). Structure, stability, and development of young children's self-concepts: A multi cohort–multi occasion study. *Child Development, 69*, 1031–1053.

Marshall, H. H. (2001). Cultural influences on the development of self-concept: Updating our thinking. *Young Children, 56*, 19–22.

Marshall, H. H. (2003). Cultural influences on the development of self-concept: Updating our thinking. In C. Copple (Ed.), *A world of difference* (pp. 167–171). Washington, DC: National Association for the Education of Young Children.

Martin, B. (1969a). *Brown bear, brown bear.* New York: Holt, Rinehart, & Winston.

Martin, B. (1969b). *Our sun is a star.* New York: Holt, Rinehart, & Winston.

Martin, B. (1969c). *David was mad.* New York: Holt, Rinehart, & Winston.

Martin, B. (1969d). *Children of the world say good morning.* New York: Holt, Rinehart, & Winston.

Martin, L., & Miller, M. (1999). *Great graphing.* New York: Scholastic.

Marzoff, D. P., & DeLoache, J. S. (1994). Transfer in young children's understanding of spatial representations. *Child Development, 65,* 1–16.

Maslow, A. (1969). *Toward a psychology of being.* New York: Van Nostrand.

McCaughrean, G. (2002). *My grandmother's clock.* New York: Clarion.

McCloskey, R. (1952). *One morning in Maine.* New York: Viking.

McCloskey, R. (1976). *Blueberries for Sal.* New York: Viking.

McConnell, J. (2000). Children's social skills and understanding of others' emotions. *Dissertation Abstracts International, 62*(5-B), 2788.

McCormick, L., Wong, M., & Yogi, L. (2003). Individualization in the inclusive preschool: A planning process. *Childhood Education, 79,* 212–217.

McCormick, T. M., & Hubbard, J. (2011). Every picture tells a story: A study of teaching methods using historical photographs with elementary students. *Journal of Social Studies Research, 35*(1), 80–94.

McDermott, J. (2003). A letter to teachers of young children. In C. Copple (Ed.), *A world of difference* (pp. 140–142). Washington, DC: National Association for the Education of Young Children.

McEwan, E. E. (1996). *Whose hat?* New York: Shaw.

Mead, M. (1970). *Culture and commitment: A study of the generation gap.* New York: American Museum of Natural History.

Meadow, S. (2010). *The child as a social person.* London, England: Routledge.

Medda, M. E. (1996). Classrooms where children learn to care. *Childhood Education, 72,* 72–74.

Merryfield, M. M. (2007). The Web and teachers' decision-making in global education. *Theory and Research in Social Education, 35,* 256–276.

Meszaros, B., & Engstrom, L. (1998). The voluntary national content standards in economics. *Social Studies and the Young Learner, 11,* 7–12.

Meyer, L., Sherman, L., & MacKinster, J. (2006). The effects of the Japan bridge project on third graders' cultural sensitivity. *Theory and Research in Social Education, 34,* 347–369.

Miller, J. (1985). Teaching map skills: Theory, research, and practice. *Social Education, 49,* 30–33.

Milne, A. A. (1955). *Now we are six.* London: Dutton.

Milne, A. A. (1991). *Winnie the Pooh.* New York: Dutton.

Minarik, E. H. (1978). *Little Bear.* New York: HarperTrophy.

Misco, T., & Shiveley, J. (2010). Seeing the forest through the trees: Some renewed thinking on dispositions specific to social studies education. *The Social Studies, 101,* 121–126.

Mitchell, L. S. (1934). *Young geographers.* New York: Bank Street College.

Mitchell, L. S. (2000). Social studies for future teachers. In N. Nager & E. K. Shapior (Eds.), *Revisiting a progressive pedagogy* (pp. 125–138). Albany: State University of New York Press.

Molenarr-Klumper, M. (2002). *Nonverbal learning disabilities.* New York: Jessica Kingsley.

Mollet, T. M., & Lewis, E. B. (1999). *My rows and piles of coins.* New York: Clarion.

Montessori, M. (1949/1995). *The absorbent mind.* New York: Henry Holt.

Morgan, W., & Streb, M. (2001). Building citizenship: How student voice in service-learning develops civic values. *Social Science Quarterly, 82,* 154.

Moriarty, R. F. (2002). Helping teachers develop as facilitators of three- to five-year-olds' science inquiry. *Young Children, 57,* 20–25.

Morris, A. (1989). *Bread, bread, bread.* New York: Lothrop, Lee, & Shepard.

Morris, A. (2002). *Grandma Susan remembers: A British-American family story.* Brookfield, CT: Millbrook.

Morris, R. V. (2000). Teaching social studies with artifacts. *Social Studies, 91,* 32–37.

Mosenthal, P. B., & Kirsch, S. (1991). Understanding general reference maps. *Journal of Reading, 34,* 60–63.

Murphy, S. J., & Greenseid, D. (1996). *Get up and go!* New York: HarperCollins.

Myers, M. E., & Myers, B. K. (2002). Holidays in the public school kindergarten: An avenue for emerging religious and spiritual literacy. *Childhood Education, 78,* 79–84.

National Assessment of Educational Progress. (2002). *NAEP in U.S. history.* Washington, DC: U.S. Department of Education.

National Association for the Education of Young Children. (1998). *Guidelines for appropriate curriculum content and assessment in programs serving children ages 3 through 8* [Position statement]. Washington, DC: Author.

National Association for the Education of Young Children. (2001). Helping young children in frightening times. *Young Children, 56,* 6–7.

National Center for History in the Schools. (1994). *National standards: History for grades K–4.* Los Angeles: Author.

National Commission on Social Studies in the Schools. (1989). *Charting a course: Social studies for the 21st century.* New York: Author.

National Council for History Education. (1998). *NCHE recommendations.* Westlake, OH: Author.

National Council for the Social Studies. (1994). *Expectations of excellence: Curriculum standards for social studies.* Washington, DC: Author.

National Council for the Social Studies. (1998/2003). *Social studies for early childhood and elementary school children: Preparing for the 21st century* [Online]. Available at www.socialstudies.org/positions/elementary.shtml

National Council for the Social Studies. (2010). *National curriculum standards for social studies: A framework for teaching, learning, and assessment.* Author: Silver Spring, MD.

National Council on Economic Education. (1997). *National content standards in economics.* New York: Author.

National Council on Economic Education. (2002). *Economics America.* Bloomington, IN: Author.

National Education Goals Panel. (1998). *Principles and recommendations for early childhood assessments.* Washington, DC: Author.

National Geographic Society. (1994). *Geography for life: National Geography standards.* Washington, DC: Author.

National Institutes for Child Health and Development Early Child Care Research Network. (1998). Early child care and self-control, compliance, and problem behavior at twenty-four and thirty-six months. *Child Development, 69,* 1145–1170.

National Parent-Teacher Association. (2002). *Talking with your child about sex.* Chicago: Author. Available at www.pta.org/parentinvolvement/healthsafety/hs_talking_ sex.asp

National Research Council. (2000). *From neurons to neighborhoods: The science of early childhood development.* Washington, DC: National Academy Press.

National Research Council. (2001). *Eager to learn: Educating our preschoolers.* Washington, DC: National Academy Press.

National Research Council and Institute of Medicine (NRC & IM), Committee on Integrating the Science of Early Childhood Development. (2000). *From neurons to neighborhoods: The science of early childhood development.* Washington, DC: National Academy Press.

Nebel, M., Jamison, B., & Bennett, L. (2009). Students as digital citizens on Web 2.0. *Social Studies and the Young Learner, 21*(4), 5–7.

NetDay News. (2005, March 8). *NetDay's 2004 survey results show 58 percent of students have cell phones, 60 percent email or IM adults on a weekly basis.* Retrieved November 13, 2005, from www.netday.org/news_2004_survey_ results.htm

New, R. S. (1999a). An integrated curriculum: Moving from the what and the how to the why. In C. Seefeldt (Ed.), *The early childhood curriculum: Current findings in theory and research* (pp. 265–288). New York: Teachers College Press.

New, R. S. (1999b). Here we call it "drop off and pick up": Transition to child care, American style. *Young Children, 54,* 34–36.

Newman, R. (1995). For parents particularly: The home-school connection. *Childhood Education, 71,* 296–298.

Nolte, D. W., Harris, R., & Harris, R. (1998). *Children learn what they live: Parenting to inspire values.* New York: Workman.

Nucci, L. P. (2001). *Education in the moral domain.* Chicago: University of Chicago Press.

Nuffield Mathematics Project. (1969). *Early experiences.* London: Macdonald Education.

Ogle, D. M. (1986). K-W-L: A teaching model that develops active reading of expository text. *Reading Teacher, 39,* 564–570.

Okagaki, L., & Diamond, K. E. (2003). Responding to cultural and linguistic differences in the belief and practices of families with young children. In C. Copple (Ed.), *A world of difference* (pp. 9–15). Washington, DC: National Association for the Education of Young Children.

Otten, M., Stigler, J. W., Woodward, J. A., & Staley, L. (2004). Performing history: The effects of a dramatic arts-based history program on student achievement and enjoyment. *Theory and Research in Social Education, 32,* 187–212.

Parker, J. G., & Asher, S. R. (1987). Peer relations and later personal adjustment: Are low accepted children at risk? *Psychological Bulletin, 10,* 357–389.

Pattnaik, J. (2003). Learning about the "other": Building a case for intercultural understanding among minority children. *Childhood Education, 78,* 204–210.

Pellowski, A. (1969). *Children and international education: Portfolio no. 6.* Washington, DC: Association for Childhood Education International.

Peter, L. (2001). *On the trail of Sacagawea.* Honesdale, PA: Caroline House/Boyds Mills.

Pettigrew, E., & Kimber, W. (1992). *Night-time.* New York: Annick.

Piaget, J. (1946). The child's concept of space. In H. E. Gruber & J. J. Voneche (Eds.), *The essential Piaget* (pp. 576–645). London: Routledge & Kegan Paul.

Piaget, J. (1952). *The child's conception of number.* New York: Humanities Press.

Piaget, J. (1959). *The language and thought of the child.* London: Routledge & Kegan Paul.

Piaget, J, (1960). *The moral judgment of the child* (M. Gaban, Trans.). Glencoe, IL: Free Press. (Original work published in 1932).

Piaget, J. (1965). *The child's conception of the world.* Totowa, NJ: Littlefield Adams.

Piaget, J. (1969). *Science of education and the psychology of the child.* New York: Viking.

Piaget, J., & Inhelder, B. (1969). *The psychology of the child.* New York: Basic Books.

Pohan, C. A. (2003). Creating caring and democratic communities in our classrooms and schools. *Childhood Education, 79,* 369–373.

Polonsky, L. (2000). *Math for the very young: A handbook of activities for parents and teachers.* Chicago: University of Chicago Press.

Popkewitz, T. S. (1999). Dewey, Vygotsky, and the social administration of the individual. *American Education Research Journal, 35,* 535–570.

Postman, N. (2000). Will our children inherit only the wind? *Theory and Research in Social Education, 28,* 580–586.

Pratt, C. (1948). *I learn from children.* New York: Harper & Row.

Prawatt, R. W. (2000). The two faces of Deweyan pragmatism: Induction versus social construction. *Teachers College Record, 102,* 805–840.

Prawatt, R. W. (2001). Dewey and Pierce, the philosopher's philosopher. *Teachers College Record, 103,* 667–721.

Prencipe, A., & Helwig, C. C. (2002). The development of reasoning about the teaching of values in school and family contexts. *Child Development, 73,* 841–856.

Ramsey, P. G. (2003). Growing up with the contradictions of race and class. In C. Copple (Ed.), *A world of difference* (pp. 5–6). Washington, DC: National Association for the Education of Young Children.

Rasmussen, S. (2009). Opening up perspectives on autonomy & relatedness in parent-children dynamics: Anthropological insights. *Culture & Psychology, 15*(4), 433–449.

Richardson, W. (2009). *Blogs, wikis, podcasts and other powerful Web tools for classrooms* (2nd ed.). Thousand Oaks, CA: Corwin Press.

Richman, G., Hope, T., & Mihala, S. (2010). Assessment and treatment of self-esteem in adolescents with ADHD. In M. H. Guindon (Ed.), *Self-esteem across the life-span: Issues and interventions* (pp. 111–123). New York: Routledge/Taylor & Francis.

Rivkin, M. S. (1995). *The great outdoors: Restoring children's right to play outside.* Washington, DC: National Association for the Education of Young Children.

Roberts, R., & Aman, C. J. (1993). Developmental differences in giving directions: Spatial frames of reference and mental rotation. *Child Development, 64,* 1258–1270.

Robison, H., & Spodek, B. (1965). *New directions in the kindergarten.* New York: Teachers College Press.

Rogers, C. (1961). *On becoming a person.* Boston: Houghton Mifflin.

Rogovin, P. (2011). First graders research stuffed animals and learn about their world. *Social Studies and the Young Learner, 24*(1), 19–23.

Ronen, T., Rahav, G., & Rosenbaum, M. (2003). Children's reactions to a war situation as a function of age and sex. *Anxiety, Stress and Coping, 16,* 59–69.

Root, P. (2003). *The name quilt.* New York: Farrar, Straus, & Giroux.

Rowland, G. E. (2002). Every child needs self-esteem: Creative drama builds self-confidence through self-expression. *Dissertation Abstracts International, 63*(1-A), 30.

Ryan, P. M. (1996). *The flag we love.* New York: Charlesbridge.

Rylant, C. (1992). *When I was young in the mountains.* New York: Dutton.

Sanders, S. W. (2002). *Active for life.* Washington, DC: National Association for the Education of Young Children.

Schickedanz, J. (1999). *Much more than the ABCs.* Washington, DC: National Association for the Education of Young Children.

Schiller, M. (1995). An emergent art curriculum that fosters understanding. *Young Children, 50,* 33–39.

Schoenfeldt, M. (2001). Geographic literacy and young learners. *Educational Forum, 66,* 26–31.

Schulze, P. A., Harwood, R. L., Schoelmerich, A., & Leyendecker, B. (2002). The cultural structuring of parenting and universal developmental tasks. *Parenting: Science and Practice, 22,* 151–178.

Schweinhart, L. J., Montie, J., Xiang, Z., Barnett, W. S., Belfield, C. R., & Nores, M. (2005). *Lifetime effects: The High/Scope Perry Preschool study through age 40* (Monographs of the High/Scope Educational Research Foundation, 14). Ypsilanti, MI: High/Scope Press.

Searls, M. J. (1997). *Allowance kit, junior!: A money system for little kids.* Washington, DC: Summit Financial.

Seefeldt, C. (1989). Perspectives on the pledge of allegiance. *Childhood Education, 65,* 131–133.

Seefeldt, C. (1993). Learning for freedom. *Young Children, 48,* 4–10.

Seefeldt, C. (1995a). Art—A serious work. *Young Children, 50,* 39–66.

Seefeldt, C. (1995b). Ready to learn, but what? *Contemporary Education, 66,* 134–139.

Seefeldt, C. (1998). Assessing young children. In C. Seefeldt (Ed.), *Continuing issues in early childhood education* (pp. 314–347). Upper Saddle River, NJ: Merrill/Prentice Hall.

Seefeldt, C. (2000). Art for young children. In C. Seefeldt (Ed.), *The early childhood curriculum: Current findings and theory* (3rd ed., pp. 201–218). New York: Teachers College Press.

Seefeldt, C. (2002). *Creating rooms of wonder.* Beltsville, MD: Gryphon House.

Seefeldt, C., & Denton, K. (1997). The family as a resource for learning. In S. S. Beck & B. Hatcher (Eds.), *Learning outside of school* (2nd ed., pp. 81–89). Olney, MD: Association for Childhood Education International.

Seefeldt, C., & Galper, A. (2000). *Active experiences for active children: Social studies.* Upper Saddle River, NJ: Merrill/Prentice Hall.

Seefeldt, C., Galper, A., & Denton, D. (1998). Former Head Start parents' characteristics, perceptions of school climate, and involvement in their children's education. *Elementary School Journal, 98,* 339–351.

Seefeldt, C., & Goldsmith, N. (1998). Family Night Out: A new way to involve low-income parents. Here's how. *Elementary School Principal, 16,* 1–4.

Seefeldt, C., & Warman, B. (1990). *Young and old together.* Washington, DC: National Association for the Education of Young Children.

Sheffield, C. C., Karp, K. S., & Brown, E. T. (2010). Building basic statistical literacy with U. S. census data. *Social Studies and the Young Learner, 22*(4), 7–11.

Shepard, L. A., Kagan, S. L., & Wurtz, E. (1998). *Goal 1: Early childhood assessments resource group recommendations.* Washington, DC: U.S. Government Printing Office.

Shepardson, D. P., & Britsch, S. J. (2000). *Young children's representations of earth materials on the science journal page.* Paper presented at the annual meeting of the National Association for Research in Science Teaching, New Orleans.

Siegler, R. S. & Alibali, M. W. (2005). *Children's thinking* (4th ed.). Upper Saddle River, NJ: Prentice Hall.

Skinner, B. F. (1974). *About behaviorism.* New York: Knopf.

Slaby, R. G., Roedell, W. C., Arezzo, D., & Hendrix, K. (1995). *Early violence prevention: Tools for teachers of young children.* Washington, DC: National Association for the Education of Young Children.

Slekar, T. D. (2009). Democracy denied: Learning to teach history in elementary school. *Teacher Education Quarterly, 36*(1), 95–110.

Sousa, F. (2000). Reconstructing children's experience when teaching and assessing them: Lessons from Dewey. *Journal of Early Childhood Teacher Education, 21,* 313–320.

Spier, P. (1980). *People*. Doubleday: Garden City, NY.

Spivack, G., & Shure, M. (1978). *Social adjustment of young children: A cognitive approach to solving real-life problems*. San Francisco: Jossey-Bass.

Steitzer, U. (1995). *Building an igloo*. New York: Holt.

Stone, J. (2003). Communicating respect. In C. Copple (Ed.), *A world of difference* (p. 9). Washington, DC: National Association for the Education of Young Children.

Stormshak, E. A., Bierman, K. L., Bruschi, C., Dodge, K. A., Cole, J. D., & the Conduct Problems Prevention Research Group. (1999). The relation between behavior problems and peer preference in different classroom contexts. *Child Development, 70*, 193–196.

Sweeney, J. (1996). *Me on the map*. New York: Dragonfly Books.

Takahashi, I. (2000). Children's understanding of their own vs. scientific views of the earth's shape. *Japanese Journal of Developmental Psychology, 11*(2), 89–99.

Taylor, B. (2002). *Mountains and volcanoes: Geography facts and experiments*. New York: Houghton Mifflin.

Teaching Tolerance Project. (2003). *Starting small: Teaching tolerance in preschool and the early grades*. Montgomery, AL: Southern Poverty Law Center.

Teichman, Y. (2001). The development of Israeli children's images of Jews and Arabs and their expression in human figure drawings. *Developmental Psychology, 37*(6), 749–761.

Thompson, R. A. & Virmani, E. A. (2010). Self and personality. In M. H. Bornstein (Ed.), *Handbook of cultural developmental science* (pp. 195–207). New York: Psychology Press.

Torney, J., Oppenheim, A. N., & Farnen, R. F. (1975). *Civic education in ten countries: An empirical study*. New York: Wiley.

Turiel, E. (2003). *The development of social knowledge: Morality and convention*. Cambridge, UK: Cambridge University Press.

Turner, A., & Allen, T. B. (1994). *Sewing quilts*. New York: Simon & Schuster.

UNESCO. (1945). *Culture of peace: A declaration on a culture of peace*. Retrieved October 22, 2008, from www.unesco.org/cpp/uk/declarations/2000.htm

United States Mint. (2011). My favorite habitat: A lesson for grades K-1. *Social Studies and the Young Learner, 23*(4), P1–P4.

Vance, E., & Weaver, P. J. (2002). *Class meetings: Young children solve problems together*. Washington, DC: National Association for the Education of Young Children.

VanFossen, P. J. (2003). Best practice economic education for young children? It's elementary! *Social Education, 67*, 90–94.

VanSledright, B. A. (2002). Fifth graders investigating history in the classroom: Results from a researcher–practitioner design experiment. *Elementary School Journal, 103*, 131–160.

Vaughan, J. (1998). *Rivers and streams*. New York: Raintree.

Viorst, J. (1978). *Alexander, who used to be rich last Sunday*. New York: Atheneum.

Virginia Standards of Learning. (2012). Retrieved August 16, 2012, from www.doe.virginia.gov/testing/sol/standards.

Vukelich, C. (1990). Where's the paper? Literacy during dramatic play. *Childhood Education, 66,* 205–210.

Vukelich, R., & Thornton, S. J. (1990). Children's understanding of historical time: Implications for instruction. *Childhood Education, 66,* 22–25.

Vygotsky, L. (1978). *Thought and language.* Cambridge, MA: MIT Press.

Vygotsky, L. (1986). *Thought and language* (Rev. ed.). Cambridge, MA: MIT Press.

Wade, R. (2003). Beyond expanding horizons: New curriculum directions for elementary social studies. *Elementary School Journal, 103,* 115–131.

Wade, R., & Yarbrough, D. (2007). Service-learning in the social studies: Civic outcomes of the 3rd–12th grade Civic Connections program. *Theory and Research in Social Education, 35,* 366–392.

Walker, B., Hafenstein, N. L., & Crow-Enslow, L. (1999). Meeting the needs of gifted learners in the early childhood classroom. *Young Children, 54,* 32–37.

Walker, S. M., & Beier, E. (1998). *The 18 penny goose.* New York: HarperCrest.

Wallach, L. R. (1995). Helping children cope with violence. *Young Children, 48,* 4–12.

Walton, R. (2002). *Bunny day: Telling time from breakfast to bedtime.* New York: HarperCollins.

Wardle, F. (2001). Supporting multiracial and multiethnic children and their families. *Young Children, 56,* 38–40.

Wardle, F. (2003). Supporting multiracial and multiethnic children and their families. In C. Copple (Ed.), *A world of difference* (pp. 33–35). Washington, DC: National Association for the Education of Young Children.

Washington, V., & Bailey, V. J. (1995). *Project Head Start.* New York: Garland.

Weikart, D. (1998). *High/Scope Curriculum. Supporting children in resolving conflicts.* Ypsilanti, MI: High/Scope Press.

Weingold, H., & Webster, R. (1964). Effects of punishment on cooperative behavior in children. *Child Development, 35,* 12–16.

Weissberg, R. P., Durlak, J. A., Dymnicki, A. B., & O'Brien, M. U. (2007). *Promoting social and emotional learning enhances school success: Implications of a meta-analysis.* Manuscript submitted for publication.

Wells, R. (2001). *Bunny money.* New York: Dial.

Whitehurst, G. J., & Lonigan, C. J. (1998). Child development and emergent literacy. *Child Development, 69,* 848–872.

Whiteside, K. (2000). *Building geography skills and community understanding with constructivist teaching methods.* Report No. SO031905. Urbana, IL: ECEE.

Wigfield, A. (Ed.). (2002). *The development of achievement motivation.* San Diego: Academic Press.

Wilen, W. W. (Ed.). (2000). *Favorite lesson plans: Powerful standards-based activities.* National Council for Social Studies: Silver Spring, MD.

Wolf, B. (1994). *Beneath the stone: A Mexican Zapotec tale.* New York: Orchard.

World of Work Series (2009). Ann Arbor, MI: Cherry Hill Press.

Wu, W., West, S. G., & Hughes, J. N. (2010). Effect of grade retention in first grade on psychosocial outcomes. *Journal of Educational Psychology, 102*(1), 135–152.

Yashima, T. (1995). *Crow boy.* New York: Viking.

Index

A
A.B.C. Task Force, 184, 197, 199, 223, 225, 295
Abstract thinking, 113
Accommodation, 133
A Conduct Curriculum for the Kindergarten and First Grade (Hill), 5
A Country Far Away (Gray & Dupasquier), 330
Active learning, 13
  of children, 28
  interest and, 16
  and play, 13–14
Activities
  culminating, 56–57
  modeling, 94–95
  of preschool and primary children, 270
  science, 55
Adaptation, 133
Additive approach to culture, 178
Adler, D. A., 315
Aesthetic education, 249
Ainsworth, M. D., 150
Albertin, J. A., 33
Alexander, Who Used to Be Rich Last Sunday (Viorst), 286
Alibali, M. W., 114
Aliki, 329
Alleman, J., 16, 19, 20, 37, 133, 214, 227, 283, 325
Allen, Gary, 312
Allen, T. B., 231

Allowance Kit, Junior! : A Money System for Little Kids (Searls), 285
Allport, G., 184
Aman, C. J., 257
American Association for Health Education (1999), 221
American Association of University Women, 295
American Psychological Association (APA), 189
Ames, L., 211
Anderson, C. B., 12
Anderson, J. M., 71
Anderson, L. W., 117
Anderson, S. R., 65
Angell, A. V., 307
Annenberg/CPB, 47
Anti-bias values, 197–199
A Picture Book of Benjamin Franklin (Adler & Wallner), 315
Appropriate Curriculum and Assessment for Young Children (Bredekamp & Rosegrant), 15
Arends, R. I., 44, 46, 55, 307
Arezzo, D., 151
Art centers
  constructing, 93
  cutting and pasting, 94
  drawing and painting, 92
  function of, 90–91
  modeling, 94–95
  sewing and weaving, 93

  strategies for, 91
  woodworking, 93–94
Art forms, 325–327
Arthus-Bertrand, Y., 252
Artifacts, 230–231
Artificialism, 241–242
Arts and crafts, 55
Arts to study past, 232–233
Asher, S. R., 169
Assessment
  authentic, 46, 58
  units, projects, or thematic learning, 57
Assessment techniques
  checklists as, 60
  informal interviews as, 60–61
  observation as, 59
  performance tasks, 61–62
  portfolios as, 64
  products as, 62
  standardized tests as, 64–65
Assimilation, 132
Attachment theory, 150
Attitudes, 19, 156. *See also* Values
  in children, 186–187
  democracy and, 38
  in democratic societies, 294–296
  toward diversity, 180, 186–187
  toward self, 294
  toward sex roles, 295–296
  toward work, 294–295
Audiovisual and technology-based experiences, 55

Audiovisual materials, 102
Audiovisual resource, 54
Auel, J., 130
Austin, A. M., 168, 169
Authentic assessment, 46, 57–58. *See also* Assessment
Autonomous morality, 191

B

Bandura, A., 157, 188
Banks, J. A., 177, 178, 181
Barnes, M. K., 286
Barry-Davis, J., 241
Barton, K., 228
Barton, K. C, 207, 209
Bauer, P. J., 114
Beaty, J. J., 169, 170
Behavioral objectives, in lesson plans, 42–43
Behavioral theory, 143–144
Beier, E., 221
Belhar, M., 150
Bell, D., 311
Bellamy, Francis, 317
Beneath the Stone: A Mexican Zapotec Tale (Wolf), 245
Beneke, S., 49, 51, 58, 296
Bennett, L., 106
Berk, L. E., 152
Berkowitz, M. W., 189
Bernes-Kinkead, D., 311
Berson, M. J, 107
Berson, M. J., 107
Berti, A. E., 279
Beskow, E., 292
Biernbaum, S., 150
Birthday celebration, 216
Biscoe, A. D., 231
Black Cowboy, Wild Horses: A True Story (Lester & Pinkney), 245
Blagojevic, B., 107
Blocks, 84, 263
Bloom, B., 117
Bloom, Benjamin, 9
Blueberries for Sal (McCloskey), 244
Bodrova, E., 14, 114, 115, 160
Body awareness, 256
Bombi, A. S., 279
Bost, K. K., 169
Bower, B., 99, 232
Boyle-Baise, M., 12, 302, 311
Bozylinsky, Hannah Heritage, 328
Bradbard, M. R., 169
Bread, Bread, Bread (Morris), 328
Bredekamp, Sue, 5, 15, 28, 42, 49, 135, 184, 303
Britsch, S. J., 262

Britt, J., 267
Bronfenbrenner, Urie, 149
Bronson, M. B., 114
Brophy, J., 16, 19, 20, 37, 133, 192, 214, 227, 283, 325
Brown, A., 114
Brown, E. T., 235
Bruner, Jerome, 8, 131, 133, 134
Buffalo Hunt (Freedman), 283
Building an Igloo (Steitzer), 85
Bulletin boards and displays, 100–101
Bunny Day: Telling Time from Breakfast to Bedtime (Walton), 212
Bunny Money (Wells), 280
Burleigh, R., 252
Byrnes, D. A., 179

C

Cabrera, Derek, 127
California Tomorrow project (1999), 155
Canals Are Water Roads (Hill), 85
Career education, 293
Carlsson-Paige, N., 152, 200, 201
Carnegie Corporation, 17
Castle, S., 55, 232
Caudill, Nancy, 316
Caulfield, M. J., 200
Caverly, S. L., 170
CDs, recording, and television, 103–104
Ceilinski, K. L., 169
Celebrations, 330–331
Center for Civic Education, 301, 302
Change
  in children, 216–219
  in nature, 216
  in neighborhood or community, 215–216
  in school, 214–215
  as social studies theme, 17
Checklists, 60
Children
  abilities of, 30
  as active learners, 28
  change in, 216–219
  with disabilities, 171
  experiences of, 29–30
  interests of, 30
  knowledge of, 27–29
  literature for, 96
  mapping skills of, 267, 268
  needs of, 28
  as resources for learning, 69
  thoughts of, 28–29
Children of the World Say Good Morning (Martin), 329
Children with special needs
  inclusion and, 34
  legislation related to, 31

  strategies for teaching, 32
  talking with families, 31
  types of, 32–34
Choice, 16
Chrisman, K., 156, 295
Christmas, 226
Citizenship. *See* Civics; Political concept
Citizenship, 18
Civics
  civic participation, 306–311
  democratic values, 302–311
  key concepts, 301–302
  overview of, 301
Civil rights, 9–10
CIVITAS, 187, 196, 307
Clan of the Cave Bear (Auel), 130
CLASP (classroom lore and artifacts study project), 217
Classification
  developmental stages and, 121–122
  function of, 113
Classroom materials
  for art centers, 90–95
  audiovisual, 102
  bulletin boards and displays, 100–101
  CDs, recording, and television, 103–104
  children's literature, 96
  commercial, 102
  for dramatic play, 86–88
  reference materials, 96–98
  selection of, 80
  technology-based, 104–107
  for vicarious experiences, 95–96
  video clips and digital images, 103
  visual discovery, 98–100
  for writing, 89–90
Classrooms. *See also* Classroom materials
  anti-bias attitudes in, 197–199
  learning centers in, 81–95
  libraries in, 89
  rules in, 307
  safety in, 108
Clemens, S. G., 151
Coake, W., 311
Cobb, M., 231
Cognitive development
  classification of information, 113, 121–122
  comparing and contrasting and, 122–123
  experiences, planning, 114
  field trips, 118–121
  firsthand experiences, 114
  generalizations, 125–127
  graphs and, 123–125
  interpreting, reflecting, and reaching conclusions and, 127–129
  jokes and riddles, 129–130

language and, 115–116
overview of, 112–113
play and, 14, 113
questioning and sensing problems, 117–118
and social-living curriculum, 6–7
Cognitive-developmental theories, 147–148
Cognitive theories of learning, 190–191
Cohen, Miriam, 168
Coleman, C. C., 169
Coley, R. L., 150
Colker, L., 13
Collaborative for Academic, Social, and Emotional Learning (CASEL), 159
Color on maps, 265
Colosi, Laura, 127
Columbus day, 224
Commercial materials, 102
Communication
  feelings and, 329
  importance of, 158–159
  strategies to encourage, 159–161
Communication skills
  conflict resolution and, 172–174
  listening and speaking, 162–163
  reading and writing, 163–164
  sharing and, 164–168
Communities
  change in, 215–216
  and culture, 179
  fieldwork in, 74–79
  guest speakers from, 79
  knowledge of, 35–37, 308
  resources and, 47, 55
  sense of, 304
  social development and, 150–152
Community service, 79
Comparing and contrasting, 122–123
Competition, 169
Concept formation. *See also* Cognitive development
  accommodation, 133
  adaptation, 133
  assimilation, 132
  guidelines for, 135–137
  key concepts in, 131–132
  matching and, 133–135
  methods to nurture, 136
  overview of, 130–131
  play and, 13–14
  spontaneous concepts, 133
Conflict resolution
  and anti-bias learning environment, 199
  during play, 159
  strategies for, 172–174
  value of, 186–187

Connell, R., 312
Consumers, 287–289
Consuming services, 290–291
Consumption, as social studies theme, 17
Continuity
  cultural universals and, 227–228
  family and, 219–221
  holiday celebrations and traditions and, 223–227
  intergenerational contacts and, 221–223
  as social studies theme, 17
  understanding, 208
Contributions approach to culture, 178
Cooperation
  competition, 169
  reinforcement, 168–169
  school size, 169
Cooperative learning, 199
Copple, C., 28, 49, 135, 145, 303
Cortez, M., 150
Couchenour, D., 156, 295
Coufal, D. C., 164
Coufal, K., 164
Craven, R., 153
Creative dramatics, 160
Critical thinking, 112, 123
Crow-Enslow, L., 34
Cruise, M. J., 221
CTB/McGraw-Hill, 17
Cultural knowledge, 36–37
Cultural regions, 272–273
Cultural universals, 20, 227–228
Culture, 17. *See also* Diversity; Values
  approaches to, 178
  communities and, 179
  definitions of, 177–179
  friendship, 179
  NCSS standard, 177
  performance expectations and, 164
  social development and, 150–151
  as social studies theme, 17
Cunningham, W., 106
Currenton, S., 159, 165
Curriculum, integrated, 219
Curriculum models
  High/Scope approach to education, 21–22
  Montessori, 22–23
  Reggio Emilia, 20–21
Cutting, A. L., 170
Cutting and pasting, 94

D

Dams Give Us Power: A Building Block Book (Hill), 94
Daniels, Anne, 56
David Was Mad (Martin), 173

Debus, R., 153
Decision making, 303
  involving parents in, 72–73
  scarcity and, 285–286
DeKlyen, M., 150
DeLoache, J. S., 255
Democratic societies. *See also* Political concepts
  children with special needs and, 31–32
  key concepts related to, 301–302
  overview of, 301
  ownership and pride in, 318
  participation skills for, 306–311
  skills requirements and, 18–19
  social-living curriculum and, 5–7
  social skills and, 5, 6
Denton, D., 69, 152
D'Entremont, L., 181
DePaola, T., 254
Derman-Sparks, L., 28, 184, 197, 199, 223, 295
DeRoach, E. F., 189, 305
Descartes, René, 153
Developmentally Appropriate Practice in Early Childhood Programs (2009), 27
Developmentally Appropriate Practice in Early Childhood Programs Serving Children from Birth Through Age 8 (Bredekamp & Copple), 5, 15
Developmentally Appropriate Practices: Serving Children from Birth Through Age 8 (Bredekamp & Copple), 135
Developmental systems theories, 149
Dever, M. T., 179, 197
Dewey, John, 3
  on ability to think, 114
  on career education, 296
  on communication, 159
  on diversity, 180
  on history teaching, 207
  influence of, 3
  on unit planning, 46
  on values, 186
Diamond, K. E., 31, 32, 34, 181
Did You Carry the Flag Today, Charley? (Caudill), 316
Diehl, D. S., 170
Dighe, Judith, 248
Digital images, 103, 232
Digital tools for social studies, 105
Directionality, 254–259
Directional terms
  cardinal directions, 257–258
  left and right, 257
  location, 258–259
  relative position, 258
  up and down, 257

Direct teaching, 167–168
Disabilities. *See* Children with special needs
DiSalvo-Ryan, D., 283
Distance and measurement, 259–260
Distribution of goods, 17, 291–293
Diversity. *See also* Culture; Values
  attitudes toward, 180, 186–187
  discovering your own views related to, 181–184
  key concepts regarding, 186
  learning about, 184–186
  overview of, 179–180
  values and, 180
Dorsey, S., 150
Downs, R. M., 269
Drama, 55
Dramatic play
  materials for, 86–88
  and social skill development, 160
  symbolic thought and, 113
Drawing and painting, 92
DSRP rules, 127
Dunn, J., 170
Durlak, J. A., 113, 160
Dymnicki, A. B., 113, 160
Dyson, A. H., 115

E

Early Childhood: Where Learning Begins, Geography (Fromboluti & Seefeldt), 271
Early childhood education, 7, 8
Earth. *See also* Geography
  aesthetic awareness, 249
  caring for, 246–251
  environment of, 242–243
  interdependency in, 248
  land and water, 243–246
  observational skills for, 247–248
  social consciousness, 249–251
Earth from Above for Young Readers (Arthus-Bertrand & Burleigh), 252
Economic concepts
  attitudes and values, 294–296
  consumers, 287–289
  consuming services, 290–291
  development of, 278–281
  distribution of goods, 291–293
  essential skills, 296
  jobs, 293–294
  production, 291–293
  scarcity and decision making, 282–287
Economic literacy, 277–278
Economics, defined, 278
Economics America (NCEE), 282
Education of All Handicapped Children Act of 1975, 31

Egan, K., 232
Elementary-Secondary Education Act (1965), 9
Ellis, D., 231
Emotional problems, 33. *See also* Children with special needs
Enactments, 54
Engstrom, L., 277
Environment
  arranged, 54
  and geography, 242–243
Environment of earth, 242–243
Erikson, Erik, 144
Erikson's theory
  autonomy, 145
  industry, 146
  initiative, 145–146
  psychosocial stages, 144–145
  trust, basic, 145
Essential skills, 296
Exceptional children. *See* Children with special needs
Exelby, B., 80
Experiences
  of children, 29–30
  incidental, 54

F

Falconer, R. C., 179, 197
Fallace, T. D., 231
Families. *See also* parents
  with children with special needs, 31
  communication with, 71
  and continuity, 219–221
  and economic activities, 283
  formal involvement, 71–73
  informal involvement of, 70–71
  as resource, 69–70
  social development and, 149–150
  wants and needs of, 282, 283
Family history book, 220
Family Nights Out, 72
Farnen, R. F., 192
Federal Preschool Program and Early Intervention Program Act of 1986, 31
Feeling trips, 119
Field trips
  feeling trip, 119
  hearing trip, 120–121
  looking trip, 119–120
  for observation experiences, 247
  small-group, 74–75
  smelling trip, 119
  specific-purpose, 75
  use of, 118
  virtual, 75
  walking, 74

Fieldwork
  activities following, 79
  benefits of, 74
  cognitive development and, 118–121
  planning for, 76–79
  repeated, 75
  small-group trips, 74–75
  specific-purpose field trips, 75
  types of, 74–76
  virtual field trips, 75
  walking trips, 74
  WOW trips, 75–76
Finlinson, A. R., 168, 169
Firefighters Fight Fires (Greene), 172
Firsthand experiences, 114, 262
Fisher, N., 170
Flack, M., 329
Flag, 316
Flavell, John, 159
Follow the Money (Leedy), 280
Formal inservice activities, 36
Formal parent-involvement activities
  decision making, 72–73
  group meetings, 72
  working with children, 72
Forman, G. E., 244
Formative assessment, 65
Fowler, A., 244
Franklin, M. B., 132
Freedman, R., 283
Freedom of thought, 304
Freud, Sigmund, 154
Friendship, 169–172, 179
Froebel, Friedrich, 84
Frog, Duck, and Rabbit (Gretz), 324
Fromboluti, C. S., 270, 271
Froschl, M., 163
Full Steam Ahead (Gibbons), 221

G

Galper, A., 16, 118, 152, 222, 277
Gandini, L., 20
Garcia, E., 14, 180
Gelman, S., 121, 130
Gender differences, 150
Geography
  and artificialism, 241–242
  caring for earth, 246–251
  direction and location and, 241, 254–269
  earth and, 241–254
  environment and, 242–243
  human-environment relationships and, 269–270
  key concepts for, 240–241
  land and water and, 243–246
  national standards for, 239–240

regions and, 241, 271–273
solar system and, 252–254
spatial interactions and, 241, 270–271
Geography Education Standards Project, 239–240
Get Up and Go! (Murphy & Greenseid), 212
Gibbons, F., 221
Gifted children, 34
Gillies, R. M., 168
Glanz, D., 223
Glassman, M., 11
Global Connections
global education and, 333–334
interconnectedness and interdependency, 323–331
key concepts in, 323
NCSS standards, 322
resources for learning about, 331–333
similarities, 325–331
technology, 331
trade, 331
Global education, 333–334
Global education curriculum, 333
Global interdependence, 18
Globes, maps and, 260–269
Goodman, J. F., 191
Goodman, M., 184
Google Earth, 267
Gorter-Reu, M. S., 71
Gouteux, S., 262
Grandma Susan Remembers (Morris), 221
Graphic organizers, 232
Graphs
activities using, 124–125
cognitive development using, 123–125
types of, 123
Greenberg, M. T., 150
Greenberg, P., 172, 304
Greene, C., 33
Greene, Carol, 172
Greenseid, D., 212
Gretz, S., 324
Gronlund, G., 64
Gross, T., 151
Group meetings, for parents, 72
Group rules, 327
Guest speakers, 79
Guidelines for Appropriate Curriculum Content and Assessment in Programs Serving Children Ages 3 Through 8 (NAEYC), 137
Gunnar, M. R., 156

H

Hafenstein, N. L., 34
Halloween, 224–225
Hanline, M. F., 113
Hanukkah, 226
Harris, R., 307
Hart, C. H., 170
Harwood, R. L., 189
Head Start programs, 9, 127, 181
Hearing impairments, 32–33
Hearing trips, 120–121
Hearne, B., 245
Helm, J. H., 46, 49, 51, 58, 69, 296
Helwig, C. C., 189, 312, 316
Hembacher, D., 221
Hendrick, J., 20
Hendrix, K., 151
Henning, M. B., 311
Here-and-now curriculum, 3–5
Here-and-now world
experiences from, 114–116
explanation of, 5
strengths and weaknesses of, 8
Hess, Robert, 313, 316
Hesse, P., 107
Hewett, K., 84, 85
Hidi, S., 16
High/Scope curriculum, 21–22
Hill, Patty Smith, 5
History
change, study of, 214–219
connection to past and, 228–233
continuity of human life, 219–228
importance of, 207
key concepts for, 207–209
methods of historian, 233–235
passage of time, 213, 214
routines and time, 211–212
science, technology, and society, 205
study of, defined, 207
time concepts, development of, 209–211
time measurement, 212
History for Grades K–4 (NCHS), 208
Holiday celebrations and traditions
Christmas, 226
Columbus day, 224
Halloween, 224–225
Hanukkah, 226
national days, 226–227
planning of, 223–224
thanksgiving, 225
Valentine's Day, 227
winter holidays, 226
Holiday curriculum, 7, 8
Holst, Carol, 284
Hope, T., 153
Hsu, M.-C., 12
Hubbard, J., 231, 232
Hughes, J. N., 146
Huijbregts, S. K., 150
Human-environment relationship, 269–270
Hunt, J. McVicker, 9

I

Identity, 140, 141f
Inclusion
of children with special needs, 31–32
goals for, 34
Individualized Education Plan (IEP), 35
Individual Transition Plan, 72
Indoctrination, 192, 317
Informal conversations, 36
Informal interviews, 60–61
Informal parent-involvement activities, 70–71
Inhelder, B., 5, 10, 190
Inquiry process, 113
Integrated curriculum, change in, 219
Intellectual development, 5
Intelligence theories, 65
Interactive bulletin boards, 100–101
Interconnectedness, 186, 323–331
Interdependency, 186, 323–331
Intergenerational contacts, 221–223
International Society for Technology in Education (ISTE), 104, 105
Internet
and mapping skills, 267
as news source, 98
safety issues related to, 108
social study resources on, 106–107
video and video clips on, 103
for virtual field trips, 75
Interpretation, 127–129
Intuitive time, 209
Isbell, R., 80
Isenberg, J., 113, 159
It Could Still Be a Tree (Fowler), 244
It's George (Cohen), 168

J

James, J. H., 233
Jantz, R. K., 14, 207, 209
Jenkins, S., 252
Jobs, 293–294
Johnson, A., 232
Johnson, E. C., 286
Johnson, S., 12
Jokes, 129–130
Journal writing, 90
Journey North, 47

K

Kagan, S. L., 65
Karp, K. S., 235

Katz, L., 46, 69
Kemple, K. M., 170
Kimber, W., 212
Kirsch, S., 262
Klein, A., 103
Klineberg, O., 185, 186
Knowledge, 16–18
 of children, 27–29
 of community, 35–37
 cultural , values and, 36–37
 of social studies, 37–38
Kochanska, G., 192
Kochenderfer, B. J., 169
Koenig, A. L., 192
Kohlberg, Lawrence, 148
Kornfeld, J., 325
Koster, J. B., 95
Kowalski, K., 185
Krathwol, D. R., 117
Kraus, R., 217
K–4 standards, 302
K-W-L chart, 39

L

Ladd, G. W., 169, 170
LaFontaine, G., 267
Lala Salama: An African Lullaby (Bozylinsky), 328
Lambert, W., 185
Land and water, 243–246
Landry, C. E., 244
Lane, F., 107
Lang, H. G., 33
Langer, S., 116
Language
 and cognitive development, 115–116
 experiences, 55
 impairments, 34
Learning activities, 45
Learning centers, 16, 55, 56
 function of, 80
 importance of, 81
 introducing children to, 81
 sample floor plan, 82
 types of, 83–95
Learning experiences
 firsthand, 114
 involving language, 115–116
 involving others, 114–115
 in units, projects, or thematic learning, 54–56
Learning theories
 current knowledge about, 9
 Piaget and, 10–11
 Vygotsky and, 11
Leedy, L., 266, 280
Lemerise, E. A., 170

Leong, D. J., 14, 114, 115, 160
Leseman, P. P. M., 150
Lesson plans
 assessment of, 46
 elements of, 41
 objectives of, 42–45
 preparation for, 42
 procedures in, 45–46
Lester, J., 245
Leventhal, D., 329
Levin, D. E., 98, 152, 172, 173, 199
Levstik, L., 16, 209, 228, 232, 233
Lewis, E. B., 280
Leyendecker, B., 189
Liben, L. S., 269
Lillard, A., 159, 165
Limited English proficiency
 strategies for children with, 34
 verbal communication and, 159
Lionni, Leo, 172
Listening skills, 162–163
Literature
 activities to accompany, 96
 benefits of, 96
 related to block play, 85
Lo, Y. F., 185
Lobdell, J., 99, 232
Location, concepts of, 259
Locke, John, 143
Locomotion, 256
Longstreet, W. S., 303
Lonigan, C. J., 116
Looking Down (Jenkins), 252
Looking trips, 119–120
Lord, Frank, 257
Loudermilk, L., 311
Lukasik, D., 311

M

Maccoby, E. E., 150
MacKinster, J., 333
Maestro, B. C., 280
Maestro, G., 280
Mapping Penny's World (Leedy), 266
Maps and globes, 260–269
Marschark, M., 33
Marsh, H. W., 153, 154
Marshall, H. H., 145, 182
Martin, B., 70, 252, 329
Martin, Bill, 173
Martin, L., 123
Marzoff, D. P, 255
Maslow, Abraham, 154
Matching
 concept formation and, 133–135
 and zone of proximal development, 11
Mathematics, 55

McCaughrean, G., 212
McCloskey, R., 84, 244
McConnell, J., 165
McCormick, L., 28
McCormick, T. M, 231, 232
McDermott, J., 32
McEwan, E. E., 172
Mead, M., 221
Meadow, S., 154
Measurement, distance and, 259–260
Medda, M. E., 193
Memorization
 function of, 130, 131
 past emphasis on, 3–4
Mental disabilities, 33. *See also* Children with special needs
Merryfield, M. M., 107, 333
Meszaros, B, 277
Metzger, S. A., 12
Meyer, L, 333
Mihala, S., 153
Miller, J., 262
Miller, M., 123
Milne, A. A., 128, 217, 314
Milton, S., 113
Minarik, E. H., 129
Misco, T., 19
Mitchell, L. S., 247
Mitchell, Lucy Sprague
 on curriculum, 131
 on environment, 35
 on fieldwork, 74
 on geography skills, 239
 on here-and-now curriculum, 3–5
 influence of, 12
 on maps use, 262, 265
 on planning, 27
 on social studies curriculum, 2–3
Modeling
 activities, 94–95
 of appropriate behaviors, 167
 of values and attitudes, 188–190
Molenarr-Klumper, M., 33
Mollet, T. M., 280
Money, 280
Montessori, M., 22, 23
Montessori curriculum, 21, 22–23
Morality of constraint, 190
Moral realism, 190
Moral reasoning, 148
Morgan, W., 306
Morris, A., 221
Morris, Ann, 328
Mosenthal, P. B., 262
Mountains and Volcanoes (Taylor), 244
Movement exploration, 256
Moyer, J., 103

Multiculturalism, 186
Murphy, S. J., 212
Music, 55
Myers, B. K., 7
Myers, M. E., 7
My Grandmother's Clock (McCaughrean), 212
My Rows and Piles of Coins (Mollet & Lewis), 280

N
Narratives/arts to study past, 232–233
Nation, 318
National Association for the Education of Young Children (NAEYC), 151, 152, 182
National Center for History in the Schools (NCHS), 7, 191, 207, 216
National Commission on Social Studies in the Schools, 196
National Council for the Social Studies (NCSS), 2, 12, 13, 15, 19, 52, 131, 140, 141, 177, 196, 205, 206, 240–241, 277, 301, 310, 322
National Council on Economic Education (NCEE), 278
National days, 226–227
National Education Goals Panel, 57
National geography standards, 239–240
National history standards, 208
National Research Council (NRC), 2, 9, 149
National Research Council and Institute of Medicine (NRC & IM), 114, 152, 244
National Standards for Civics and Government, 18, 302
National standards for geography, 239–240
Nature, change in, 216
Needs
  of children, 28
  wants and, 285
Neff, L., 286
New, R. S., 305
New Directions in the Kindergarten, 9
Newman, R., 36
Night-Time (Pettigrew & Kimber), 212
No Child Left Behind Act (NCLB), 6, 11–12
Nolte, D. W., 307
Nucci, L. P., 188
Nuffield Mathematics Project (1969), 260

O
Objects from past, 231
O'Brien, M. U., 160

Observation
  as assessment tools, 59
  skills development in, 120, 247–248
Okagaki, L., 181
O'Mahony, C., 20
One Morning in Maine (McCloskey), 244
One Riddle, One Answer (2000), 130
Online resources, 106–107
On the Trail of Sacagawea (Peter), 221
Operational time, 209
Oppenheim, A. N., 192
Otten, M., 233
Our Sun Is a Star (Martin), 252
Ownership, 318

P
Padavich, D. L., 192
Pantomime activities, 160
Parents
  with children with special needs, 31
  and consumer education, 290
  formal involvement of, 71–73
  informal involvement, 70–71
  as resource, 69–70
  social skill development, 150
Parker, J. G., 169
Passage of time, 213, 214
Past
  narratives and arts to study, 232–233
  people as resources to study, 229
  primary source documents, 229–232
  understanding of, 208, 228–229
Patterns of Thinking method, 127
Pattnaik, J., 16
Peace, culture of, 199–201
Pelle's New Suit (Beskow), 292
Performance tasks, 61–62
Perry, J. L., 231
Personal identity, 17
Personal names (general identity), 154–155
Peter, L., 221
Pettigrew, E., 212
Pfister, R., 168, 169
Phelps, P. C., 113
Photographs, 231–232
Physical activities, 55
Physical disabilities, 33. See also Children with special needs
Physical regions, 271–272
Physical self, 155–157
Piaget, Jean, 5, 73, 132, 209, 260
  as cognitive-developmental theorists, 147–148
  on informal interviews, 61
  on moral values, 190
  philosophy of, 21–22

  on play, 13
  and spontaneous concepts, 133
  theories of, 10–11
Piagetian theory, 278
Pictures, to study past, 232
Pinkney, J., 245
Planning
  for individual lessons, 41–46
  for spontaneity, 40–41
  for units, projects, and thematic learning, 46–57
Play, 13–14
  dramatic, 86–88
  following fieldwork, 78
  with maps, 265
  sand/water, 83–84
  sociodramatic, 113
Playing store, 288
Pledge of Allegiance, 317
Podany, W., 311
Podcasts, 106
Pohan, C. A., 2
Political concepts. See also Civics
  overview of, 311–312
  research, 312–313
  symbols of democratic government, 315–317
  and voting, 313–315
Polonsky, L., 123
Popkewitz, T.S., 14
Portfolios, 64
Postman, N., 107
Pratt, Caroline, 84
Prawatt, R. W., 114, 130
Prejudice reduction activities, 199
Pre-kindergarten standards, 17
Prencipe, A., 189, 316
Preoperational stage
  economic concepts and, 281
  geography skills, 242
  time concept and, 210
Price, J. M., 170
Pride, 318
Primary source documents
  artifacts, 230–231
  photographs, 231–232
  visual discovery, 231–232
Production, 291–293
Products, 62, 63
Progressive education, 3–5
Projects
  assessment of, 57
  explanation of, 46
  goals of, 48–49
  methods for planning, 49–57
Prosocial skills, 153
Psychoanalytic theory, 6

Q

Questioning/sensing problems, 117–118
Quisenberry, N., 113, 159

R

Rahav, G., 151
Ramsay, S., 170
Ramsey, P. G., 184
Rasmussen, S., 145
Rating scales, 60
Reaching Potentials (Bredekamp & Rosegrant), 15
Reading applications, 163–164
Recycling, 250
Reference materials, 96–98
Reggio Emilia curriculum model, 20–21
Reggio Emilia programs, 49
Regions, 241
    cultural, 272–273
    physical, 271–272
Reinforcement theory, 190
Repeated fieldwork, 75
Resource person, 36
Resources
    children as, 69
    community as, 73–79
    families as, 69–70
    school as, 73
    technology, 104–107
Respect, 305
Reuse of materials, 250
Richardson, W., 104, 105, 107, 108
Richman, G., 153
Riddles, 129–130
Rivers and Streams (Vaughan), 244
Rivkin, M. S., 246
Roberts, J., 170
Roberts, R., 257
Robison, H., 9
Roedell, W. C., 151
Rogers, Carl, 154
Role-play, 161
Ronen, T., 151
Root, P., 231
Rosegrant, T., 42
Rosenbaum, M., 151
Routines in teaching, 211–212
Rowland, G. E., 159
Rubrics in teacher education (example), 62, 63
Ryan, P. M., 316
Rylant, C., 232

S

Sand and social studies, 83–84
Scarcity and decision making, 282–287
Schellinger, K., 113
Schickedanz, J., 90
Schiller, M., 164
Schoelmerich, A., 189
Schoenfeldt, M., 239
School community, pride and, 318
Schools. *See also* Classrooms
    change in, 214–215
    resources within, 73
    self-concept and, 153
    social development and, 152–153
Schulze, P. A., 189
Schweinhart, L. J., 22
Science, 55, 205
Searls, M. J., 285
Security, 166–167
Seefeldt, C., 1, 65, 69, 91, 152, 207, 222, 277
Self-concept
    assessment of, 158
    defined, 153
    explanation, 154
    personal names (general identity), 154–155
    physical self, 155–157
    school and, 153
    self-efficacy/self-worth, 157–158
Self-esteem, 153, 155
Self-identity, 153
Sensorimotor space, 255
Sensorimotor stage
    economic concepts and, 281
    geography skills and, 242
    time concept and, 210
Sensory experiences
    cognitive development and, 114
    field trips promoting, 118–121
Serriere, S. C., 12
Service projects, 309
Services, 291–293
Seven Brave Women (Hearne), 245
Sewing and weaving, 93
Sewing Quilts (Turner & Allen), 231
Sharing
    behaviors, fostering, 166
    direct teaching, 167–168
    goal of, 164–165
    level identification, 165–166
    models, 167
    physical environment, 167
    security, 166–167
Sheffield, C. C., 235
Shepard, L. A., 65
Shepardson, D. P., 262
Sherman, L., 333
Shiveley, J., 19
Shure, M., 147
Siegler, R. S., 114
Similarities
    in art forms, 325–327
    basic needs, 328
    in celebrations, 330–331
    explanation of, 323, 325
    in group rules, 327
    in languages, 328–330
    in social organization, 327–328
Skills, 18–19
    and career education, 296
    essential, 296
    observational, 247–248
Skinner, B. F., 143, 190
Slaby, R. G., 151
Slekar, T. D., 14, 305
Small-group field trips, 74–75
Smelling trips, 119
Smith, L. P., 232
Social action approach to culture, 178
Social-cognitive theories, 146–147
Social consciousness, 249–251
Social development
    community and, 150–152
    factors affecting, 149
    family and, 149–150
    school and, 152–153
Socialization, theories of
    behavioral theory, 143–144
    cognitive-developmental theories, 147–148
    developmental systems theories, 149
    Erikson's theory of psychosocial development, 144–146
    social–cognitive theories, 146–147
    Vygotsky's sociocultural theory, 148–149
Social-living curriculum, 5–7
Social organization, 327–328
Social skills, 55. *See also* Socialization, theories of
    communication and, 158–164
    community, role of, 150–152
    conflict resolution and, 172–174
    cooperation and, 168–169
    development of, 140, 141–142
    family, 149–150
    focus on, 18–19
    friendship and, 169–172
    individual development and identity, 140, 141
    school, role of, 152–153
    self-concept and, 153–158
    sharing and, 164–168
    social-living curriculum and, 5–7
    as social studies approach, 8t
    for units, projects, or thematic learning, 55
Social skills checklist, 60f

Social studies. *See also* Social studies curriculum
  active learning, 13–14
  attitudes and values, 19
  current approaches, 12–23
  defined, 2
  integrated nature of, 14
  interest of children in, 16
  knowledge about, 16–18
  meaningfulness, 15
  past approaches to, 3–12
  progressive education, 3–5
  purposes of, 1–3
  scope and sequence, 19–20
  skills, 18–19
  teachers' knowledge of, 37–38
Social studies curriculum
  concepts, 8
  here-and-now, 3–5
  holiday, 7
  models for early childhood education, 20–23
  social forces affecting, 8–12
  social-living, 5–7
  spiral, 4
  technology-based materials for, 106
Solar system
  climate conditions, 253–254
  movement in space, 252–253
Sousa, F., 114
Space, 256
Speaking, 162–163
Special needs. *See* Children with special needs
Specific-purpose field trips, 75
Speech impairments, 34
Speltz, M. L., 150
Spier, Peter, 273
Spiral curriculum, 4
Spivack, G., 147
Spodek, B., 9
Spontaneity, 40–41
Spontaneous concepts, 133
Sprung, B., 163
Sputnik launch, 8–9
Stacey, S., 31, 32, 34
Staley, L., 232
Standard American English (SAE), 329
Standardized tests, 64–65
Standards
  civic education, 18–19
  focus on, 18
  national geography, 239–240
  national history, 208
  NCSS on culture, 177
  NCSS VIII (science/rechnology/society), 205

pre-kindergarten, 17
social studies, 37
Stewart, D., 12
Stigler, J. W., 232
Stormshak, E. A., 167
Streb, M., 306
Surback, E., 103
Swimmy (Lionni), 172
Symbols, 315–317

T
Takahashi, I., 252
Tavecchio, L. W. C., 150
Taylor, B., 244
Taylor, R. D., 113
Teacher–child interaction, 166
Teacher–child planning, 38–39
Teacher-initiated question, 54
Teachers, social studies knowledge of, 37–38
Teaching Tolerance Project (2003), 200
Technology, 331
  comfort development by, 105–106
  online resources, 106–107
  selecting technological tools and resources for, 107
  as social studies theme, 17
  standards, 104–105
  teaching content, 107
  units, projects, or thematic learning using, 55
Technology-based experiences, 55
Teichman, Y., 185
Television, 103–104
Tell Me a Story Mama (Johnson), 232
Thanksgiving, 225
The Chocolate Train (Kornfeld), 325
The Cloud Book (dePaola), 254
The Empire State Building (Holland), 94
The Flag We Love (Ryan), 316
The Growing Story (Kraus), 217
The Laughing Classroom (2002), 130
The Lot at the End of My Block (Lewis & Cartwright), 85
Thematic learning
  assessment of, 57
  explanation of, 46
  goals of, 48–49, 48f
  planning for, 49–57
Theme selection, 49
The Name Quilt (Root), 231
The National Standards for Civics and Government (Center for Civic Education), 306
The 18 Penny Goose (Walker & Beier), 221
The Process of Education, 131

The Quilt-Block History of Pioneer Days: With Projects Kids Can Make (Cobb & Ellis), 231
The Story of Money (Maestro & Maestro), 280
The Story of Ping (Flack), 329
The Two of Them (Aliki), 329
Thinking. *See* Cognitive development
Thinking at Every Desk (2009), 127
Thompson, R. A., 146
Thornton, S. J., 209
Thoughts of children, 28–29
Time
  concept development, 209–211
  measuring, 212
  passage of time, 213, 214
  routines in teaching, 211–212
  as social studies theme, 17
Timelines, 217
Tool-maps, 265
Torney, J., 192, 316
Torney, Judith, 313
Tourist curriculum, 223
Trade, 331
Transdisciplinary theme, 53
Transformation approach to culture, 178
Transforming Early Childhood and Assessment (Bredekamp & Rosegrant), 15
Transition Demonstration, 72
Tunnels Go Underground: A Building Block Book (Hill), 85
Turner, A., 231

U
Uncle Willie and the Soup Kitchen (DiSalvo-Ryan), 283
Units
  assessment of, 57
  example of, 46
  explanation of, 41, 46
  goals of, 48–49, 48f
  methods for planning, 49–57

V
Valentine's Day, 227
Value analysis theory, 193–195
Value clarification theory, 193
Values, 19, 38, 180. *See also* Attitudes
  and attitudes, 186–187
  clarification theory on, 193
  cognitive theories of learning, 190–191
  cultural knowledge and, 36–37
  encouragement of anti-bias, 197–199
  indoctrination of, 192
  instructions in, 195–196
  modeling of, 188–190
  reinforcement of, 190
  value analysis theory, 193–195

Vance, E., 324
VanSledright, B. A., 233
Vaughan, J., 244
Vaughn, B. E., 169
Velvet Revolutions, 103
Video clips and digital images, 103
Violence, 200
Viorst, J., 286
Virmani, E. A., 146
Virtual field trips, 75
Visual discovery
  classroom materials, 98–100
  to study past, 231–232
Visual impairments, 32
Voting, 313–315
Vukelich, C., 87
Vukelich, R., 209
Vygotsky, Lev, 5, 7, 13, 73
  background and theories of, 11
  on cognitive development, 113, 115
  on concept formation, 130
  on continuity of life, 223
  on matching, 15
  sociocultural theory by, 148–149
  on thematic learning, 46
  on thought process, 115
  zone of proximal development and, 134

W
Wade, R., 4, 18, 19, 308
Walker, B., 34
Walker, S. M., 221
Walking field trips, 74
Wall, S., 150
Wallach, L. R., 151
Wallner, J. W., 315
Walton, R., 212
Wants and needs, 282–285
War, 199–201
Warman, B., 221, 222
War on Poverty, 9
Washington, W. N., 169
Water play, 83–84
Waters, E., 150
We Are Best Friends (Aliki), 168
Weaver, P. J., 324
Webquests, 106
Webster, R., 168
Weikart, D., 21
Weingold, H., 168
Weissberg, R. P., 113, 160
Welfare, 303
Wellington, M., 329
West, S. G., 146
What Is Your Language? (Leventhal & Wellington), 329

When I Was Young in the Mountains (Rylant), 232
Whitaker, M. L., 179
Whitehurst, G. J., 116
Whiteside, K., 262
Whose Hat? (McEwan), 172
Wigfield, A., 16
Wolf, B., 245
Wong, M., 28
Woods Hole Conference (1959), 8
Woodward, J. A., 232
Woodworking, 93–94
World of Work Series, 294
WOW trips, 75–76
Writing applications, 163–164
Writing area, 89–90
Writing for communication, 116
Wu, W., 146
Wurtz, E., 65

Y
Yarbrough, D., 308
Yashima, Taro, 163
Yogi, L., 28
Young Citizens of the World (2009), 311
Young Geographers (Mitchell), 131